index

1. Structure	**7**
Mechanics	9
Structural analysis	17
Structure	20
Bulk-active structure	22
Frame	29
Vector-active structure	36
Surface-active structure	42
Form-active structure	47
Tubular structure	53
Foundation	54
Sitework	64
2. Building	**69**
Building	71
Roof	78
Stair	93
Elevator	101
Door	103
Window	110
Nonbearing partition	116
Façade	119
Finish floor	132
Ceiling	140
Thermal insulation	143
Damp proofing	144
Sound	146
Building typology	149

3. Con	
Wood	159
Metal	170
Concrete	175
Brick	182
Concrete block	185
Nail	189
Screw	191
Bolt	193
Tool	197
4. Installations	**201**
HVAC	203
Solar energy	213
Electricity	216
Light	221
Plumbing	229
Fire safety	241
5. Geometry	**245**
Euclidean geometry	247
Drawing	255
Topographic survey	261
6. Alphabetical Index	**265**

Structure

Mechanics
Structural analysis
Structure
Bulk-active structure
Frame system
Vector-active structure
Surface-active structure
Form-active structure
Tubular structure
Foundation
Sitework

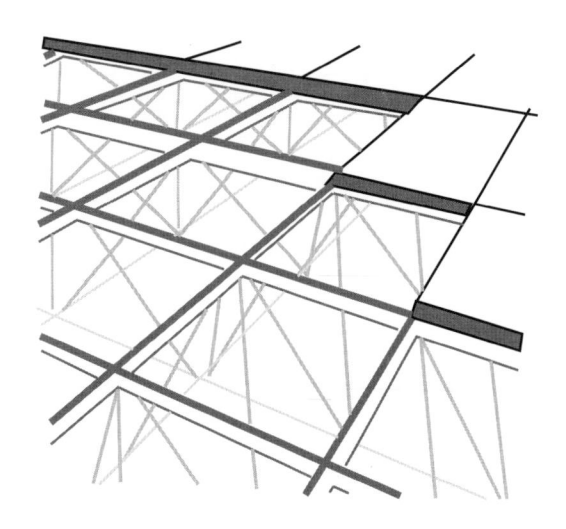

mechanics

The area of physics that studies the effects of forces on bodies or systems, both static and in motion.

force
An action to which a body is submitted, tending to produce or producing alterations to its shape, movement, or position in space.

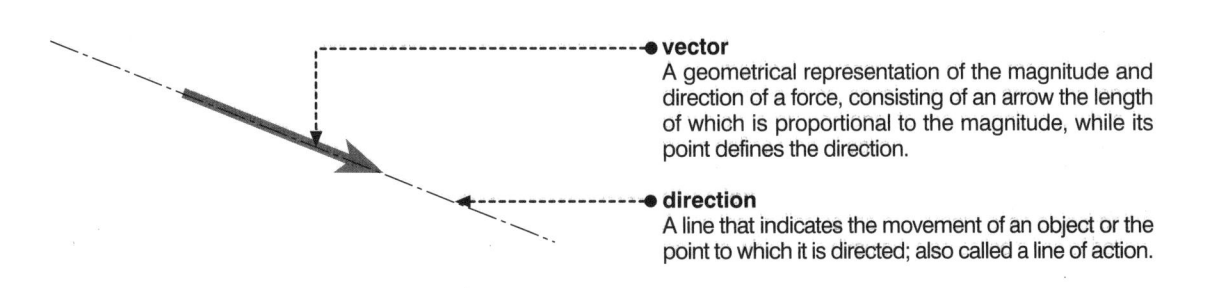

vector
A geometrical representation of the magnitude and direction of a force, consisting of an arrow the length of which is proportional to the magnitude, while its point defines the direction.

direction
A line that indicates the movement of an object or the point to which it is directed; also called a line of action.

Direction of forces

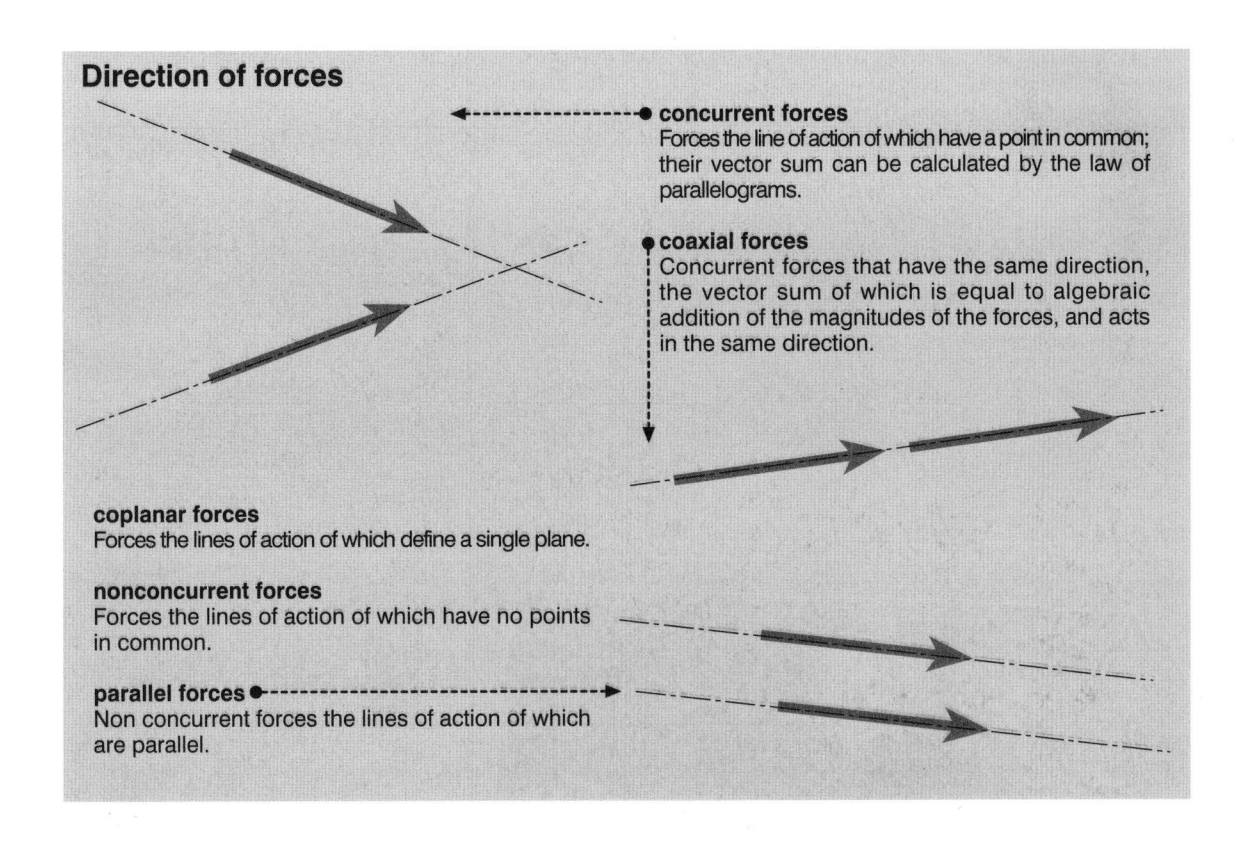

concurrent forces
Forces the line of action of which have a point in common; their vector sum can be calculated by the law of parallelograms.

coaxial forces
Concurrent forces that have the same direction, the vector sum of which is equal to algebraic addition of the magnitudes of the forces, and acts in the same direction.

coplanar forces
Forces the lines of action of which define a single plane.

nonconcurrent forces
Forces the lines of action of which have no points in common.

parallel forces
Non concurrent forces the lines of action of which are parallel.

mechanics

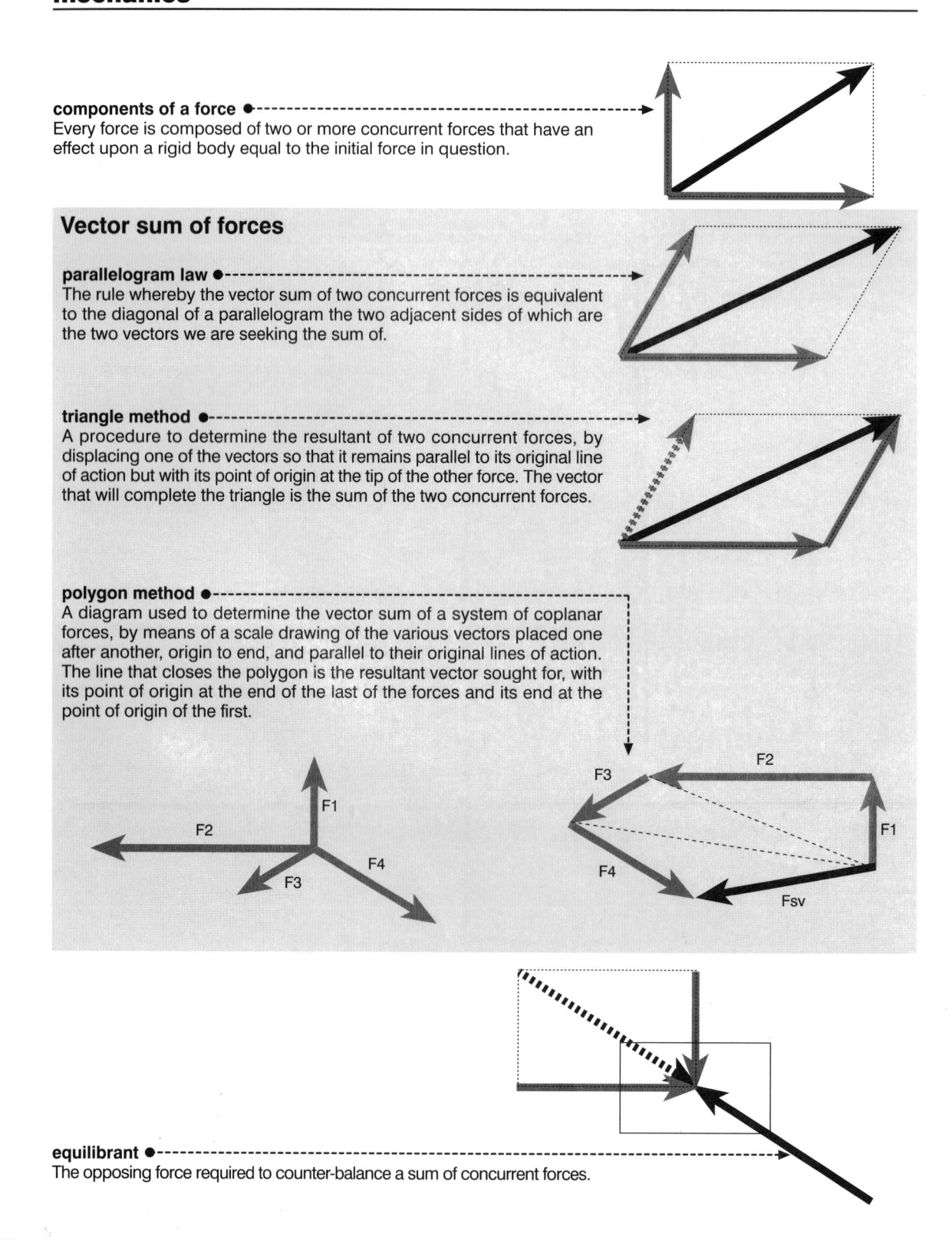

components of a force •- ▶
Every force is composed of two or more concurrent forces that have an effect upon a rigid body equal to the initial force in question.

Vector sum of forces

parallelogram law •- ▶
The rule whereby the vector sum of two concurrent forces is equivalent to the diagonal of a parallelogram the two adjacent sides of which are the two vectors we are seeking the sum of.

triangle method •- ▶
A procedure to determine the resultant of two concurrent forces, by displacing one of the vectors so that it remains parallel to its original line of action but with its point of origin at the tip of the other force. The vector that will complete the triangle is the sum of the two concurrent forces.

polygon method •- ▶
A diagram used to determine the vector sum of a system of coplanar forces, by means of a scale drawing of the various vectors placed one after another, origin to end, and parallel to their original lines of action. The line that closes the polygon is the resultant vector sought for, with its point of origin at the end of the last of the forces and its end at the point of origin of the first.

equilibrant •- ▶
The opposing force required to counter-balance a sum of concurrent forces.

mechanics

Newton's Laws

Newton's first Law, principle of inertia
Physical law which states that a body tends to remain in a state of rest or uniform rectilinear motion unless an external force acts upon it.

inertia
The tendency of a body to remain at rest or in uniform rectilinear motion unless an external force is applied upon it.

stability
That property by which a shape or a structure resists sliding, overturning, falling, or warping, tending to maintain a given position in space.

translation
A uniform, rectilinear displacement of a body, without rotation or inclination.

rotation
A circular displacement of a bdy around its own axis.

equilibrium
The state of rest of a body due to the perfect balance of all the forces acting upon it.

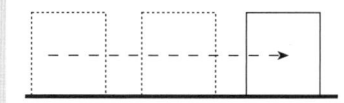

translational equilibrium
The resultant of all the forces that act upon a solid body adding up to zero.

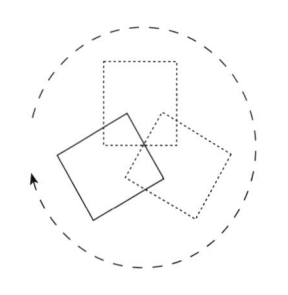

Newton´s second law of motion
A physical law which states that the sum of forces acting on a body is equal to the mass of the body times the acceleration produced by the said forces, with motion in the direction of the resultant of the forces.

Force (F) = mass (m) x acceleration (a).

weight (w) = mass (m) x gravitational acc. (g).

gravity
The force of attraction that the terrestrial mass exerts on a body close to its surface.

center of gravity
The point of origin of the resultant force of all the gravitational forces a body is submitted to. When this resultant vector force passes within its supporting base, the body remains stable.

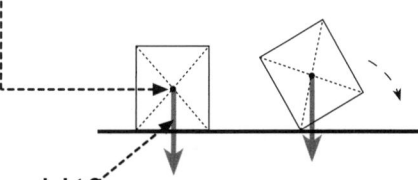

weight
The force of gravitational attraction that the earth exerts upon a body, equal to the mass of the body times the gravitational acceleration in that particular location.

law of action and reaction
A physical law stating that two bodies acting upon one another exert two forces of equal magnitude in opposite directions along the same line of action.

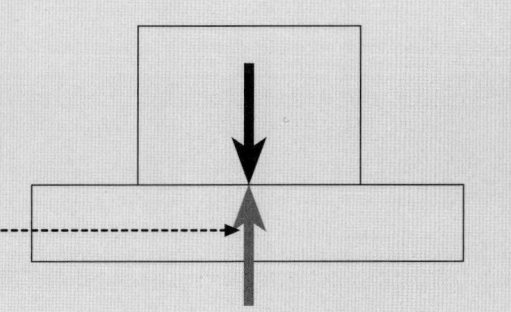

reactive force
An external force caused by the action of one body on another, also called a reaction

mechanics

moment
The property by which a force tends to cause a body's rotation around a point or line; its magnitude is equal to the force times the perpendicular distance from the point, or line, to the line of action of the force.

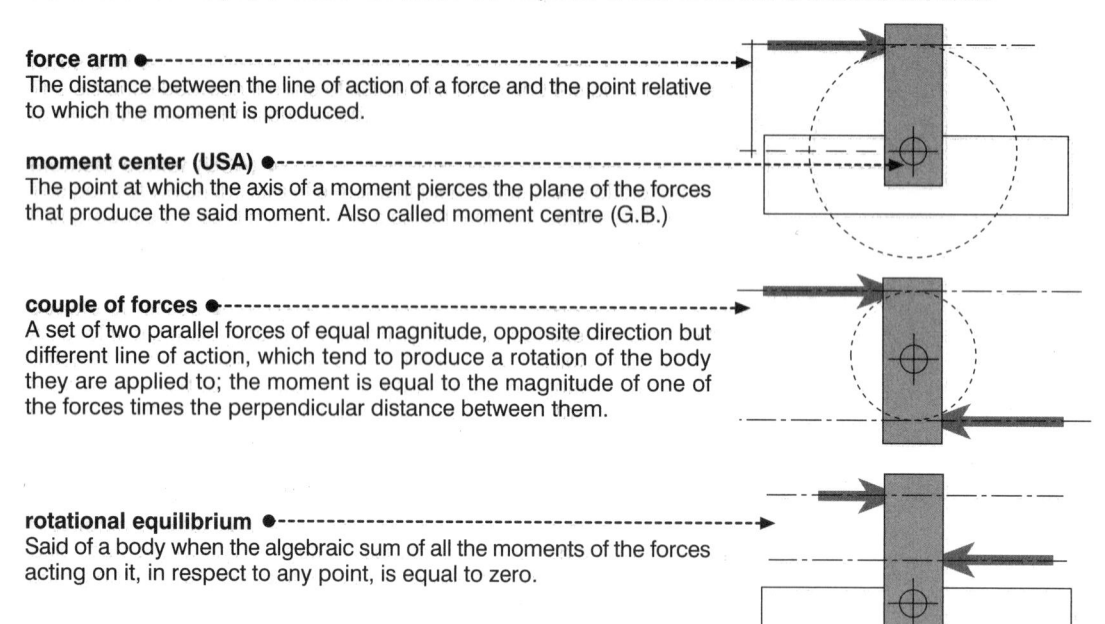

force arm
The distance between the line of action of a force and the point relative to which the moment is produced.

moment center (USA)
The point at which the axis of a moment pierces the plane of the forces that produce the said moment. Also called moment centre (G.B.)

couple of forces
A set of two parallel forces of equal magnitude, opposite direction but different line of action, which tend to produce a rotation of the body they are applied to; the moment is equal to the magnitude of one of the forces times the perpendicular distance between them.

rotational equilibrium
Said of a body when the algebraic sum of all the moments of the forces acting on it, in respect to any point, is equal to zero.

load
Force or set of forces that act upon a structure or structural element.

applied force
An external force that acts directly on a body.

axial load, axial force
The force that acts upon the longitudinal axis of a structural member and is applied at the center of the member's cross section, producing a uniform stress.

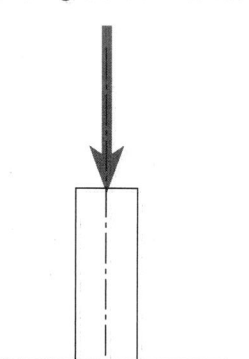

eccentric load, eccentric force
A load applied asymmetrically in respect to the central axis of a pillar or column, producing a bending moment.

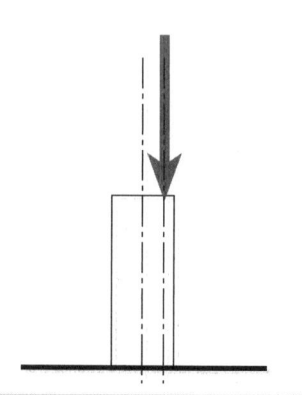

transverse force, transverse load
A force or load applied in a direction perpendicular to the longitudinal axis of a structural member, tending to produce a bend, a breakage or a displacement.

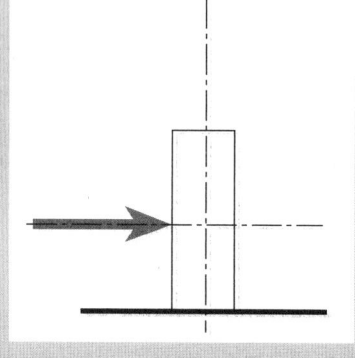

mechanics

actions

compression
The action of the forces that hold a body by applying pressure on its ends, tending to a reduction of the volume of elastic bodies.

compression member
A part subjected to a longitudinal compression

tension
1. The action of the forces that keep a body stretched by pulling in opposite directions from the ends of its longitudinal axis, tending to elongate it.

tension member
An element or part of a structure submitted to traction forces.

bending
The curvature or sag of a structural member, as a result of the load it is submitted to.

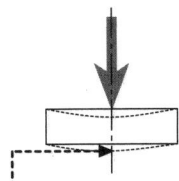

deflection
1. V shaped sign as a reference point or the limit of a geometrical element. 2. Deformation of a structural member due to a load applied upon it. 3. lateral displacement of an element due to wind or other external forces.

bending member
A part submitted to transversal forces causing it to bend or sag.

buckling
The elastic instability resulting in lateral deformation of the longitudinal axis of a structural member under compression, due to a disproportion between the compressing force and the diameter or rigidity of the member; it generally occurs suddenly.

buckling load
The axial load at which a column or other straight structural member begins to bend at the middle.

twist
The turn of a body around its longitudinal axis due to opposite torsion moments. 2. Deformation of a plank or piece of lumber due to an opposite bend in its two longitudinal edges. Also called torsion.

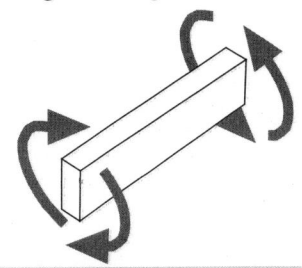

shear
1. A deformation in which two internal planes of an object slide along the plane of contact.
2. The lateral deformation resulting from an external force.

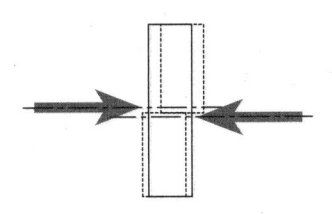

mechanics

Stresses and moments

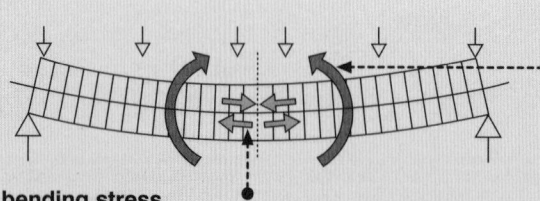

bending moment
The moment that results from the bending of part of a beam or other structural member; it is equal to the sum of the moments attached to the center of gravity of that part.

bending stress
The combination of traction and compression forces developed across the transversal section of a structural member resisting a transversal force.

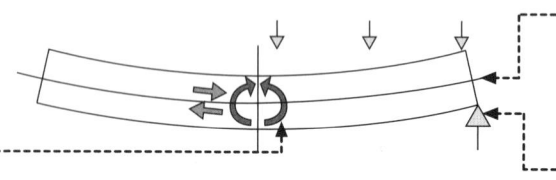

phantom line
An imaginary line inside a structural member subjected to bending, where neither tension nor compression occur and where no deformation takes place. Also called the neutral axis.

resisting moment
The moment of inertia of the area of the cross section of a structural member divided by the distance between the neutral grain and the end grain; also called the section modulus.

bearing
Any part of a beam, truss or other structural member that rests on a support.

point of support
The point of a structural member at which the load is transmitted in the form of a force to the support element.

shearing stress
Internal forces developing inside a body in response to shearing forces; they are tangential to the surface upon which they are exerted.

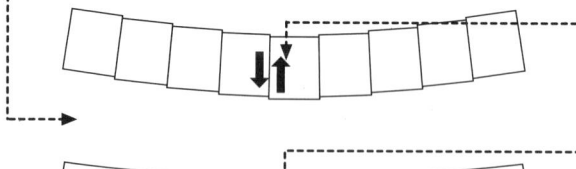

vertical shearing stress
The shearing stress that develops throughout the cross section of a structural member to resist a transversal or vertical shearing force.

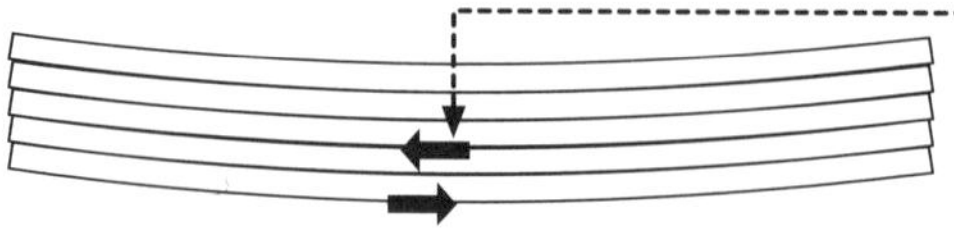

longitudinal shearing stress
The shearing stress that develops throughout a structural element subjected to transversal loads; it is equal to the vertical stress at that same point. Also called a horizontal shearing stress.

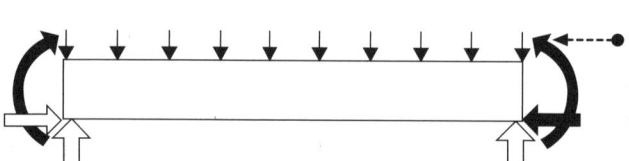

free-body diagram
Graphic representation of the system of external forces applied and the reactive forces that act upon a body or a particular part of a structure.

mechanics

axial stress
A stress that is perpendicular to the plane on which the traction or compression force is applied, and distributed evenly throughout its entire surface.

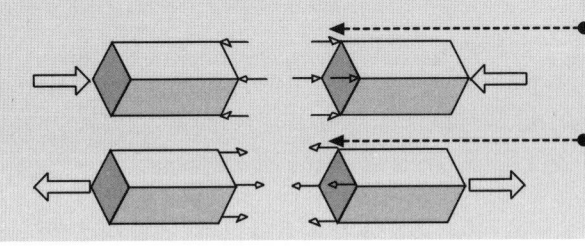

compressive stress
The stress that resists shortening by an external compressive force

tensile stress
A stress developed in the cross section of a part which is resisting elongation, and which tends to narrow the said crossed section.

shear diagram
A representation of the variations in the magnitude of the shearing force in a structural member, for a given system of loads and support conditions.

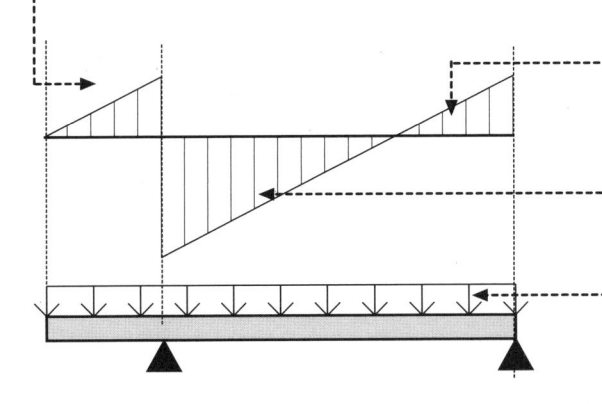

positive shear
The resultant of the forces that act vertically upwards on the left hand side of a given structure.

negative shear
The resultant of the forces that act vertically downwards on the left hand side of a given structure

uniformly distributed load
A load the magnitude of which has been evenly distributed. Also called evenly a distributed load.

moment diagram
The graphic representation of the alterations in magnitude of the bending moment throughout the axis of a structural member subjected to a determined set or system of transversal loads and with given conditions of support.

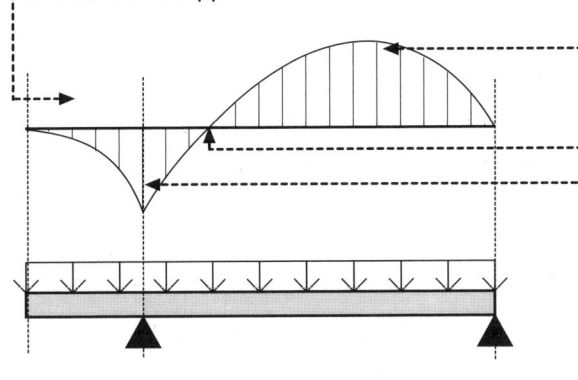

positive moment
The bending moment that produces a concave curve in a part of a structure; also called a positive bending moment.

inflection point
The point at which the curvature of a structure changes from convex to concave and vice versa, and at which the bending moment is zero.

negative bending moment (USA)
The bending moment that produces a convex curve in a part of a structure; also called a hogging moment.

mechanics

stress-strain diagram
Graphic representation showing the relation between the values of overall fatigue and those of the corresponding deformation in a given material.

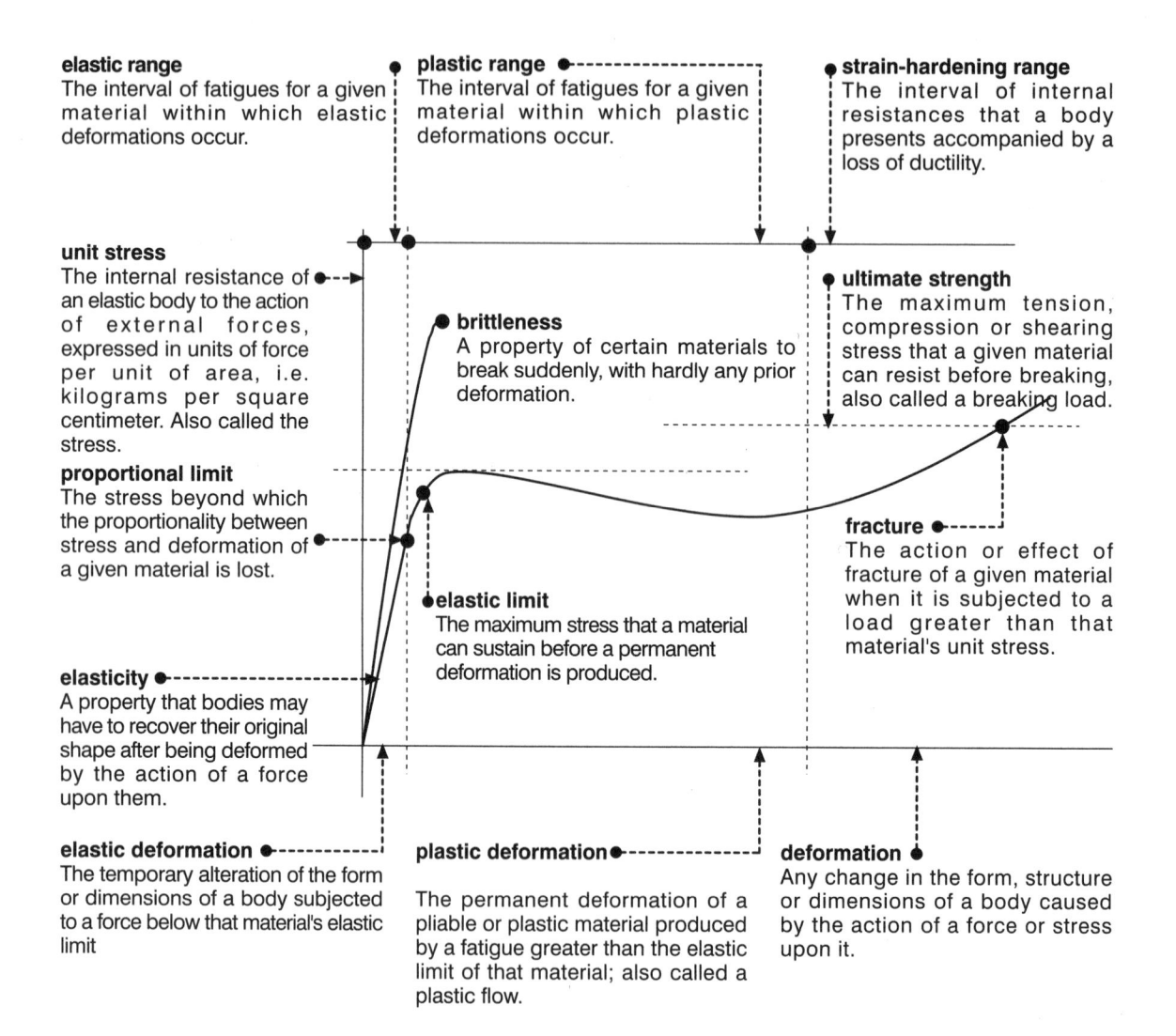

elastic range
The interval of fatigues for a given material within which elastic deformations occur.

plastic range
The interval of fatigues for a given material within which plastic deformations occur.

strain-hardening range
The interval of internal resistances that a body presents accompanied by a loss of ductility.

unit stress
The internal resistance of an elastic body to the action of external forces, expressed in units of force per unit of area, i.e. kilograms per square centimeter. Also called the stress.

brittleness
A property of certain materials to break suddenly, with hardly any prior deformation.

ultimate strength
The maximum tension, compression or shearing stress that a given material can resist before breaking, also called a breaking load.

proportional limit
The stress beyond which the proportionality between stress and deformation of a given material is lost.

elastic limit
The maximum stress that a material can sustain before a permanent deformation is produced.

fracture
The action or effect of fracture of a given material when it is subjected to a load greater than that material's unit stress.

elasticity
A property that bodies may have to recover their original shape after being deformed by the action of a force upon them.

elastic deformation
The temporary alteration of the form or dimensions of a body subjected to a force below that material's elastic limit.

plastic deformation
The permanent deformation of a pliable or plastic material produced by a fatigue greater than the elastic limit of that material; also called a plastic flow.

deformation
Any change in the form, structure or dimensions of a body caused by the action of a force or stress upon it.

permanent set
The permanent deformation in length of an elastic material after removal of the force that produced the deformation, expressed in percentage of the original length.

Hooke's law
A law according to which the deformation of an elastic body is proportional to the force acting on it, so long as the stress does not exceed the elastic limit.

yield point
The maximum stress above which a material will suffer plastic deformations, that will continue without an increase in the given stress.

structural analysis

Process by which a problem is reduced to its first causes, such as the localization of the forces that act upon a structure.

load combination
A general calculation of an element or structure, including the deadweight and the non-favorable occupancy loads that only act occasionally upon certain parts of the structure.

static load
A load applied gradually to a structure until it reaches its maximum, corresponding then to the maximum deformation of the structure.

concentrated load
The load that acts upon a very small area or a particular point of a structure.

distributed load
The load that is applied to the whole length of a structural member or to a part of it.

dynamic load
The load applied to a structure, often accompanied by sudden changes of intensity and position; under the action of a dynamic load the structure develops inertial forces and its maximum deformation does not necessarily coincide with the maximum intensity of the force applied.

impact load
The dynamic effect that a movable or static structure is subjected to when violent contact occurs with another body, with an applied force of only momentary duration.

impact factor
The factor by which the effect of a static load is to be multiplied to approach the effect of the same load applied dynamically.

critical buckling load
The maximum axial load that can be applied to a column or pillar before causing it to buckle. Also called the Euler buckling load.

local buckling
The lateral bend or buckling of a structural member subjected to compression forces tending to produce the collapse of the member.

effective length
The distance between two inflection points of a structural member subjected to buckling.

effective length factor
The factor that permits the modification of the real length of a column according to the conditions of support at its ends so as to determine its virtual length.

clear span
The distance between the internal sides of two supporting members.

structural analysis

load flow
The process that explains the way in which a structure gathers and distributes the loads resulting from external forces, directing them towards the foundations; the loads originate in the roof and each load becomes a force that acts upon the lower members. Also called the load trace.

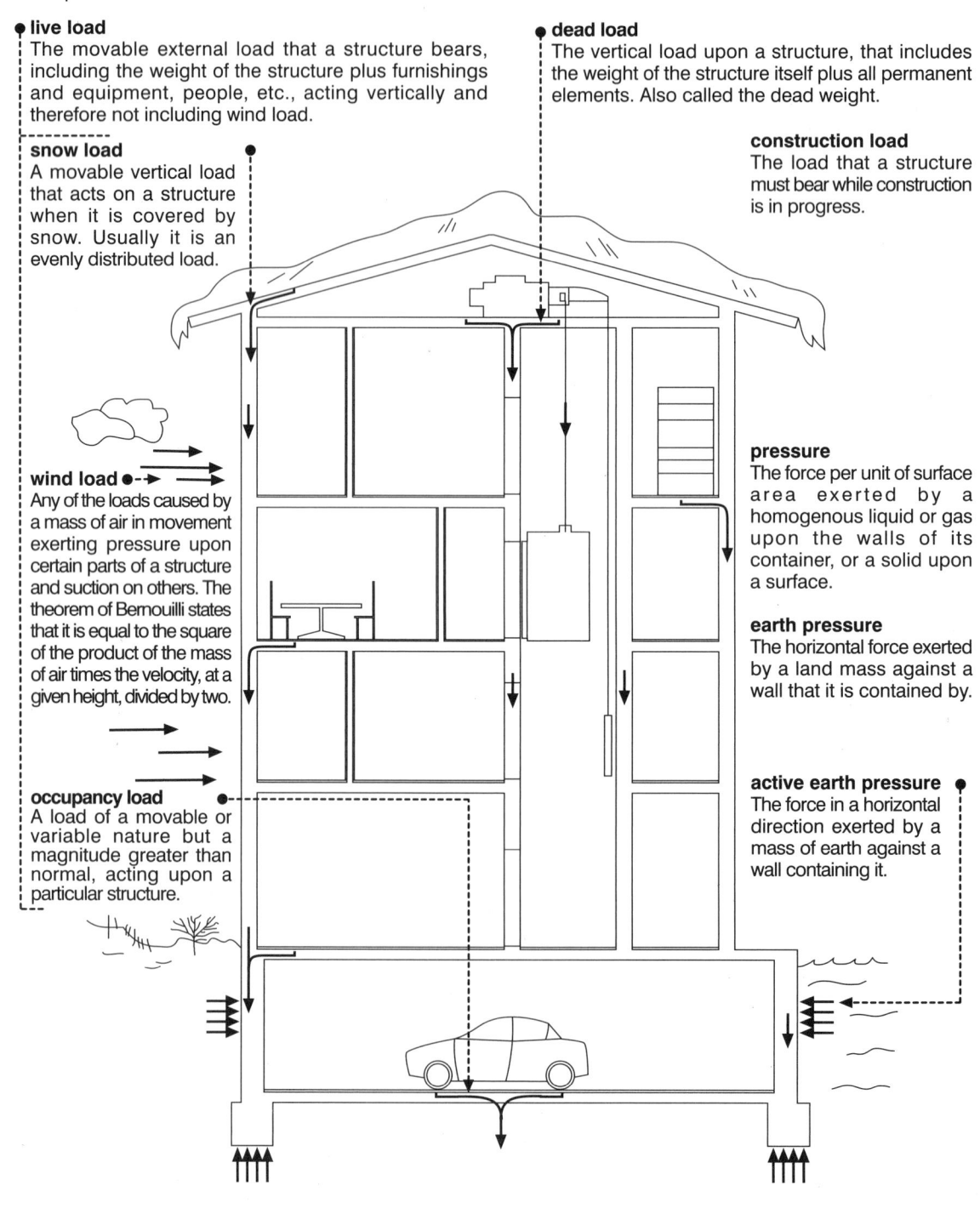

live load
The movable external load that a structure bears, including the weight of the structure plus furnishings and equipment, people, etc., acting vertically and therefore not including wind load.

snow load
A movable vertical load that acts on a structure when it is covered by snow. Usually it is an evenly distributed load.

wind load
Any of the loads caused by a mass of air in movement exerting pressure upon certain parts of a structure and suction on others. The theorem of Bernouilli states that it is equal to the square of the product of the mass of air times the velocity, at a given height, divided by two.

occupancy load
A load of a movable or variable nature but a magnitude greater than normal, acting upon a particular structure.

dead load
The vertical load upon a structure, that includes the weight of the structure itself plus all permanent elements. Also called the dead weight.

construction load
The load that a structure must bear while construction is in progress.

pressure
The force per unit of surface area exerted by a homogenous liquid or gas upon the walls of its container, or a solid upon a surface.

earth pressure
The horizontal force exerted by a land mass against a wall that it is contained by.

active earth pressure
The force in a horizontal direction exerted by a mass of earth against a wall containing it.

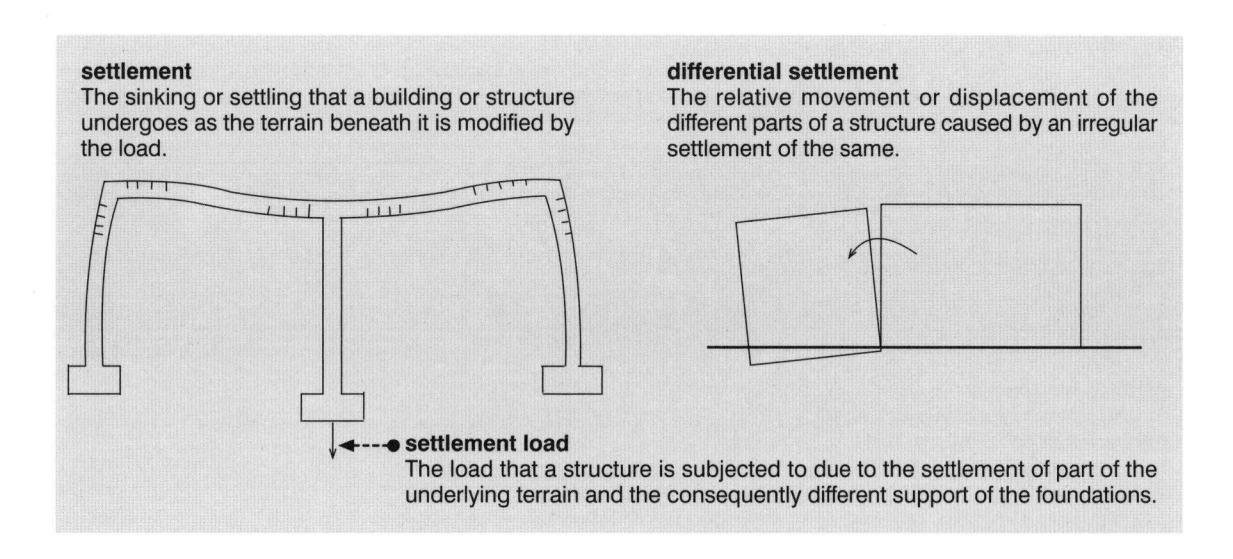

structural analysis

settlement
The sinking or settling that a building or structure undergoes as the terrain beneath it is modified by the load.

differential settlement
The relative movement or displacement of the different parts of a structure caused by an irregular settlement of the same.

settlement load
The load that a structure is subjected to due to the settlement of part of the underlying terrain and the consequently different support of the foundations.

earthquake
A series of longitudinal and transversal vibrations that occur throughout the crust of the earth's surface due to movements of the tectonic plates along the fault lines.

seismic force
Any of the forces caused by earth movements resulting from earthquakes; the design of horizontal structural components is vital, as these are the least resistant to this type of movements.

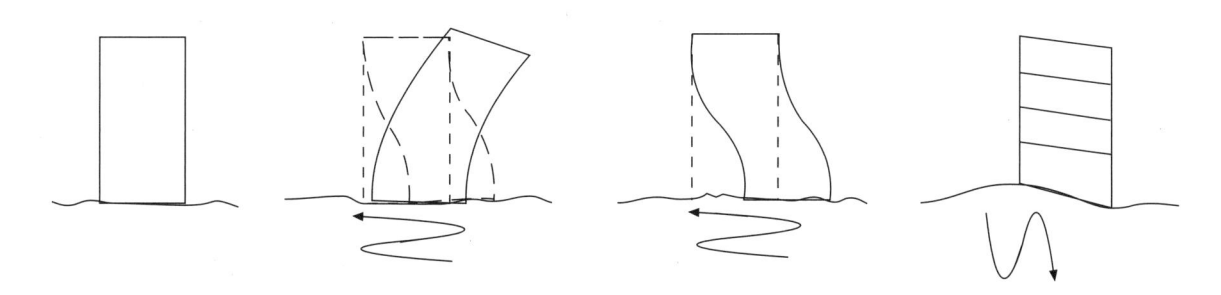

earthquake load
The force that the structure of a building is subjected to by an earthquake.

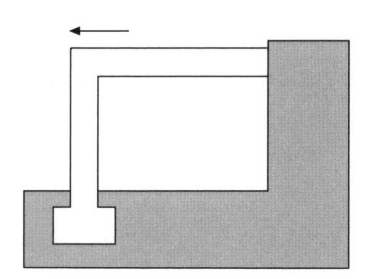

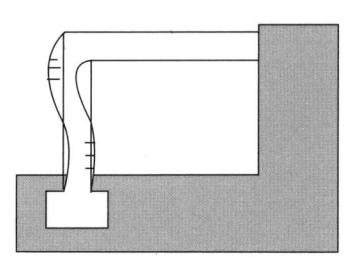

structure, f

The system of interconnected structural members that sustain and give form to a building. Also called a **frame, framework, shell, skeleton construction.**

---

structural member
Each of the constitutive parts of a structure posessing a unitary character, displaying itself as such under the action of an applied load.

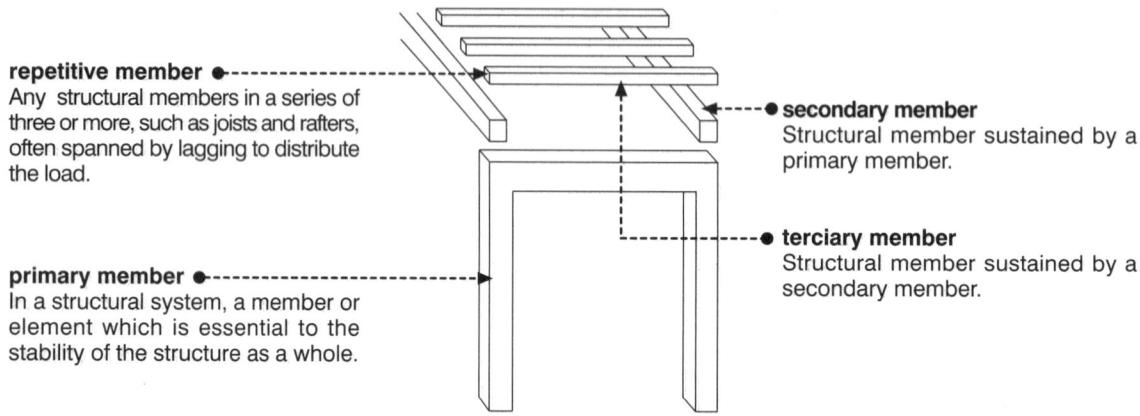

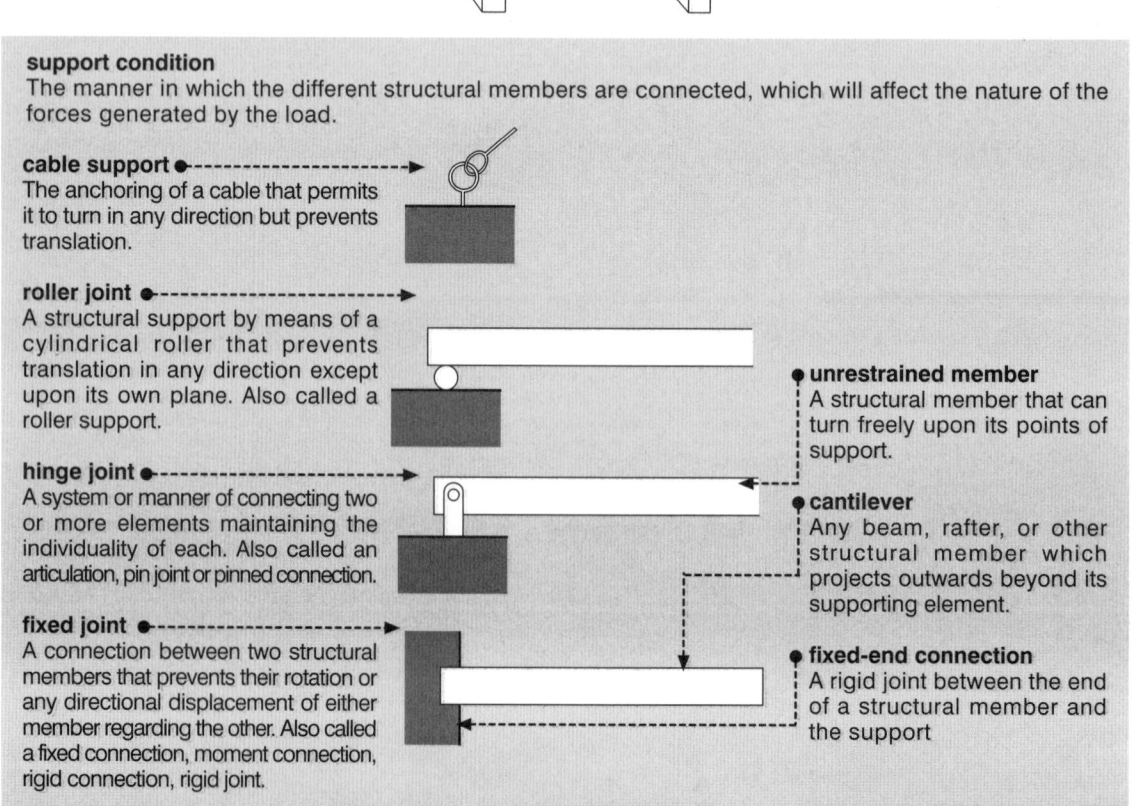

repetitive member
Any structural members in a series of three or more, such as joists and rafters, often spanned by lagging to distribute the load.

primary member
In a structural system, a member or element which is essential to the stability of the structure as a whole.

secondary member
Structural member sustained by a primary member.

terciary member
Structural member sustained by a secondary member.

support condition
The manner in which the different structural members are connected, which will affect the nature of the forces generated by the load.

cable support
The anchoring of a cable that permits it to turn in any direction but prevents translation.

roller joint
A structural support by means of a cylindrical roller that prevents translation in any direction except upon its own plane. Also called a roller support.

hinge joint
A system or manner of connecting two or more elements maintaining the individuality of each. Also called an articulation, pin joint or pinned connection.

fixed joint
A connection between two structural members that prevents their rotation or any directional displacement of either member regarding the other. Also called a fixed connection, moment connection, rigid connection, rigid joint.

unrestrained member
A structural member that can turn freely upon its points of support.

cantilever
Any beam, rafter, or other structural member which projects outwards beyond its supporting element.

fixed-end connection
A rigid joint between the end of a structural member and the support

structure

structural pattern
A placement or pattern of the vertical support elements throughout a structure so as to allow for an appropriate distribution of the beams, and of the internal spaces and functions.

regular structure
Structural systems characterized by the symmetrical configuration of their structural members and other components, resistance to lateral forces, avoidance of discontinuities or breaks affecting the rigidity and resistance of the whole.

irregular structure
Structural systems characterized by having irregularities, in their footprint, elevation or both; an analysis is required to determine the torsions that may arise due to lateral forces.

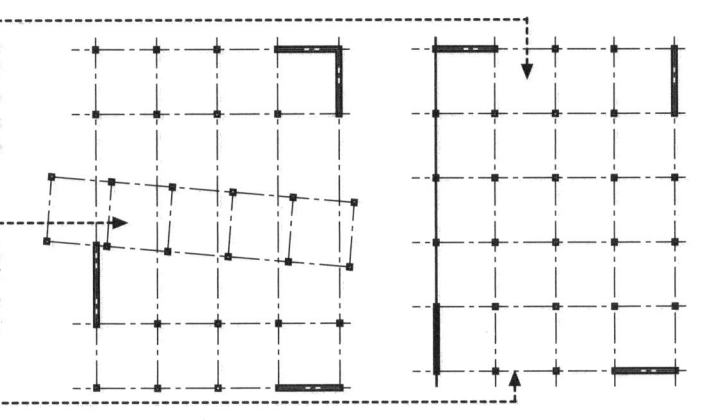

structural grid
A reticule that determines the main points and lines of support throughout a structural system.

linear structure
A structural member the length of which is more significant than its other dimensions.

two-way structure
A structure or structural member which has the particularity of being able to act in two or more directions.

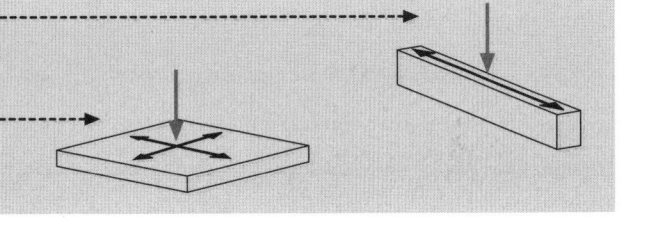

determinate structure
A structure that can be analyzed according to the laws of statics; the suppression of any of its links leads to collapse.

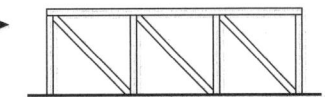

indeterminate structure
A structure requiring more than the necessary elements to remain stable; the suppression of one of them does not lead to collapse but modifies the conditions of static function.

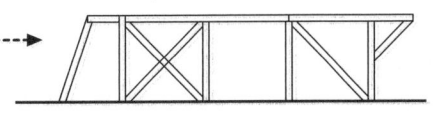

unstable structure
A structure the members of which are distributed in such a way that there is danger of collapse or failure if a force is applied upon it.

structural failure
Any external or internal condition that prevents a structure or structural member from fulfilling the function for which it was designed.

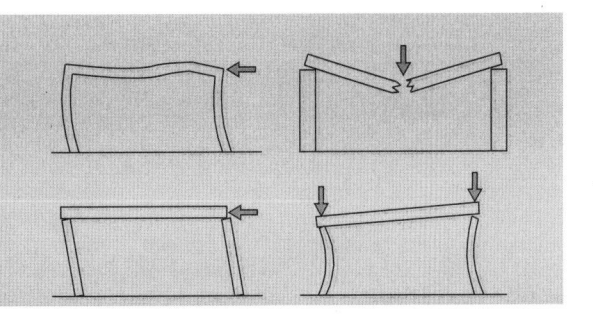

bulk-active structure

A structure or structural member that transmits the external forces acting on it, according to the mass and the continuity of the material it is composed of.

pillar
A rigid vertical support, generally of stone, concrete or steel, used as a sustaining structural member or as a monument if it is standing alone; when its cross section is circular it is usually referred to as a column.

column
A vertical, relatively slender structural member, usually with a circular cross-section, designed to undergo compressive stress, supporting axial loads applied at its ends.

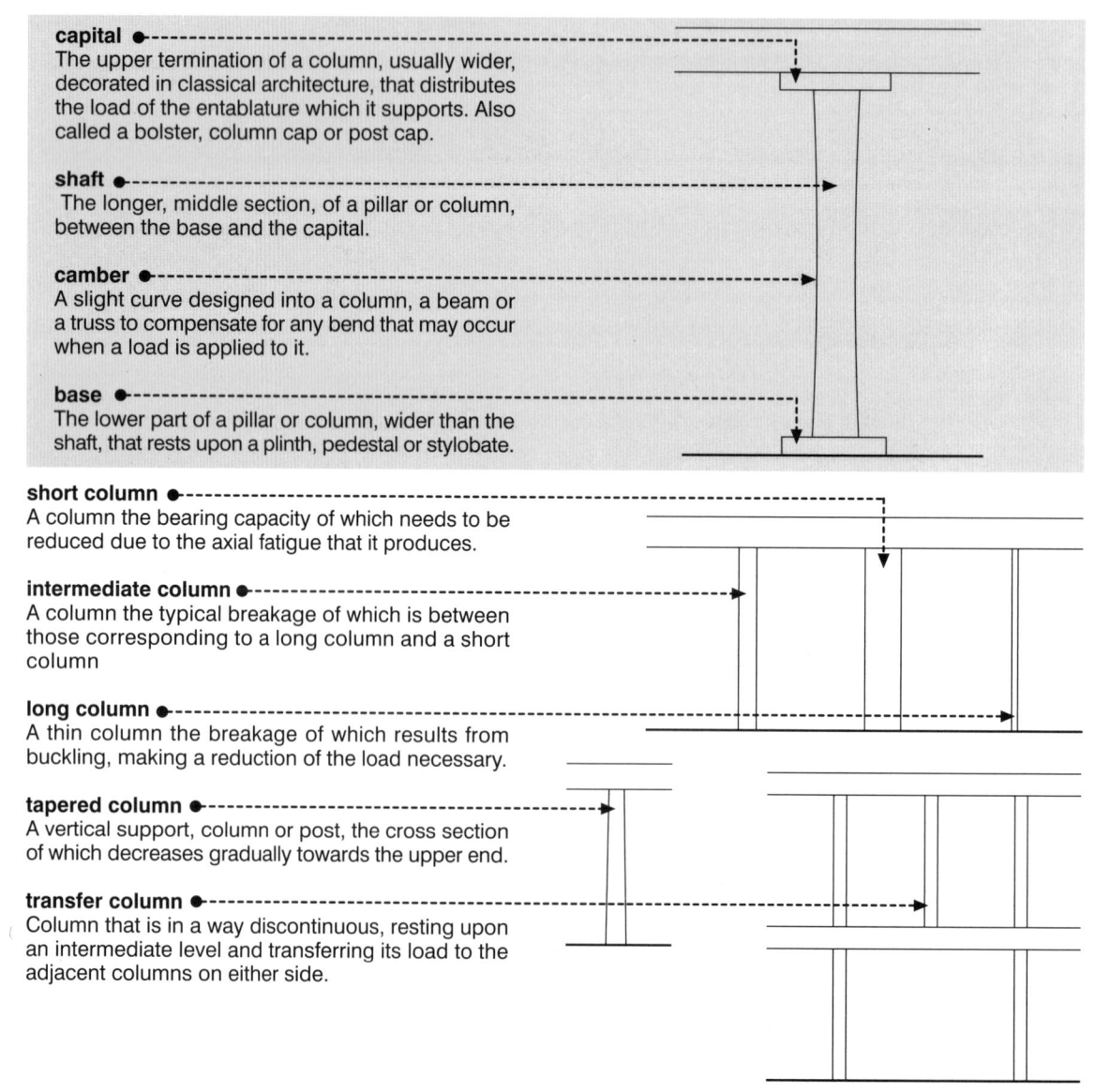

capital
The upper termination of a column, usually wider, decorated in classical architecture, that distributes the load of the entablature which it supports. Also called a bolster, column cap or post cap.

shaft
The longer, middle section, of a pillar or column, between the base and the capital.

camber
A slight curve designed into a column, a beam or a truss to compensate for any bend that may occur when a load is applied to it.

base
The lower part of a pillar or column, wider than the shaft, that rests upon a plinth, pedestal or stylobate.

short column
A column the bearing capacity of which needs to be reduced due to the axial fatigue that it produces.

intermediate column
A column the typical breakage of which is between those corresponding to a long column and a short column

long column
A thin column the breakage of which results from buckling, making a reduction of the load necessary.

tapered column
A vertical support, column or post, the cross section of which decreases gradually towards the upper end.

transfer column
Column that is in a way discontinuous, resting upon an intermediate level and transferring its load to the adjacent columns on either side.

bulk-active structure

solid column
A column made of a single timber or of laminated wood, or rectangular and having no hollow space within its exterior surfaces.

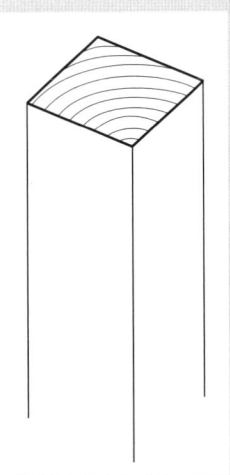

spaced column
A wooden column made of several parallel planks held separate along the whole length by wooden blocks which also keep them connected.

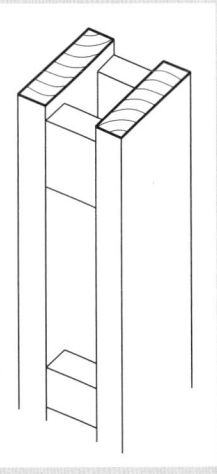

box column
A pillar or column built of wooden planks around a square or rectangular hollow space.

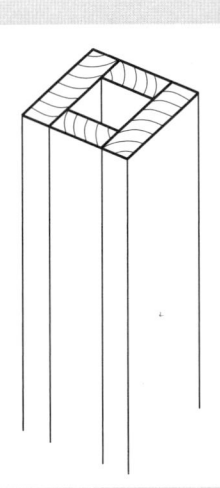

built-up column
A wooden column made of several boards glued together plus two or more parallel planks.

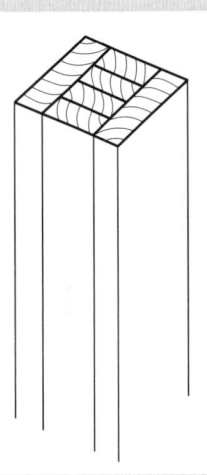

engaged column
A pillar or column that only partly emerges from a wall it is built into. Also called a pilaster or respond.

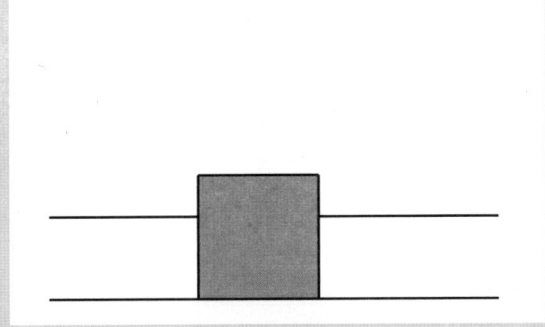

attached column
A column that emerges more than three quarters out of the wall it is built into.

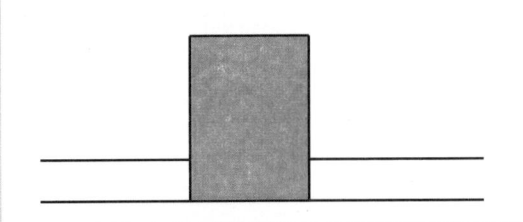

bulk-active structure

reinforced concrete pile
A vertical structural member made of reinforced concrete, for the support of upper floors or roofs. Its cross sectional area is 96 square inches (25 cm x 25 cm).

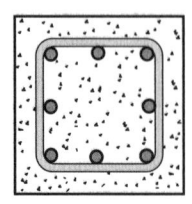

spiral column
A concrete pillar or column reinforced with a spiral network of steel rods so as to increase the resistance to compression and avoid buckling.

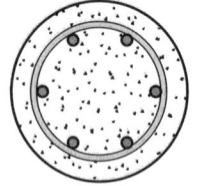

pipe column
A steel tube used as an upright post, that can be filled with concrete.

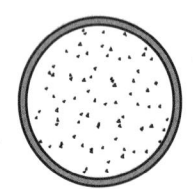

composite pillar
A steel pillar totally encased in reinforced concrete with a perimetral spiral network to prevent buckling.

compound column
A pillar made of structural steel coated with a 64 mm (2 1/2 inches) layer of concrete.

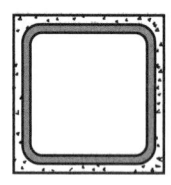

steel column
A post made of steel angles, in a single piece or in a composite manner, the cross section design of which determines its particular performance under load.

box beam
A beam or girder made up of various steel or timber parts leaving the center hollow. Also called a box girder.

composite beam
A steel structural member built up of several component parts.

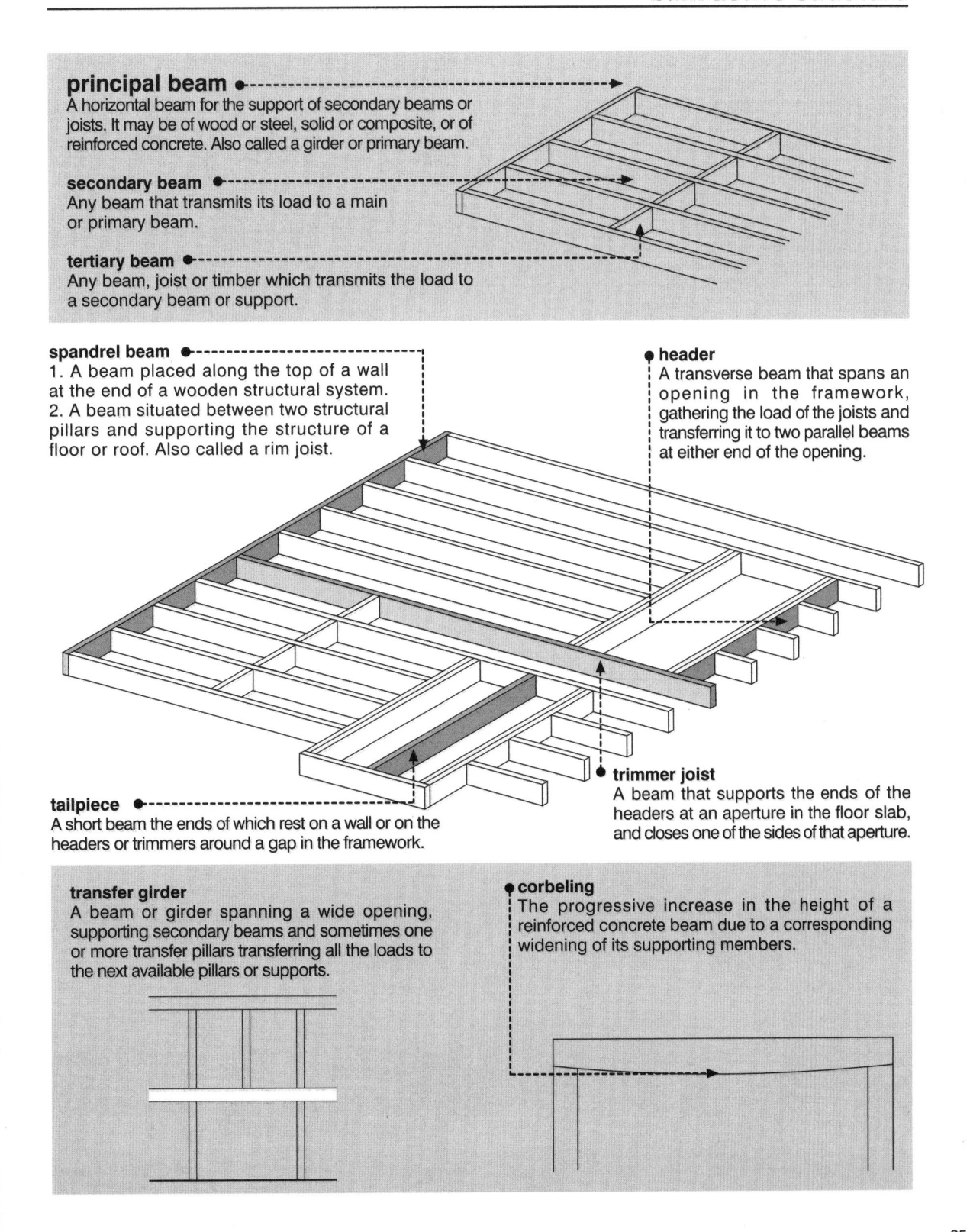

bulk-active structure

principal beam
A horizontal beam for the support of secondary beams or joists. It may be of wood or steel, solid or composite, or of reinforced concrete. Also called a girder or primary beam.

secondary beam
Any beam that transmits its load to a main or primary beam.

tertiary beam
Any beam, joist or timber which transmits the load to a secondary beam or support.

spandrel beam
1. A beam placed along the top of a wall at the end of a wooden structural system.
2. A beam situated between two structural pillars and supporting the structure of a floor or roof. Also called a rim joist.

header
A transverse beam that spans an opening in the framework, gathering the load of the joists and transferring it to two parallel beams at either end of the opening.

tailpiece
A short beam the ends of which rest on a wall or on the headers or trimmers around a gap in the framework.

trimmer joist
A beam that supports the ends of the headers at an aperture in the floor slab, and closes one of the sides of that aperture.

transfer girder
A beam or girder spanning a wide opening, supporting secondary beams and sometimes one or more transfer pillars transferring all the loads to the next available pillars or supports.

corbeling
The progressive increase in the height of a reinforced concrete beam due to a corresponding widening of its supporting members.

bulk-active structure

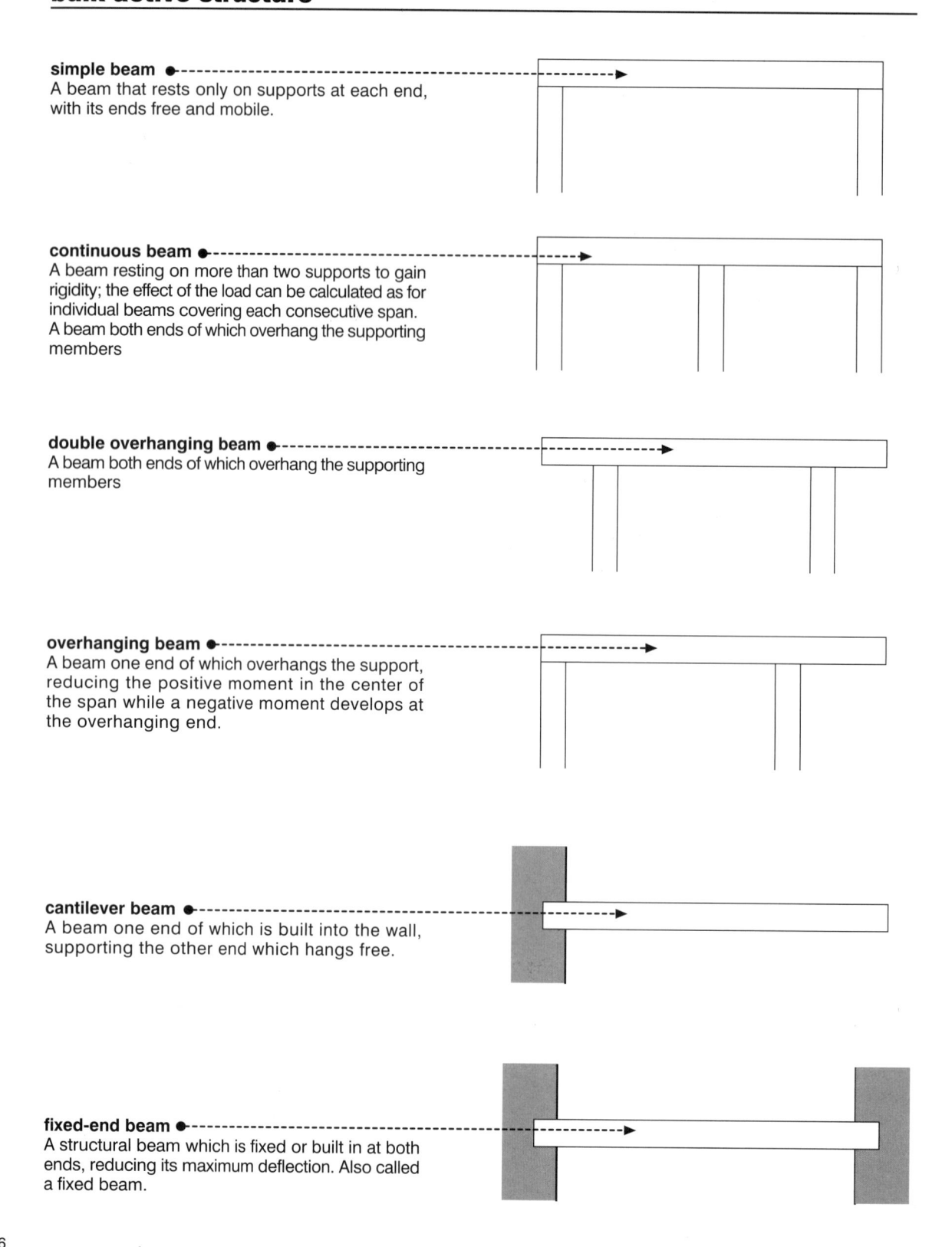

simple beam
A beam that rests only on supports at each end, with its ends free and mobile.

continuous beam
A beam resting on more than two supports to gain rigidity; the effect of the load can be calculated as for individual beams covering each consecutive span. A beam both ends of which overhang the supporting members

double overhanging beam
A beam both ends of which overhang the supporting members

overhanging beam
A beam one end of which overhangs the support, reducing the positive moment in the center of the span while a negative moment develops at the overhanging end.

cantilever beam
A beam one end of which is built into the wall, supporting the other end which hangs free.

fixed-end beam
A structural beam which is fixed or built in at both ends, reducing its maximum deflection. Also called a fixed beam.

bulk-active structure

reinforced concrete beam
A concrete beam capable of resisting the forces that act upon it due to the outstanding joint functions of concrete with the steel reinforcement bars and transverse stirrups.

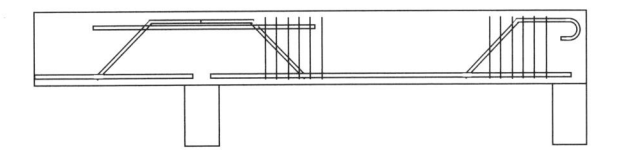

ledger beam
A concrete beam with lateral projections for the support of other structural members.

T-beam
A concrete beam the lower part of which projects beneath it, adding greater resistance to deflection and shearing stress.

inverted T-beam
A prestressed reinforced concrete beam with a lower lateral projection or flange, in the form of an inverted T.

L-beam
A prestressed reinforced concrete beam with a lower projection or flange on one side only; its cross section forms an L.

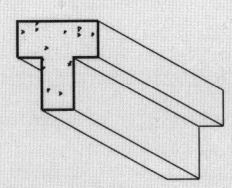

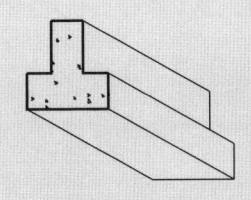

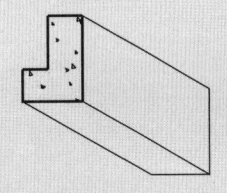

compound girder
1. A beam made of various layers of wood joined with glue, screws or bolts to make up a more sturdy structural member. 2. A steel beam made up of various lighter steel parts, soldered or bolted together.

I-beam
A beam consisting of a wooden plank which forms the beam's web, to which two wooden flanges have been attached along the upper and lower edges. Also called an I joist.

box beam
A beam made up of several components with an empty center. Also called a box girder.

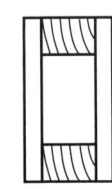

trussed beam
A wooden beam the bearing capacity of which is aided be a system of tie rods and braces, in the form of a truss.

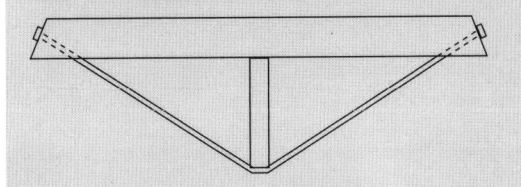

trussed joist
A horizontal truss, usually of wood, used to support floors, and the web of which is a system of diagonal steel connectors.

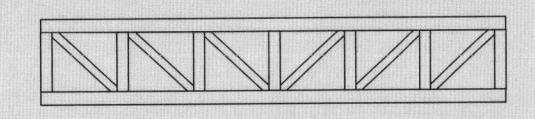

bulk-active structure

steel beam
A beam consisting in a combination of several layers of steel components

flange
Wide lateral projection perpendicular to the web of the beam, to add rigidity and support.

web
Flat central element of a beam that carries almost all of the vertical load.

flange angle
The angles, usually 90 degrees, that perform as the upper and lower flanges, or as the connection between the web and the flanges of a beam.

cover plate
One or more layers of steel plate added over the flanges of a beam to increase its girth and rigidity regarding lateral forces.

flitchplate
A steel sheet welded or riveted to the web of a composite beam to increase its capacity to bear vertical loads, or enclosed between the layers of a composite wooden beam for the same purpose.

open-web steel joist
A steel beam the web of which has been lightened to save steel in cases where the bending stress is greater than the shear; there are various types, such as the bar joist, open web joists, trussed joist.

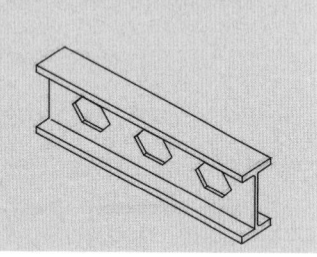

castellated beam
A composite steel beam made by cutting a zigzag through the web of a beam, displacing the two halves so that only the peaks meet; welded together, the depth of the web of the beam will have been increased without adding to the weight.

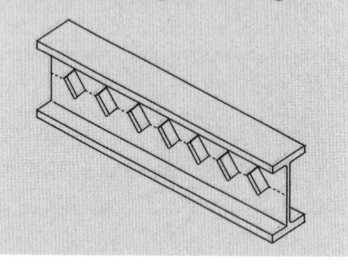

beam pocket
A cavity or gap in the vertical face of a wall constructed to receive the head of a beam.

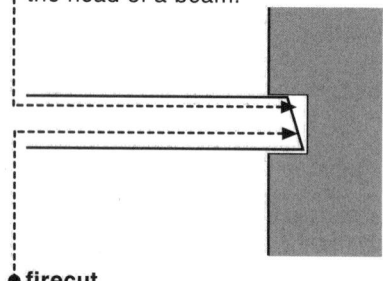

firecut
A diagonal cut at the head of a beam which prevents damage to the wall in case of fire.

box beam
A steel beam with a hollow center. Also called a box girder.

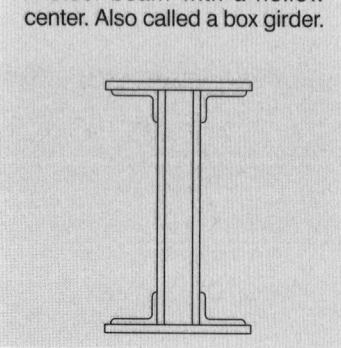

H beam
A steel beam in the form of an H.

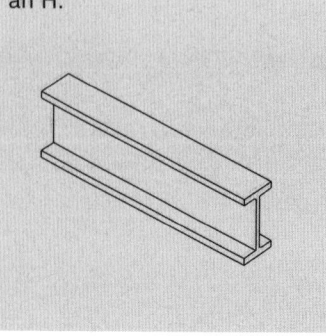

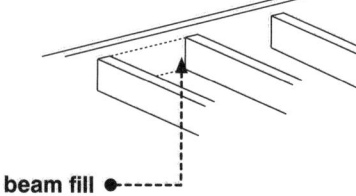

beam fill
The material used to fill the gaps between the beams at the supports, giving added fire resistance; may be brickwork or other masonry.

frame system

A structural system consisting of a set of interconnected linear elements to make up a whole, with the function of bearing the gravitational load and the lateral forces.

Frame structure

A frame structure designed to bear vertical gravitational and lateral transversal loads affecting the span of the frame in question.

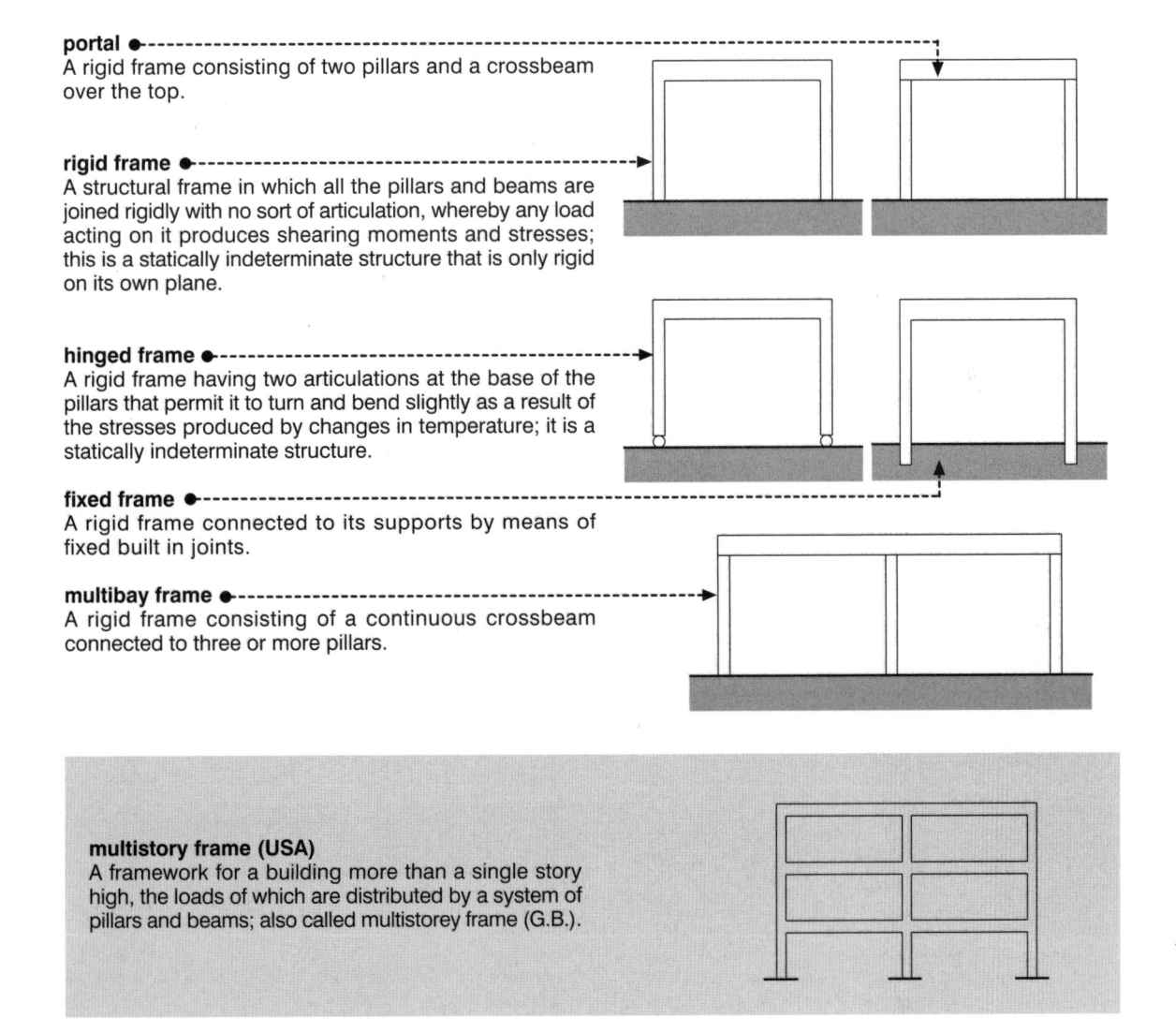

portal
A rigid frame consisting of two pillars and a crossbeam over the top.

rigid frame
A structural frame in which all the pillars and beams are joined rigidly with no sort of articulation, whereby any load acting on it produces shearing moments and stresses; this is a statically indeterminate structure that is only rigid on its own plane.

hinged frame
A rigid frame having two articulations at the base of the pillars that permit it to turn and bend slightly as a result of the stresses produced by changes in temperature; it is a statically indeterminate structure.

fixed frame
A rigid frame connected to its supports by means of fixed built in joints.

multibay frame
A rigid frame consisting of a continuous crossbeam connected to three or more pillars.

multistory frame (USA)
A framework for a building more than a single story high, the loads of which are distributed by a system of pillars and beams; also called multistorey frame (G.B.).

frame system

lateral stability
The capacity of an object to resist the lateral forces without overturning, buckling or collapsing.

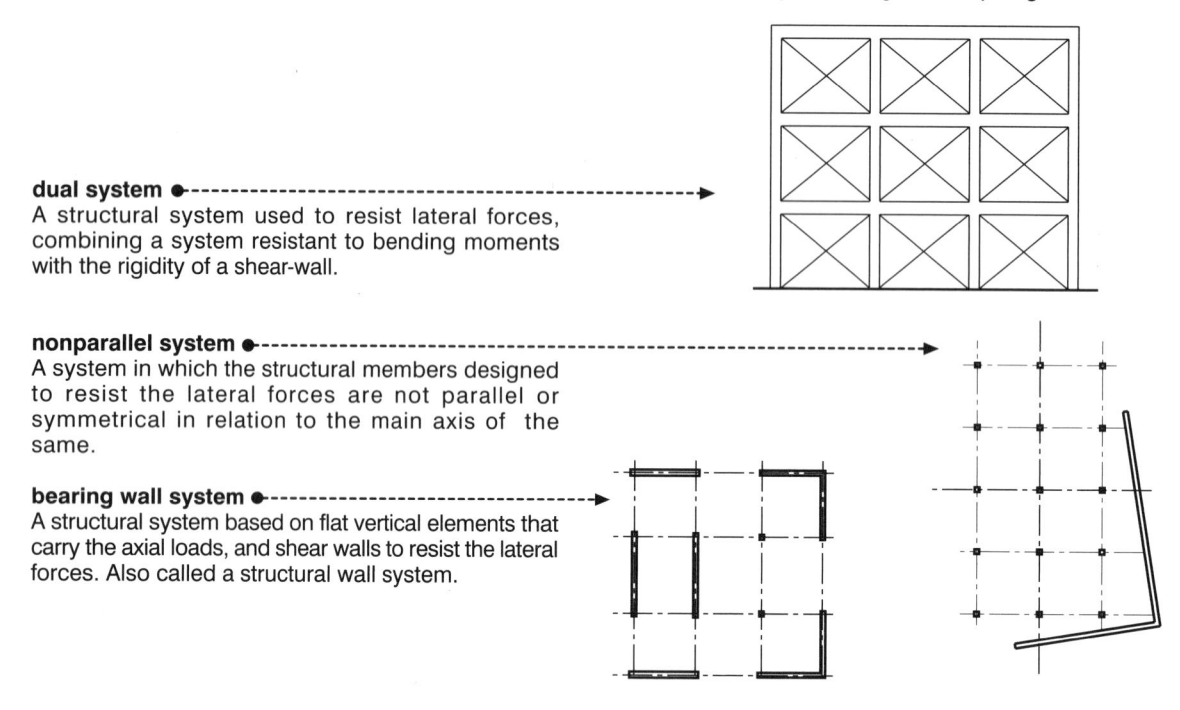

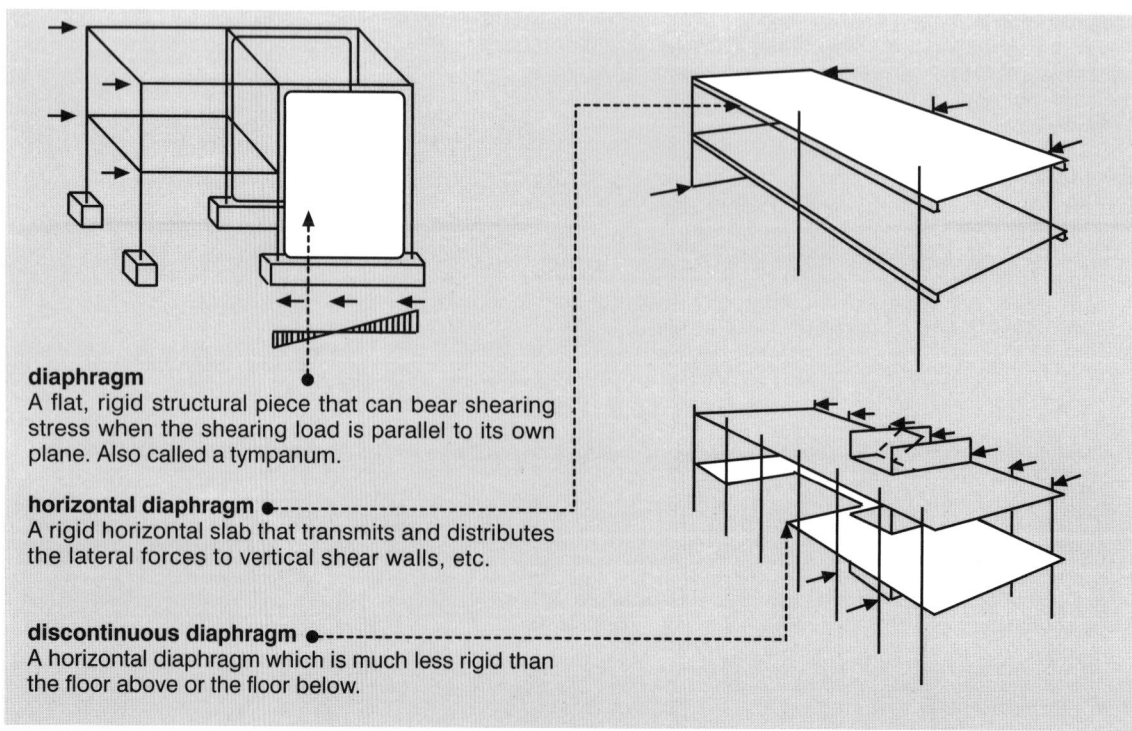

dual system
A structural system used to resist lateral forces, combining a system resistant to bending moments with the rigidity of a shear-wall.

nonparallel system
A system in which the structural members designed to resist the lateral forces are not parallel or symmetrical in relation to the main axis of the same.

bearing wall system
A structural system based on flat vertical elements that carry the axial loads, and shear walls to resist the lateral forces. Also called a structural wall system.

diaphragm
A flat, rigid structural piece that can bear shearing stress when the shearing load is parallel to its own plane. Also called a tympanum.

horizontal diaphragm
A rigid horizontal slab that transmits and distributes the lateral forces to vertical shear walls, etc.

discontinuous diaphragm
A horizontal diaphragm which is much less rigid than the floor above or the floor below.

frame system

bracing
A system of braces between joists or similar structural members that help to distribute the load and prevent the structure from being deformed.

Braced frame structure
A building's framework in which the resistance to lateral forces or other potential instabillities are counteracted by diagonal, triangular or any other type of bracing.

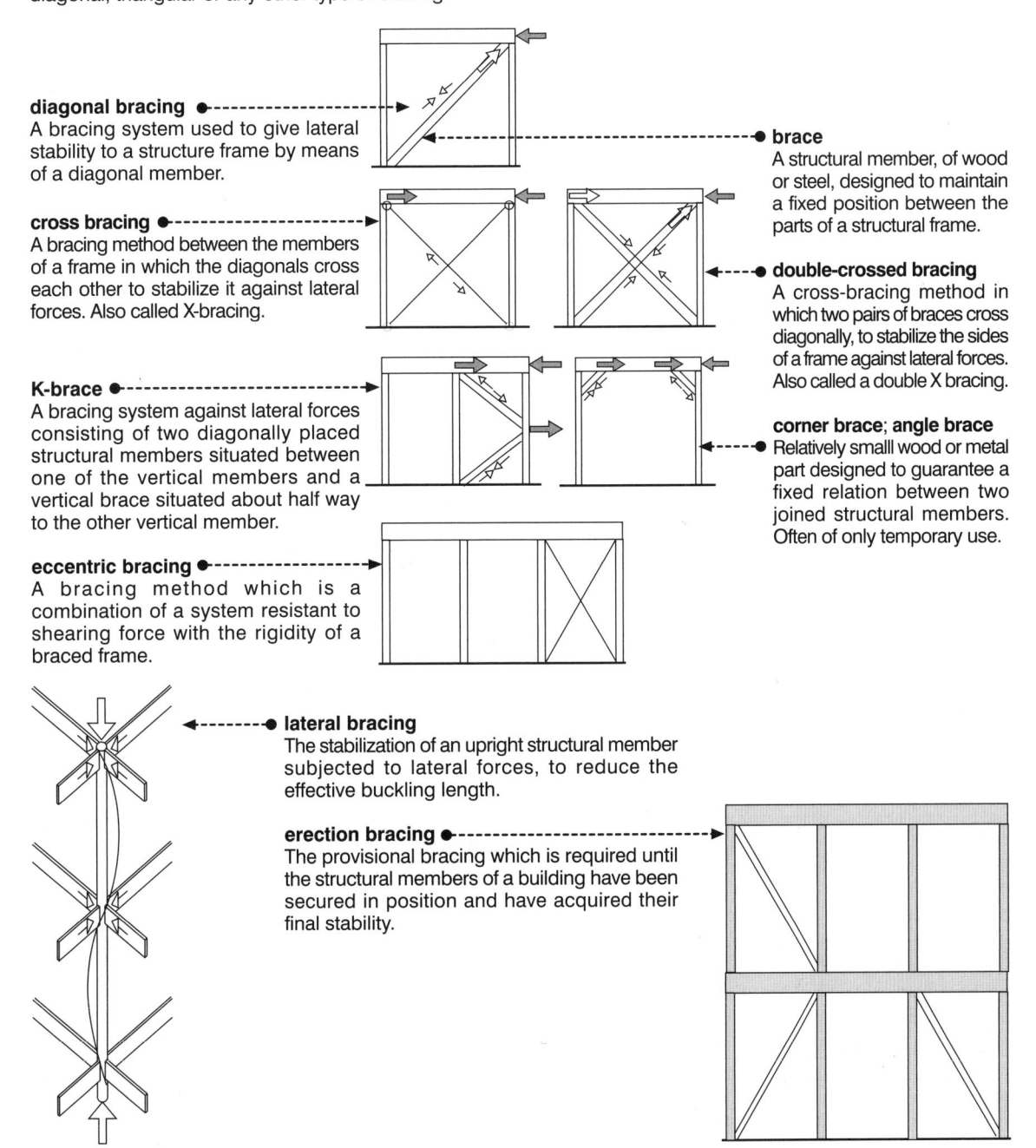

diagonal bracing
A bracing system used to give lateral stability to a structure frame by means of a diagonal member.

cross bracing
A bracing method between the members of a frame in which the diagonals cross each other to stabilize it against lateral forces. Also called X-bracing.

K-brace
A bracing system against lateral forces consisting of two diagonally placed structural members situated between one of the vertical members and a vertical brace situated about half way to the other vertical member.

eccentric bracing
A bracing method which is a combination of a system resistant to shearing force with the rigidity of a braced frame.

brace
A structural member, of wood or steel, designed to maintain a fixed position between the parts of a structural frame.

double-crossed bracing
A cross-bracing method in which two pairs of braces cross diagonally, to stabilize the sides of a frame against lateral forces. Also called a double X bracing.

corner brace; angle brace
Relatively smalll wood or metal part designed to guarantee a fixed relation between two joined structural members. Often of only temporary use.

lateral bracing
The stabilization of an upright structural member subjected to lateral forces, to reduce the effective buckling length.

erection bracing
The provisional bracing which is required until the structural members of a building have been secured in position and have acquired their final stability.

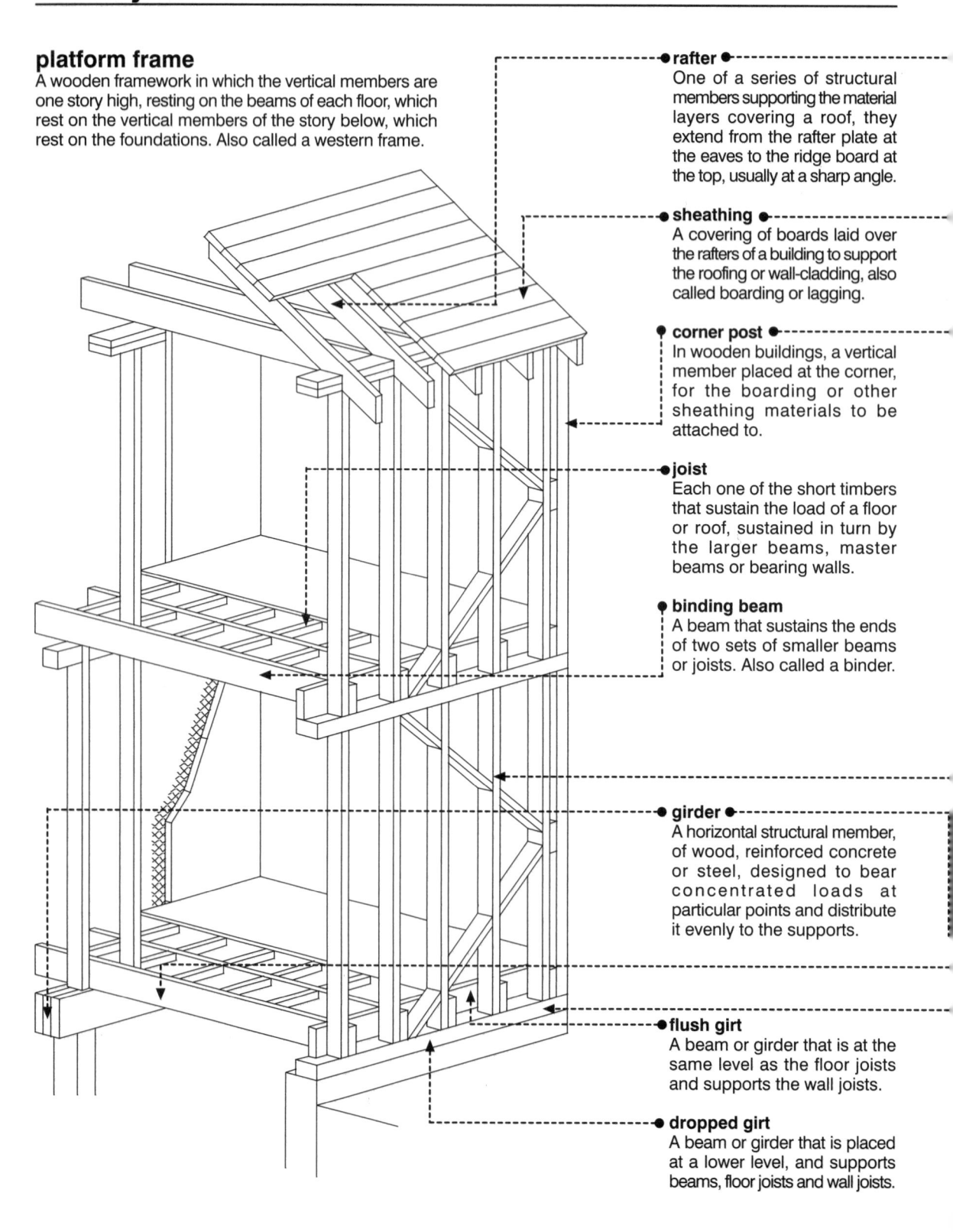

frame system

platform frame
A wooden framework in which the vertical members are one story high, resting on the beams of each floor, which rest on the vertical members of the story below, which rest on the foundations. Also called a western frame.

rafter
One of a series of structural members supporting the material layers covering a roof, they extend from the rafter plate at the eaves to the ridge board at the top, usually at a sharp angle.

sheathing
A covering of boards laid over the rafters of a building to support the roofing or wall-cladding, also called boarding or lagging.

corner post
In wooden buildings, a vertical member placed at the corner, for the boarding or other sheathing materials to be attached to.

joist
Each one of the short timbers that sustain the load of a floor or roof, sustained in turn by the larger beams, master beams or bearing walls.

binding beam
A beam that sustains the ends of two sets of smaller beams or joists. Also called a binder.

girder
A horizontal structural member, of wood, reinforced concrete or steel, designed to bear concentrated loads at particular points and distribute it evenly to the supports.

flush girt
A beam or girder that is at the same level as the floor joists and supports the wall joists.

dropped girt
A beam or girder that is placed at a lower level, and supports beams, floor joists and wall joists.

frame system

balloon frame
A wooden framework of a building in which all the vertical structural members of the outer walls cover the whole height, from the sleeper to the head. All the beams are nailed to the vertical members. Also called a balloon framing

girt
A horizontal structural member parallel to the floor joists, used to connect the vertical joists of a wooden braced frame structure.

post
A vertical structural member used to resist longitudinal compression, especially in post-and-beam or post-and-lintel construction.

stilt *m*
A vertical structural member used to resist longitudinal compression, especially in post-and-beam or post-and-lintel construction. Any vertical structural member that makes up the skeleton or structure of a wall or partition.

beam
A horizontal structural member used to carry and transfer the vertical loads to which it is subjected.

sleeper
1. The lowest horizontal member of a wooden frame structure, lying directly on the foundations or the ground. 2. A horizontal member fixed or placed on the upper part of a wall to support and distribute the load of the beams.

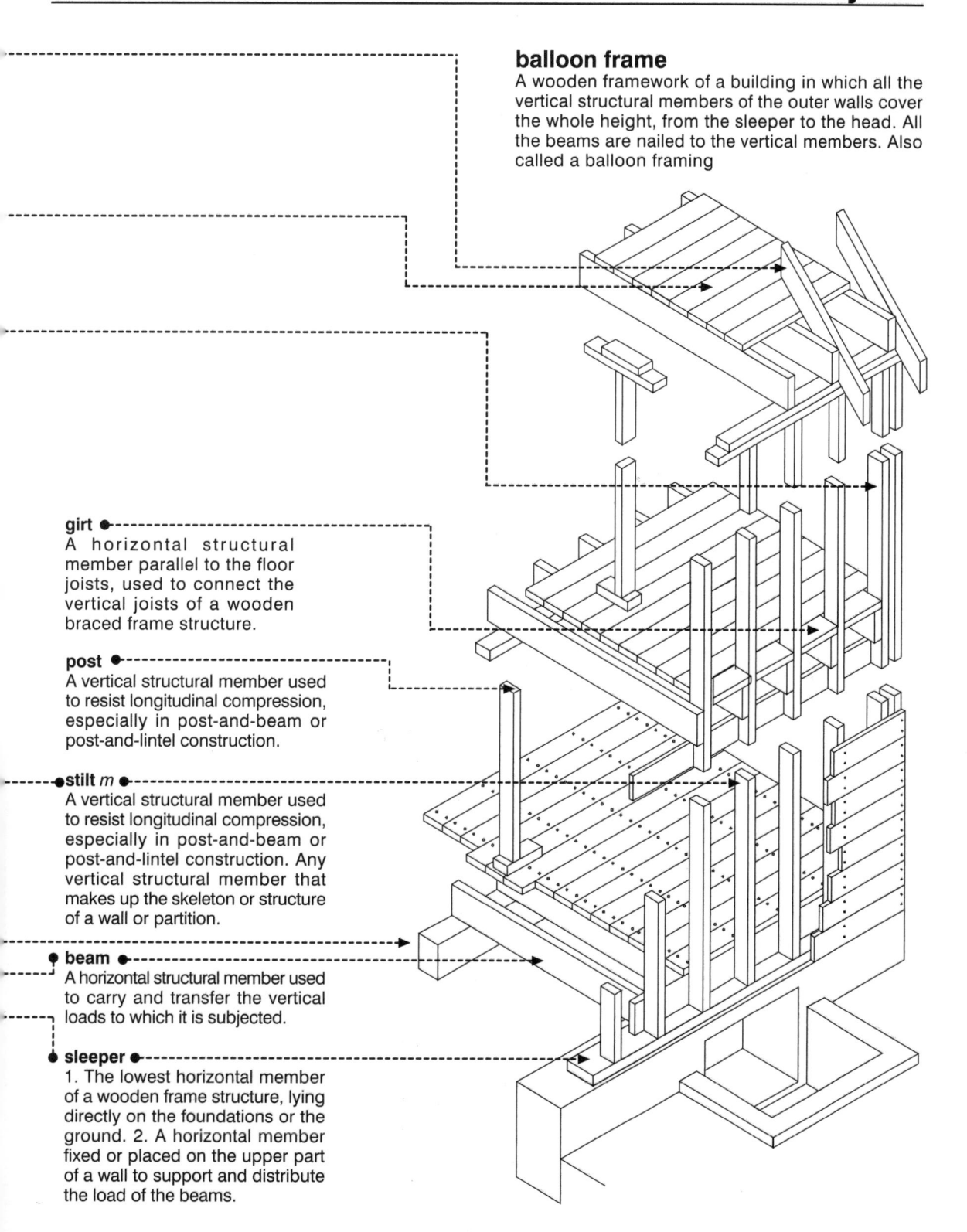

frame system

framing anchor
Any of a variety of metal devices designed to join the structural members of light wooden framework constructions.

holddown
A steel bolt in the form of an angle embedded in the foundation with the threaded end emerging, to secure a wooden frame structure firmly onto the foundations, against wind or earth movements.

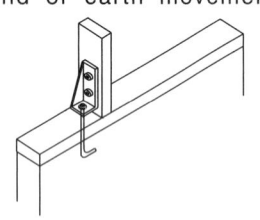

sill anchor
A metal device that attaches a wooden sleeper or sill to a slab or foundation wall of concrete.

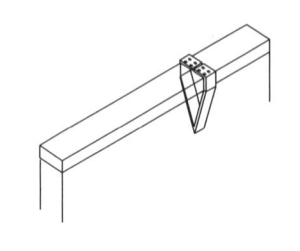

base anchor
A metal device designed to hold the base of a wooden structure to the ground, either permanently or in an adjustable manner.

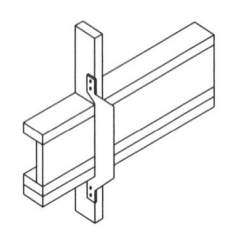

joist to beam anchor

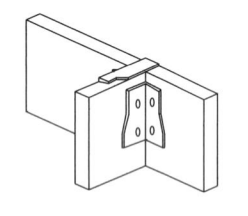

runner to post anchor

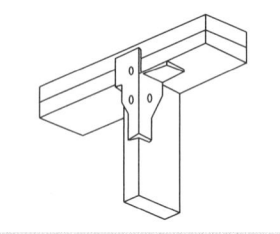

beam to header anchor

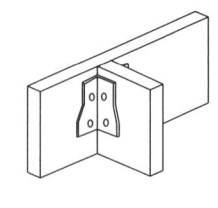

rafter to spandrel anchor

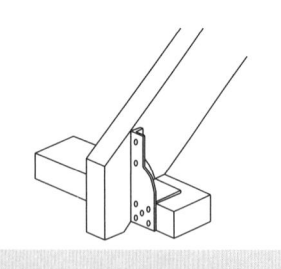

dintel to post anchor

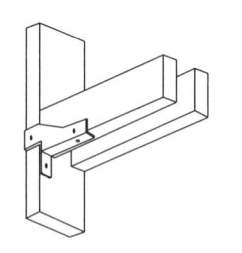

beam to girder anchor

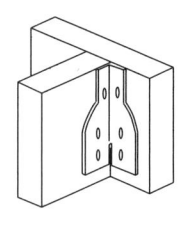

Butt-end anchor and anchor bolts

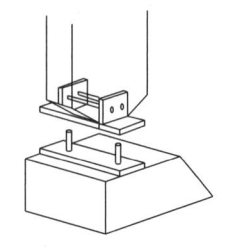

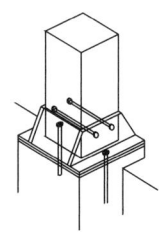

frame system

truss to spandrel anchor

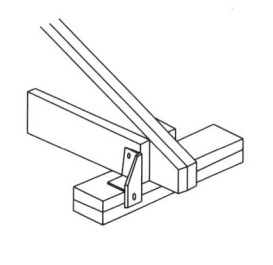

post to sleeper anchor

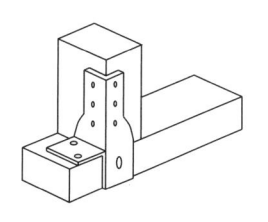

beam to girder anchor

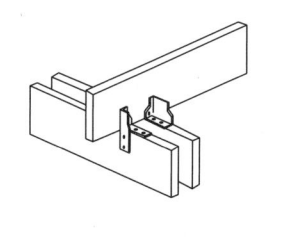

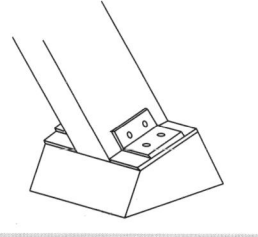

cap plate
A steel plate over the top of a column or pillar that usually bears a load.

filler plate
A piece of steel sheet or plate used to fill the open gaps between structural members or parts of structural members.

splice plate
A segment of steel plate riveted or welded onto the join between two steel supports.

base plate
A steel plate under the bottom of a column or pillar that usually bears a load.

tie bar joint
A joint that consists in welding or riveting the web of a beam to a support or to another beam by means of two angles; it is resistant to shearing stress.

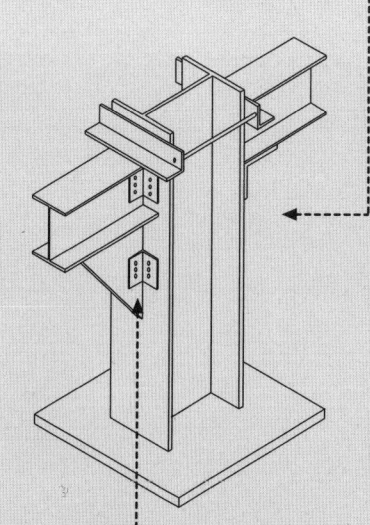

seat angle
A short steel angle iron welded onto the web of a vertical structural member as a support for another member.

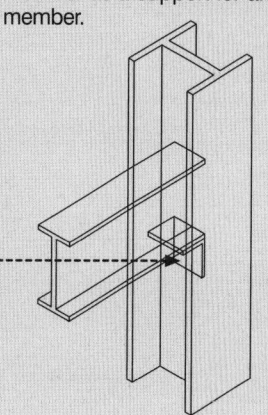

angle cleat
A metallic piece used to join two structural members at a 90º angle.

35

vector-active structure

A framework or structural system that transfers the external forces acting on it by means of a particular distribution of its members and the compression and tension stresses they are subjected to.

roof framing
Any of the various trussed structures designed to support a roof, consisting of rods subjected to tension and compression forces. Also called a principal or truss.

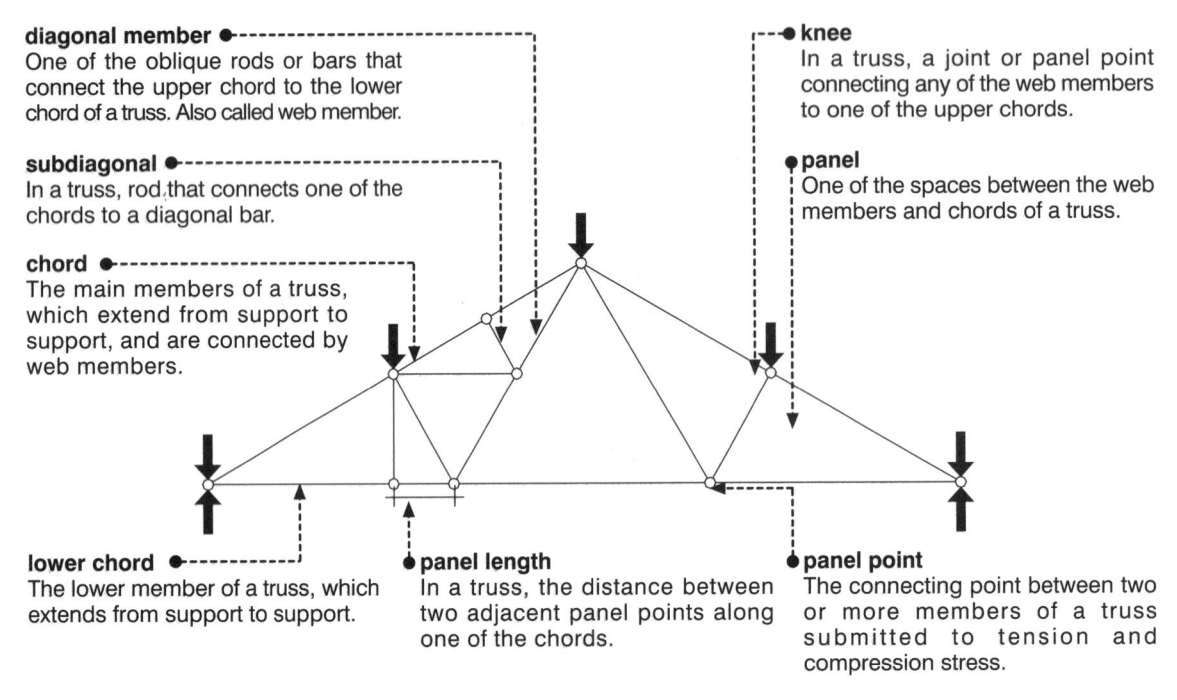

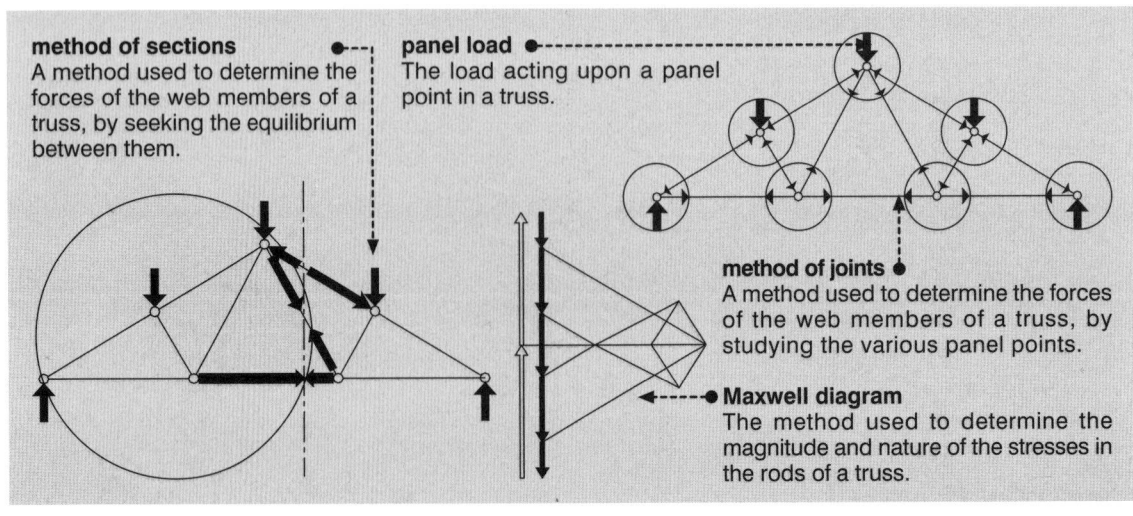

diagonal member
One of the oblique rods or bars that connect the upper chord to the lower chord of a truss. Also called web member.

subdiagonal
In a truss, rod that connects one of the chords to a diagonal bar.

chord
The main members of a truss, which extend from support to support, and are connected by web members.

knee
In a truss, a joint or panel point connecting any of the web members to one of the upper chords.

panel
One of the spaces between the web members and chords of a truss.

lower chord
The lower member of a truss, which extends from support to support.

panel length
In a truss, the distance between two adjacent panel points along one of the chords.

panel point
The connecting point between two or more members of a truss submitted to tension and compression stress.

method of sections
A method used to determine the forces of the web members of a truss, by seeking the equilibrium between them.

panel load
The load acting upon a panel point in a truss.

method of joints
A method used to determine the forces of the web members of a truss, by studying the various panel points.

Maxwell diagram
The method used to determine the magnitude and nature of the stresses in the rods of a truss.

vector-active structure

pitched truss
A trussed frame for a roof, the upper chords of which are sloped.

trussed rafter
A triangular wooden truss used for roofs; the web members are joined by means of spiked timber connectors.

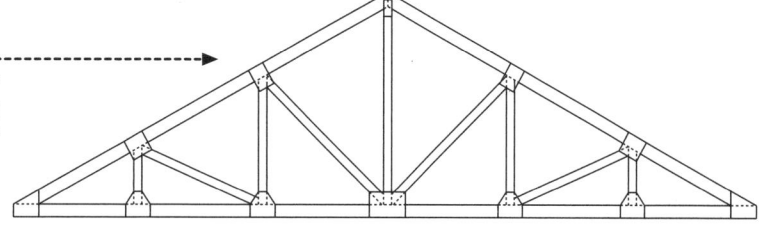

composite truss
A type of truss the compression members of which are wood and the tension members are metal, generally steel.

truss rod
a metal web member designed to absorb tension forces between the chords of a truss. Also called a straining piece.

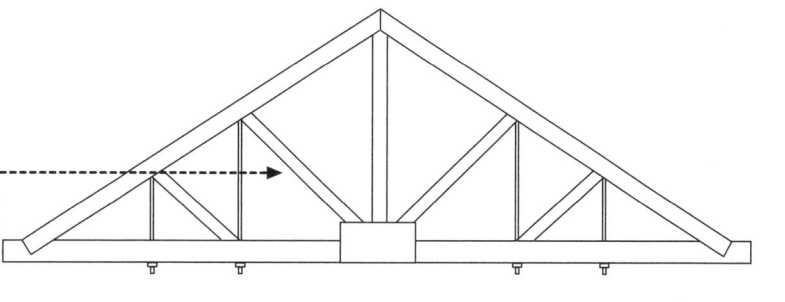

couple
A roof frame consisting of two rafters joined at the apex and connected across the bottom.

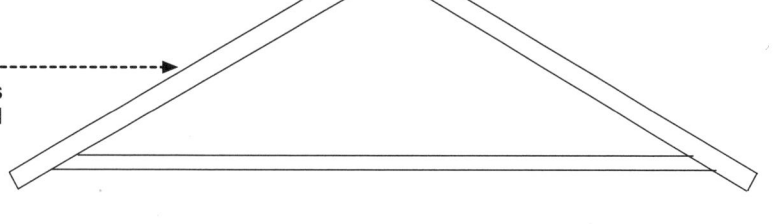

king-post truss
A triangular roof frame consisting of two oblique members joined at the ridge and the opposite ends connected by the tie beam, from the middle of which the king post connects with the ridge.

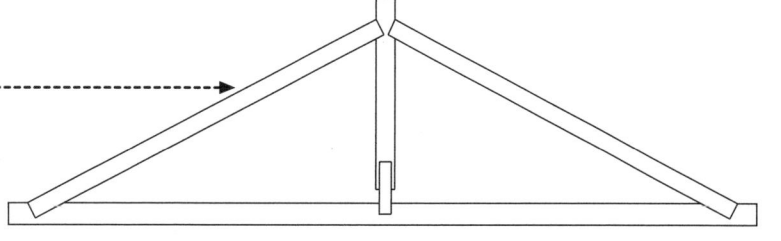

queen truss
A triangular roof frame which has two vertical posts between the tie beam and the rafters, usually connected horizontally by a straining piece.

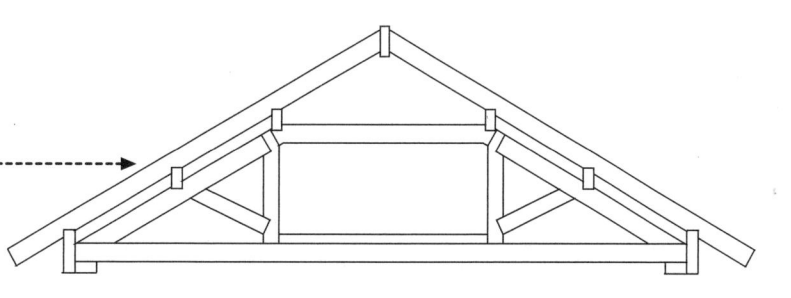

vector-active structure

Warren truss
An arched or straight truss, with parallel upper and lower chords, and web members forming equilateral angles.

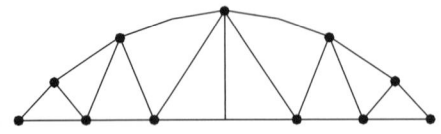

bowstring truss
A truss consisting of a curved element the two ends of which are connected by a straight lower chord.

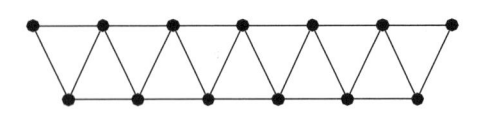

parallel-chord truss
A truss the lower and upper chords of which are parallel and horizontal.

Belfast truss
A type of arched truss made of wood, the lower chord of which is horizontal.

Howe truss
A truss consisting of horizontal upper and lower members among which the verticals take tension stress and the diagonals take compression.

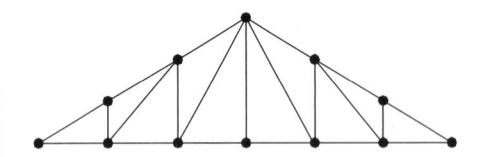

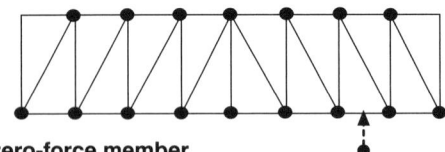

zero-force member
A member of a truss that receives no direct load, and the elimination of which would not destabilize the structure.

Pratt truss
A truss the vertical members of which take compression stress, while the oblique ones take the tension stress, slanting towards the center from either side.

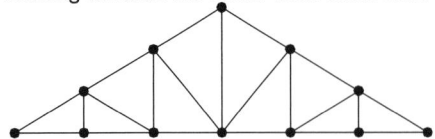

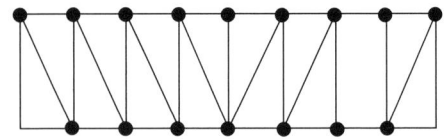

Fink truss
A Belgian truss with subdiagonal members designed to reduce the length of the compression members.

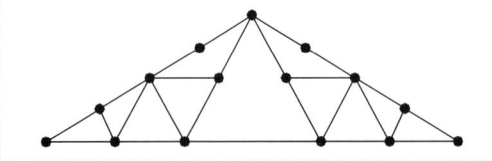

Belgian truss
A symmetrical truss especially designed to support a pitched roof; all its web members are slanted.

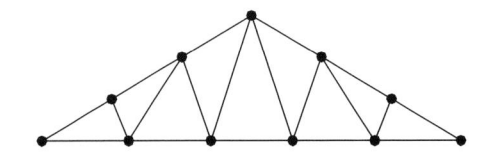

vector-active structure

crescent truss
A truss the upper and lower chords of which are non-concentric curves that have two points in common at the two opposite ends of the truss.

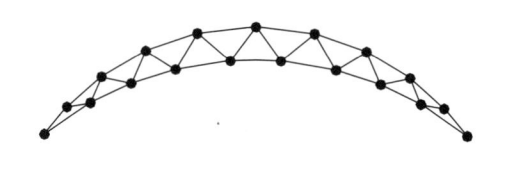

scissors truss
A pitched roof truss, the tension members of which cross each other, connecting the base of the lower chord and an intermediate point of the opposite upper chord.

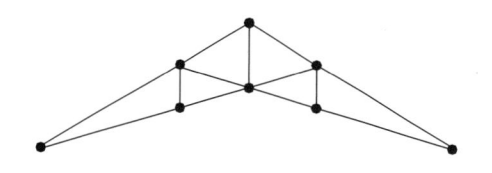

fan truss
A roof truss the vertical and diagonal suspension members of which radiate out from a series of points along the lower chord, like the struts of a fan.

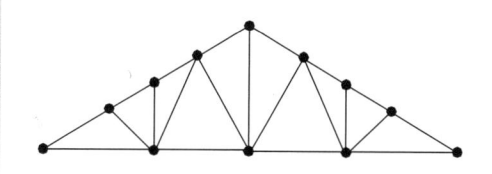

Vierendeel girder
An open web beam consisting of a series of upper and lower chords connected by rigid vertical rods, without diagonals. Also called a Vierendeel truss.

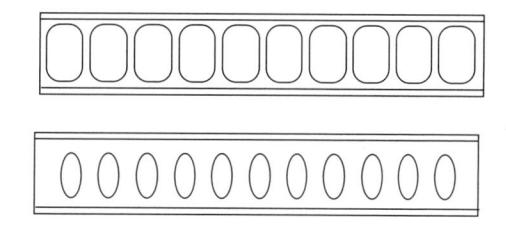

hammer-beam roof
A roof frame that rests upon hammer beams.

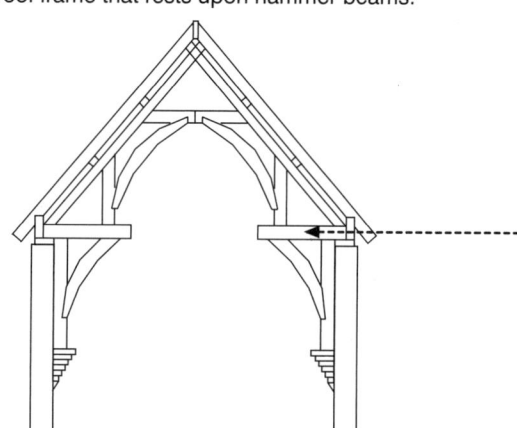

hammer beam
A short horizontal member joined to the base of the principal rafter, instead of a tie beam.

vector-active structure

space frame
A rigid three-dimensional structure consisting of a lattice of tension and compression members, as opposed to two dimensional structures with all members on a single plane. Also called a space truss.

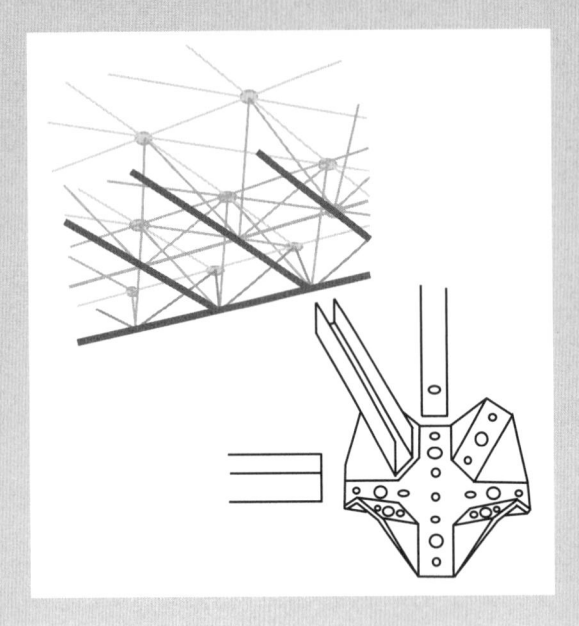

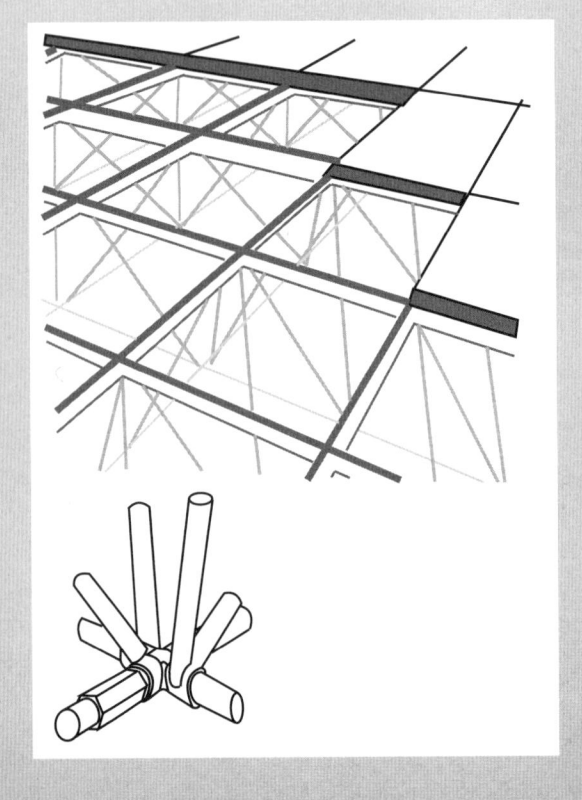

vector-active structure

dome
A curved structure covering a space, as the roof or an inner vault; it often has a spherical shape, that distributes the load evenly on all sides.

geodesic dome
A type of dome developed by R. Buckminster Fuller, consisting in a multiplicity of light steel tension and compression members, equal in length, parallel to the lines of three great circles that intersect at 60° angles, subdividing the entire surface into equilateral triangles.

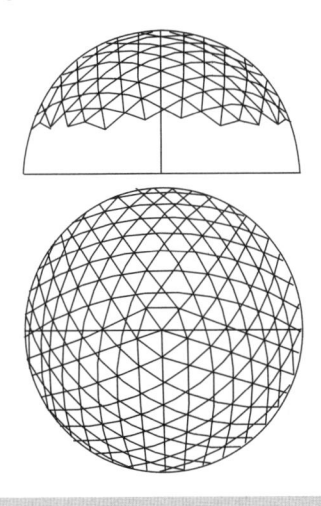

radial dome
A dome sustained by radial steel members connected by horizontal members forming concentric circles.

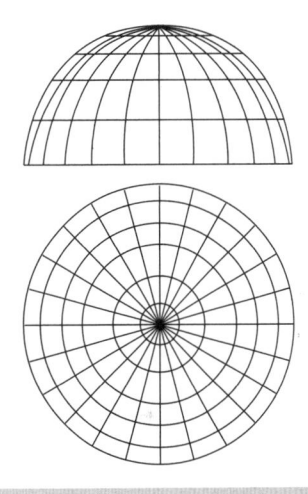

lattice dome
A dome sustained by steel members distributed in horizontal concentric circles connected by radial ribbing crossed by opposite diagonal members, subdividing the surface into a lattice of isosceles triangles.

Schwedler dome
A dome with a structure following the pattern of longitude and latitude lines, subdivided by diagonals from joint to joint.

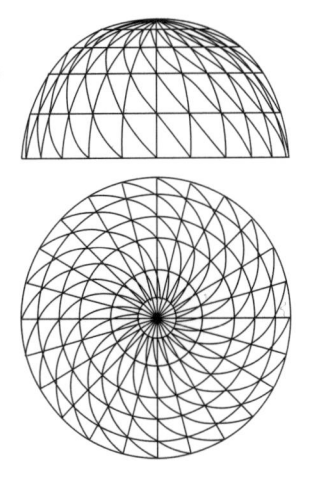

surface-active structure

A structure or structural member that transfers the external forces acting on it due to its continuity and consistency as a single surface.

concrete slab
A flat structural member made of concrete.

reinforced concrete slab
A flat concrete slab in which steel rods or grid have been embedded, greatly increasing its resistance to the forces acting on it, due to the particular tensile and compressive interaction of concrete and steel.

two-way slab
Concrete slab with steel reinforcement in two directions and ribbing around all four edges.

one-way slab
A rectangular concrete slab which extends further in a particular direction, so the loads should usually be distributed across the shorter span.

ribbed slab
A reinforced concrete slab consisting in a network of ribs resting on larger ribs or beams at the perimeter.

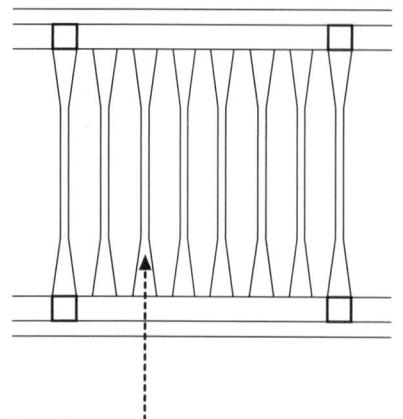

distribution rib
A structural supporting rib or beam perpendicular to the main direction of a ribbed slab, used to distribute the load over a larger surface.

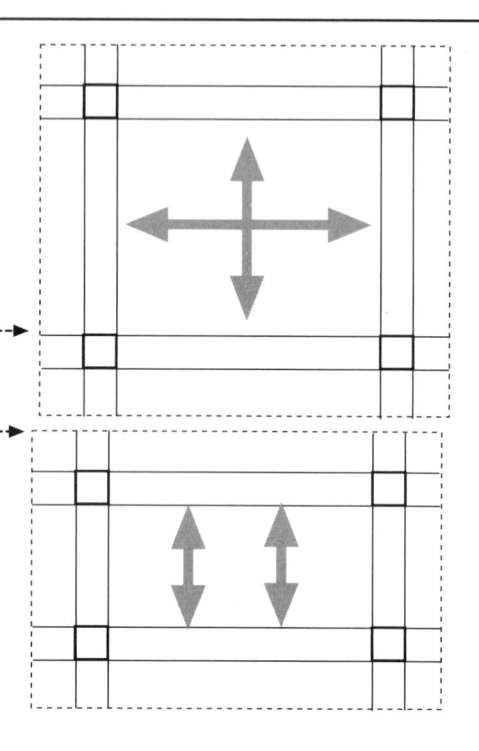

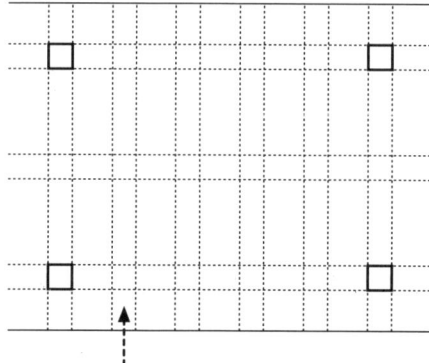

flat slab
A concrete slab that is reinforced in two or more directions, usually without incorporated bearing joists or beams transferring the load to the support elements.

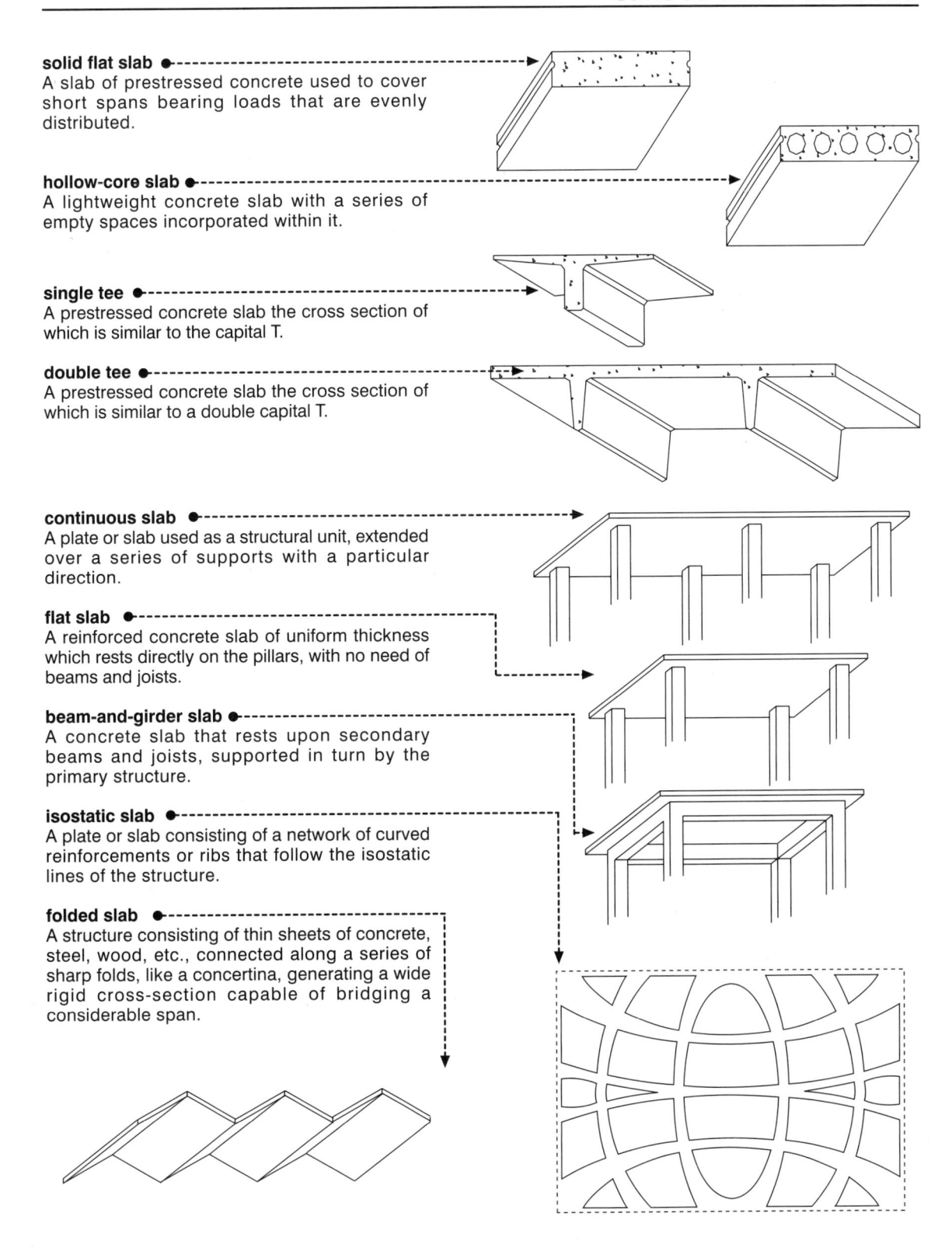

surface-active structure

solid flat slab
A slab of prestressed concrete used to cover short spans bearing loads that are evenly distributed.

hollow-core slab
A lightweight concrete slab with a series of empty spaces incorporated within it.

single tee
A prestressed concrete slab the cross section of which is similar to the capital T.

double tee
A prestressed concrete slab the cross section of which is similar to a double capital T.

continuous slab
A plate or slab used as a structural unit, extended over a series of supports with a particular direction.

flat slab
A reinforced concrete slab of uniform thickness which rests directly on the pillars, with no need of beams and joists.

beam-and-girder slab
A concrete slab that rests upon secondary beams and joists, supported in turn by the primary structure.

isostatic slab
A plate or slab consisting of a network of curved reinforcements or ribs that follow the isostatic lines of the structure.

folded slab
A structure consisting of thin sheets of concrete, steel, wood, etc., connected along a series of sharp folds, like a concertina, generating a wide rigid cross-section capable of bridging a considerable span.

surface-active structure

vault
A type of covering for spaces, based on the principal of the arch, made of masonry or reinforced concrete.

barrel vault
A vault the cross section of which is approximately semicircular, resting on two parallel walls or lines of pillars. Also called a cradle, tunnel or wagon vault.

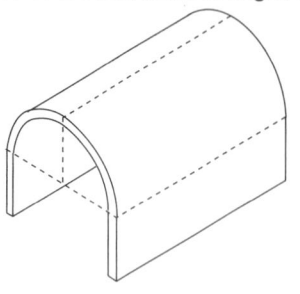

conical vault
A vault with a semicircular cross section the diameter of which is wider at one end than the other.

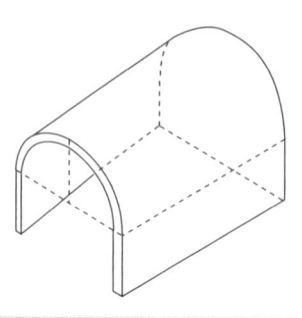

rampant vault
A continuous or tunnel vault in which the abutment is higher on one side than the other, so as to support an inclined plane.

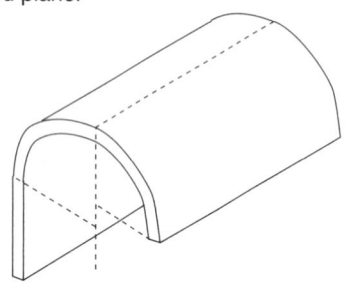

pendentive dome
A vault or dome that rests upon four pendentives.

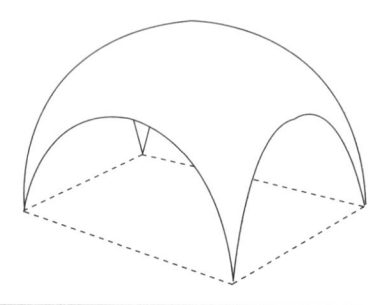

stilted vault
A vault in which the center of the curve (A) is above the abutment or impost line (B).

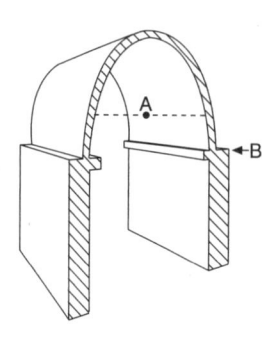

cul-de-four
A half or quarter-sphere vault or dome, as that covering an apse or niche.

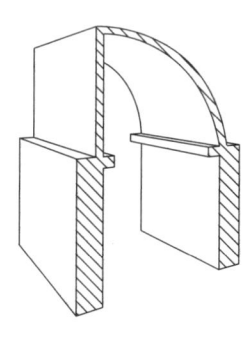

surface-active structure

cross vault
A vault formed by the intersection of two barrel vaults.

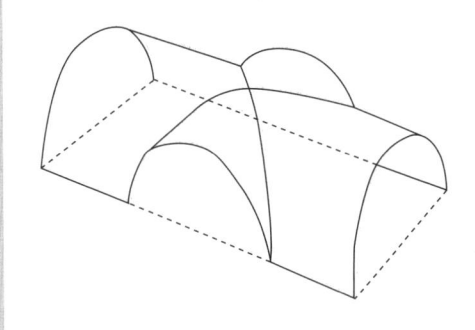

cloister vault
A vault consisting of four quarter cylindrical surfaces enclosing the intersection of two barrel vaults, with recessed groins at the diagonal lines of intersection. Also called a coved vault.

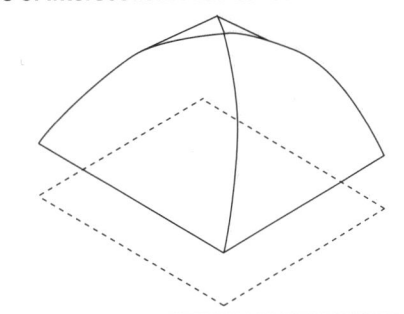

fan vault
A conical vault usually spanning a corner, the ribs of which spread like a fan.

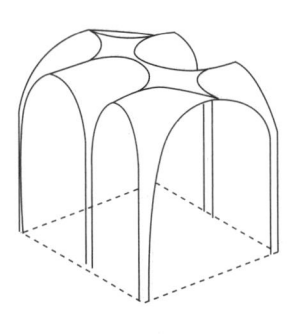

rib vault
A vault sustained or decorated by a structure of ribs or nerves.

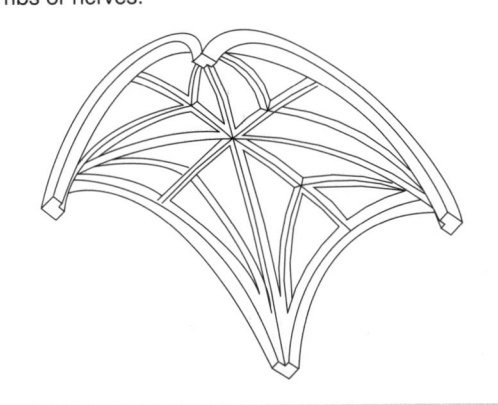

annular vault
A barrel vault the parallel sustaining walls of which enclose a curved space.

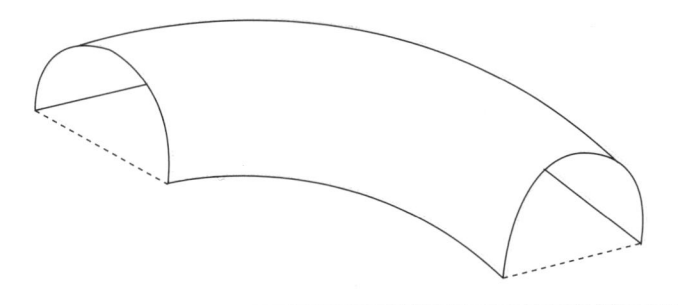

surface-active structure

wall
A continuous vertical surface of masonry or concrete, erected to enclose or subdivide a space, and often bearing a share of the load of the beams, upper floors or the roof.

bearing wall
A wall built to support the loads expected to act upon it. Also called a load-bearing wall.

load-bearing partition
An interior wall that supports a structural load. Also called a bearing partition.

return wall
Short stretch of wall perpendicular to, and often at the end of, a longer wall, to which it adds greater structural stability.

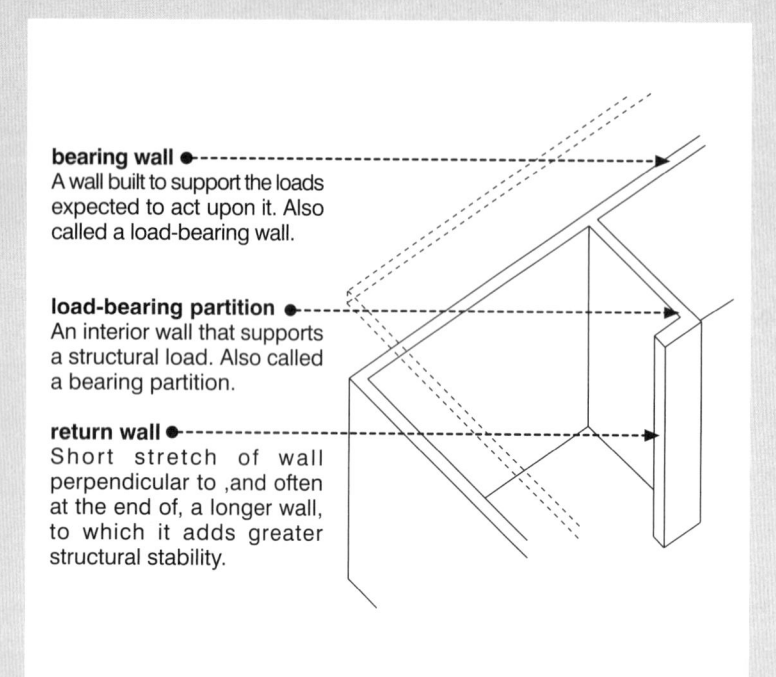

faced wall
A wall that consists of two sheets of masonry linked together so that both are structurally active.

cavity wall
A double masonry wall built on either side of a hollow space, sometimes filled with an insulating material, and with occasional links across the space to bind the two sides.

composite wall
A wall in which the use of two different materials is combined.

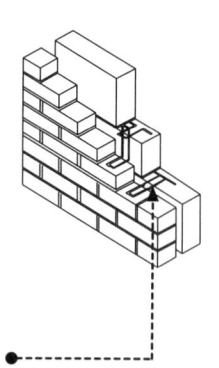

solid masonry
A thick wall made of solid masonry, in which all gaps are filled completely with mortar.

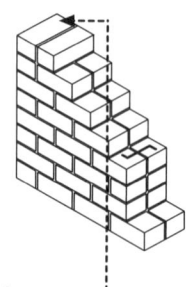

veneered wall
A wall that has of a non-structural outer facing or veneer fixed onto the bearing wall.

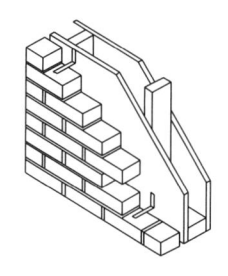

tie
A building device designed to prevent the movement or separation of two sides of a wall or other structural item.

bond course
A course of masonry that links together the two faces of a bearing wall.

form-active structure

A structure or structural member that transfers the external forces acting on it by means of the shape or form of that structure.

funicular structure
A structure designed to support given loads by means of lateral or compression forces.

funicular shape
The form described by a chord or chain suspended from supports at each end and with loads acting on it, so that the form depends on the magnitude and distribution of the loads. Also called catenary curve.

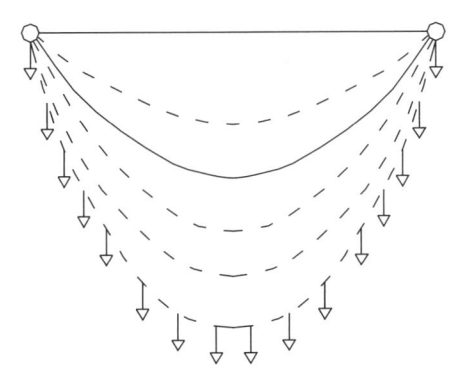

funicular curve
The curved line described by a chord or chain suspended between two fixed points and subjected to a given evenly distributed load.

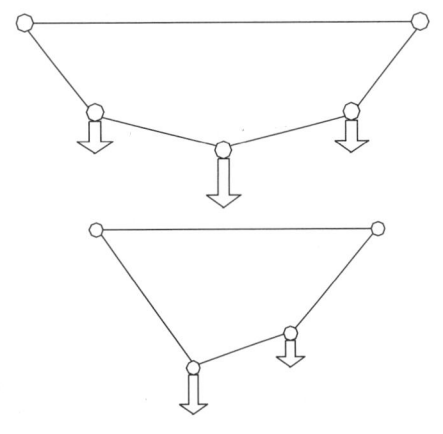

funicular polygon
The form described by a chord suspended between two points and subjected to given loads at particular points.

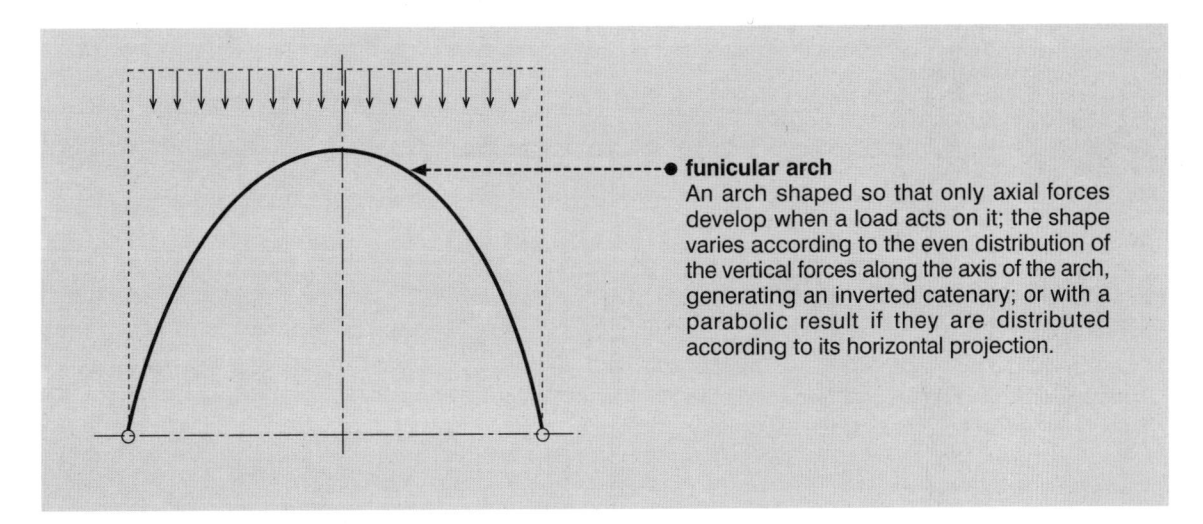

funicular arch
An arch shaped so that only axial forces develop when a load acts on it; the shape varies according to the even distribution of the vertical forces along the axis of the arch, generating an inverted catenary; or with a parabolic result if they are distributed according to its horizontal projection.

form-active structure

arch
A curved structure that spans the opening between two structural columns, pillars or pilasters that support the vertical load.

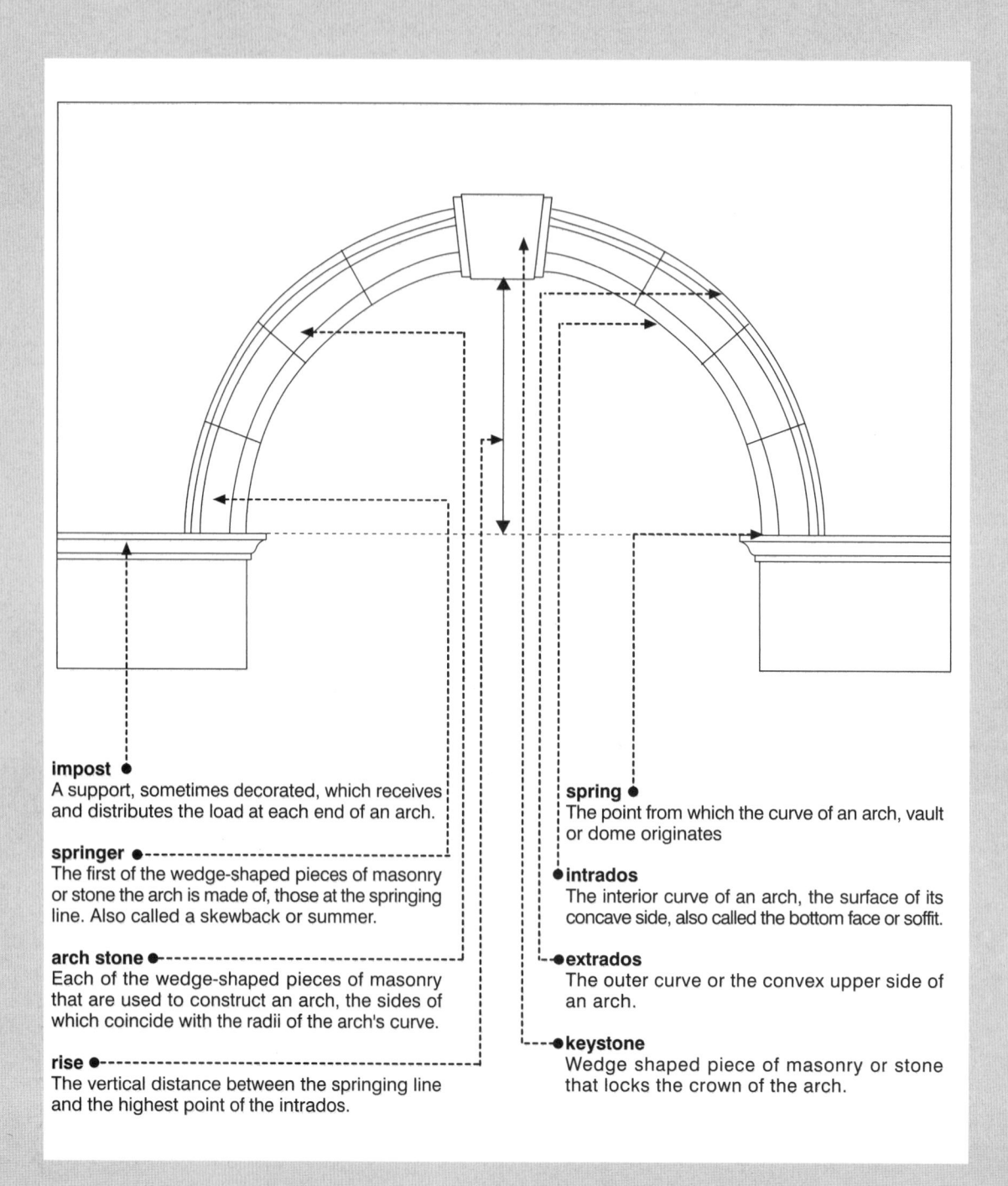

impost
A support, sometimes decorated, which receives and distributes the load at each end of an arch.

springer
The first of the wedge-shaped pieces of masonry or stone the arch is made of, those at the springing line. Also called a skewback or summer.

arch stone
Each of the wedge-shaped pieces of masonry that are used to construct an arch, the sides of which coincide with the radii of the arch's curve.

rise
The vertical distance between the springing line and the highest point of the intrados.

spring
The point from which the curve of an arch, vault or dome originates

intrados
The interior curve of an arch, the surface of its concave side, also called the bottom face or soffit.

extrados
The outer curve or the convex upper side of an arch.

keystone
Wedge shaped piece of masonry or stone that locks the crown of the arch.

form-active structure

round arch
An arch the intrados of which forms a semicircle. Also called a Roman arch.

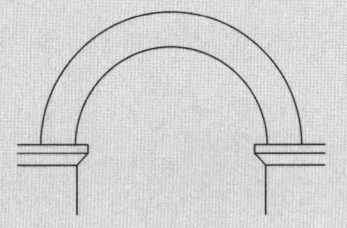

surbased arch
An arch which has been traced from one or more centers lower than the springing line; also called a segmental arch.

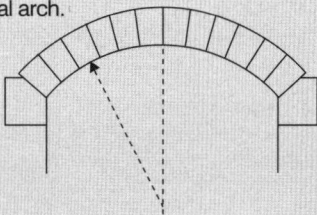

basket arch
An arch in the form of a false ellipse with two quarter circles at the ends, based on three tangent circles with different centers. Also called an anse de panier.

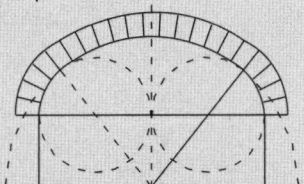

stilted arch
An arch the curve of which begins above the springing line, so the rise is greater than half the span.

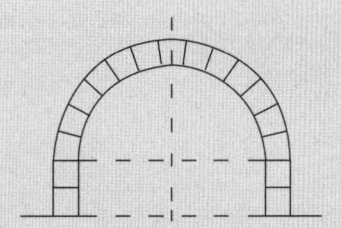

equilateral arch
An arch with two centers at the opposite springing points and the radius equal to the span of the arch. Also called a two centered arch.

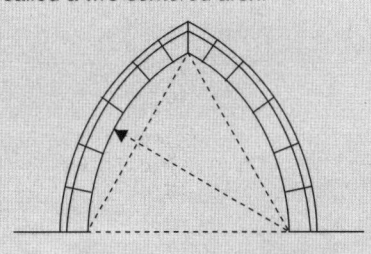

horseshoe arch
An arch with a curve slightly larger than a semicircle, so the span widens above the springing line.

elliptical arch
An arch with an elliptical intrados.

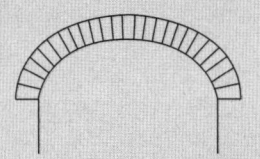

two-hinged arch
A two-hinged arch-shaped structure, supported on mobile joints.

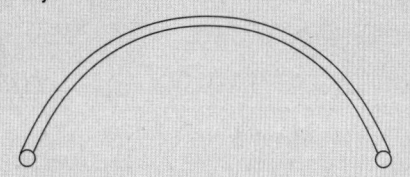

form-active structure

cable structure
A structure in which cables are the main load bearing member.

suspension structure
A structure consisting of prestressed cables suspended between compression members which transfer the load acting on it.

cable-stayed structure
A structure consisting of upright masts which sustain cables forming a radial or parallel pattern to support the horizontal structural members.

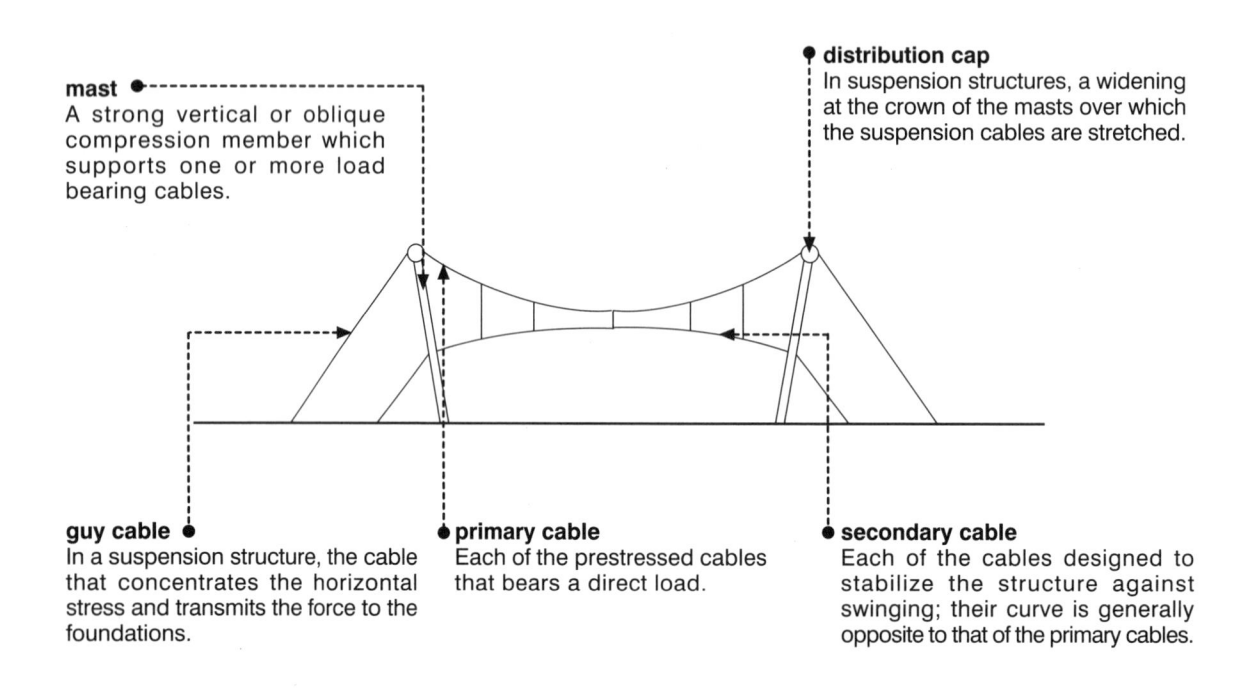

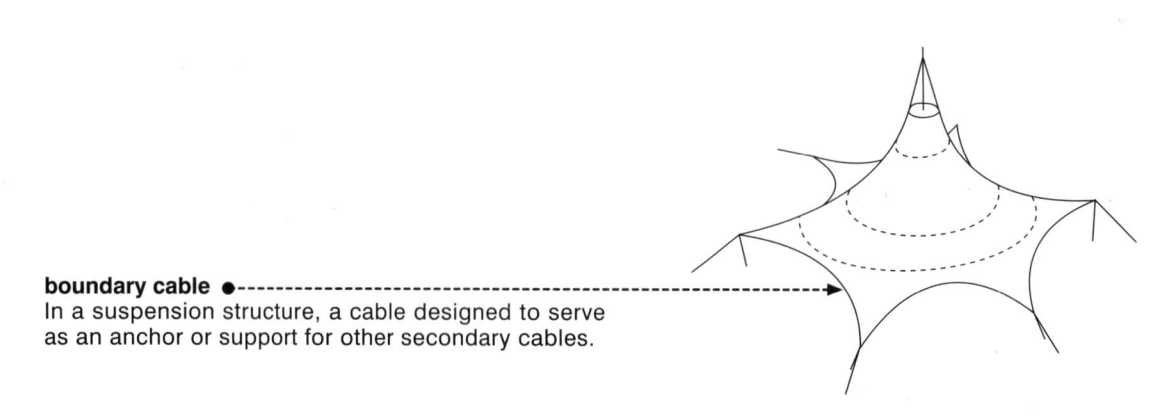

mast
A strong vertical or oblique compression member which supports one or more load bearing cables.

distribution cap
In suspension structures, a widening at the crown of the masts over which the suspension cables are stretched.

guy cable
In a suspension structure, the cable that concentrates the horizontal stress and transmits the force to the foundations.

primary cable
Each of the prestressed cables that bears a direct load.

secondary cable
Each of the cables designed to stabilize the structure against swinging; their curve is generally opposite to that of the primary cables.

boundary cable
In a suspension structure, a cable designed to serve as an anchor or support for other secondary cables.

form-active structure

lenticular structure
A lens shaped structure in which the outward pressure of an arch is counterbalanced by the inward tension of a cable, in such a way that the horizontal stress to the supports is nullified.

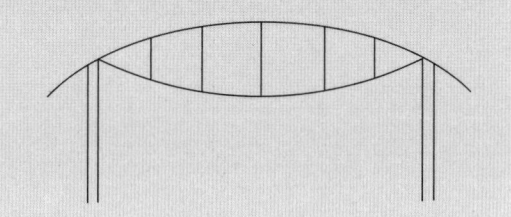

double-cable structure
A structure provided with a double set of cables, an upper and a lower one, with a different curve, designed to improve the rigidity of the system and its resistance to swinging.

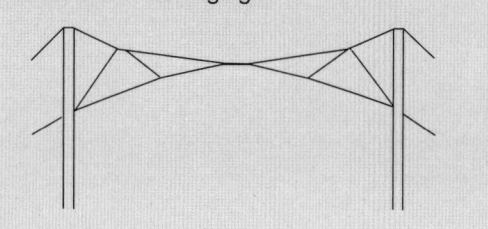

net structure
A structure the surface of which consists of a dense network of cables.

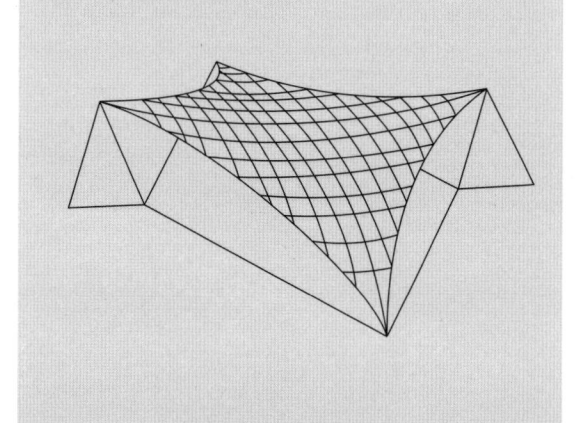

tent structure
A membrane structure prestressed so as to remain tensed under any foreseeable load or conditions of external forces, and which has sharp curves in opposite directions.

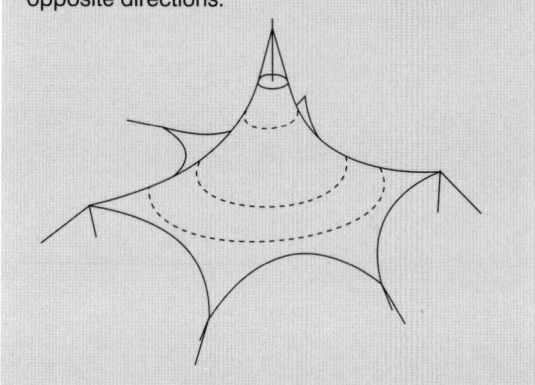

single-curvature structure
A suspension structure consisting of a system of parallel cables employed to support beams or other similar structural members.

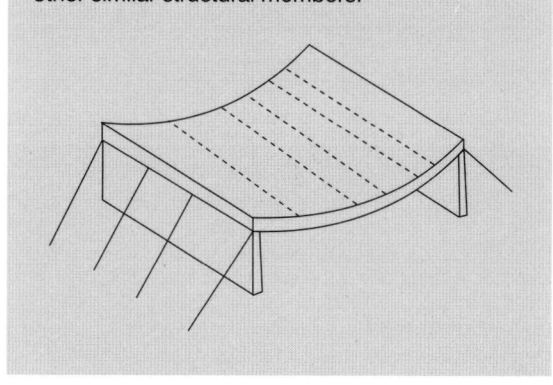

double-curvature structure
A suspension structure consisting of cables that cross each other following different curves; the oscillation frequency of each cable is different, creating a system less prone to vibrations.

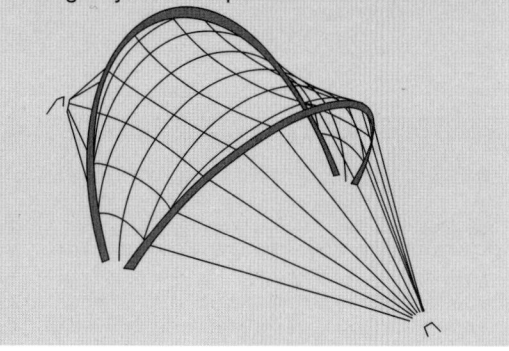

form-active structure

air-supported structure

air-supported structure
A structure consisting of a very large membrane of strong watertight fabric or material supported by air pressure slightly above normal atmospheric pressure. Attached to the ground so as to prevent any possible leaks, access to the interior has to be through air locks.

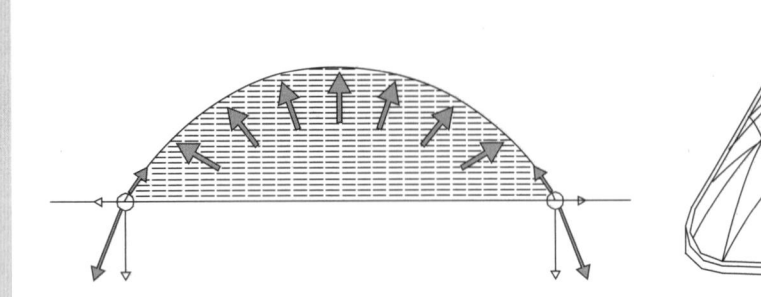

air-inflated structure
A pneumatic structure supported by air pressure introduced into the supporting members; to prevent its natural tendency to sag in the middle, a series of compression rings or ties are distributed along its length.

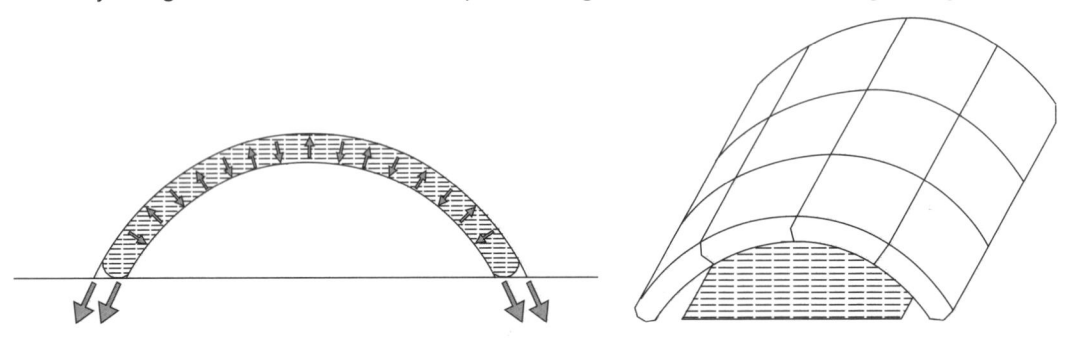

cable-restrained pneumatic structure
A structure supported by air pressure, in which a system of cables is employed to prevent the membrane from adopting the inflated profile it would naturally acquire.

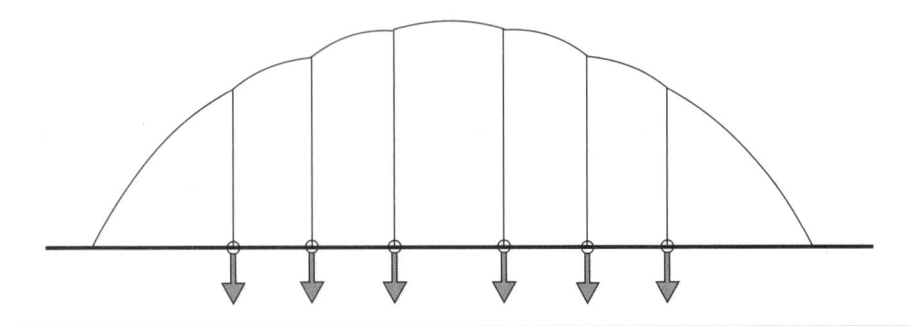

tube structure

A structure consisting of perimetral systems which enable it to resist lateral forces, and which is braced internally by means of rigid frames.

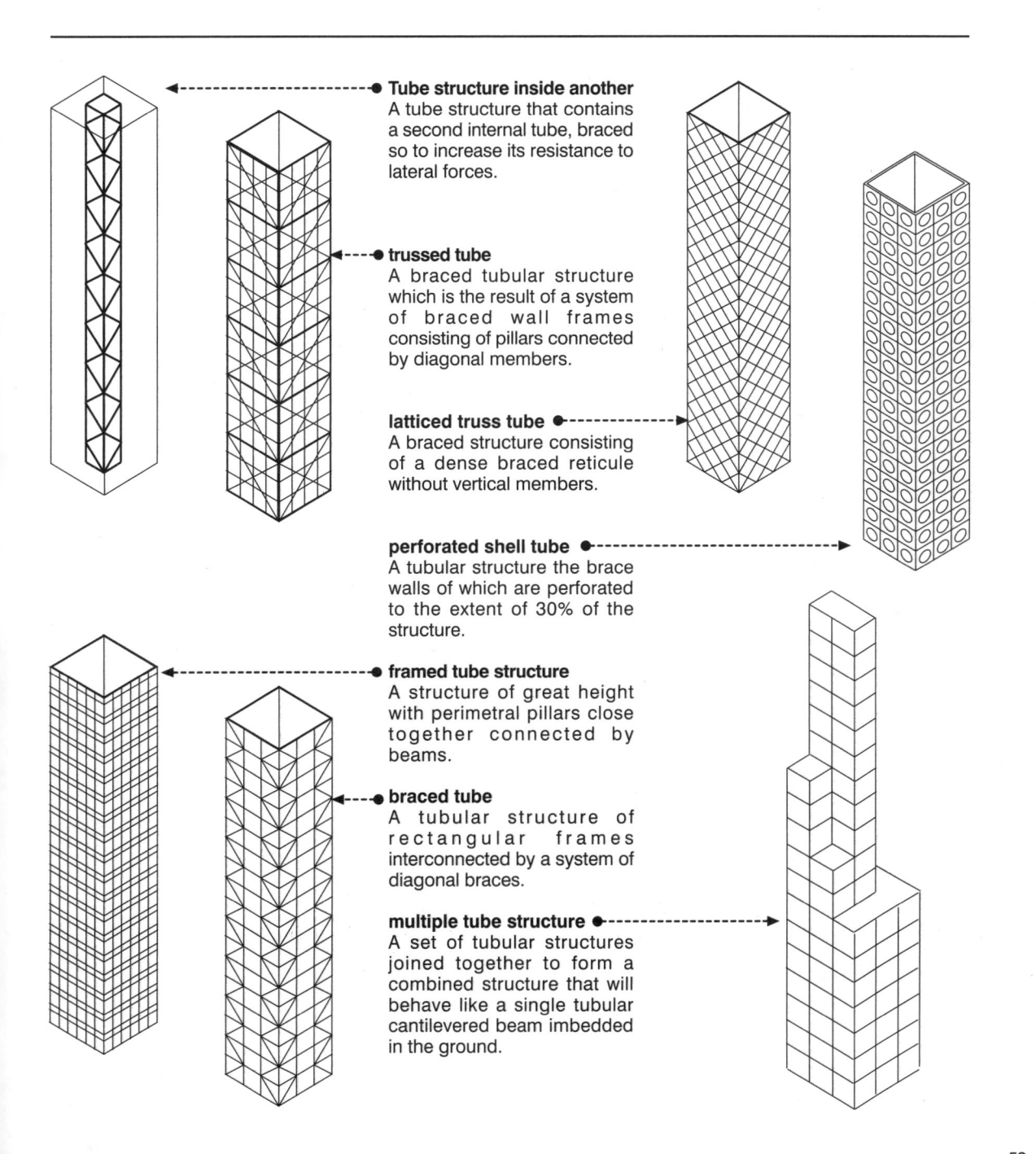

Tube structure inside another
A tube structure that contains a second internal tube, braced so to increase its resistance to lateral forces.

trussed tube
A braced tubular structure which is the result of a system of braced wall frames consisting of pillars connected by diagonal members.

latticed truss tube
A braced structure consisting of a dense braced reticule without vertical members.

perforated shell tube
A tubular structure the brace walls of which are perforated to the extent of 30% of the structure.

framed tube structure
A structure of great height with perimetral pillars close together connected by beams.

braced tube
A tubular structure of rectangular frames interconnected by a system of diagonal braces.

multiple tube structure
A set of tubular structures joined together to form a combined structure that will behave like a single tubular cantilevered beam imbedded in the ground.

foundation

The lowest underlying part of a building's structure, frequently underground, that connects or anchors the building to the ground and transfers the load directly to the bearing stratum.

---

footing
That part of the foundation of a structure which transfers the load directly to the ground, usually widened so as to distribute the load over a bigger surface and reduce settling.

Solid pyramidal footing

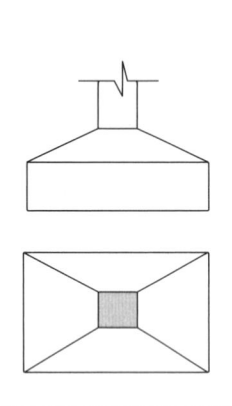

solid stoped footing

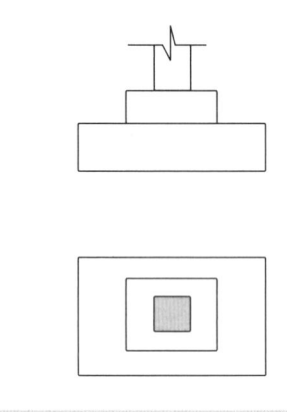

straight solid footing

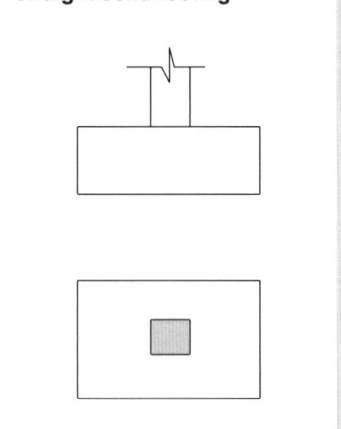

lightweight footing

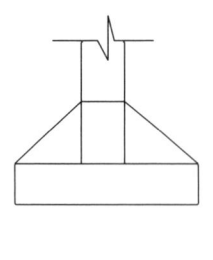

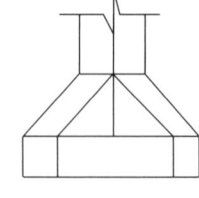

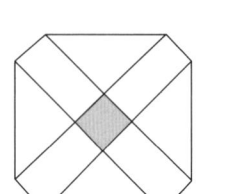

flexible footing
Footing that has stretched without reaching the elastic limit, so as to spread the load.

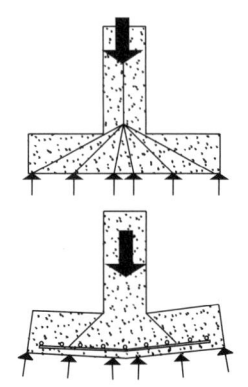

foundation

continuous footing
A length of strap footing for the support of a line of pillars.

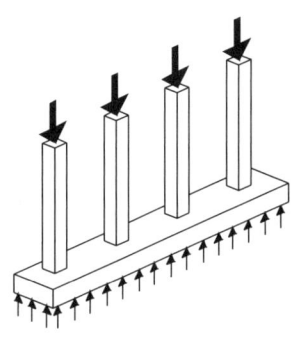

ground beam
A heavy reinforced concrete girder supporting the outer walls of a building, resting at ground level on isolated footing pieces, or directly on the ground as strap footing.

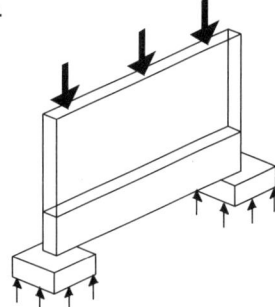

isolated footing
An isolated foot of concrete foundation that supports an external pillar.

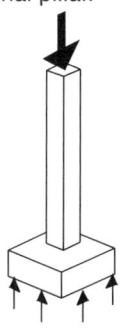

strap footing
An uninterrupted foundation wall which distributes the load evenly to the ground. Also called strip footing, strip foundation.

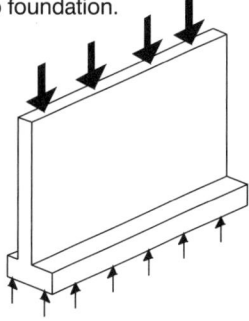

combined footing
A slab of concrete footing or foundation that supports the load of more than one pillar.

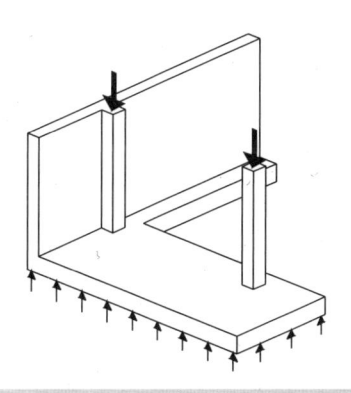

cantilever footing
A piece of concrete footing that is connected to another, so as to balance a load which is not symmetrically placed. Also called strap footing.

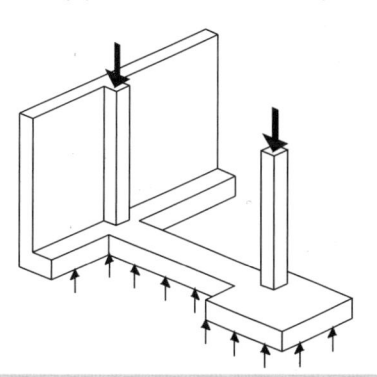

foundation

shallow foundation
A type of foundation or footing that is just beneath the lower parts of a structure and rests directly on the ground, transferring the load of the building by vertical compression.

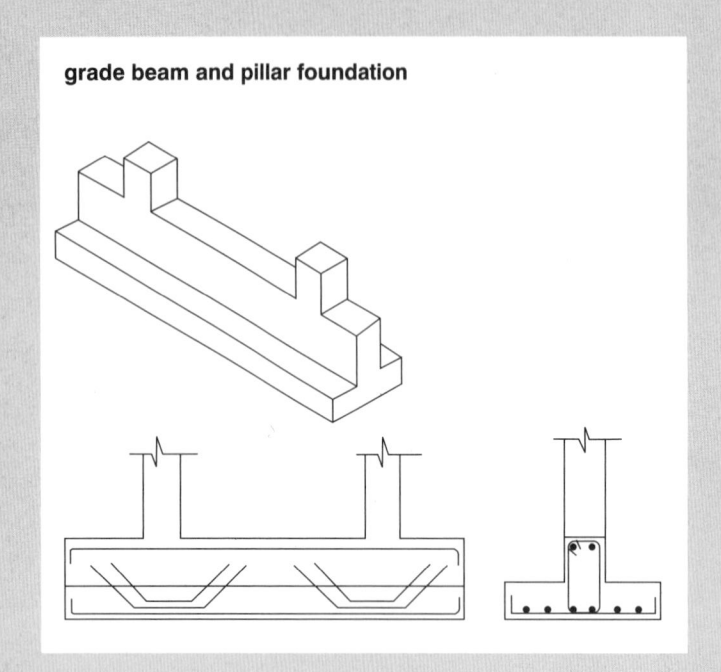

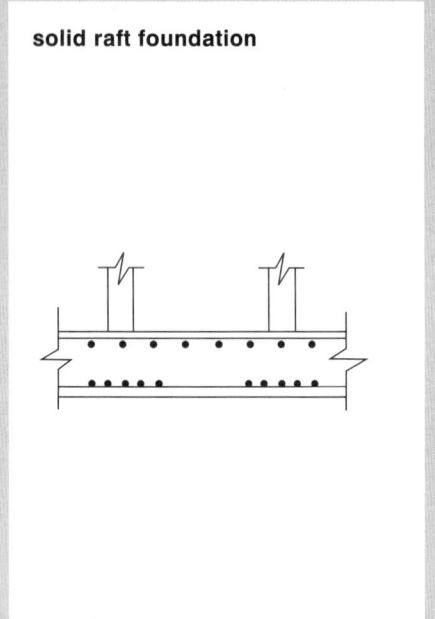

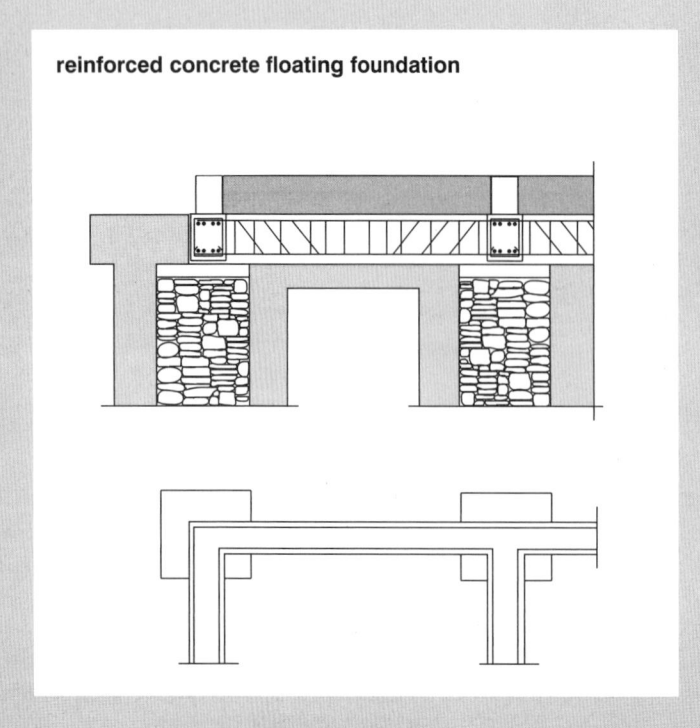

grade beam and pillar foundation

solid raft foundation

reinforced concrete floating foundation

cellular foundation

foundation

sunken foot raft foundation

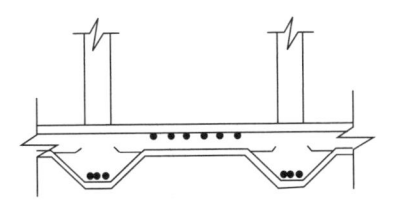

raised foot raft foundation

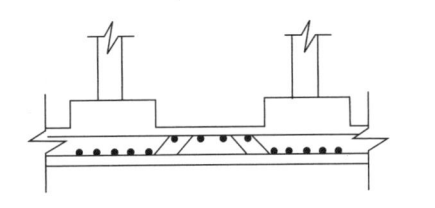

sunken rib raft foundation

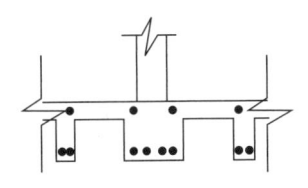

raised rib raft foundation

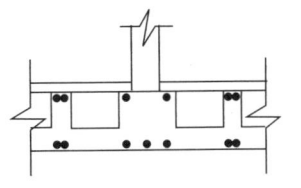

hollow raft foundation

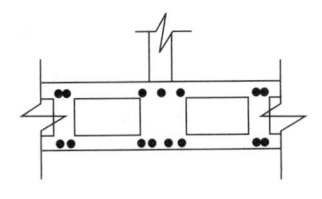

box foundation

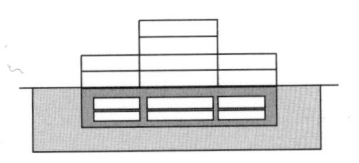

ribbed foundation raft with a flange

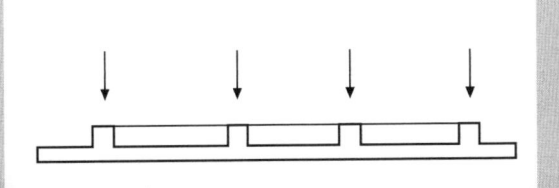

ribbed foundation raft with a grade beam.

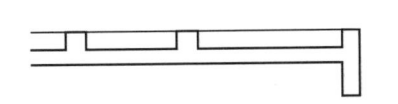

57

foundation

gravity wall
A dam or retaining wall, of concrete or masonry, which relies in its own weight and internal strength for stability, to resist displacement or overturning.

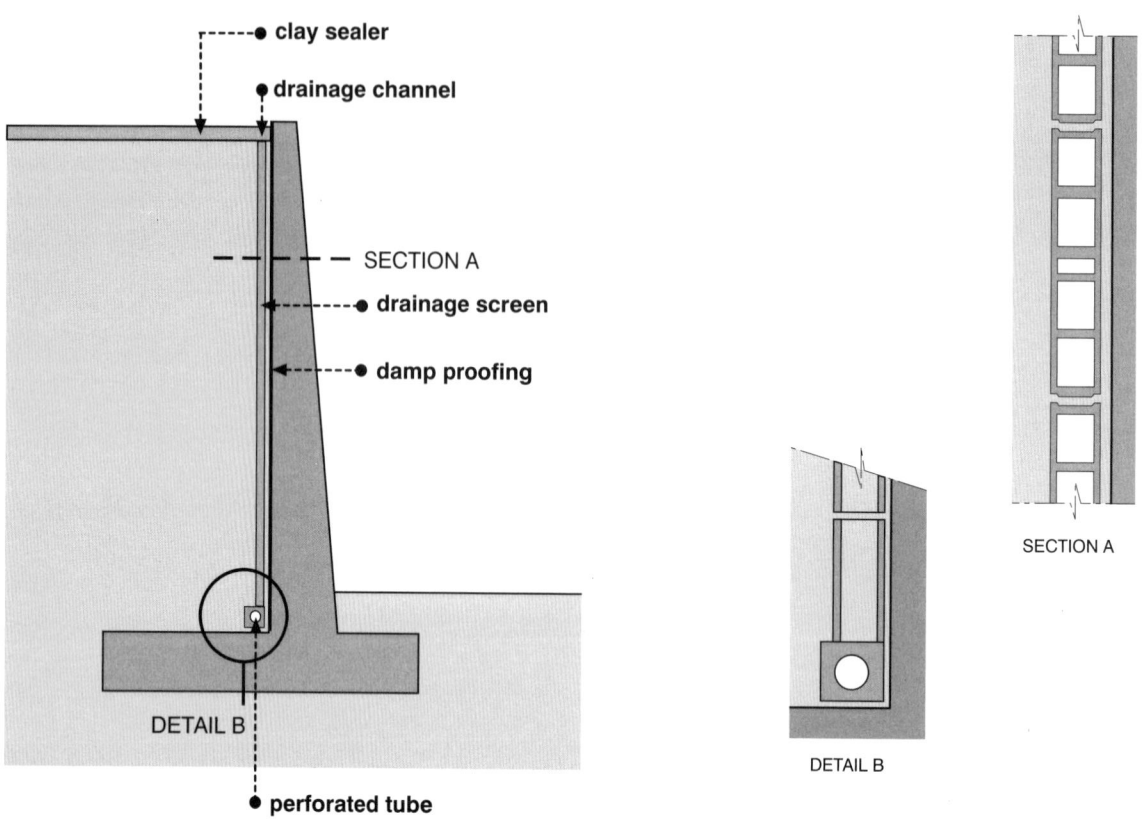

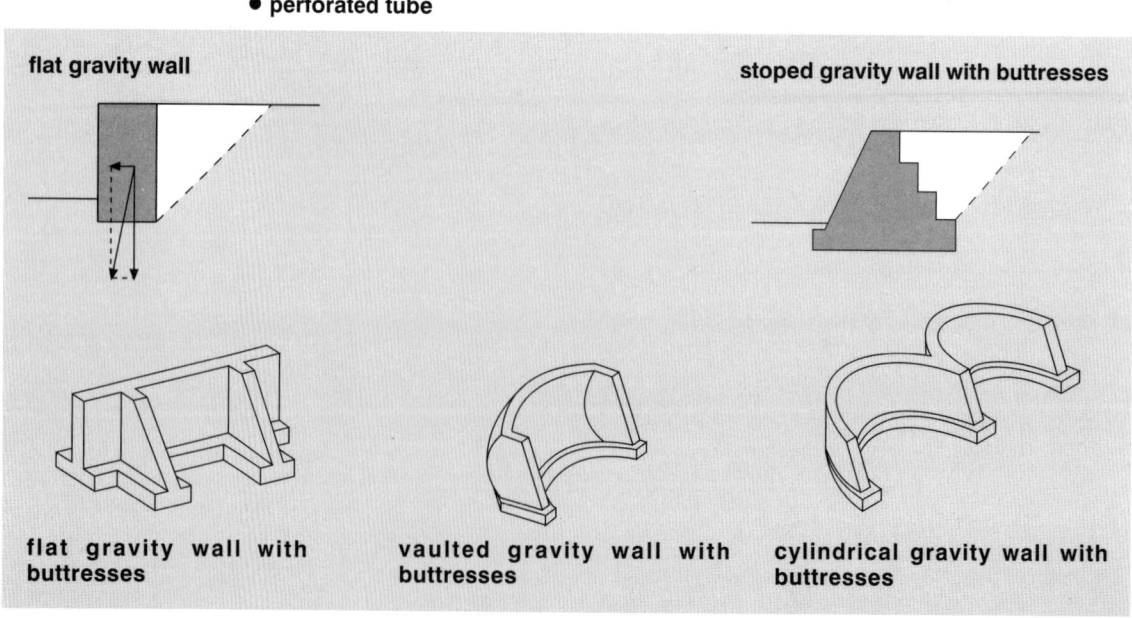

- clay sealer
- drainage channel
- SECTION A
- drainage screen
- damp proofing
- DETAIL B
- perforated tube

SECTION A

DETAIL B

flat gravity wall

stoped gravity wall with buttresses

flat gravity wall with buttresses

vaulted gravity wall with buttresses

cylindrical gravity wall with buttresses

foundation

pile
A wood, steel, or reinforced concrete pillar, usually less than two feet (60 cm) in diameter, embedded or driven into the ground, to withstand vertical load or provide lateral support.

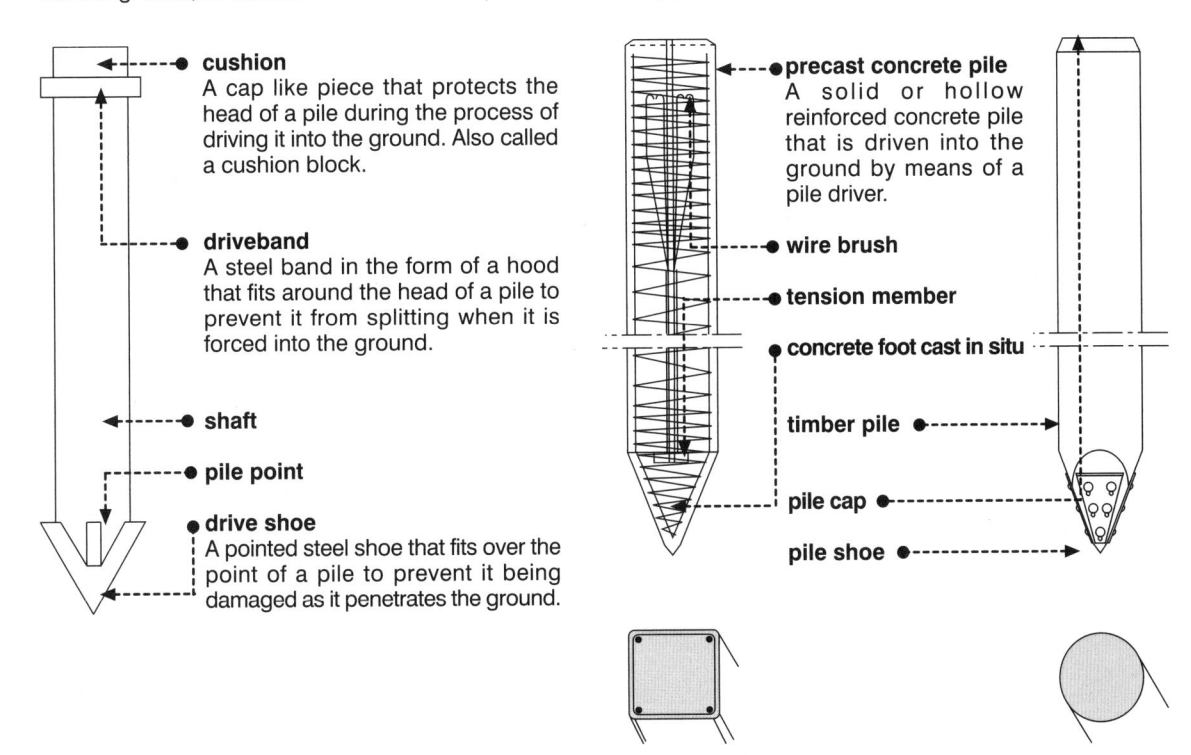

- **cushion** — A cap like piece that protects the head of a pile during the process of driving it into the ground. Also called a cushion block.
- **driveband** — A steel band in the form of a hood that fits around the head of a pile to prevent it from splitting when it is forced into the ground.
- **shaft**
- **pile point**
- **drive shoe** — A pointed steel shoe that fits over the point of a pile to prevent it being damaged as it penetrates the ground.
- **precast concrete pile** — A solid or hollow reinforced concrete pile that is driven into the ground by means of a pile driver.
- **wire brush**
- **tension member**
- **concrete foot cast in situ**
- **timber pile**
- **pile cap**
- **pile shoe**

pile points and shoes

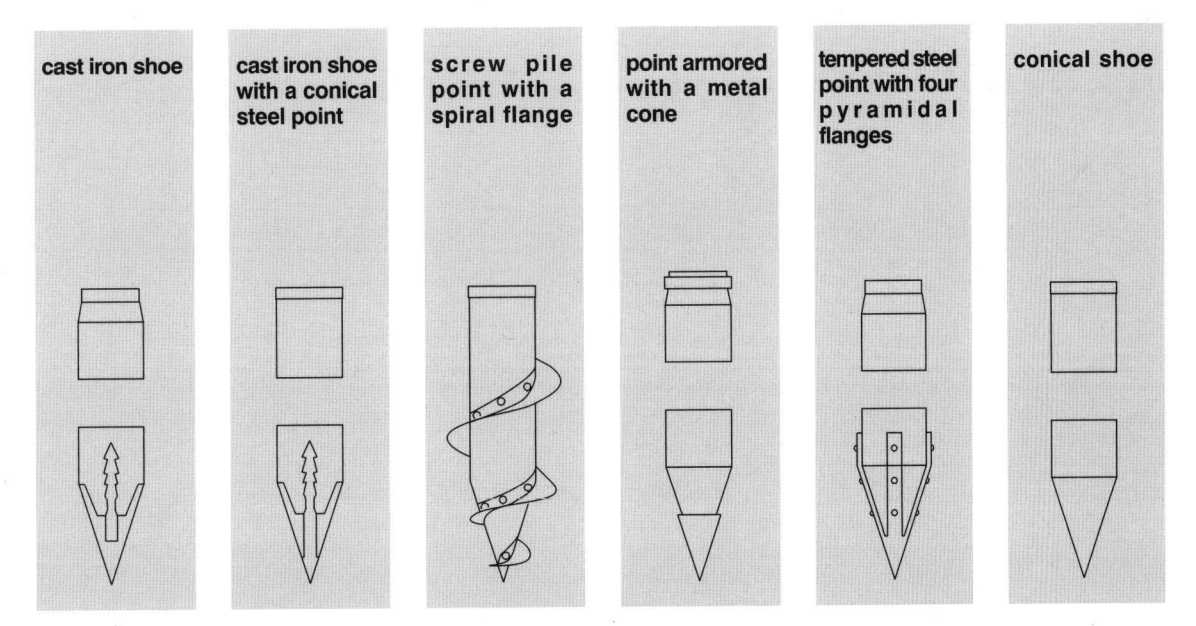

- cast iron shoe
- cast iron shoe with a conical steel point
- screw pile point with a spiral flange
- point armored with a metal cone
- tempered steel point with four pyramidal flanges
- conical shoe

59

foundation

- **pedestal pile**
  A concrete pile cast-in-place, ending in a widened bulb or belled foot, to increase the surface of support and the satisfactory resistance of the bearing stratum. Also called a belled caisson pile.

- **uncased pile**
  A reinforced concrete pile built by driving steel casing, usually cylindrical, into the ground until the satisfactory bearing stratum is found, at which point the concrete is introduced under pressure or rammed in as the casing is removed.

- **cased pile**
  A reinforced concrete pile built by driving a steel tube into the ground until a satisfactory bearing stratum is found, and filling it with concrete. The tube remains in place as part of the reinforcement.

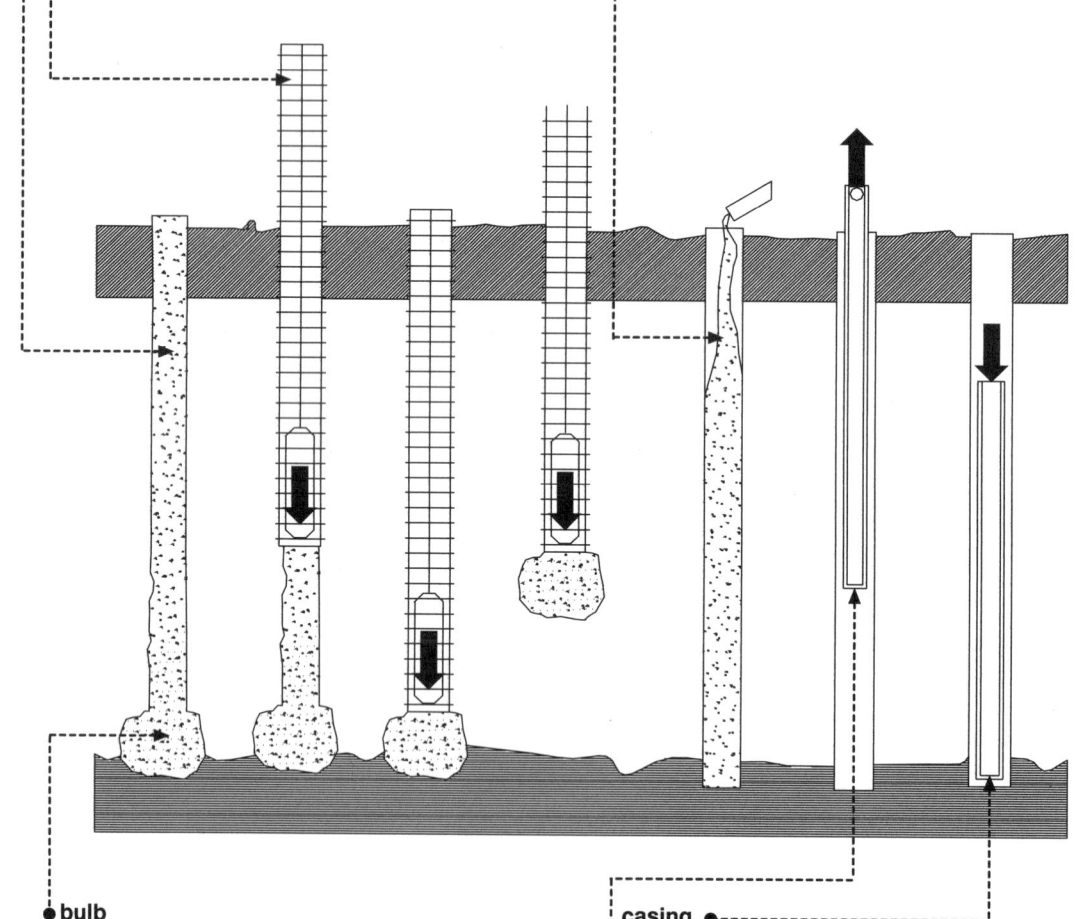

- **bulb**
  A bulb or bell shaped mass at the foot of a reinforced concrete pile serving to increase the load distribution onto the bearing stratum. Also called a bell.

- **casing**
  A cylindrical steel tube driven into the ground providing greater rigidity to a reinforced concrete pile.

- **mandrel**
  A temporary internal support inserted within the casing of a pile to take the impact of the driving process. It is then removed to make place for the concrete.

foundation

raft pile system

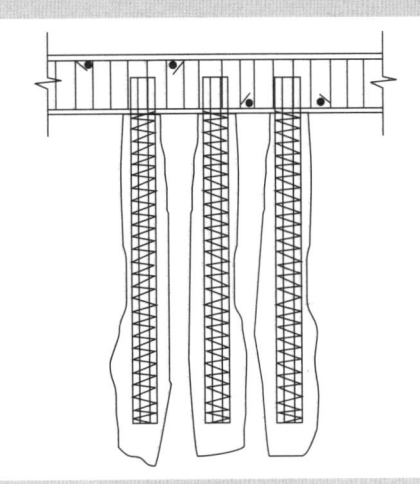

raft connecting two piles

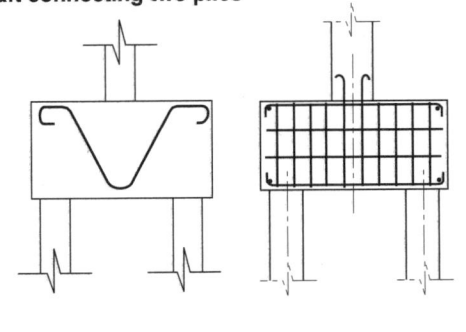

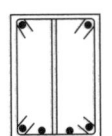

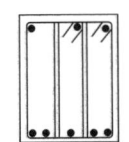

raft connecting three piles

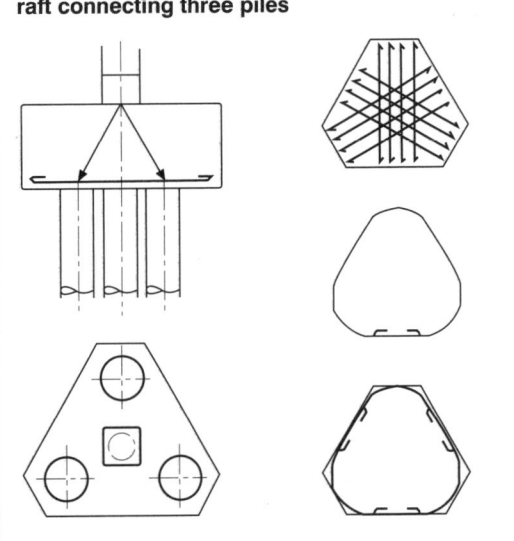

raft connecting four piles

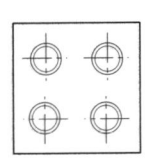

raft connecting five piles

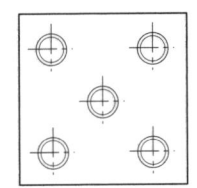

raft connecting six piles

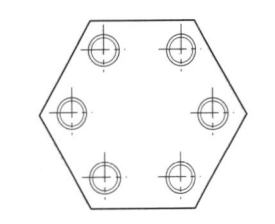

foundation

slurry wall
A concrete wall built inside a trench with the purpose of retaining the soil, and to serve as a permanent foundation wall.

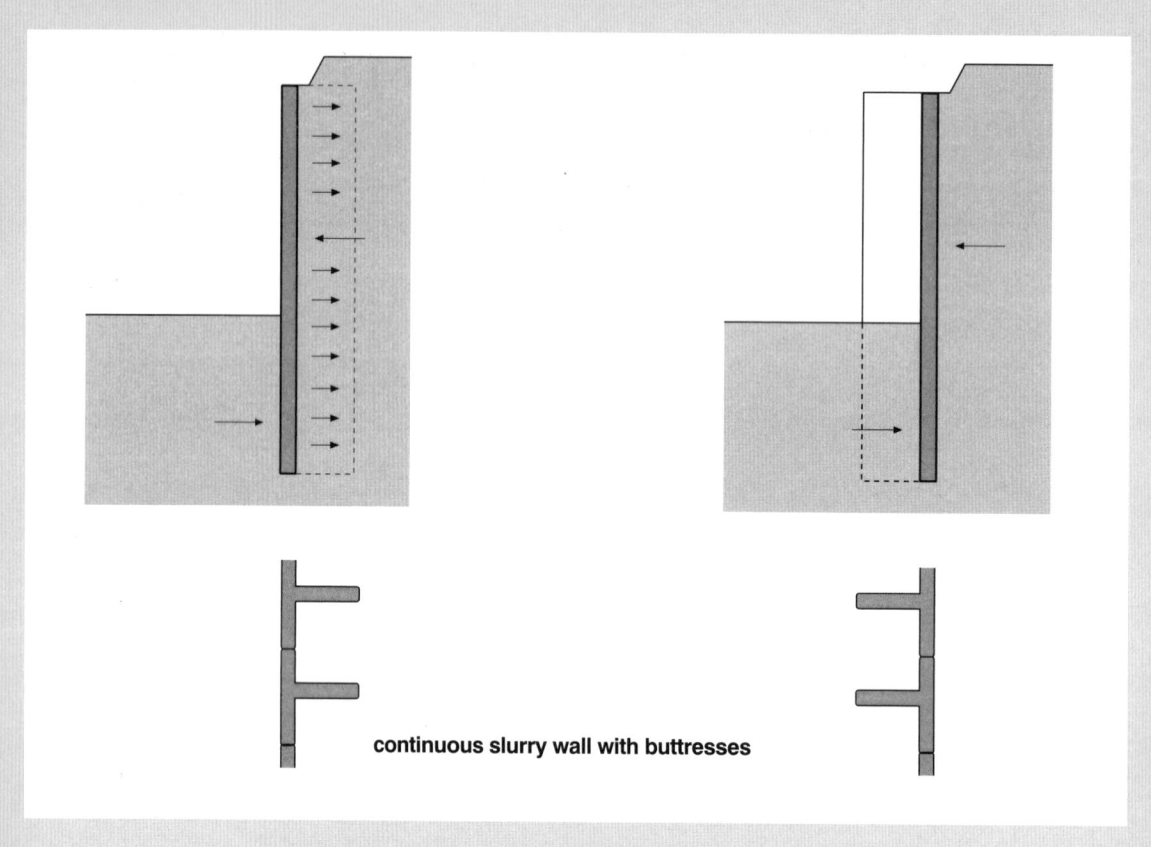

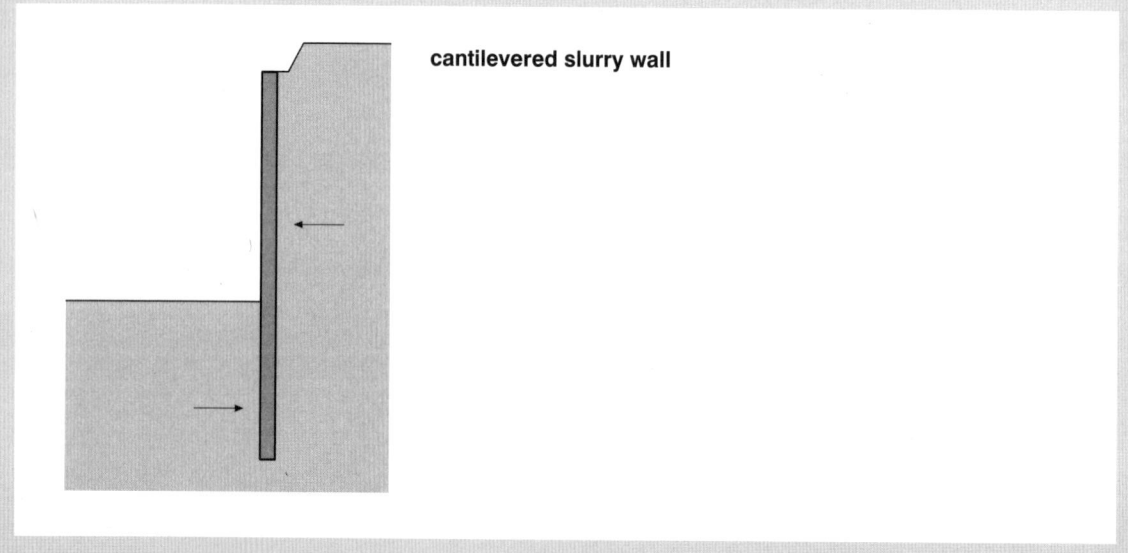

continuous slurry wall with buttresses

cantilevered slurry wall

foundation

deep foundation
A type of foundation consisting in excavating the underlying layers that are unsuitable for resisting load, down to a level with a satisfactory load bearing capacity.

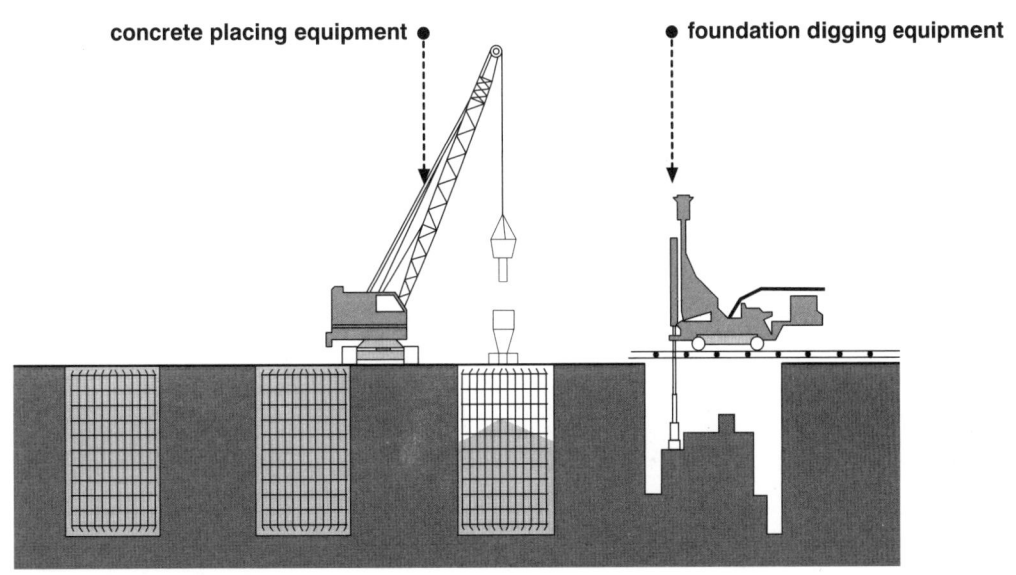

concrete placing equipment

foundation digging equipment

gradual progressive placing of the unevenseries

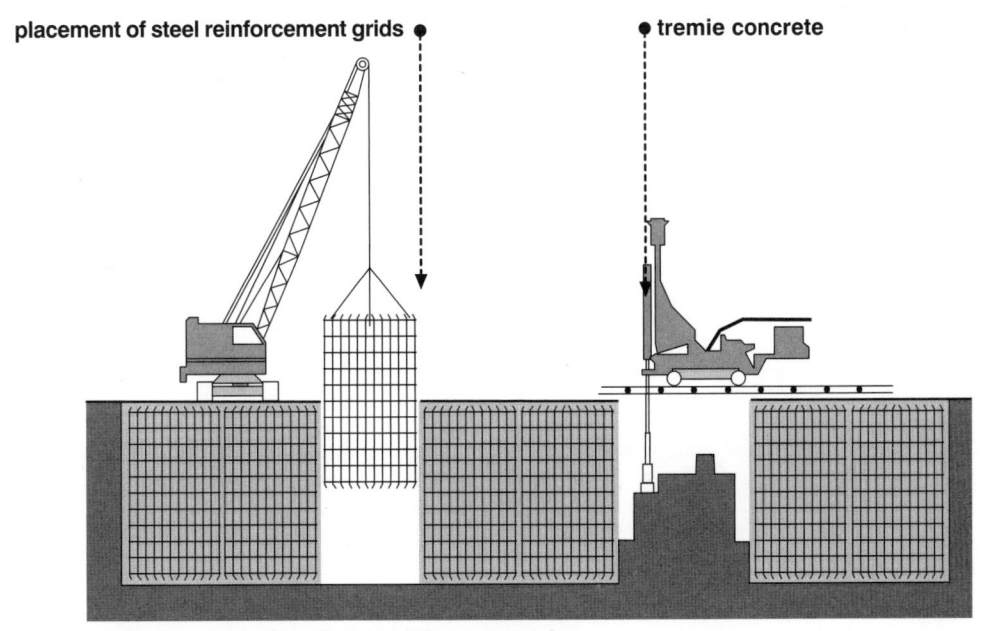

placement of steel reinforcement grids

tremie concrete

gradual progressive placing of the even series

sitework

Any and all of the various tasks that have to be completed to prepare a site for the operations of building.

soil class
The numerical classification or grading of soil according to its texture: (1) gravel, (2) sand or sandy soil, (3) clay or claylike soil, (4) average plasticity soil, (5) highly plastic soil, (6) highly compressible soil.

crushed gravel
The gravel that results from the mechanical crushing of rocks or boulders.

pea gravel
A fine grade gravel, generally between 6,4 and 9,5 mm (1/4 and 1/3 of an inch) which has been sifted under given conditions.

pebble
A rounded stone of small size, the surface of which has been worn by erosion.

crushed rock
Stones that have resulted from the mechanical crushing of rocks. Also called crushed stone.

coarse aggregate
Aggregate retained by 4.76 mm (No 4) sieve.

broken stone
A coarse natural or manufactured aggregate (crushed rock), retained by a 3 in. (76 mm) sieve and passing by a nº 4 (4.76 mm). Also called gravel or coarse aggregate.

fine aggregate
A hard and inert material used for the preparation of concrete or mortar, sifted by a 4,76 mm sieve. Also called sand.

sand clay
A type of sand containing approx. 10% of clay, often used as a base or seat material.

inorganic silt
A material composed of non plastic granules with diameters of between 0.002 and 0.05 mm, that do not counteract a drying process. Also called rock flour.

loam
A rich soil consisting of sand, silt or clay (or any proportion of these) with humus, also called topsoil, as opposed to deeper layers that contain a smaller proportion of organic matter.

clay loam
A soil that contains a proportion of clay of between 25% and 40%, with between 20% and 45% of sand.

clay
An earthy material composed mainly of hydrated silicates of aluminum; it is very plastic when wet, and contracts and hardens through calcination.

bentonite
A clay formed by the decomposition of volcanic ash; it is capable of absorbing an enormous quantity of water and of multiplying its volume accordingly.

loess
A fine windborne silt of little consistency.

organic soil
A soil that contains a high proportion of organic matter; it is generally very compressible and offers poor bearing capacity.

plastic soil
A soil showing a degree of plasticity.

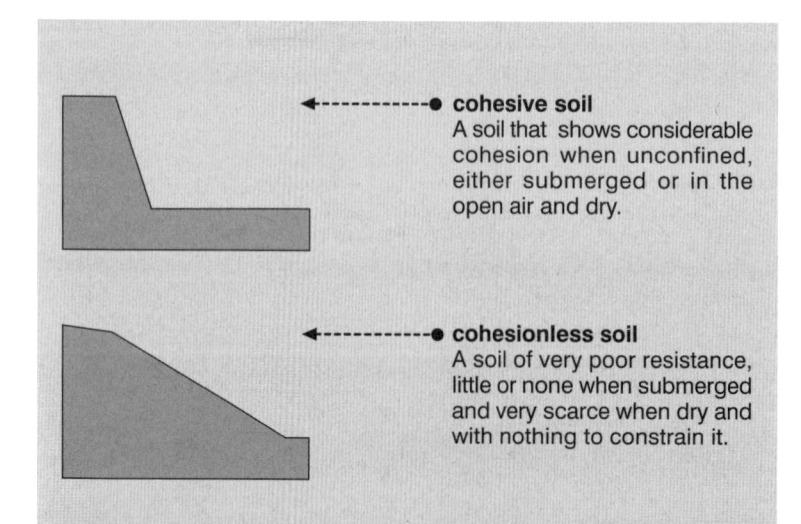

cohesive soil
A soil that shows considerable cohesion when unconfined, either submerged or in the open air and dry.

cohesionless soil
A soil of very poor resistance, little or none when submerged and very scarce when dry and with nothing to constrain it.

site work

excavation
A hollow, trench or hole that results from the action of digging.

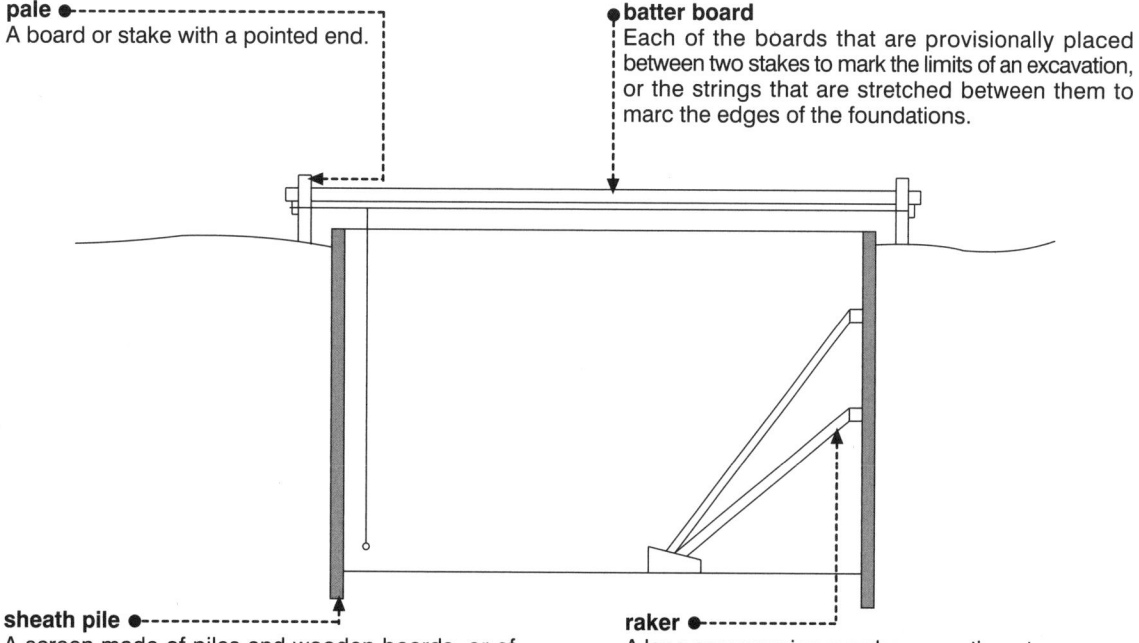

pale
A board or stake with a pointed end.

batter board
Each of the boards that are provisionally placed between two stakes to mark the limits of an excavation, or the strings that are stretched between them to marc the edges of the foundations.

sheath pile
A screen made of piles and wooden boards, or of sheets of steel or concrete driven into the ground, in order to contain the soil and prevent water from penetrating.

raker
A long compression member, sometimes temporary, placed obliquely against the wall of a building to give it support.

slurry wall
A concrete wall built inside a trench with the purpose of retaining the soil, and to serve as a permanent foundation wall.

blow
The emergence of water and solid matters in an excavation, due to excessive water pressure on the outside.

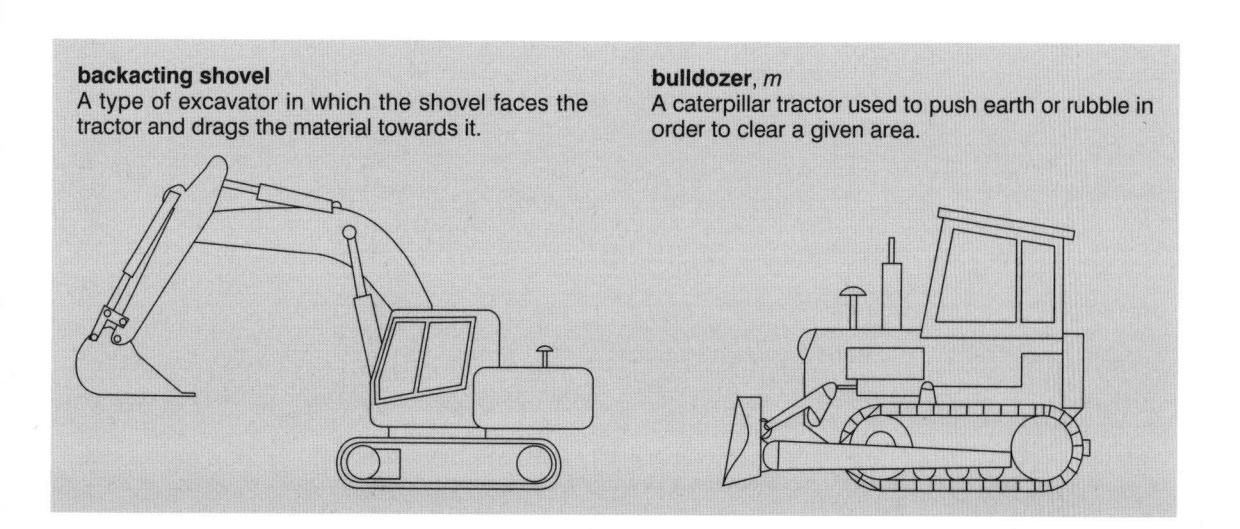

backacting shovel
A type of excavator in which the shovel faces the tractor and drags the material towards it.

bulldozer, m
A caterpillar tractor used to push earth or rubble in order to clear a given area.

site work

earthwork
Any mechanical or manual operations undertaken which involve moving the earth to alter or prepare the layout of the site.

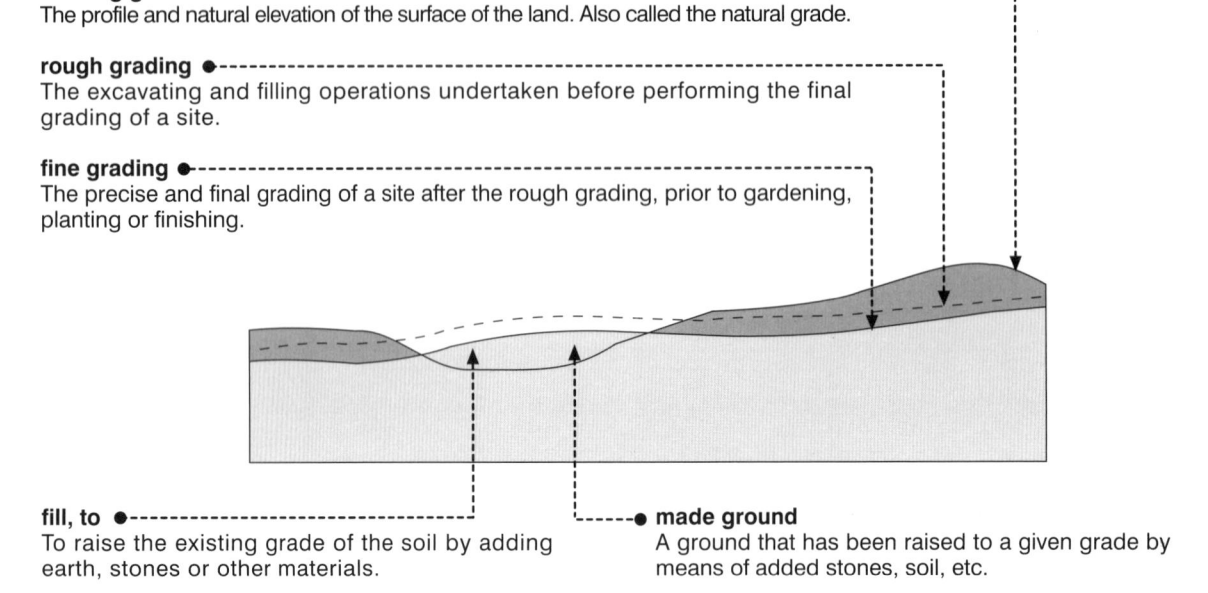

existing grade
The profile and natural elevation of the surface of the land. Also called the natural grade.

rough grading
The excavating and filling operations undertaken before performing the final grading of a site.

fine grading
The precise and final grading of a site after the rough grading, prior to gardening, planting or finishing.

fill, to
To raise the existing grade of the soil by adding earth, stones or other materials.

made ground
A ground that has been raised to a given grade by means of added stones, soil, etc.

controlled fill
A landfill that is added in layers and supervised to ensure that it meets the specifications regarding cohesiveness and to control the humidity content of each of the layers, as well as its thickness and bearing capacity.

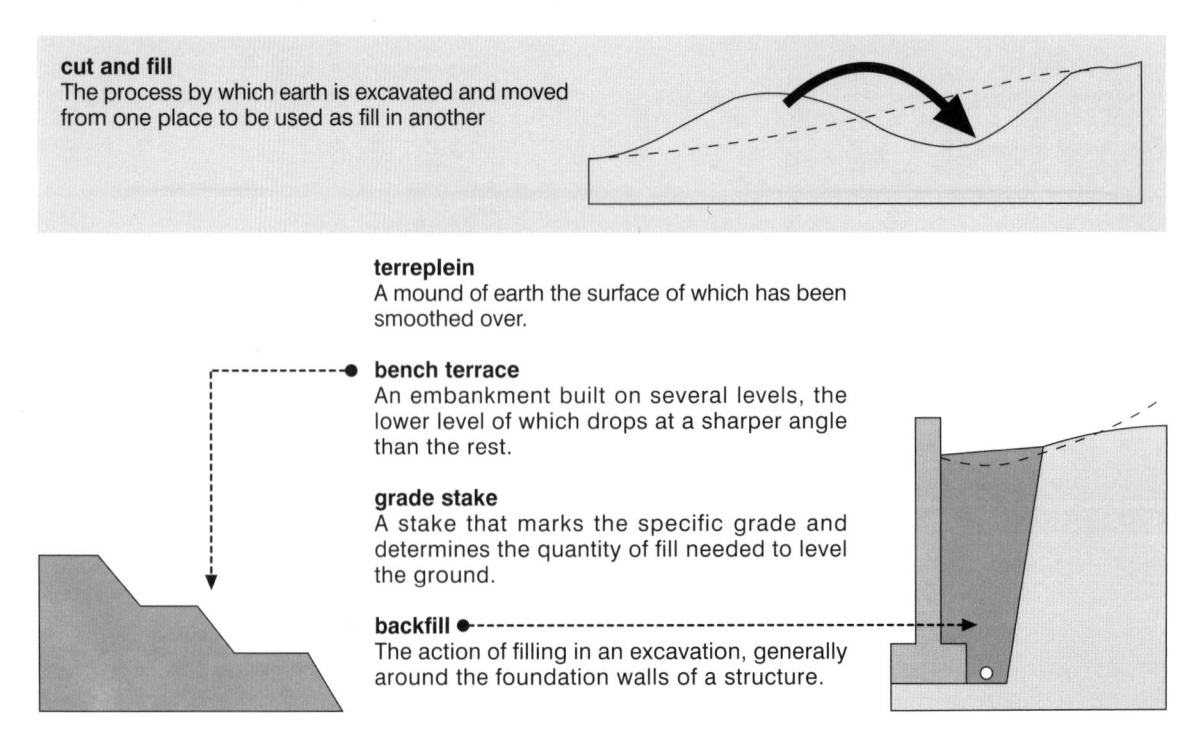

cut and fill
The process by which earth is excavated and moved from one place to be used as fill in another

terreplein
A mound of earth the surface of which has been smoothed over.

bench terrace
An embankment built on several levels, the lower level of which drops at a sharper angle than the rest.

grade stake
A stake that marks the specific grade and determines the quantity of fill needed to level the ground.

backfill
The action of filling in an excavation, generally around the foundation walls of a structure.

site work

retaining wall
A wall built of concrete, masonry or wood in order to contain a mass of earth or fill liable to slide and resist the corresponding lateral forces that act upon it.

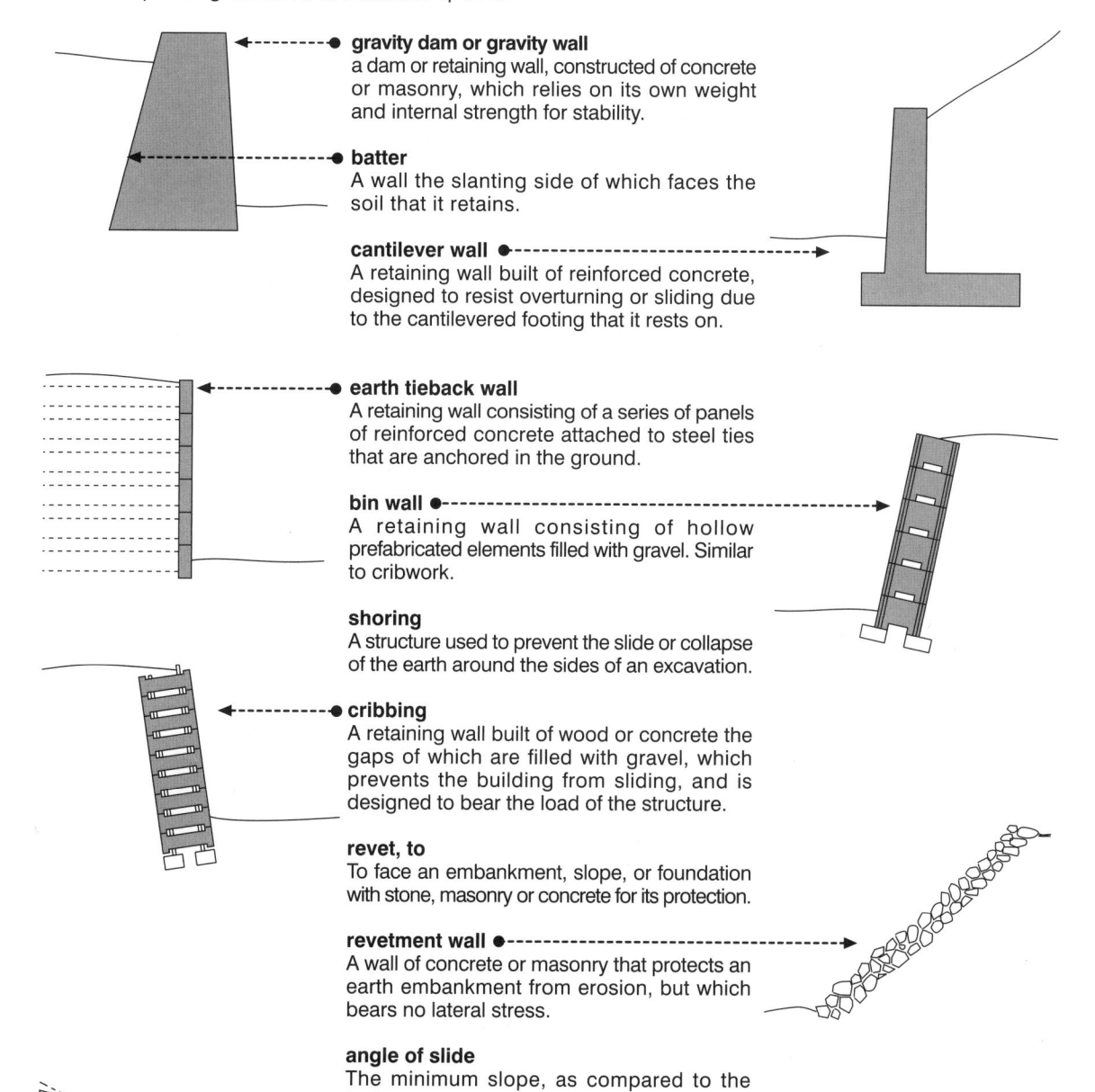

gravity dam or gravity wall
a dam or retaining wall, constructed of concrete or masonry, which relies on its own weight and internal strength for stability.

batter
A wall the slanting side of which faces the soil that it retains.

cantilever wall
A retaining wall built of reinforced concrete, designed to resist overturning or sliding due to the cantilevered footing that it rests on.

earth tieback wall
A retaining wall consisting of a series of panels of reinforced concrete attached to steel ties that are anchored in the ground.

bin wall
A retaining wall consisting of hollow prefabricated elements filled with gravel. Similar to cribwork.

shoring
A structure used to prevent the slide or collapse of the earth around the sides of an excavation.

cribbing
A retaining wall built of wood or concrete the gaps of which are filled with gravel, which prevents the building from sliding, and is designed to bear the load of the structure.

revet, to
To face an embankment, slope, or foundation with stone, masonry or concrete for its protection.

revetment wall
A wall of concrete or masonry that protects an earth embankment from erosion, but which bears no lateral stress.

angle of slide
The minimum slope, as compared to the horizontal, beyond which a given granular soil begins to slide.

angle of repose
The maximum slope a given granular soil can rest at without starting to slide.

Building

Building
Roof
Stair
Elevator (USA)
Door
Window
Nonbearing partition
Façade
Finish floor
Ceiling
Thermal insulation
Damp proofing
Sound
Building typology

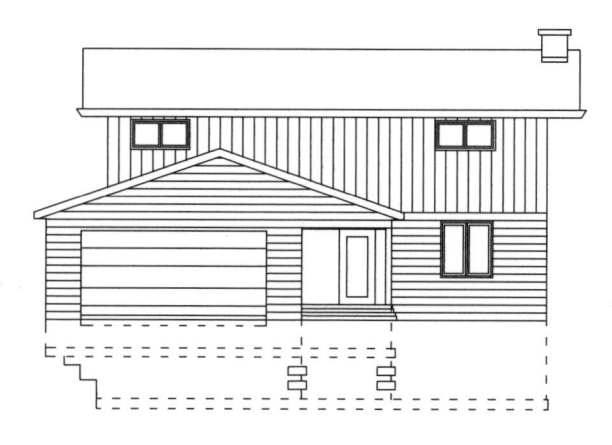

building

A habitable structure or construction of a more or less permanent nature, as opposed to ones that are movable or designed for a purpose other than their occupancy.

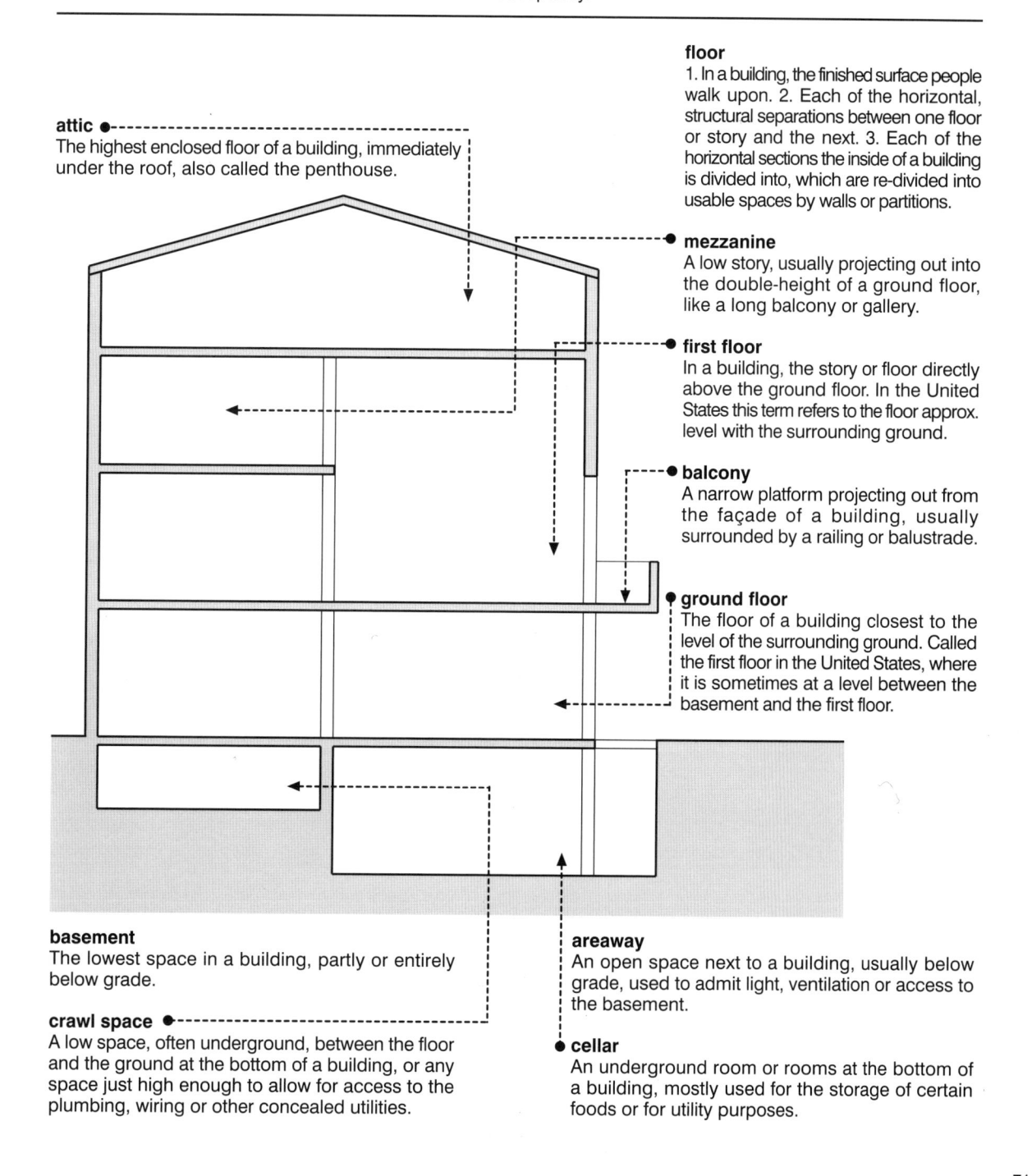

attic
The highest enclosed floor of a building, immediately under the roof, also called the penthouse.

floor
1. In a building, the finished surface people walk upon. 2. Each of the horizontal, structural separations between one floor or story and the next. 3. Each of the horizontal sections the inside of a building is divided into, which are re-divided into usable spaces by walls or partitions.

mezzanine
A low story, usually projecting out into the double-height of a ground floor, like a long balcony or gallery.

first floor
In a building, the story or floor directly above the ground floor. In the United States this term refers to the floor approx. level with the surrounding ground.

balcony
A narrow platform projecting out from the façade of a building, usually surrounded by a railing or balustrade.

ground floor
The floor of a building closest to the level of the surrounding ground. Called the first floor in the United States, where it is sometimes at a level between the basement and the first floor.

basement
The lowest space in a building, partly or entirely below grade.

crawl space
A low space, often underground, between the floor and the ground at the bottom of a building, or any space just high enough to allow for access to the plumbing, wiring or other concealed utilities.

areaway
An open space next to a building, usually below grade, used to admit light, ventilation or access to the basement.

cellar
An underground room or rooms at the bottom of a building, mostly used for the storage of certain foods or for utility purposes.

building

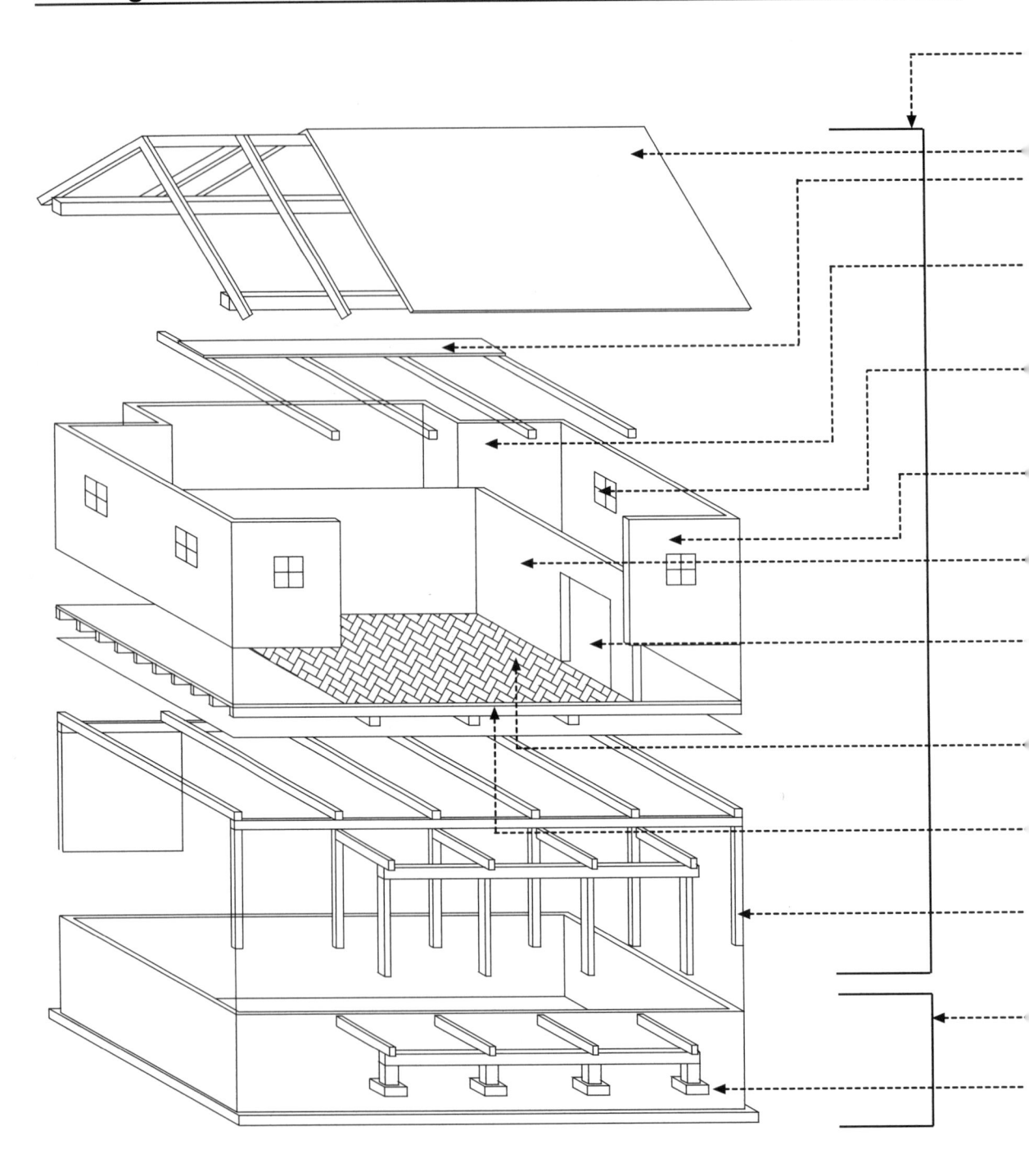

building

- **superstructure**
  That part of a structure that rises above its foundations.

- **roof**
  The structure that encloses the exterior of the upper part of a building.

- **ceiling**
  The overhead covering or decorative finish often used to conceal ducts, the supporting structure of the roof or of the floor above.

- **wall**
  A continuous vertical surface of masonry or concrete, erected to enclose or subdivide a space, and often bearing a share of the load of beams, upper floors or a roof.

- **window**
  An aperture in the wall of a building to allow light and ventilation inside, usually having a fixed frame and one or more sashes that may move in a variety of ways.

- **façade**
  Any of the outer walls of a building exposed to the weather. Also called an external wall.

- **nonbearing partition**
  An interior wall built for the purpose of dividing the space into suitable volumes, but bearing no other load than its own.

- **door**
  A movable barrier that closes the access to a space; made of wood, glass or metal, moving on hinges, sliding or folding, it usually has some closing mechanism such as a lock.

- **finished floor**
  A material, with decorative or hygienic properties, covering the walkable substrate of a given space.

- **floor**
  In a building or room, the underlying horizontal finished surface people walk on.

- **structure**
  The combination of structural members that contribute to form and support the integrity of a building. Also called the frame, framework, shell, skeleton construction.

- **substructure**
  The underlying structure, usually underground, that supports a building, connecting it to the ground and the bearing stratum.

- **foundation**
  The lowest underlying part of a building's structure, frequently underground, that connects or anchors the building to the ground and transfers the load directly to the bearing stratum.

stoop
A raised platform one or more steps above the surrounding ground, leading to the entrance of a house.

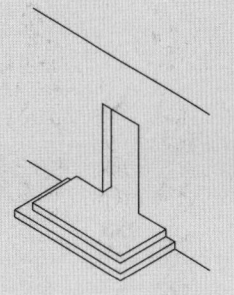

porch
A semi enclosed annex structure to shelter the building's entrance; usually roofed, sometimes of some size as in a veranda, the sides may be screened with glass.

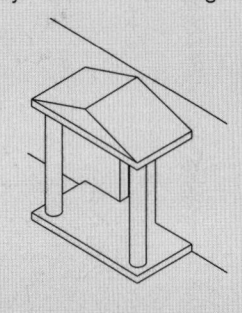

portico
A monumental porch or decorative structure dignifying the access to a building; it often consists of a colonnade supporting a roof.

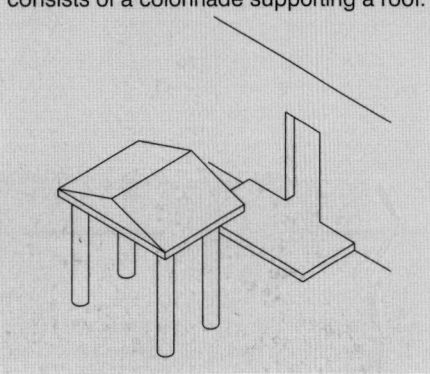

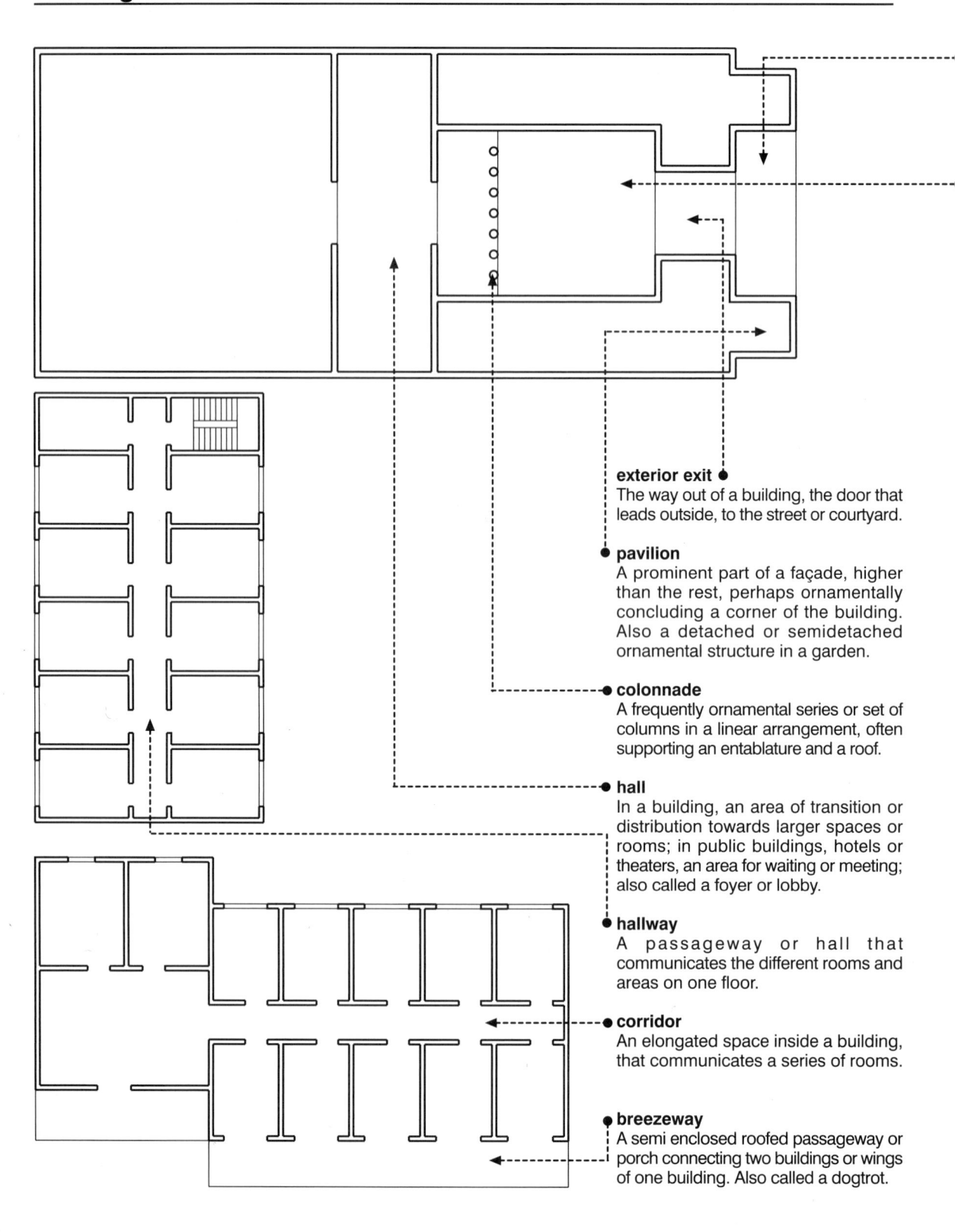

building

exterior exit
The way out of a building, the door that leads outside, to the street or courtyard.

pavilion
A prominent part of a façade, higher than the rest, perhaps ornamentally concluding a corner of the building. Also a detached or semidetached ornamental structure in a garden.

colonnade
A frequently ornamental series or set of columns in a linear arrangement, often supporting an entablature and a roof.

hall
In a building, an area of transition or distribution towards larger spaces or rooms; in public buildings, hotels or theaters, an area for waiting or meeting; also called a foyer or lobby.

hallway
A passageway or hall that communicates the different rooms and areas on one floor.

corridor
An elongated space inside a building, that communicates a series of rooms.

breezeway
A semi enclosed roofed passageway or porch connecting two buildings or wings of one building. Also called a dogtrot.

building

forecourt
An open area or plaza at the front of a building or between buildings, usually as an entrance or arrival area.

courtyard
An open court in the center of a building, which surrounds it on all sides.

atrium
An open space within a building, which light penetrates from above through a glazed roof or skylight.

peristyle
A colonnade that surrounds a courtyard or the exterior of a building.

court
An open space in or next to one or more buildings, that partly surround it.

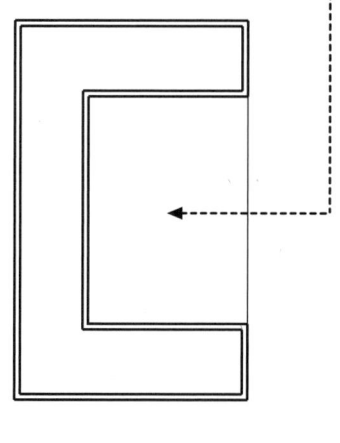

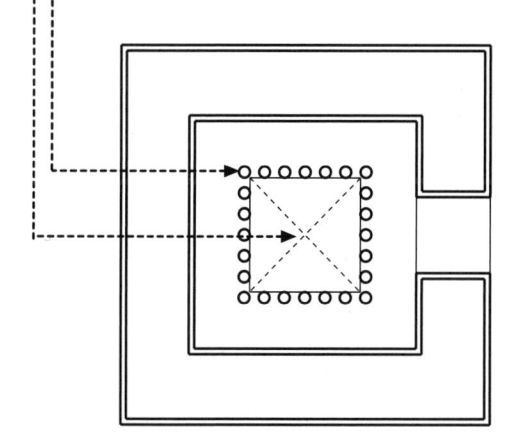

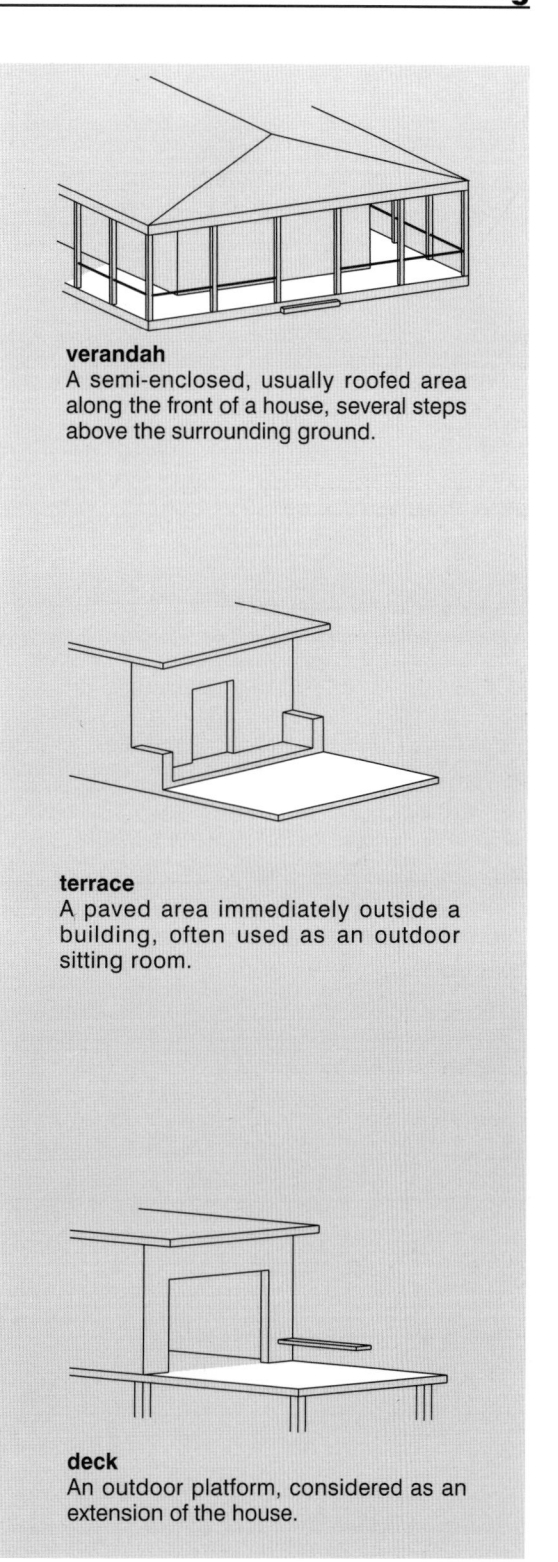

verandah
A semi-enclosed, usually roofed area along the front of a house, several steps above the surrounding ground.

terrace
A paved area immediately outside a building, often used as an outdoor sitting room.

deck
An outdoor platform, considered as an extension of the house.

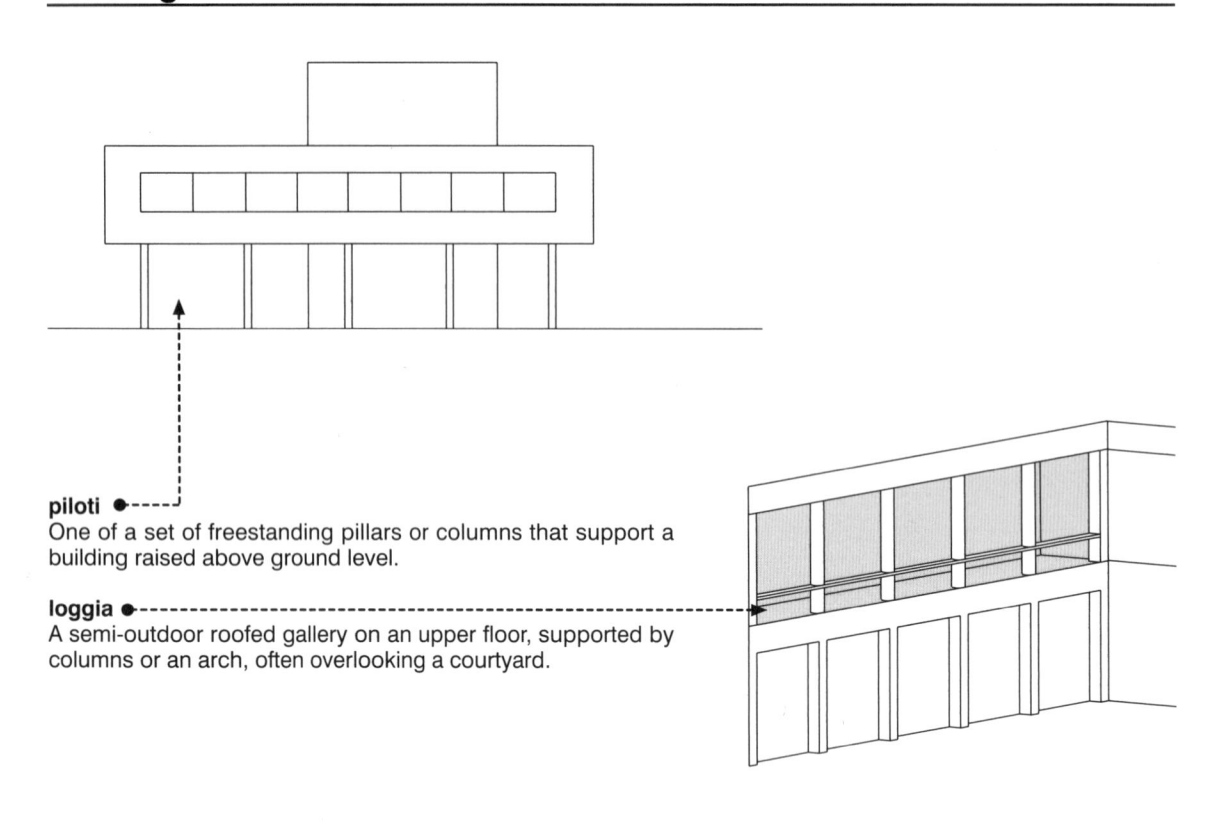

building

piloti
One of a set of freestanding pillars or columns that support a building raised above ground level.

loggia
A semi-outdoor roofed gallery on an upper floor, supported by columns or an arch, often overlooking a courtyard.

closed plan
The distribution plan of a closed space, with doors to interconnect the resulting spaces.

open plan
The floor plan of a building that has the minimum number of interior subdivisions between the different functional areas.

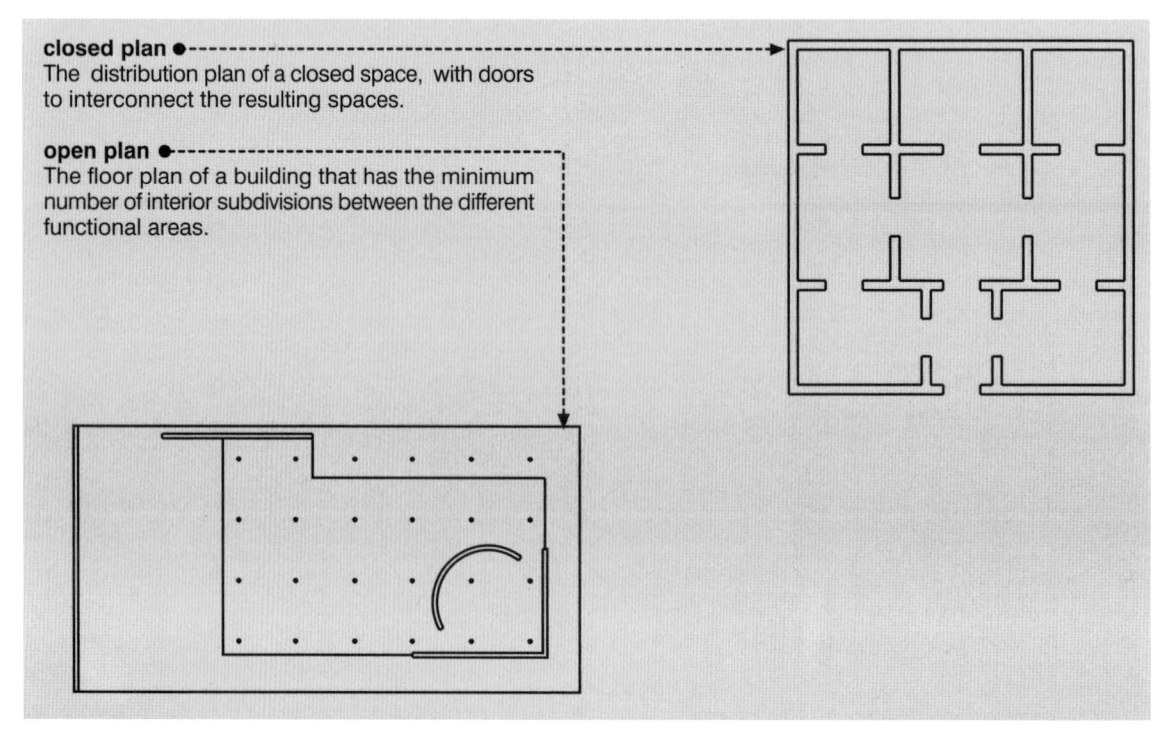

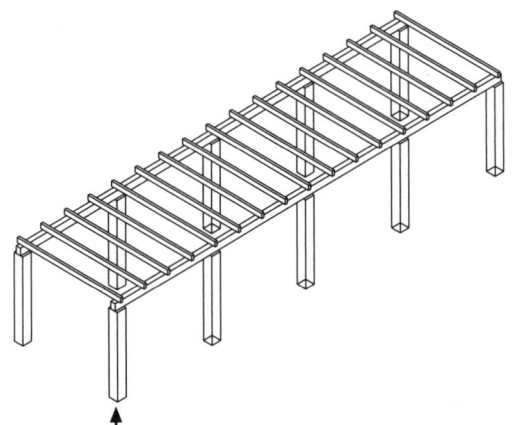

building

pergola
In a garden, a structure consisting of two lines of columns or posts supporting an open roof made of light beams or lattice work so as to support climbing plants

parterre
1. One of the flowerbeds in a formal garden, divided and outlined by paths, often creating a geometrical pattern. 2. In a theater, the rows of seats at the rear of the main floor or parquet, also called parquet circle or orchestra circle.

arbor (USA)
Within a garden, an area that is sheltered by hedges or trees, or surrounded by shrubbery or climbing plants; also called arbour (G.B.).

trellis
A light structure of latticework used as a separation, and often as a support for climbing plants.

folly
A structure built to create a focus of interest in a view or landscape, without fulfilling any functional purpose whatever.

gazebo
An ornamental roofed structure with open sides standing isolated in a garden, to provide shade, shelter or repose.

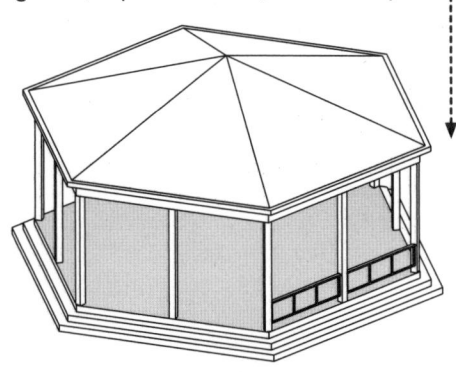

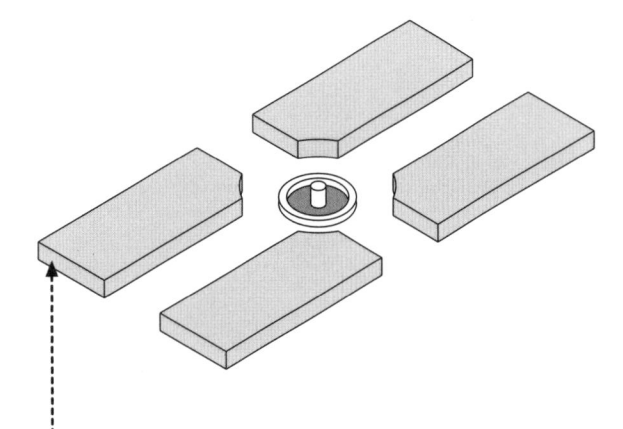

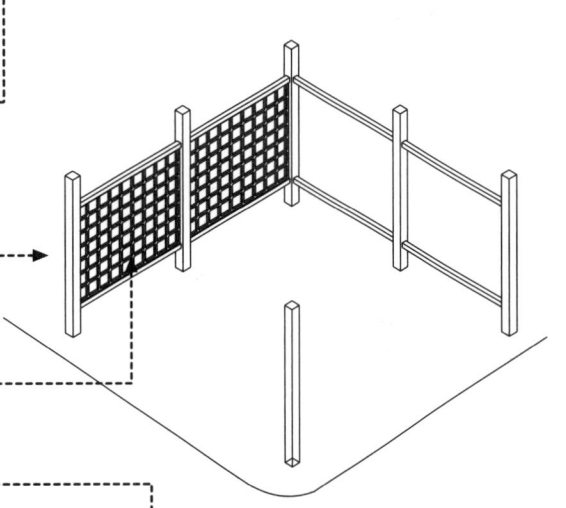

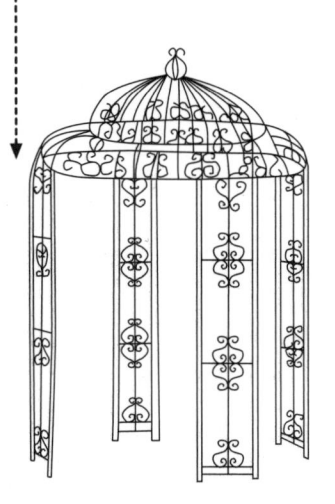

roof

The structure that encloses the exterior
of the upper part of a building

pitched roof
A roof having one or more of its planes sloped at a significant angle.

pitch
The slope or angle of a roof expressed in measures of vertical rise per measure of length, such as inches or centimeters per foot or meter.

rise
The amount of vertical rise found between the cornice and the apex of a particular roof.

pediment
1. In a classical gabled façade, the triangular finish between the horizontal cornice and the end of the roof. 2. A similar ornamental detail over a door or window.

rake
The projecting pitched edge of a roof.

saddle
Any hollow backed element or saddle-like structure designed to roof the intersection between two slopes of a pitched roof, shedding the rain to either side.

hip
The convex angle formed by the intersection of two adjacent roof planes.

valley
The covering of the concave intersection of two adjacent roof planes, where rainwater gathers from both sides.

eave
That part of a roof which projects outward beyond the wall, often ended in a gutter that leads the rainwater towards the drain.

ridgecap
The horizontal line between two opposite slopes of a pitched roof. The material covering of the ridge between two opposite slopes of a pitched roof.

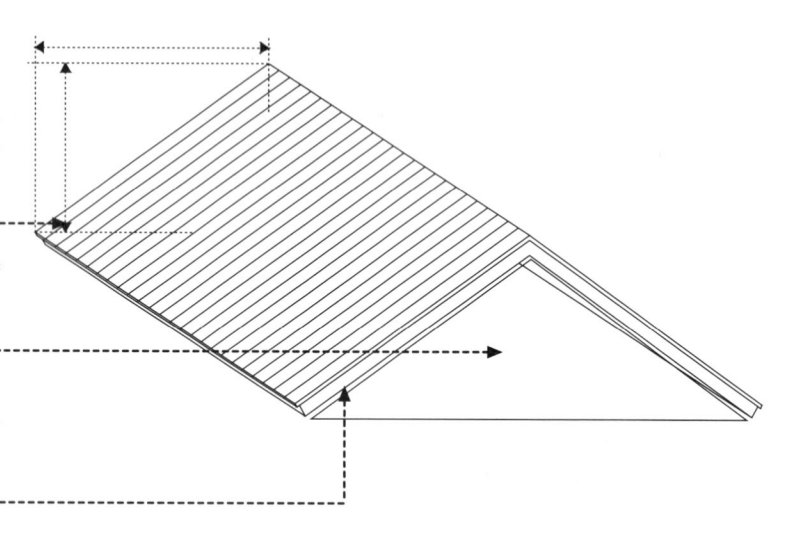

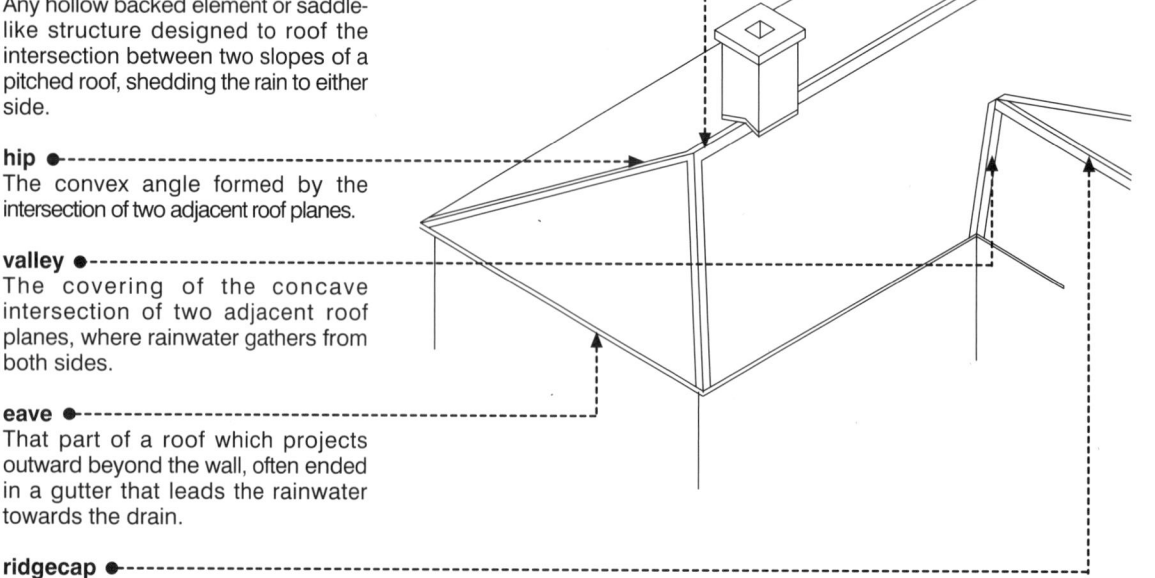

roof

hipped roof
A pitched roof having four sloped sides that meet along convex ridges. Also called a hip roof.

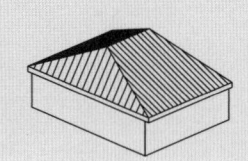

gable roof
A roof having two sloped sides that intersect along a ridge at the top, shedding the rainwater in two opposite directions.

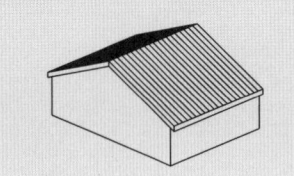

mansard roof
A roof consisting of more than one plane on each side, the lower sections of which are the steepest.

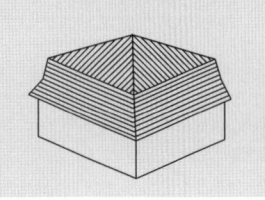

curb roof
A pitched roof with two sides that slope away from the ridge in two successive angles, the lower of which is nearly vertical. Also called a gambrel, mansard or French roof.

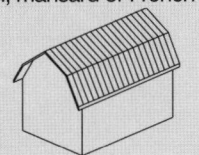

butterfly roof
A two-sided pitched roof sloping in towards the central valley or gutter that leads the rain water to a downspout.

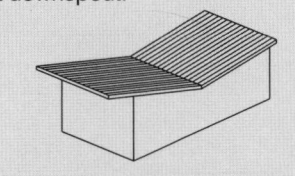

pent roof
A pitched roof with only one side, one slope and one plane, also called a shed roof.

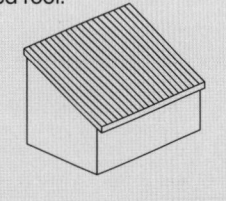

whaleback roof
A two-sided pitched roof curving gradually down from the ridge, in the form of a gothic arch. Also called a rainbow roof.

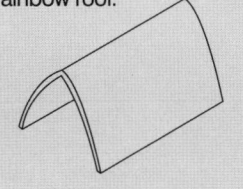

barrel roof
A semi cylindrical roof covering a space similar to a barrel vault.

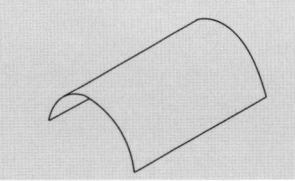

jerkinhead
Cubierta a dos aguas que posee la parte superior de los hastiales reemplazados por copetes.

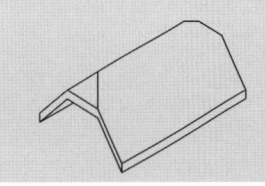

lean-to
A small extension to a building with a one-sided pitched roof resting on the wall of the building, against which it "leans".

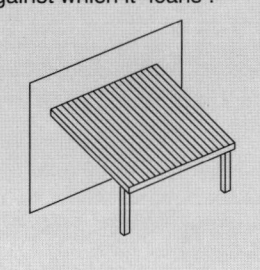

pavilion roof
A ridgeless pitched roof, the various sides of which slope away from their one common point, at the apex.

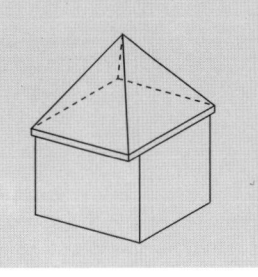

sawtooth roof
A roof consisting of parallel strips across the building, creating a corresponding succession of gables along the two opposite façades; the north side of these strips is often glazed.

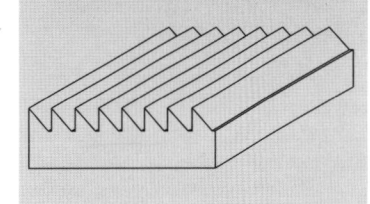

roof

close couple roof
A roof structure of opposite pitched rafters with their top ends resting on a central ridgeboard.

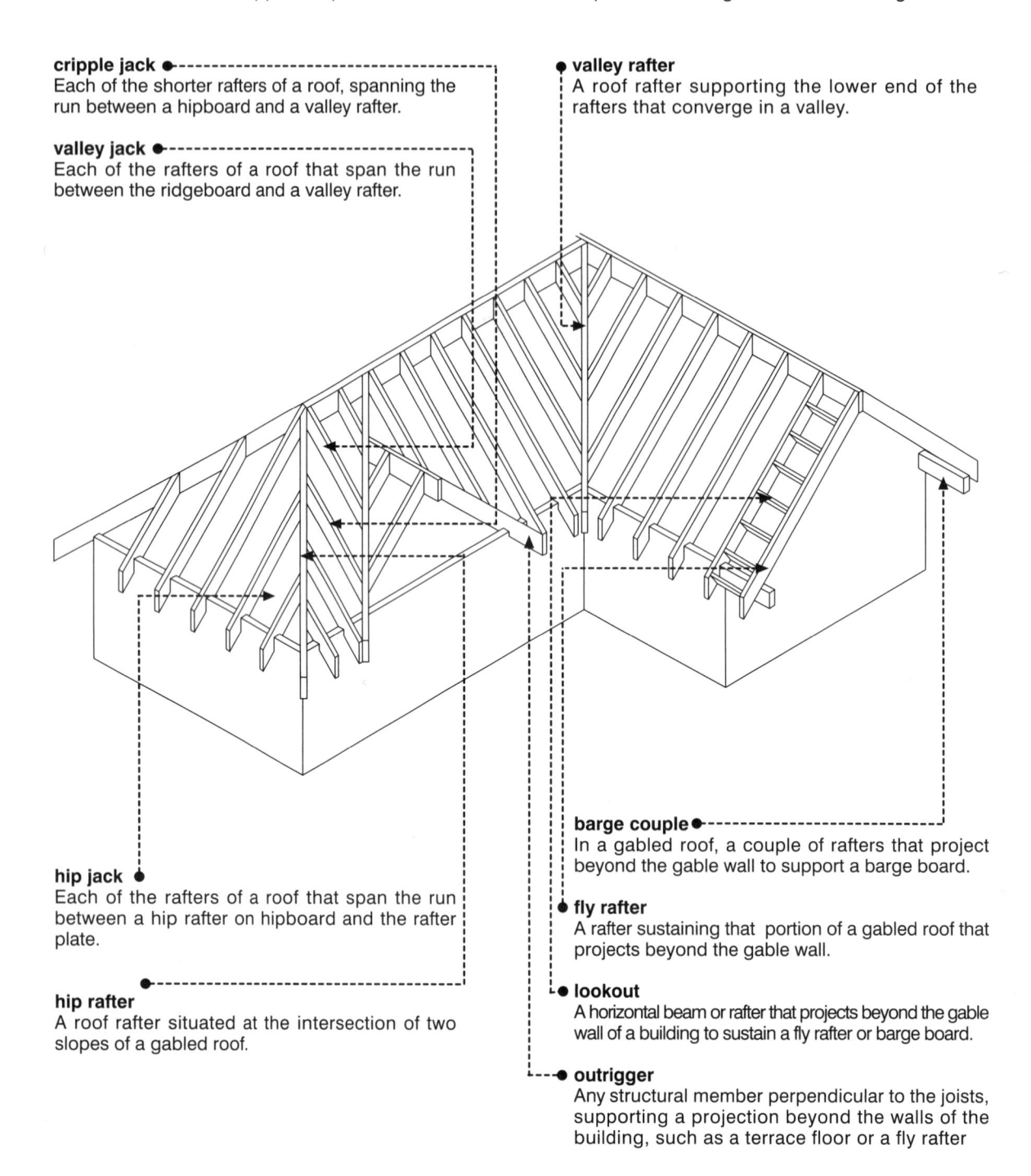

cripple jack
Each of the shorter rafters of a roof, spanning the run between a hipboard and a valley rafter.

valley jack
Each of the rafters of a roof that span the run between the ridgeboard and a valley rafter.

valley rafter
A roof rafter supporting the lower end of the rafters that converge in a valley.

hip jack
Each of the rafters of a roof that span the run between a hip rafter on hipboard and the rafter plate.

hip rafter
A roof rafter situated at the intersection of two slopes of a gabled roof.

barge couple
In a gabled roof, a couple of rafters that project beyond the gable wall to support a barge board.

fly rafter
A rafter sustaining that portion of a gabled roof that projects beyond the gable wall.

lookout
A horizontal beam or rafter that projects beyond the gable wall of a building to sustain a fly rafter or barge board.

outrigger
Any structural member perpendicular to the joists, supporting a projection beyond the walls of the building, such as a terrace floor or a fly rafter

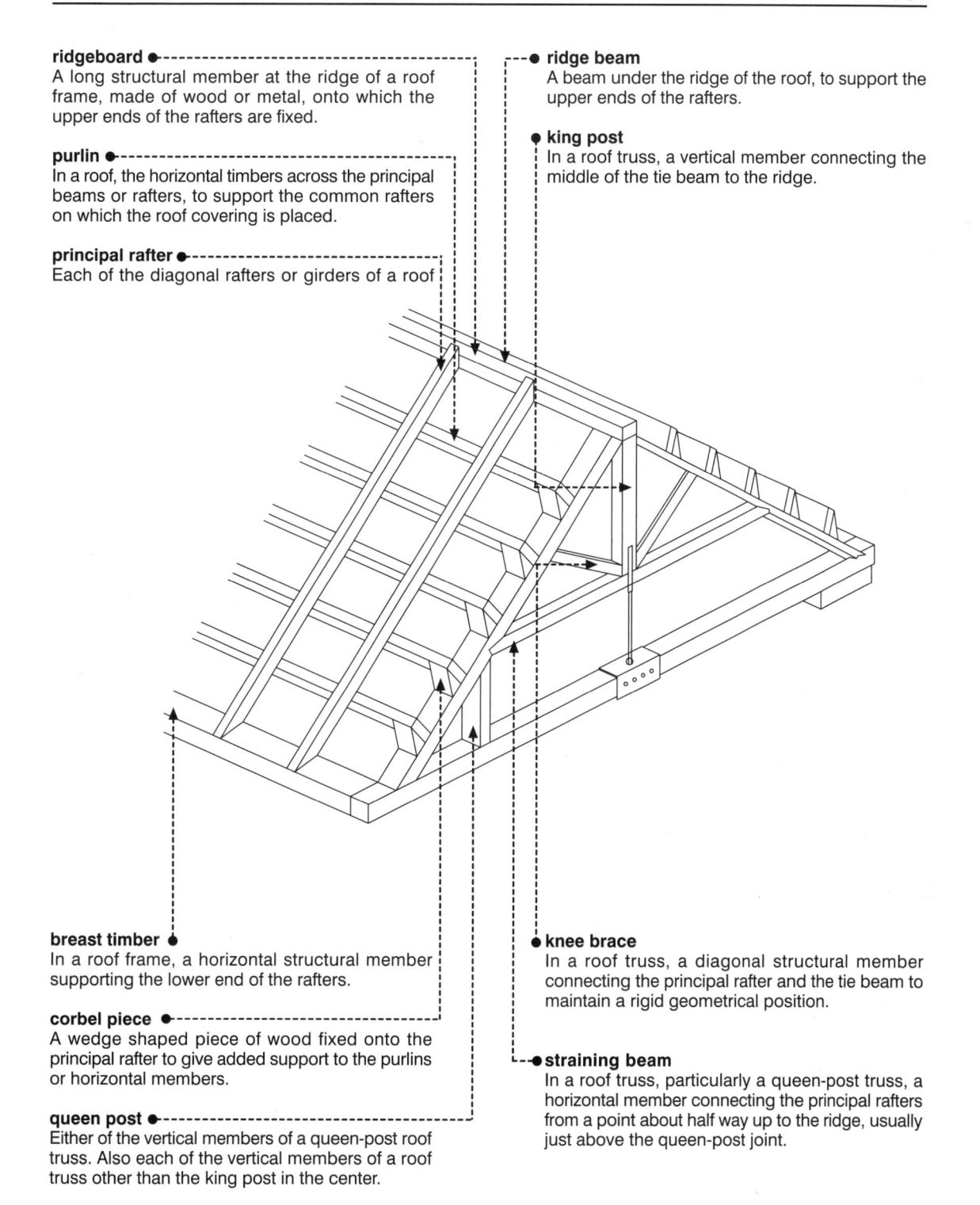

roof

ridgeboard
A long structural member at the ridge of a roof frame, made of wood or metal, onto which the upper ends of the rafters are fixed.

purlin
In a roof, the horizontal timbers across the principal beams or rafters, to support the common rafters on which the roof covering is placed.

principal rafter
Each of the diagonal rafters or girders of a roof

ridge beam
A beam under the ridge of the roof, to support the upper ends of the rafters.

king post
In a roof truss, a vertical member connecting the middle of the tie beam to the ridge.

breast timber
In a roof frame, a horizontal structural member supporting the lower end of the rafters.

corbel piece
A wedge shaped piece of wood fixed onto the principal rafter to give added support to the purlins or horizontal members.

queen post
Either of the vertical members of a queen-post roof truss. Also each of the vertical members of a roof truss other than the king post in the center.

knee brace
In a roof truss, a diagonal structural member connecting the principal rafter and the tie beam to maintain a rigid geometrical position.

straining beam
In a roof truss, particularly a queen-post truss, a horizontal member connecting the principal rafters from a point about half way up to the ridge, usually just above the queen-post joint.

roof

roofing
Any of the various materials used to ensure that the top of a building is weatherproof and that storm water is shed correctly towards an appropriate drainage system.

roofing tile
A watertight building unit for roof covering; a wide range of designs, assembly methods and materials suit it to different conditions and purposes.

slate
A metamorphic rock of clay sediments in horizontal layers that cleave well, producing thin, hard, watertight plates.

shingle
Each of the thin elongated pieces, fixed in an overlapping pattern, to weatherproof a pitched roof or an exterior.

asbestos shingle
A fireproof roofing material made mainly of asbestos.

asphalt shingle
A type of shingle made of a semi rigid base like fiberglass or felt, covered with asphalt and with an outer finish of mineral granules.

fiberglass shingle (USA)
A type of shingle made of fiberglass impregnated with asphalt, with an outer finish of colored ceramic particles; also called fibreglass shingle (G.B.)

corrugated metal
A sheet metal roofing, corrugated to improve its mechanical resistance and to shed water away from the anchoring points.

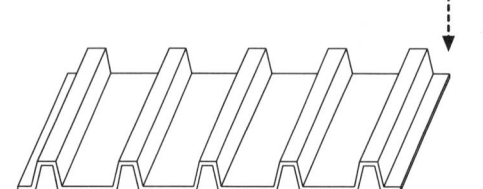

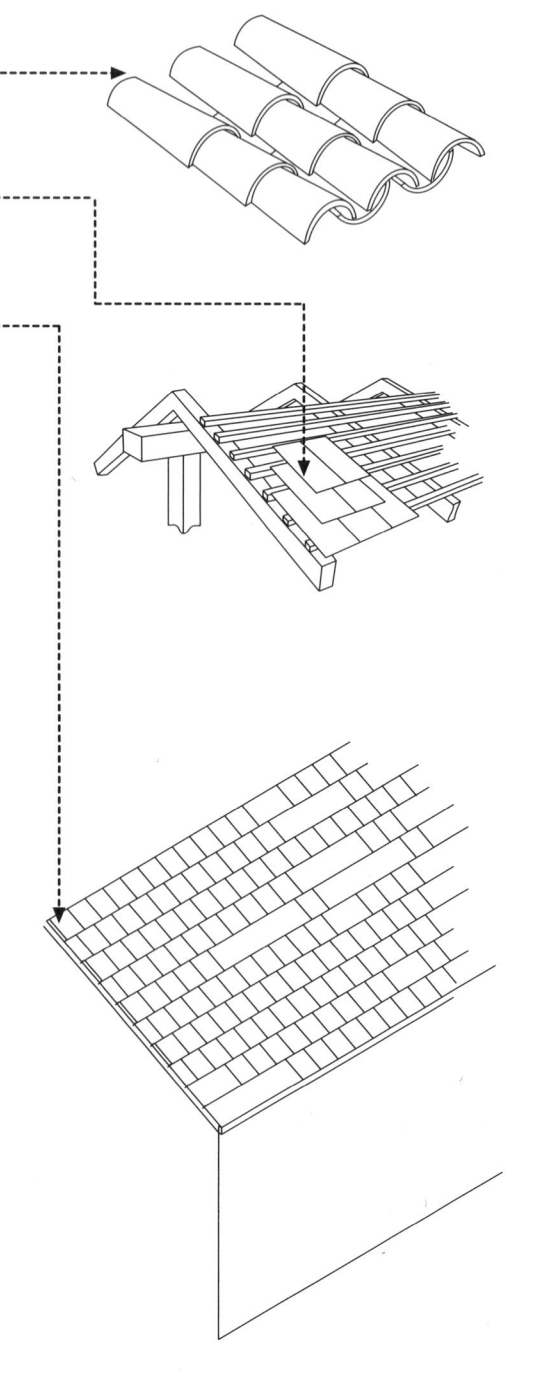

roof

mission tile
A semicircular tile, usually clay, to be used combining them both ways up.

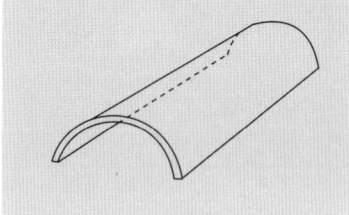

interlocking tile
A rectangular roofing tile with a groove under one side that fits over the flange on the side of the next tile.

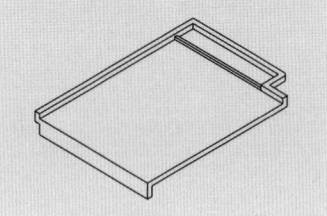

pantile
A roofing tile the cross section of which is shaped like an S, so the convexity of one overlaps the concavity of the next.

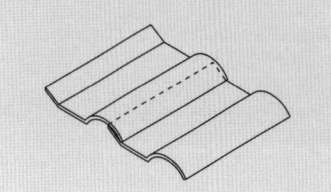

ridge tile
A convex tile used to cover the ridge of a roof, also called a crown tile.

field tile
Any of the regular tiles or shingles that cover one of the sides of a roof.

hip tile
A convex tile used to cover the hips of a hipped roof.

eaves course
The first or lowest course of tiles on a roof, probably covering the eaves.

shingle tile
A small flat roofing shingle, each course fixed overlapping the last.

starter tile
A short roofing tile placed under the eaves course so as to give it the same slope as the rest of the run.

tilting fillet
A thin wedge shaped piece of wood introduced under the eaves course of a pitched roof to ensure the tiles lie parallel to the courses above them. See doubling piece or arris fillet.

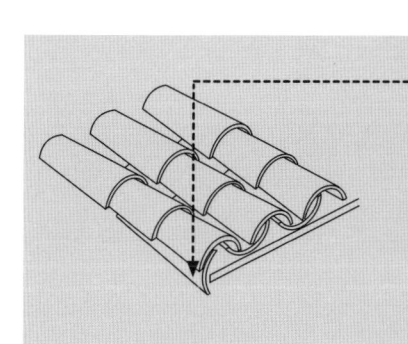

rake tile
A roof tile fixed in such a way as to conceal the edge of the roof.

angle tile
A special roof tile with an L-shaped cross section made to cover the edge of a roof. Also called an arris tile.

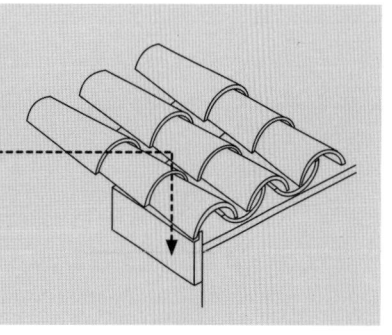

roof

open valley
In a pitched roof, a valley over which the shingles have not been interwoven, leaving the metal gutter visible.

drip edge
A strip of material extending further out from other parts of a roof to shed the rain water clear of the building.

rake
A wooden board or strip of appropriate material along the sloped edge of a gable, to conceal the edge of the siding.

starting course
On a pitched roof, a course of tiles laid over the eaves, before and under the first course itself.

underlayment
A layer of weatherproof material laid beneath the tiles or shingles.

laced valley
An interwoven placement of tiles, shingles or slates to weatherproof the concave join of a roof's two fields.

valley flashing
A sheet metal strip laid under the intersection of two sides of a roof, acting as a gutter.

common lap
A distribution of the shingles on a roof in which each successive course is displaced sideways by half a shingle in respect to the course it covers.

sidelap
The amount by which one roof shingle overlaps another along its side.

Dutch lap
In shingle or slate roofs, an overlap in which each piece covers a strip of the tile below it and of the one beside it.

cocking piece
A strip of wood placed over the rafters at the eaves to tilt upward the first courses of the roof. Also called a sprocket.

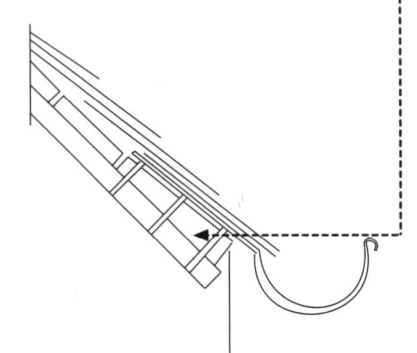

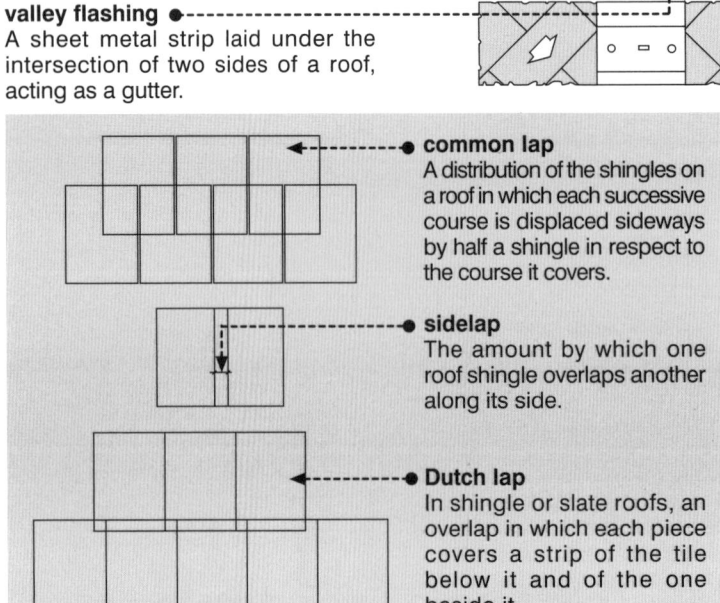

84

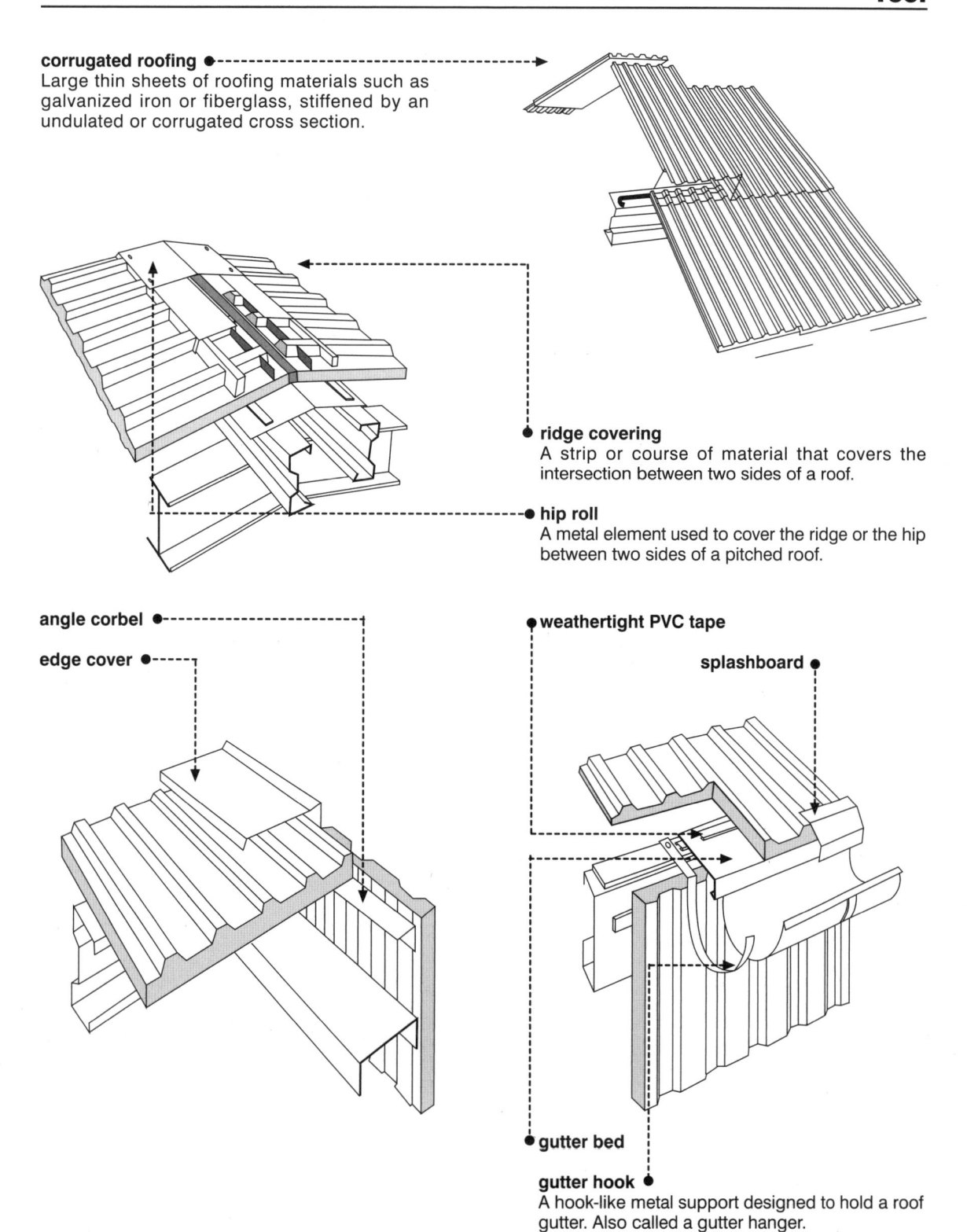

roof

corrugated roofing
Large thin sheets of roofing materials such as galvanized iron or fiberglass, stiffened by an undulated or corrugated cross section.

ridge covering
A strip or course of material that covers the intersection between two sides of a roof.

hip roll
A metal element used to cover the ridge or the hip between two sides of a pitched roof.

angle corbel

edge cover

weathertight PVC tape

splashboard

gutter bed

gutter hook
A hook-like metal support designed to hold a roof gutter. Also called a gutter hanger.

roof

roof anchoring with jointed L hooks on steel purlins

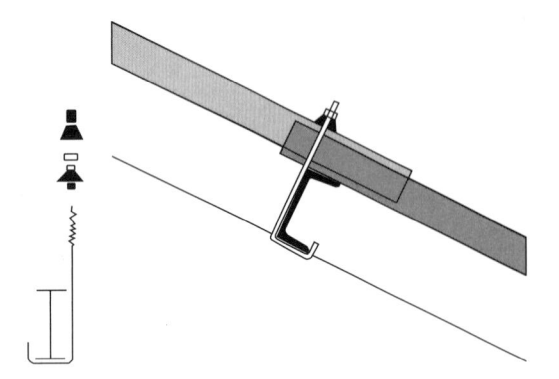

roof anchoring with screws in wood purlins

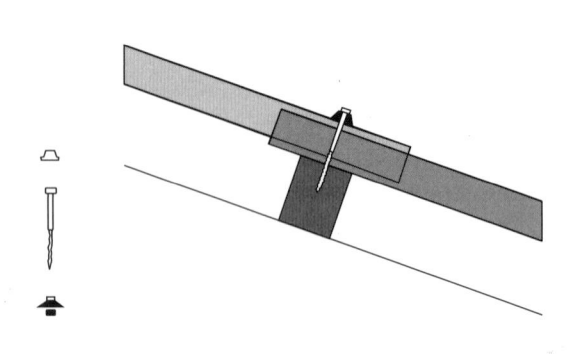

roof anchoring with L hooks on steel purlins

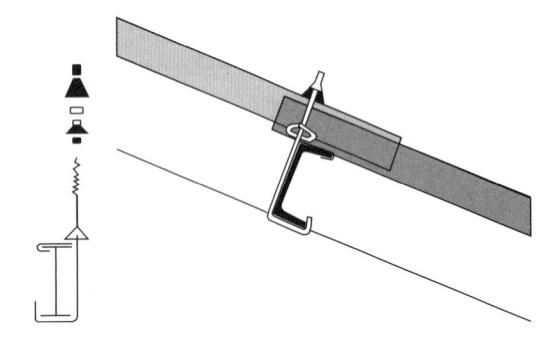

roof anchoring with jointed hooks in wood purlins

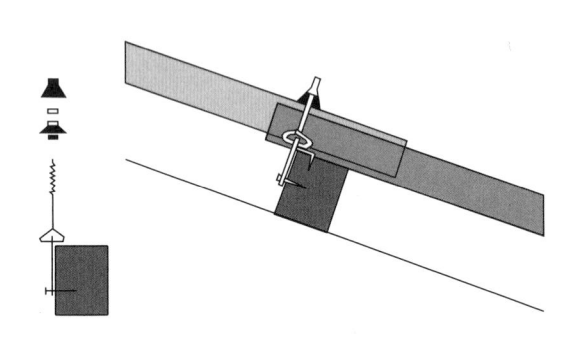

roof anchoring with U hooks on tubular steel purlins

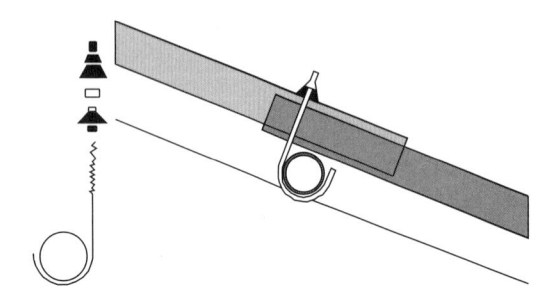

roof

flat roof
A roof that has just enough slope to shed the storm water, generally less than a 10% angle.

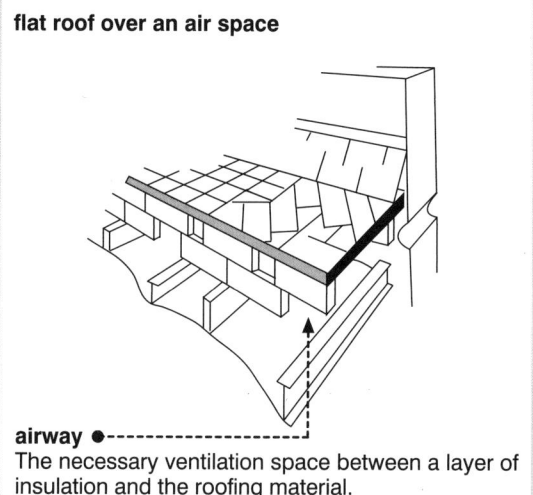

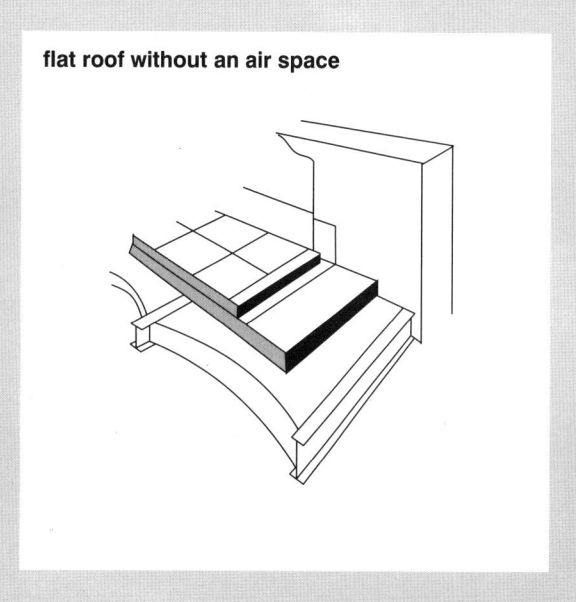

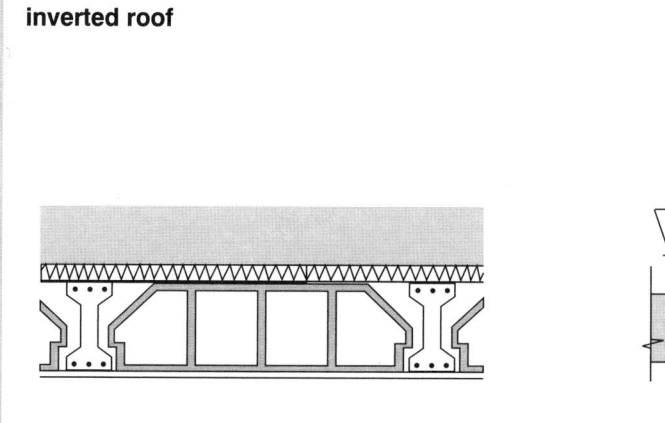

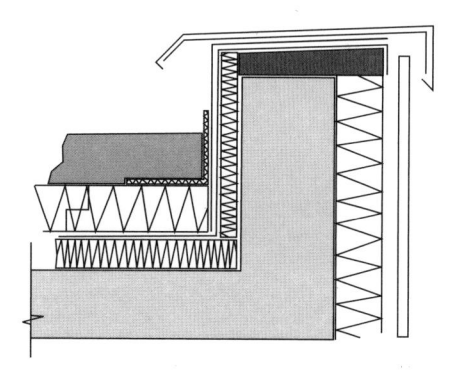

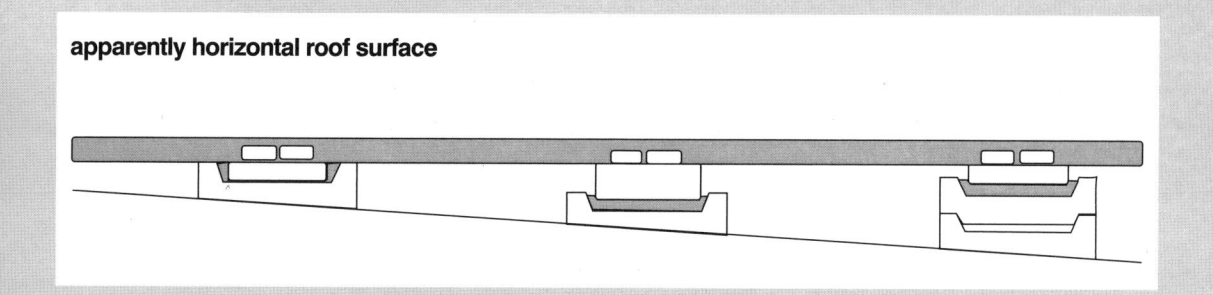

flat roof over an air space

airway
The necessary ventilation space between a layer of insulation and the roofing material.

flat roof without an air space

inverted roof

apparently horizontal roof surface

roof

flashing
Any watertight material used to prevent the entrance of water and improve drainage, in particular between the roof and a wall, or different roof slopes, or around windows and doors.

counterflashing
A thin strip of watertight material, often metal, built into the masonry so as to cover the exposed edge of the base flashing on a roof. Also called cap flashing.

parapet
A low wall consisting of that part of a building's exterior walls that rises above the level of the roof

base flashing
A watertight material used to cover and protect the seam between a roof and an adjacent wall.

cant strip
A strip of material laid under the roofing, to soften the angle where water could gather between the roof and a wall or parapet.

masonry flashing
A way of making the joins on a roof watertight without using metal strips.

built-up roofing
A roofing method consisting in alternate layers of asphalt rolled roofing and asphalt mastic under a final layer of mineral aggregates or gravel bound with asphalt. Also called composition roofing, felt and gravel roofing or gravel roofing.

wear course
A layer of mineral aggregates that protect a watertight covering from weather related abrasion.

cap sheet
A type of asphalt impregnated felt faced with a layer of asphalt-bound mineral aggregates, used as a final layer of roofing.

base sheet
A sheet of asphalt impregnated felt used as a first layer of impermeable material to make a roof watertight.

elastomeric roofing
A single sheet of elastomeric material attached onto the roof deck with a binding agent.

gravel stop
A strip of material, usually a metal flange attached to the rim of a built up roof to act as a drip and prevent loose fragments of gravel or roof surface being washed off. Also called a gravel strip or slag strip.

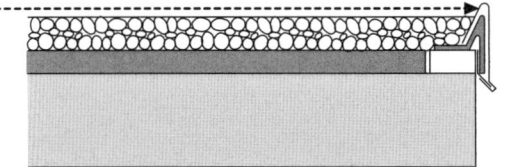

roof

gutter
A half round or square channel to gather storm water from the roof and lead it to a downspout. Also called the eaves trough or roof gutter.

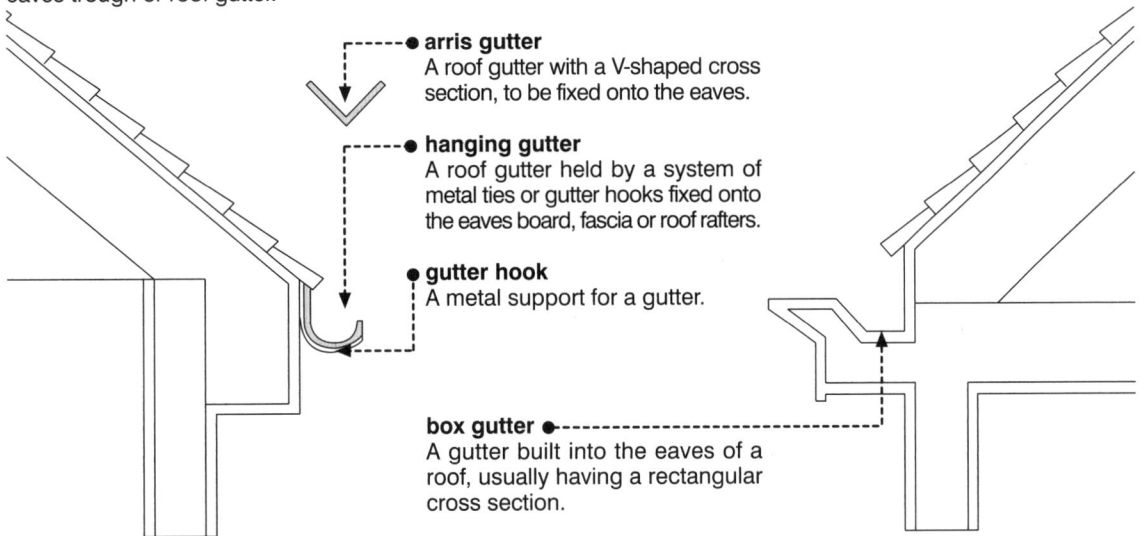

arris gutter
A roof gutter with a V-shaped cross section, to be fixed onto the eaves.

hanging gutter
A roof gutter held by a system of metal ties or gutter hooks fixed onto the eaves board, fascia or roof rafters.

gutter hook
A metal support for a gutter.

box gutter
A gutter built into the eaves of a roof, usually having a rectangular cross section.

downspout
A vertical pipe leading rainwater from a roof gutter to the drainage system or the ground. Also called a drainspout or leader.

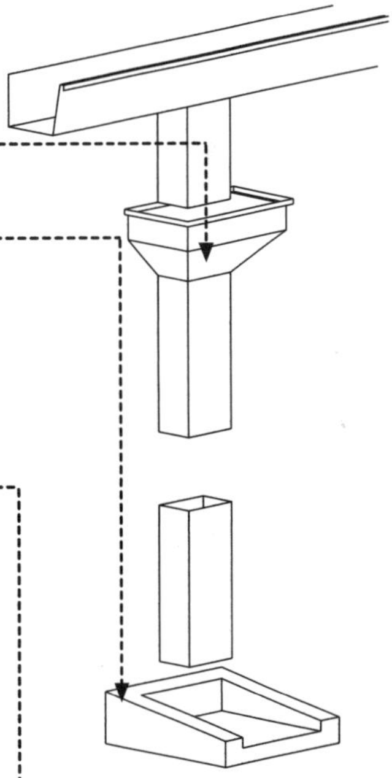

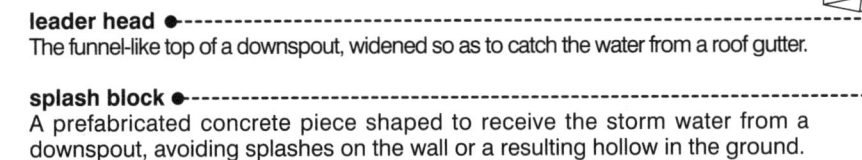

leader head
The funnel-like top of a downspout, widened so as to catch the water from a roof gutter.

splash block
A prefabricated concrete piece shaped to receive the storm water from a downspout, avoiding splashes on the wall or a resulting hollow in the ground.

sump
As part of a roof draining system, a receptacle or cavity designed to gather stormwater and lead it into a downspout.

gargoyle
A waterspout projecting out of the wall of a building (often grotesquely carved, especially in gothic architecture) to eject storm water from the roof.

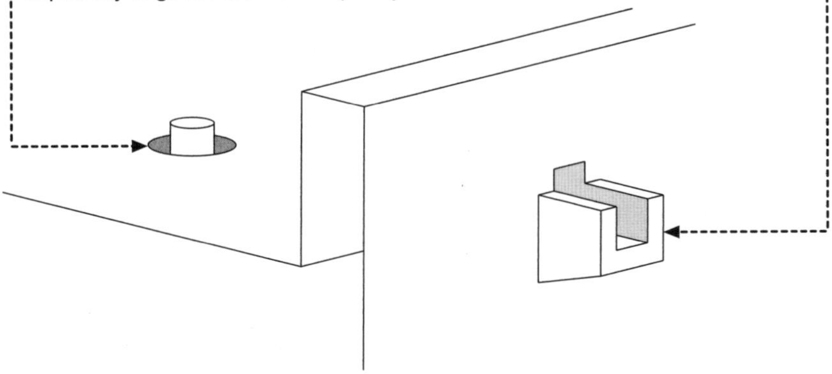

roof

dormer window
A vertical window in one of the slopes of a pitched roof, housed under a small gable or projection built to cover it.

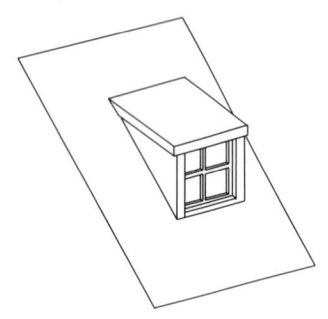

dormer
A weatherproof projection out of the slope of a pitched roof, usually built to cover a dormer window.

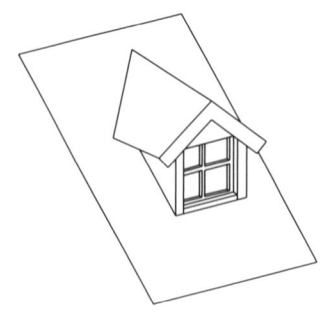

gable dormer
A dormer that is covered by a gabled roof.

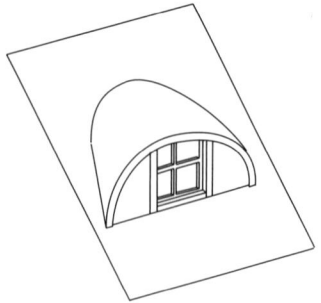

eyebrow
A dormer without definable walls, covered by a gentle convex curve of the same roof slope it projects from.

monitor roof
On the roof of a building, often over the ridge, a construction made to house one or more vertical windows to brighten or ventilate the space below.

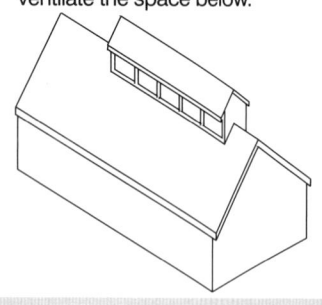

internal dormer
A window that is recessed into the slope of a pitched roof.

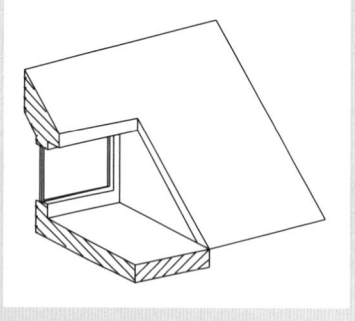

cricket
A small hip or gable to lead the stormwater around some obstacle (such as a chimney) in the slope of a pitched roof.

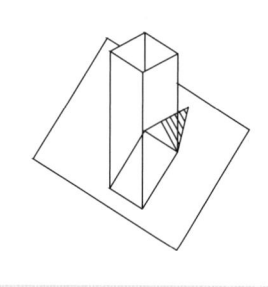

skylight
A glazed opening in a roof, built to allow light into the space below it.

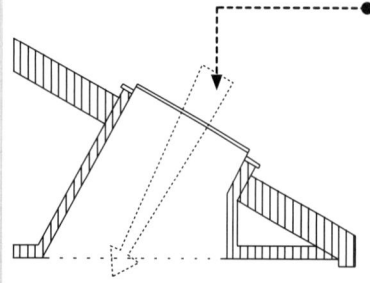

clerestory (USA)
A window or line of windows near the top of the walls of a high space, to shed light upon the central area; also called clerestorey (G.B.).

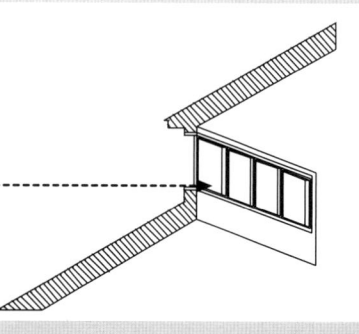

roof

skylight
An opening in a roof, glazed or covered with a translucent material, allowing light and often ventilation into the space below. Also called a rooflight.

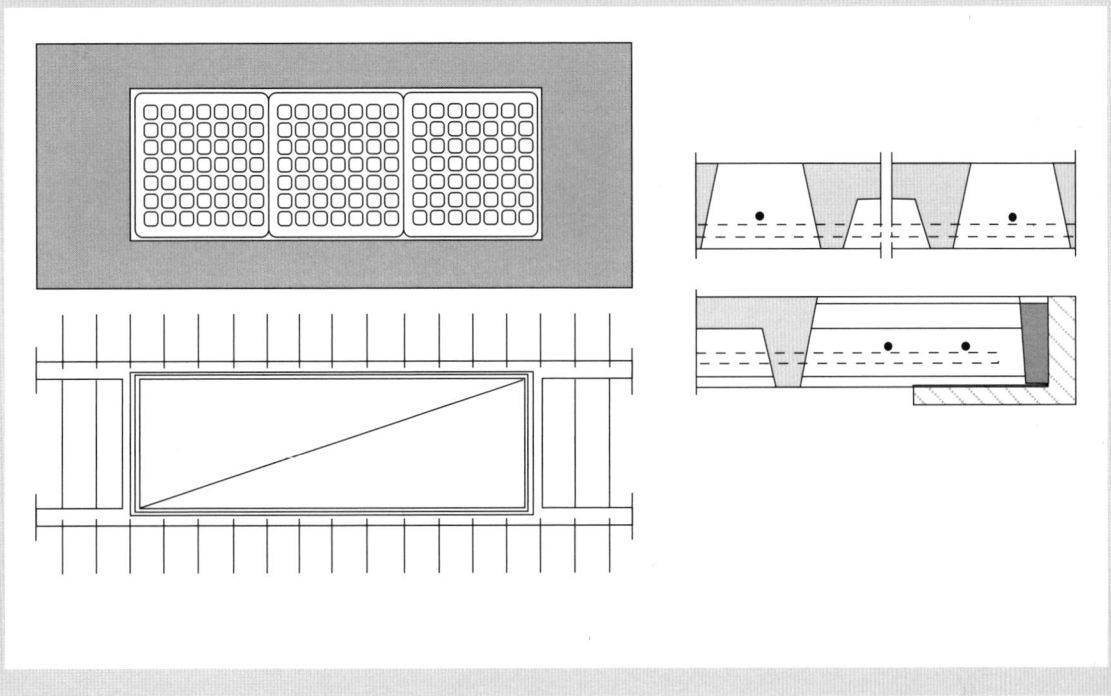

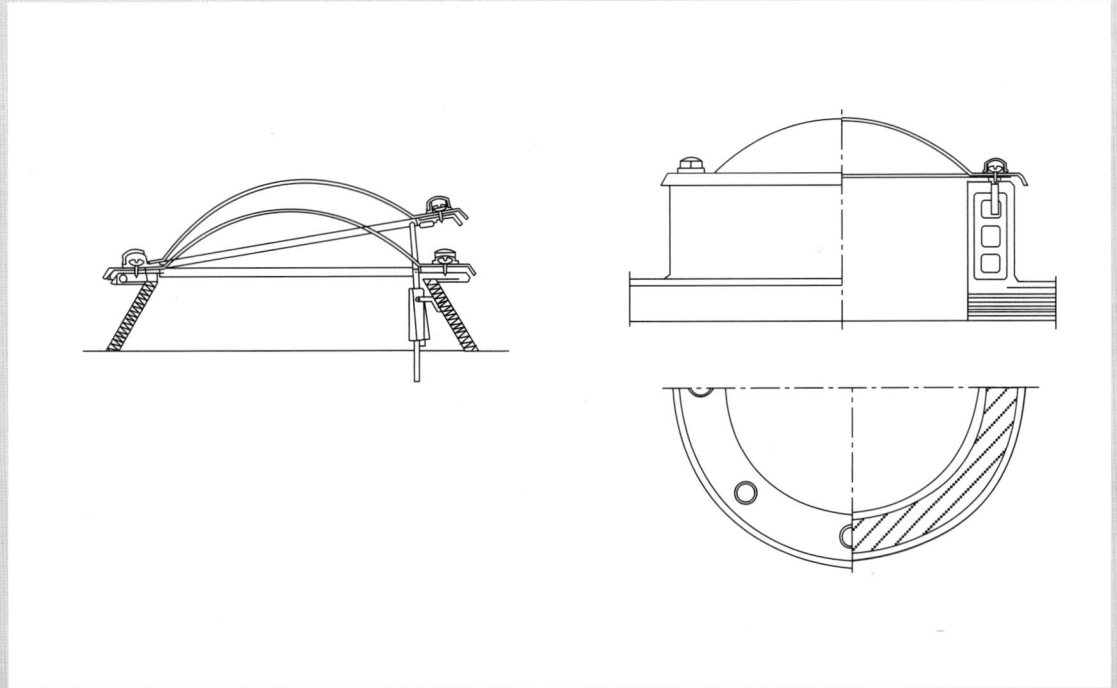

roof

chimney hood
The device at the top of a chimney, constructed or prefabricated, made to prevent rain from entering and enabling smoke to exit efficiently. According to the shape, also called a chimney bonnet, chimney cap, chimney cowl, chimney pot.

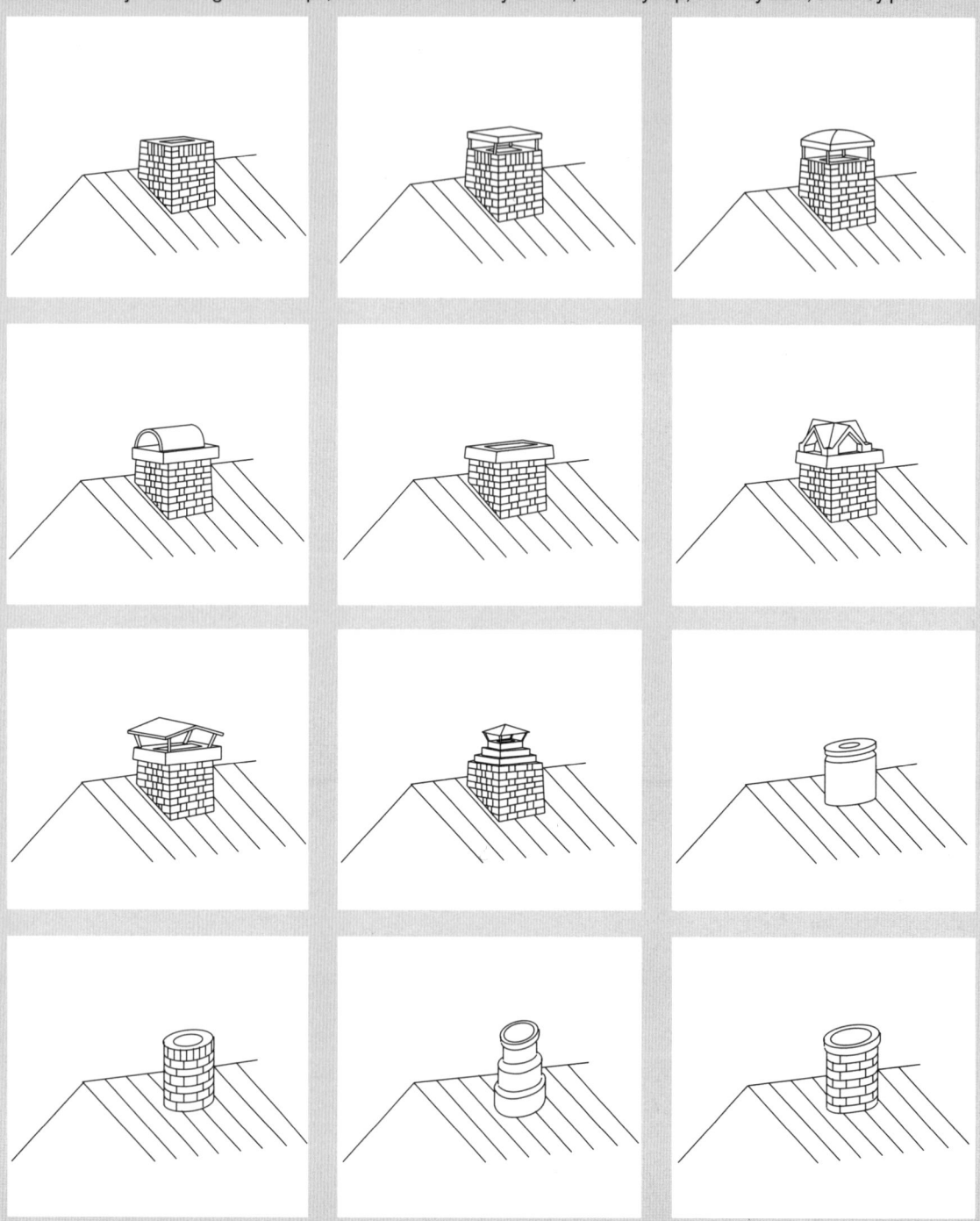

stair

A gradually rising sequence of steps or stairs leading from one level to another, from one landing to the next, or from one floor to the next above it.

staircase
A flight or a sequence of flights of stairs partly enclosed by walls, plus the handrail, the banisters and any other supports involved.

closed stairway
A flight or a sequence of flights of stairs entirely enclosed by walls.

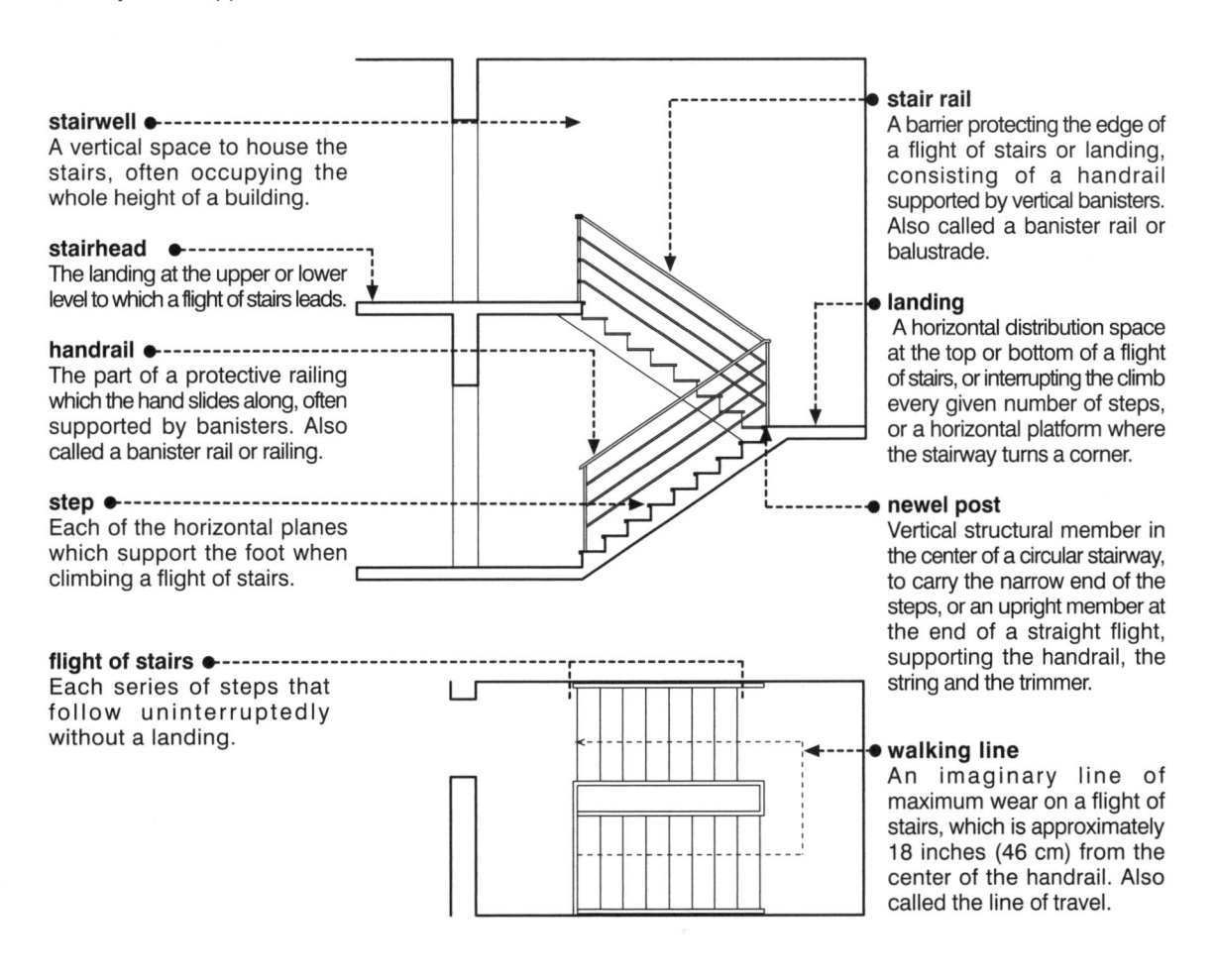

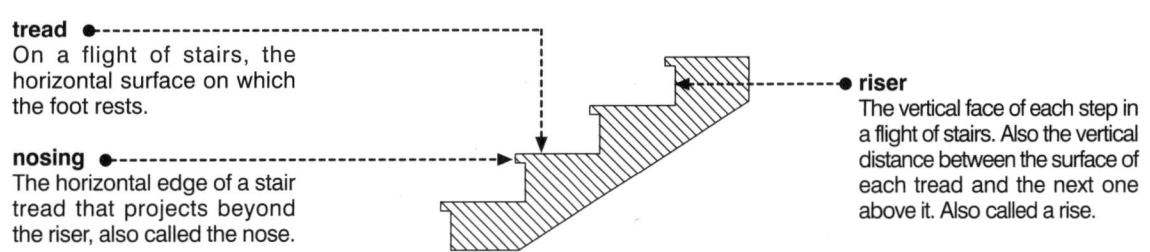

stairwell
A vertical space to house the stairs, often occupying the whole height of a building.

stairhead
The landing at the upper or lower level to which a flight of stairs leads.

handrail
The part of a protective railing which the hand slides along, often supported by banisters. Also called a banister rail or railing.

step
Each of the horizontal planes which support the foot when climbing a flight of stairs.

flight of stairs
Each series of steps that follow uninterruptedly without a landing.

tread
On a flight of stairs, the horizontal surface on which the foot rests.

nosing
The horizontal edge of a stair tread that projects beyond the riser, also called the nose.

stair rail
A barrier protecting the edge of a flight of stairs or landing, consisting of a handrail supported by vertical banisters. Also called a banister rail or balustrade.

landing
A horizontal distribution space at the top or bottom of a flight of stairs, or interrupting the climb every given number of steps, or a horizontal platform where the stairway turns a corner.

newel post
Vertical structural member in the center of a circular stairway, to carry the narrow end of the steps, or an upright member at the end of a straight flight, supporting the handrail, the string and the trimmer.

walking line
An imaginary line of maximum wear on a flight of stairs, which is approximately 18 inches (46 cm) from the center of the handrail. Also called the line of travel.

riser
The vertical face of each step in a flight of stairs. Also the vertical distance between the surface of each tread and the next one above it. Also called a rise.

stair

balustrade
A series of balusters supporting a horizontal or slanted handrail, to provide safety near the edge of a balcony or stairway.

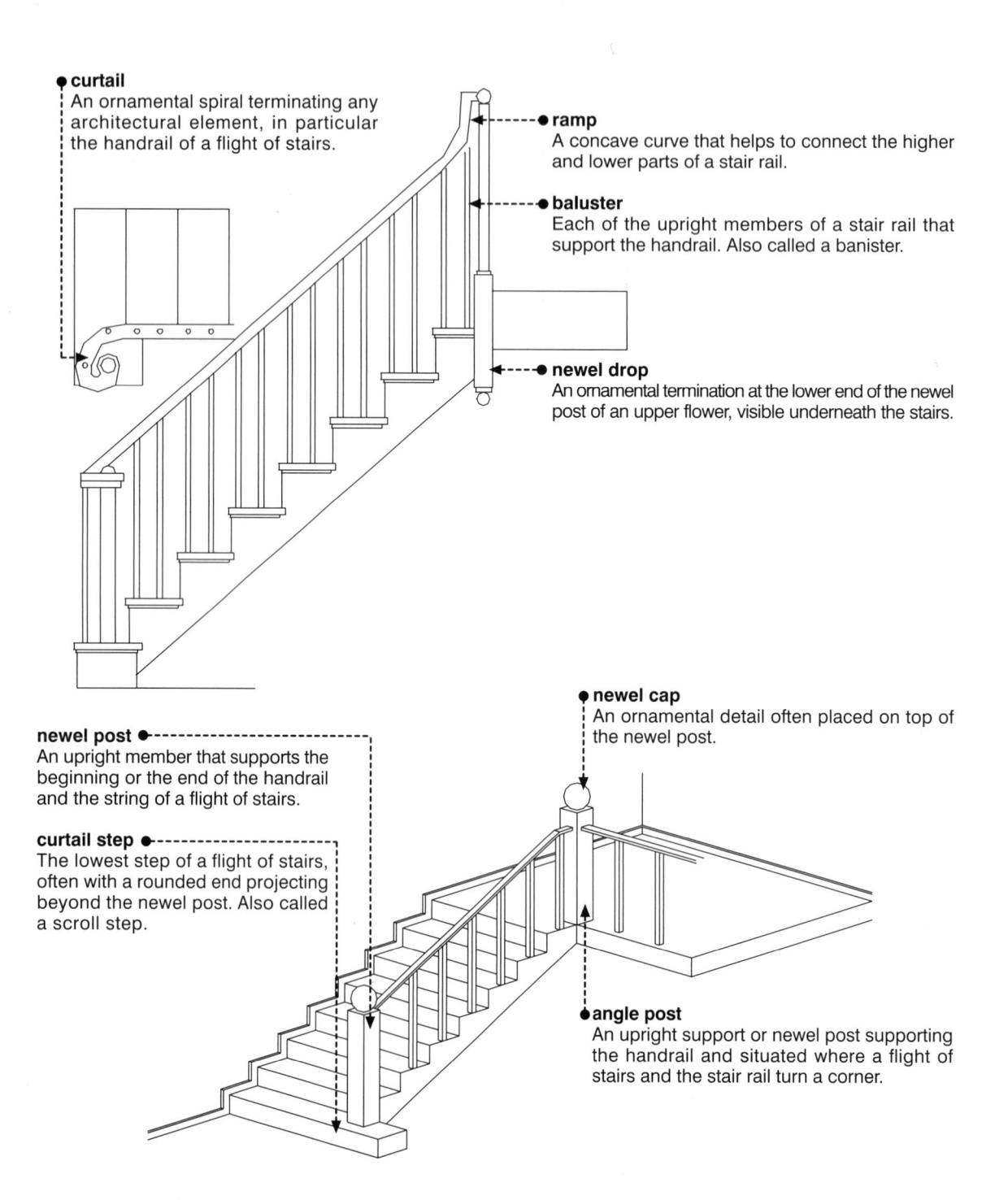

curtail
An ornamental spiral terminating any architectural element, in particular the handrail of a flight of stairs.

ramp
A concave curve that helps to connect the higher and lower parts of a stair rail.

baluster
Each of the upright members of a stair rail that support the handrail. Also called a banister.

newel drop
An ornamental termination at the lower end of the newel post of an upper flower, visible underneath the stairs.

newel post
An upright member that supports the beginning or the end of the handrail and the string of a flight of stairs.

curtail step
The lowest step of a flight of stairs, often with a rounded end projecting beyond the newel post. Also called a scroll step.

newel cap
An ornamental detail often placed on top of the newel post.

angle post
An upright support or newel post supporting the handrail and situated where a flight of stairs and the stair rail turn a corner.

stair

bridge board
In a wooden staircase, the board that defines the slope, and is shaped to support the treads and the risers of each flight of steps.

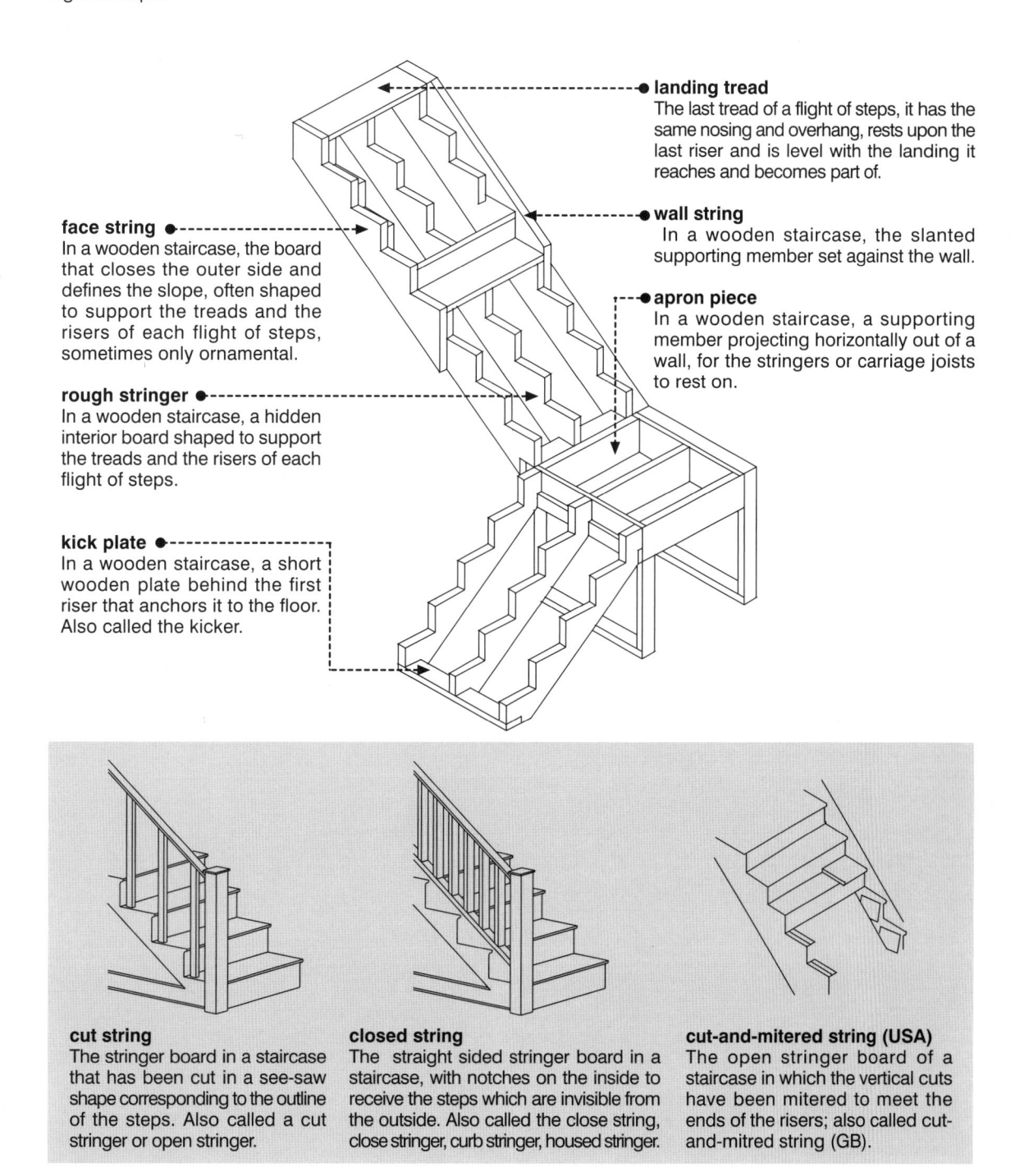

landing tread
The last tread of a flight of steps, it has the same nosing and overhang, rests upon the last riser and is level with the landing it reaches and becomes part of.

face string
In a wooden staircase, the board that closes the outer side and defines the slope, often shaped to support the treads and the risers of each flight of steps, sometimes only ornamental.

wall string
In a wooden staircase, the slanted supporting member set against the wall.

apron piece
In a wooden staircase, a supporting member projecting horizontally out of a wall, for the stringers or carriage joists to rest on.

rough stringer
In a wooden staircase, a hidden interior board shaped to support the treads and the risers of each flight of steps.

kick plate
In a wooden staircase, a short wooden plate behind the first riser that anchors it to the floor. Also called the kicker.

cut string
The stringer board in a staircase that has been cut in a see-saw shape corresponding to the outline of the steps. Also called a cut stringer or open stringer.

closed string
The straight sided stringer board in a staircase, with notches on the inside to receive the steps which are invisible from the outside. Also called the close string, close stringer, curb stringer, housed stringer.

cut-and-mitered string (USA)
The open stringer board of a staircase in which the vertical cuts have been mitered to meet the ends of the risers; also called cut-and-mitred string (GB).

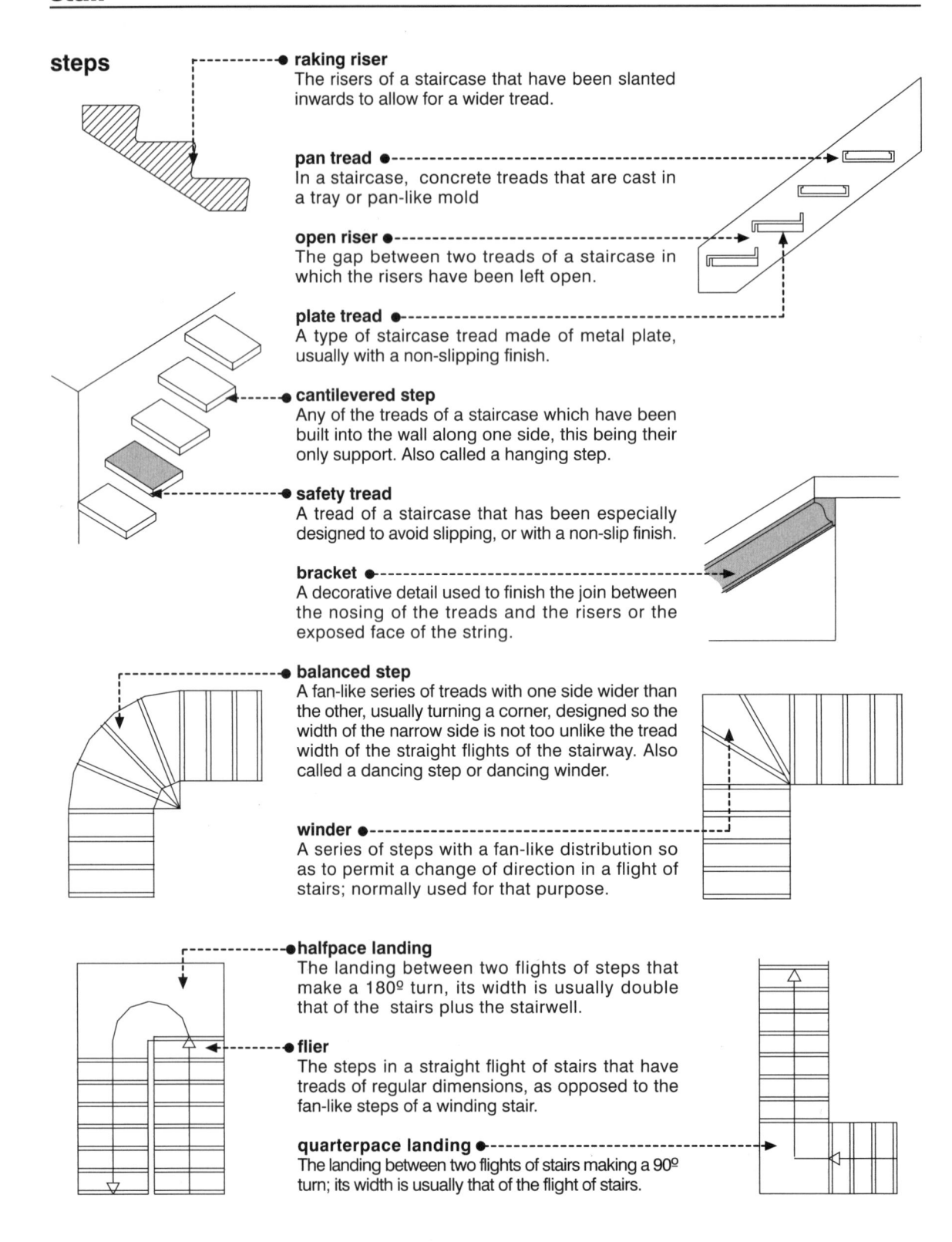

stair

steps

raking riser
The risers of a staircase that have been slanted inwards to allow for a wider tread.

pan tread
In a staircase, concrete treads that are cast in a tray or pan-like mold

open riser
The gap between two treads of a staircase in which the risers have been left open.

plate tread
A type of staircase tread made of metal plate, usually with a non-slipping finish.

cantilevered step
Any of the treads of a staircase which have been built into the wall along one side, this being their only support. Also called a hanging step.

safety tread
A tread of a staircase that has been especially designed to avoid slipping, or with a non-slip finish.

bracket
A decorative detail used to finish the join between the nosing of the treads and the risers or the exposed face of the string.

balanced step
A fan-like series of treads with one side wider than the other, usually turning a corner, designed so the width of the narrow side is not too unlike the tread width of the straight flights of the stairway. Also called a dancing step or dancing winder.

winder
A series of steps with a fan-like distribution so as to permit a change of direction in a flight of stairs; normally used for that purpose.

halfpace landing
The landing between two flights of steps that make a 180º turn, its width is usually double that of the stairs plus the stairwell.

flier
The steps in a straight flight of stairs that have treads of regular dimensions, as opposed to the fan-like steps of a winding stair.

quarterpace landing
The landing between two flights of stairs making a 90º turn; its width is usually that of the flight of stairs.

stair

riser/tread ratio
The ratio that permits safe and comfortable use of a flight of stairs; the formula is T+2R=61-63 cm.

preferred angle
For comfort and safety, the preferred angle or slope of a flight of stairs lies between 26° and 36°; for a ramp not more than 5° are advisable.

critical angle
The maximum angle at which a staircase can rise before becoming uncomfortable and unsafe is 50°, and 20° for a ramp.

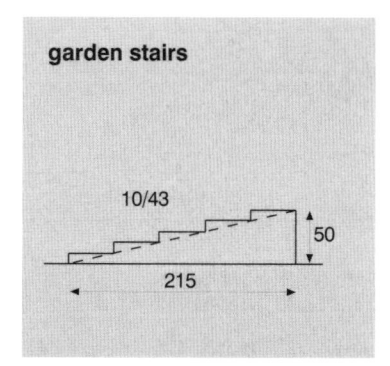

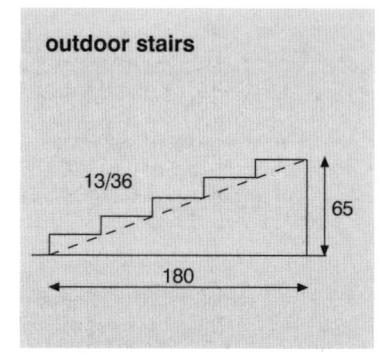

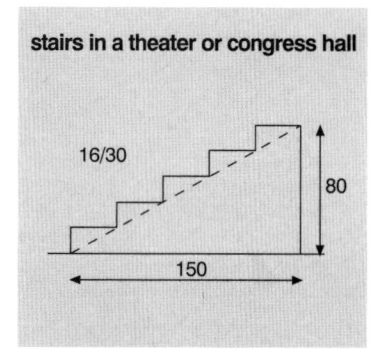

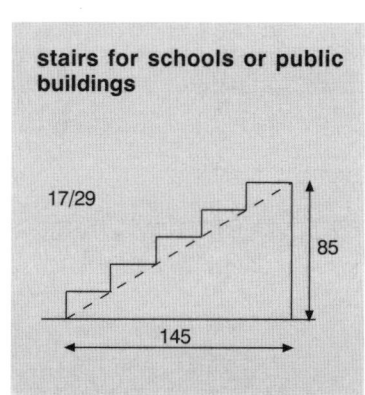

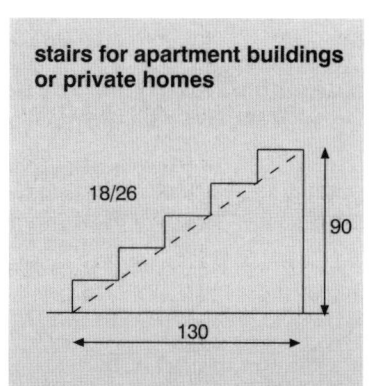

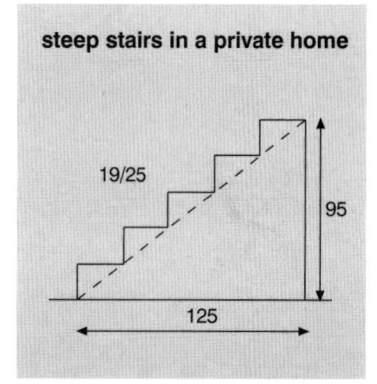

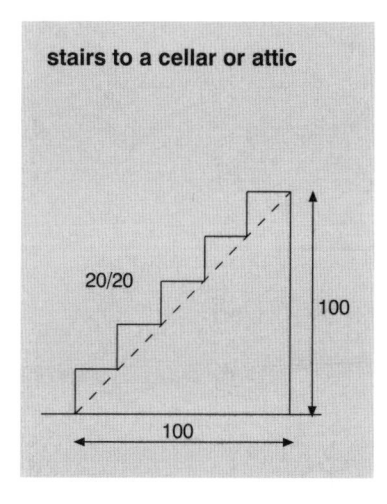

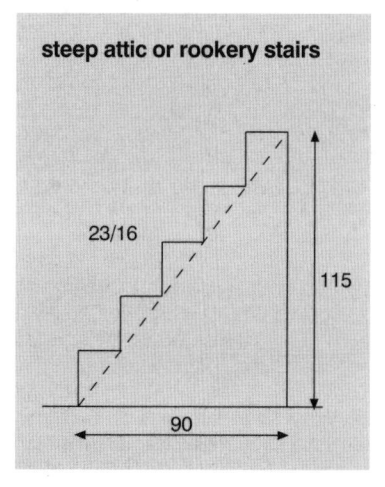

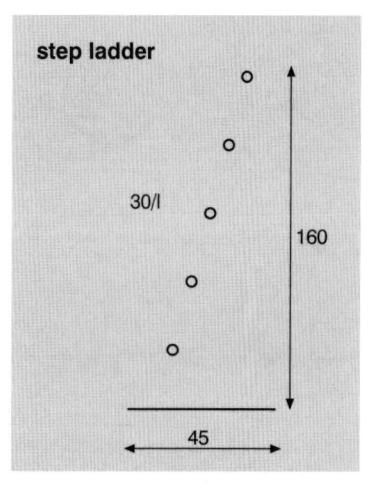

garden stairs — 10/43, 50, 215

outdoor stairs — 13/36, 65, 180

stairs in a theater or congress hall — 16/30, 80, 150

stairs for schools or public buildings — 17/29, 85, 145

stairs for apartment buildings or private homes — 18/26, 90, 130

steep stairs in a private home — 19/25, 95, 125

stairs to a cellar or attic — 20/20, 100, 100

steep attic or rookery stairs — 23/16, 115, 90

step ladder — 30/l, 160, 45

97

stair

Types of stairs

straight-run stair
A straight flight of stairs between two different levels.

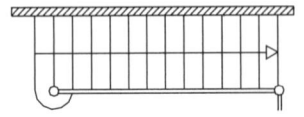

quarter-turn stair
A flight of stairs that turns 90º at a landing as it rises to connect two different levels. Also called an L stair.

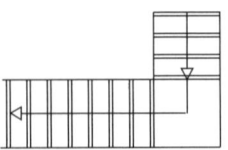

dogleg stair
A stair that turns 180º at a landing with no stairwell so the upper and lower balusters are on the same vertical plane. Also called a doglegged stair or dogleg staircase.

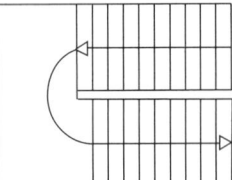

half-turn stair
A stair consisting of two straight flights going in opposite directions with a landing at the turn.

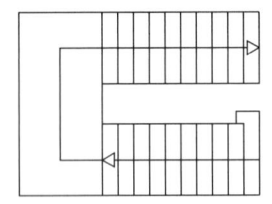

double-L stair
A half-turn stair that turns 90º at each of the two landings it has between two levels of the building.

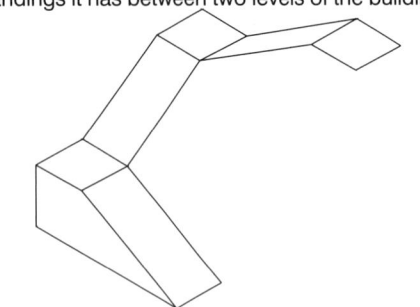

double-return stair
A stair that starts with a single wide flight of steps up to a landing where it divides into two further flights leading in opposite directions up to the next level.

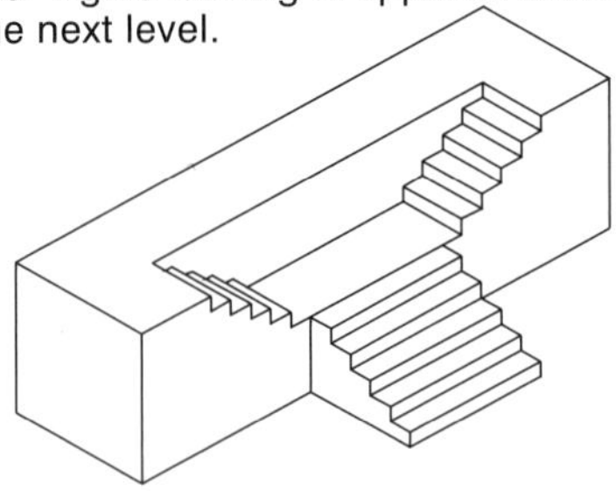

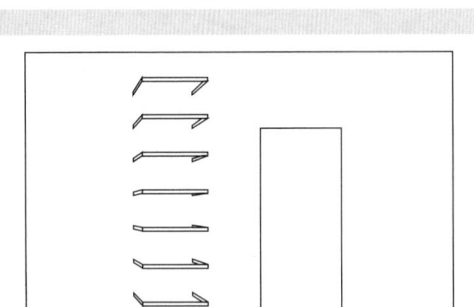

dog
A short iron bar bent 90º at both ends and driven into two pieces which it holds together, or fixed into a wall, one over another, making a ladder.

stair

spiral stair
A stairway that rises turning continually around a centre, with fanlike steps and without landings. Also called a caracole, circular staircase, winding staircase, corkscrew stair, spiral staircase.

circular stair
A spiral staircase with a circular floor plan.

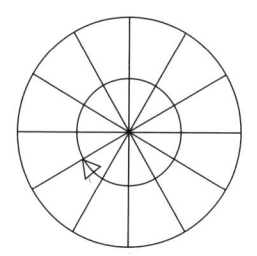

elliptical stair
A spiral staircase that winds around an elliptical newel or an elliptical stairwell.

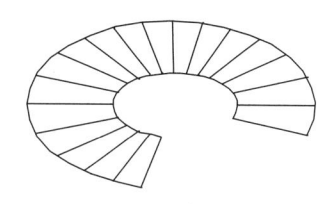

spiral stair
A stairway that rises winding continually around a central post or newel that supports the fanlike steps. Also called a caracole, circular staircase, winding staircase, spiral staircase.

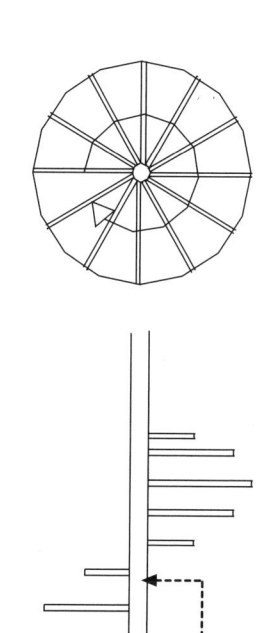

geometrical stair
A spiral staircase that winds around a hollow space or well, instead of a solid newel post.

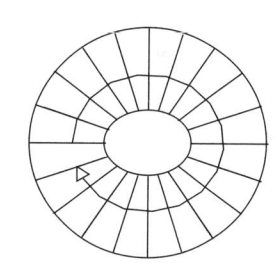

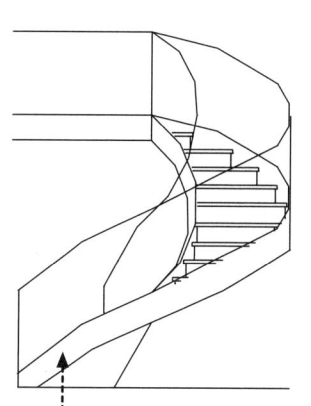

newel
The post or central pivot of a spiral stair supporting the narrow side of the steps, which fan out from it.

wreathe piece
A portion of a stairway that turns around a hollow space.

stair

escalator
A mechanical stairway the steps of which are attached to a continually moving chain belt, so as to raise or lower passengers from one level to another.

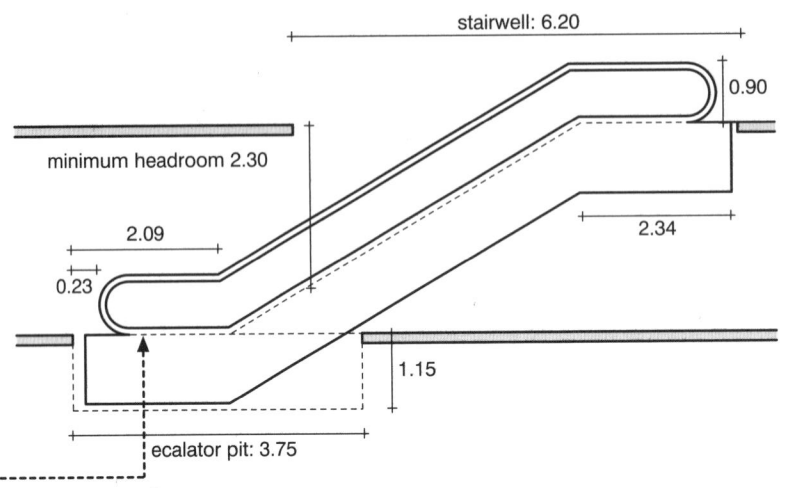

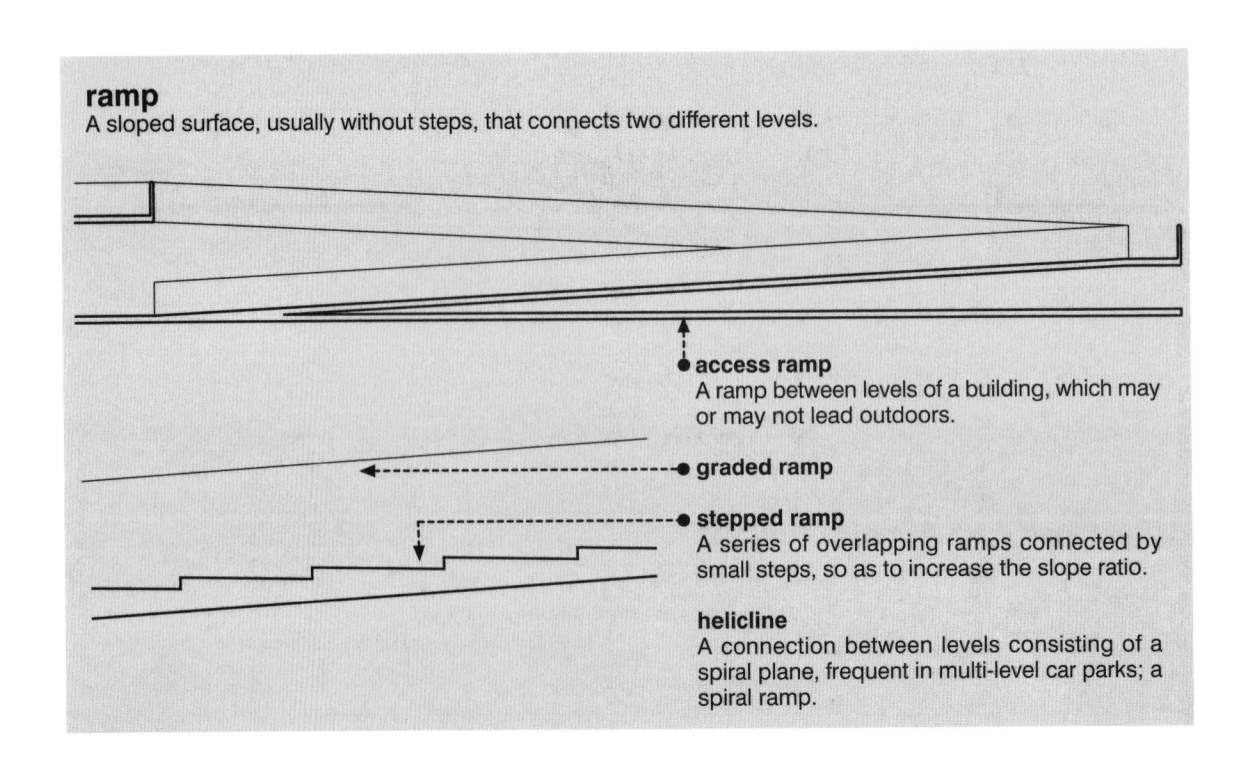

stairwell: 6.20
0.90
minimum headroom 2.30
2.09
2.34
0.23
1.15
ecalator pit: 3.75

combplate
At either end of an escalator, a stationary plate or threshold designed to mesh with the grooved surface of the steps or moving treadway.

ramp
A sloped surface, usually without steps, that connects two different levels.

access ramp
A ramp between levels of a building, which may or may not lead outdoors.

graded ramp

stepped ramp
A series of overlapping ramps connected by small steps, so as to increase the slope ratio.

helicline
A connection between levels consisting of a spiral plane, frequent in multi-level car parks; a spiral ramp.

elevator (USA)

A platform or cabin used to transport loads or passengers up or down from one level of a building to another. Also called a lift (GB).

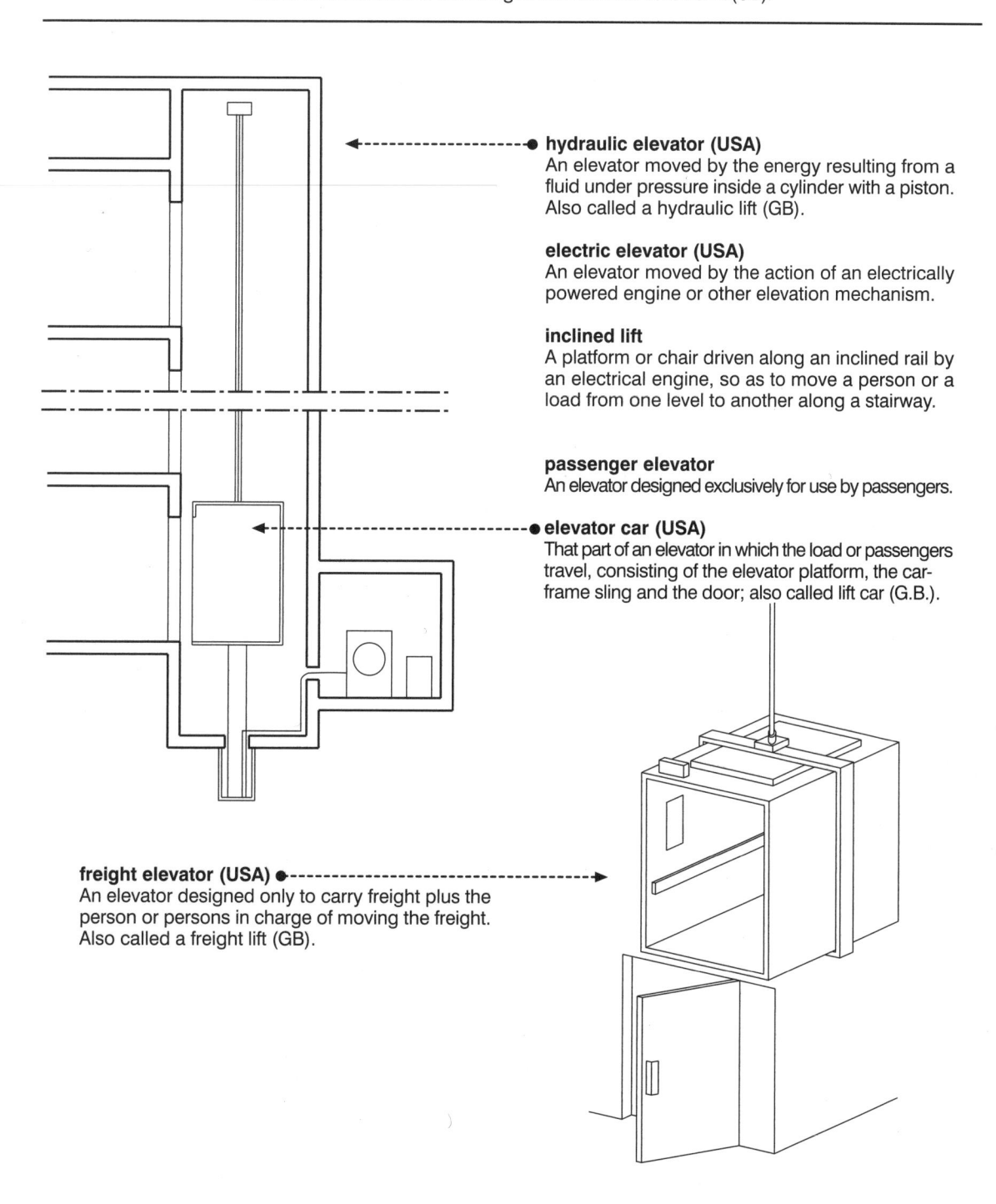

hydraulic elevator (USA)
An elevator moved by the energy resulting from a fluid under pressure inside a cylinder with a piston. Also called a hydraulic lift (GB).

electric elevator (USA)
An elevator moved by the action of an electrically powered engine or other elevation mechanism.

inclined lift
A platform or chair driven along an inclined rail by an electrical engine, so as to move a person or a load from one level to another along a stairway.

passenger elevator
An elevator designed exclusively for use by passengers.

elevator car (USA)
That part of an elevator in which the load or passengers travel, consisting of the elevator platform, the car-frame sling and the door; also called lift car (G.B.).

freight elevator (USA)
An elevator designed only to carry freight plus the person or persons in charge of moving the freight. Also called a freight lift (GB).

elevator

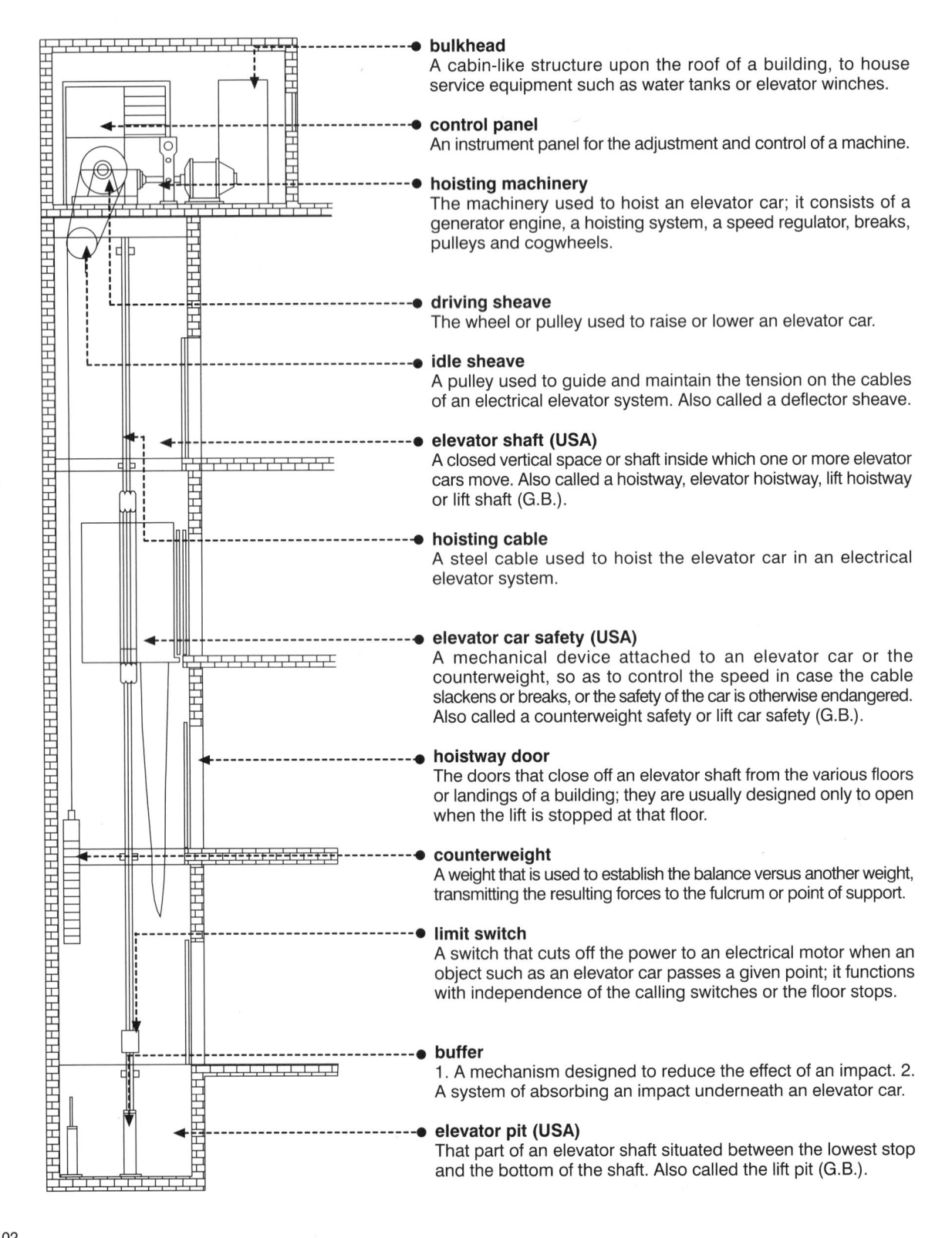

- **bulkhead**
  A cabin-like structure upon the roof of a building, to house service equipment such as water tanks or elevator winches.

- **control panel**
  An instrument panel for the adjustment and control of a machine.

- **hoisting machinery**
  The machinery used to hoist an elevator car; it consists of a generator engine, a hoisting system, a speed regulator, breaks, pulleys and cogwheels.

- **driving sheave**
  The wheel or pulley used to raise or lower an elevator car.

- **idle sheave**
  A pulley used to guide and maintain the tension on the cables of an electrical elevator system. Also called a deflector sheave.

- **elevator shaft (USA)**
  A closed vertical space or shaft inside which one or more elevator cars move. Also called a hoistway, elevator hoistway, lift hoistway or lift shaft (G.B.).

- **hoisting cable**
  A steel cable used to hoist the elevator car in an electrical elevator system.

- **elevator car safety (USA)**
  A mechanical device attached to an elevator car or the counterweight, so as to control the speed in case the cable slackens or breaks, or the safety of the car is otherwise endangered. Also called a counterweight safety or lift car safety (G.B.).

- **hoistway door**
  The doors that close off an elevator shaft from the various floors or landings of a building; they are usually designed only to open when the lift is stopped at that floor.

- **counterweight**
  A weight that is used to establish the balance versus another weight, transmitting the resulting forces to the fulcrum or point of support.

- **limit switch**
  A switch that cuts off the power to an electrical motor when an object such as an elevator car passes a given point; it functions with independence of the calling switches or the floor stops.

- **buffer**
  1. A mechanism designed to reduce the effect of an impact. 2. A system of absorbing an impact underneath an elevator car.

- **elevator pit (USA)**
  That part of an elevator shaft situated between the lowest stop and the bottom of the shaft. Also called the lift pit (G.B.).

door

A movable barrier that closes the access to a space; made of wood, glass or metal, moving on hinges, sliding or folding, it usually has some closing mechanism such as a lock.

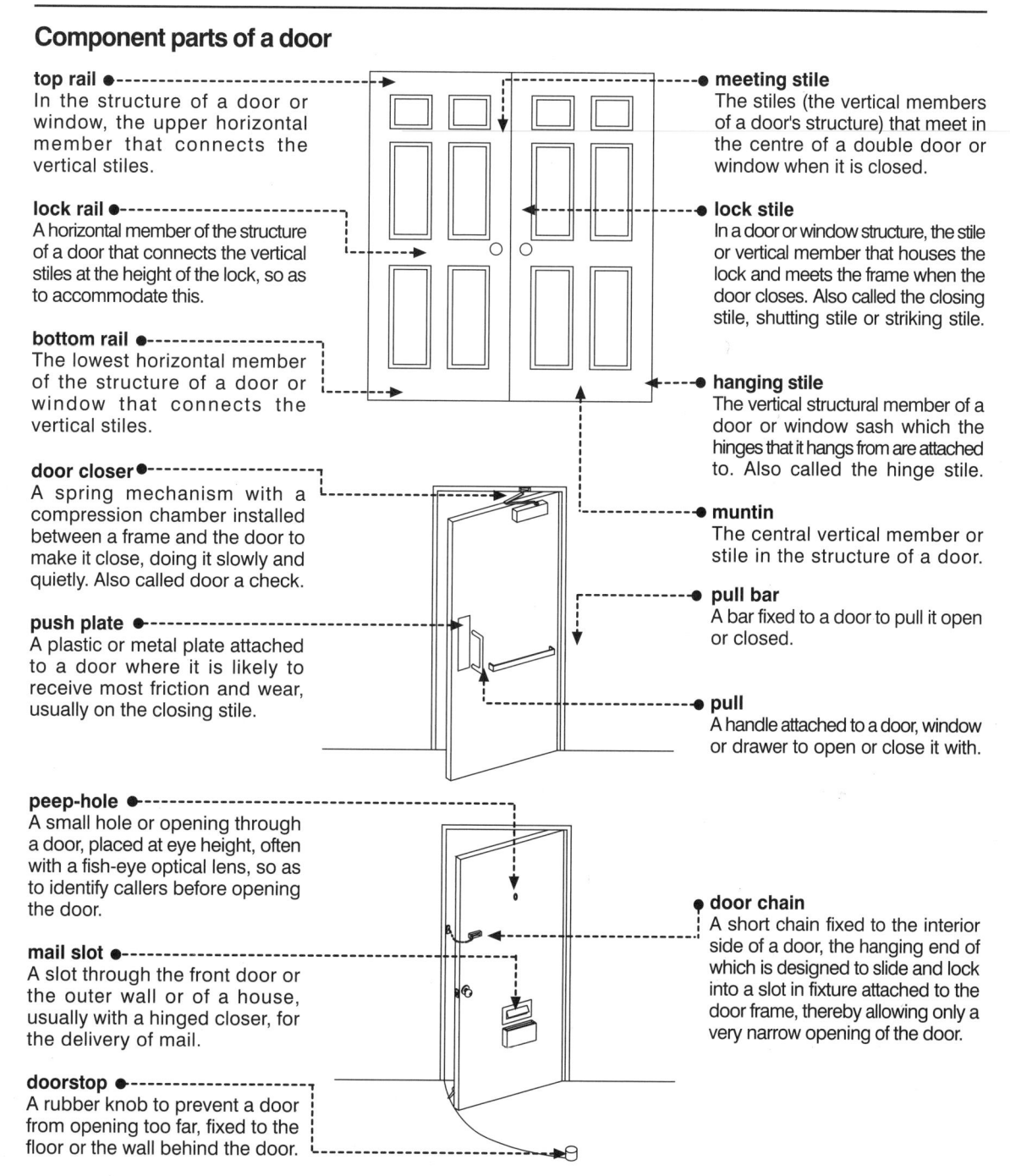

Component parts of a door

top rail
In the structure of a door or window, the upper horizontal member that connects the vertical stiles.

lock rail
A horizontal member of the structure of a door that connects the vertical stiles at the height of the lock, so as to accommodate this.

bottom rail
The lowest horizontal member of the structure of a door or window that connects the vertical stiles.

door closer
A spring mechanism with a compression chamber installed between a frame and the door to make it close, doing it slowly and quietly. Also called door a check.

push plate
A plastic or metal plate attached to a door where it is likely to receive most friction and wear, usually on the closing stile.

peep-hole
A small hole or opening through a door, placed at eye height, often with a fish-eye optical lens, so as to identify callers before opening the door.

mail slot
A slot through the front door or the outer wall or of a house, usually with a hinged closer, for the delivery of mail.

doorstop
A rubber knob to prevent a door from opening too far, fixed to the floor or the wall behind the door.

meeting stile
The stiles (the vertical members of a door's structure) that meet in the centre of a double door or window when it is closed.

lock stile
In a door or window structure, the stile or vertical member that houses the lock and meets the frame when the door closes. Also called the closing stile, shutting stile or striking stile.

hanging stile
The vertical structural member of a door or window sash which the hinges that it hangs from are attached to. Also called the hinge stile.

muntin
The central vertical member or stile in the structure of a door.

pull bar
A bar fixed to a door to pull it open or closed.

pull
A handle attached to a door, window or drawer to open or close it with.

door chain
A short chain fixed to the interior side of a door, the hanging end of which is designed to slide and lock into a slot in fixture attached to the door frame, thereby allowing only a very narrow opening of the door.

103

door

types of doors

hinged door
A door that is hung on hinges, allowing it to turn to a 90° (or greater) angle versus its closed position.

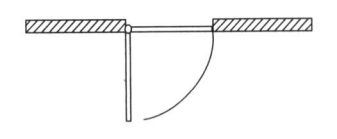

swinging door
A door that will swing open to both sides of an opening, usually with a springed hinge to make it return to the closed position.

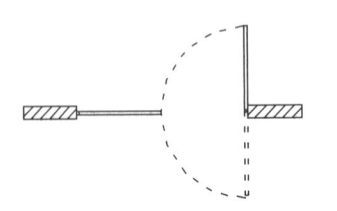

overhead door
A door which rolls, folds or swings upward, disappearing above the doorhead.

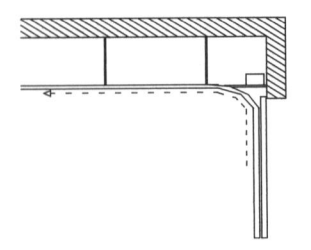

folding door
A door consisting of several articulated leaves that fold back, like an accordion, when open; it's use is often dictated by lack of space. Also called an accordion or multifolding door.

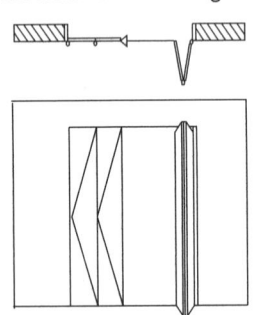

revolving door
A door consisting of four pieces that meet crosswise at a central axis, around which they revolve encased in a circular vestibule, effectively preventing drafts.

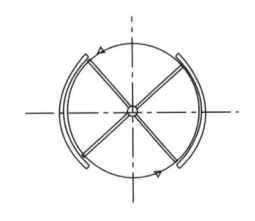

sliding door
A door that slides horizontally, on a rail parallel to the wall.

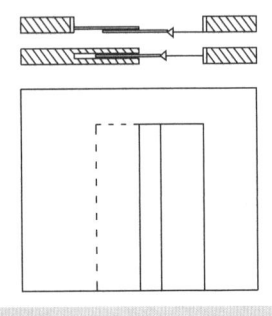

pivoted door
A door that swings on pivots, centrally placed or not, as opposed to one hung on hinges or sliding.

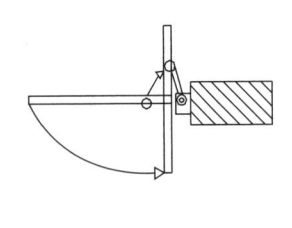

double door
A door with two leaves hanging on hinges from opposite sides of the door frame, and usually meeting in the centre.

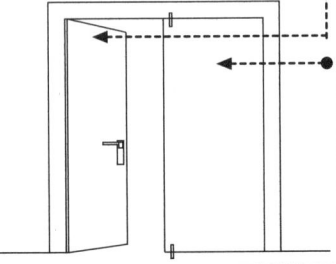

- **active leaf**
In a double door, the leaf with the latch or closing mechanism, the leaf most usually opened; sometimes both leaves may be active. Also called the active door.

- **inactive leaf**
In a double door, the leaf that usually remains closed, bolted to the floor and the doorhead, and has a device to receive the bolt of the latch on the active leaf. Also called an inactive door or standing leaf.

door

left-hand door
A door that opens inward, and is hinged on the left hand side going in.

left-hand reverse door
A door that opens outward and is hinged on the left hand side going in.

right-hand door
A door that opens inward, and is hinged on the right hand side going in.

right-hand reverse door
A door that opens outward, and is hinged on the right hand side going in.

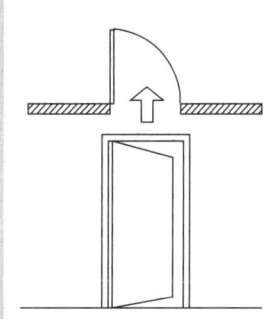

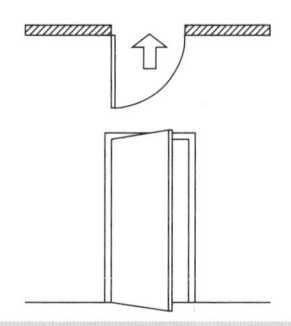

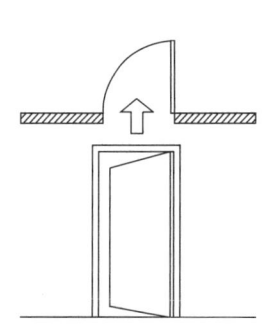

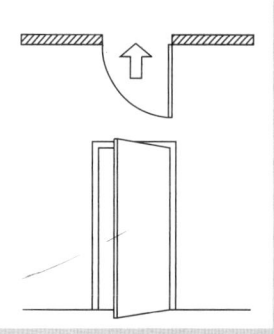

batten door
A door made of vertical boards held together by horizontal members and made rigid with the addition of diagonal ones.

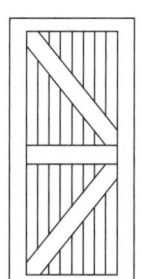

French door
A door consisting of a solid frame that contains a lighter structure to hold panes of glass; often used as a double door: Also called a casement door.

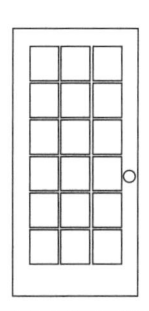

Dutch door
A door having two separate halves, one above the other, that open independently. When only the top is open the door functions as a window.

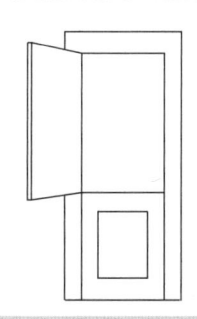

paneled door (USA)
A door with a structure of vertical and horizontal members (stiles and rails) framing several thinner panels, often with molded details. Also called a panel door or panelled door (GB).

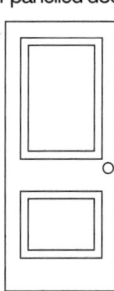

louvered door
A door in which the panels are louvers, usually with horizontal blades, permitting air to circulate when the door is closed.

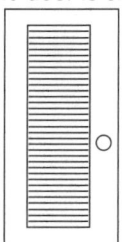

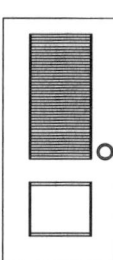

Venetian door
A door, often glazed, having three leaves, a wide central one between two narrow, usually fixed sides.

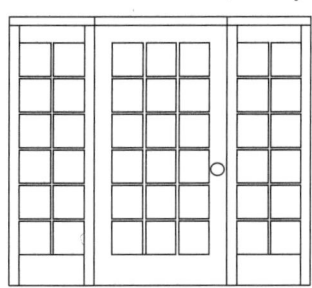

door

lock
A mechanism used to securely close a door or window; it consists of a bolt or combination of bolts moved by a key.

cylinder
In a door lock, the cylindrical piece containing the keyway and the tumblers that the correct key can enter and move.

cam
In a lock, a rotating piece at the end of the cylinder which the correct key can turn to engage the locking mechanism.

key
A small metal instrument shaped with grooves and teeth so that it alone can enter a lock and move the bolt.

keyway
A shaped aperture in the cylinder of a lock designed to fit and guide the correct key.

strike plate
A metal plate, fixed onto the doorjamb, having one or more holes or recesses to receive the bolts of the latch and doorlock. Also called a strike.

deadbolt
A type of bolt, square in cross section, that is only moved by the door key, door handle or doorknob.

latch bolt
A spring bolt with a beveled side, so that as the door meets the doorjamb the bolt is pressed back; when it reaches the socket in the frame that is ready for it, the bolt springs forth again, locking the door unless the bolt is drawn back by turning the door handle.

lock case
That part of a lock in which the mechanism and the bolts are located.

spindle
The rod or shaft which turns something, such as that between the door handle and mechanism of a latch on a door.

doorhandle
A lever, often decorated, designed to action the mechanism that opens a door; if spherical, called a doorknob

box strike
A metal box that is recessed into the doorjamb to receive the head of the bolts of the latch or lock when the door is closed.

latch
A door closing mechanism by means of a metal piece that slides or drops from the door into a cavity or socket in the door frame; it can usually be opened from both sides.

regular bevel
The bevel, or slanted profile, of the head of a spring bolt in a door that opens inward.

reverse bevel
The bevel, or slanted profile, of the head of a spring bolt in a door that opens outward.

escutcheon
A decorative plate to protect the orifice around a keyhole or a door handle. Also called a scutcheon or faceplate.

faceplate
1. A protective and decorative plate placed on the wall around an electrical socket or switch. 2. A metal plate on the lock edge of a door, through which the bolt slides. Also called a lock front.

door

mortise lock
A lock designed to be housed in a cavity, or mortise, inside the lockstile of the door.

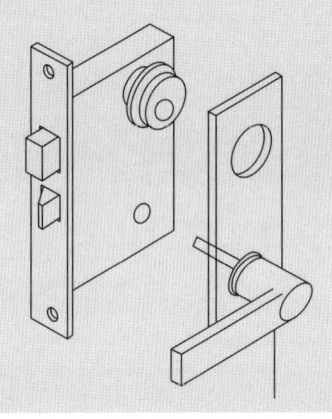

unit lock
A lock designed as a unit to be installed in a notch cut out of the door edge, requiring minimal assembly work.

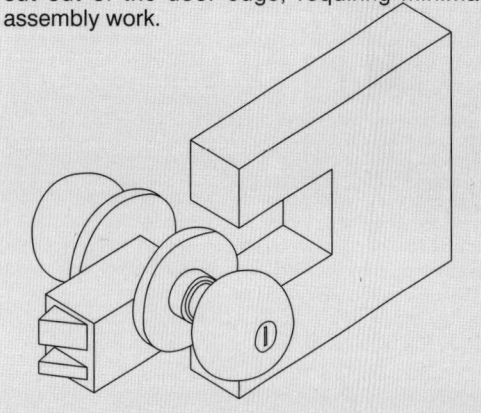

rim lock
A lock that is attached to the surface of the door, as opposed to mortised into its edge.

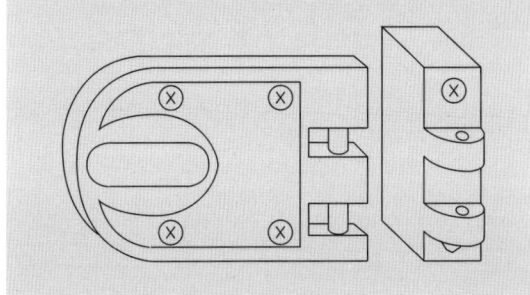

barrel bolt
A mechanism for closing doors or windows from one side, consisting of a bolt that slides along a housing or cylinder, pulled manually by a handle.

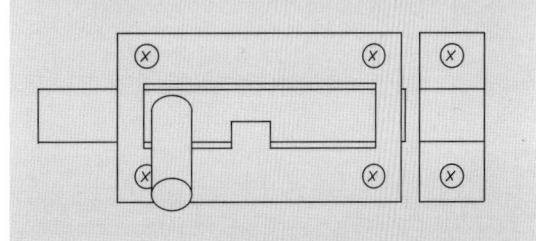

cylinder lock
A lock that is inserted in two perpendicular cylinders, one going through the face of the door, the other mortised into the door edge.

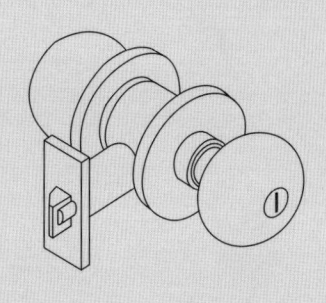

door

hinge
A device consisting of two metal plates, usually rectangular, connected along one of their edges by a movable pivot or pin so they can fold against each other; used to connect doors or windows to their frames, or lids to boxes, so they can swing open.

lift-off hinge
A hinge consisting of two separable leaves or sides, one holding the pin or pivot, the other sliding onto it; thus the door or window can be lifted free of the frame without having to disassemble the hinge.

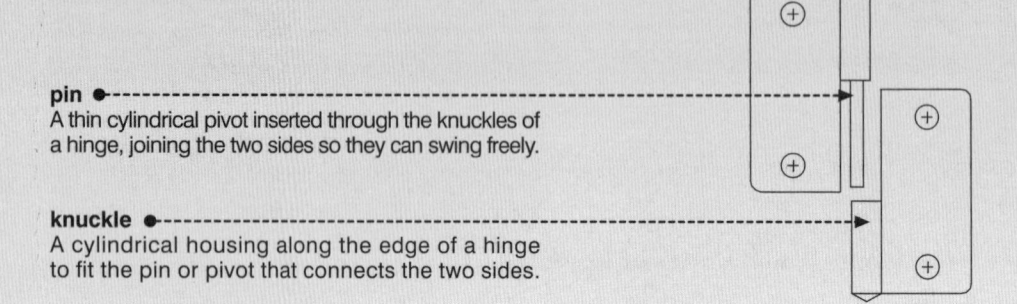

pin
A thin cylindrical pivot inserted through the knuckles of a hinge, joining the two sides so they can swing freely.

knuckle
A cylindrical housing along the edge of a hinge to fit the pin or pivot that connects the two sides.

backflap hinge
A hinge designed to have both leaves attached directly onto the face of the door and jamb, without mortising. Also called a flap hinge or full surface hinge.

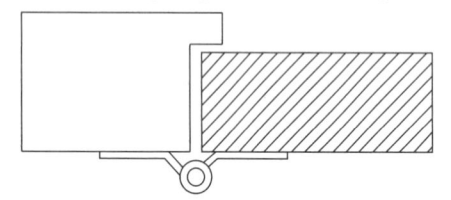

half-surface hinge
A hinge having one of its leaves attached within the doorjamb and the other mounted on the surface of the door.

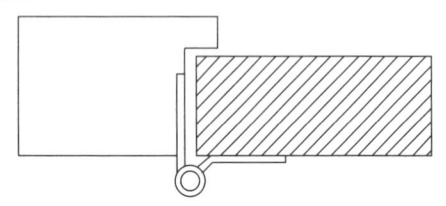

mortise hinge
A hinge that has both leaves mortised onto the sides in contact of the door jamb and the edge of the door.

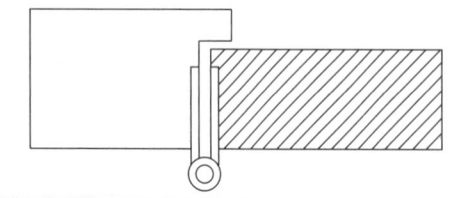

half-mortise hinge
A hinge having one of its leaves fixed to the face of the doorjamb and the other mortised onto the edge of the door.

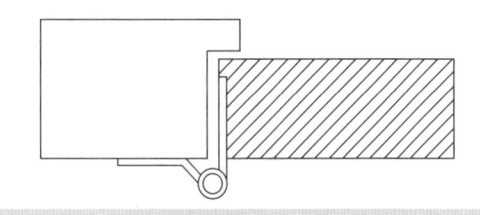

strap hinge
A surface mounted hinge with long strap-like leaves stretching away from the pin onto the door jamb and the door.

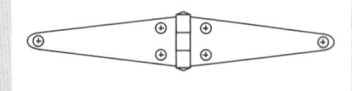

dovetail hinge
A strap hinge in which the opposite ends of the strap, or leaves, are wider than the central part holding the pin.

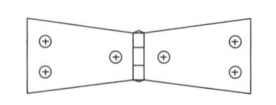

T-hinge
A surface hinge shaped like a T, with the horizontal strap fixed to the door, and the cross of the T (wider and shorter) fixed vertically to the doorframe.

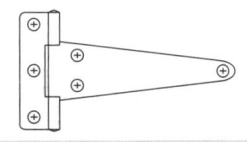

door

olive knuckle hinge
A lift-off hinge of the pivot type having a compact oval-shaped knuckle.

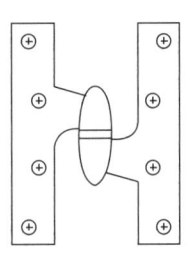

rising hinge
A door hinge with a spirally grooved knuckle or with an oblique knuckle joint so that the door rises as it opens, possibly so as to clear a carpet or a rise in the floor.

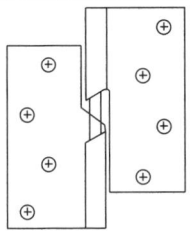

ball-bearing hinge
A hinge equipped with ball-bearings so as to reduce friction.

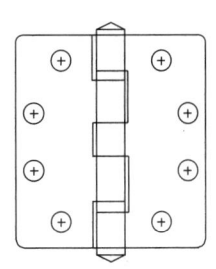

continuous hinge
A hinge that covers the whole adjacent length of the objects it is attached to. Also called a piano hinge.

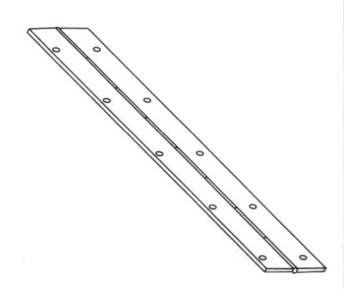

spring hinge
A hinge the knuckle of which contains a spring that automatically draws the door closed.

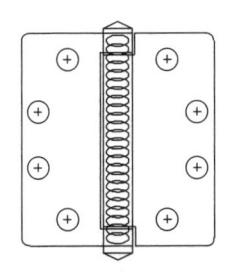

H-hinge
A type of strap hinge with the leaves parallel to the pivot, so when the hinge is open it looks like a letter H. Also called a parliament hinge.

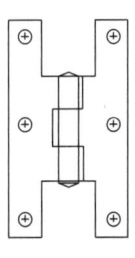

butt hinge
A hinge consisting of two adjacent rectangular leaves held together by meshed knuckles turning on a pin, it is usually attached to the face of the door and the doorjamb. Also called a butt.

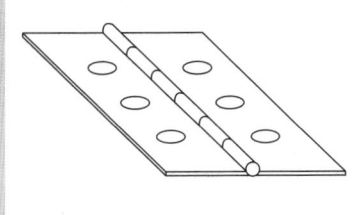

loose-pin hinge
A butt hinge consisting of three parts: two leaves with their respective knuckles and a pin which is removable to avoid trouble when unhinging the door.

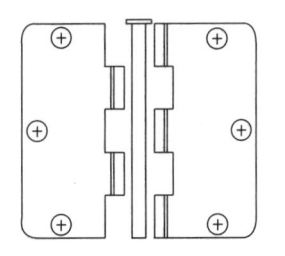

invisible hinge
A hinge that is designed so that no part of it is visible when the door is closed. Also called a concealed hinge.

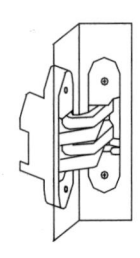

window

An aperture in the wall of a building to allow light and ventilation inside, usually having a fixed frame and one or more sashes that may move in a variety of ways.

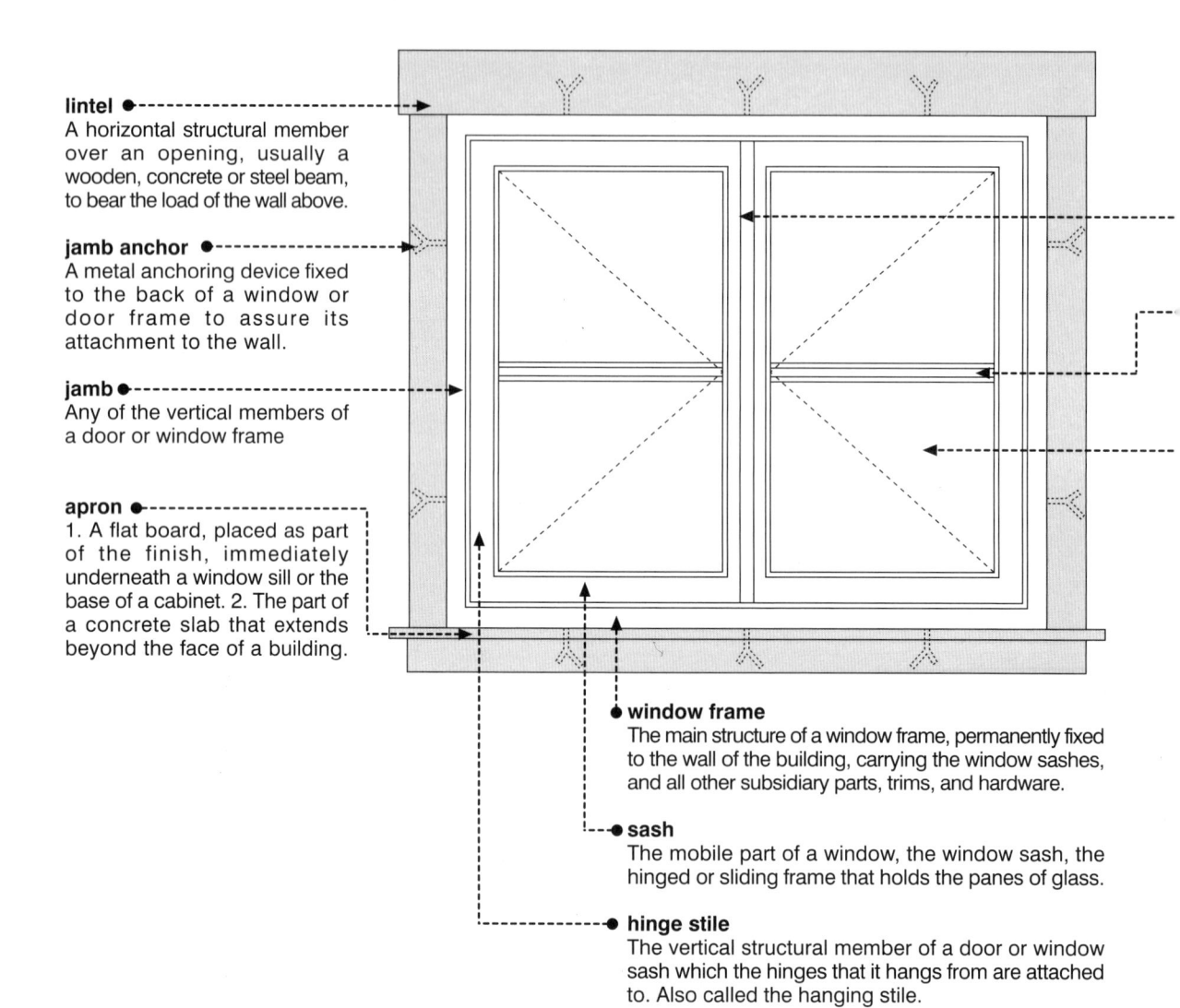

lintel
A horizontal structural member over an opening, usually a wooden, concrete or steel beam, to bear the load of the wall above.

jamb anchor
A metal anchoring device fixed to the back of a window or door frame to assure its attachment to the wall.

jamb
Any of the vertical members of a door or window frame

apron
1. A flat board, placed as part of the finish, immediately underneath a window sill or the base of a cabinet. 2. The part of a concrete slab that extends beyond the face of a building.

window frame
The main structure of a window frame, permanently fixed to the wall of the building, carrying the window sashes, and all other subsidiary parts, trims, and hardware.

sash
The mobile part of a window, the window sash, the hinged or sliding frame that holds the panes of glass.

hinge stile
The vertical structural member of a door or window sash which the hinges that it hangs from are attached to. Also called the hanging stile.

110

window

stile
Any of the vertical members of the structure of the leaf of a door or a window sash.

muntin
The usually slender, vertical or horizontal, secondary members of a glazed door or window that hold the panes of glass. Also called a division bar, glazing bar, sash bar, window bar.

sash
That part of a window or door that, by turning on hinges, swinging, or sliding, serves to open and close the opening. Also called a leaf.

pane
Each of the glazed segments into which a window sash or a glazed door is divided.

drip molding
A groove on the under side of the bottom rail of a window or door, to shed drops of water outside of the frame.

sill
The lower horizontal structural member of a window or door frame.

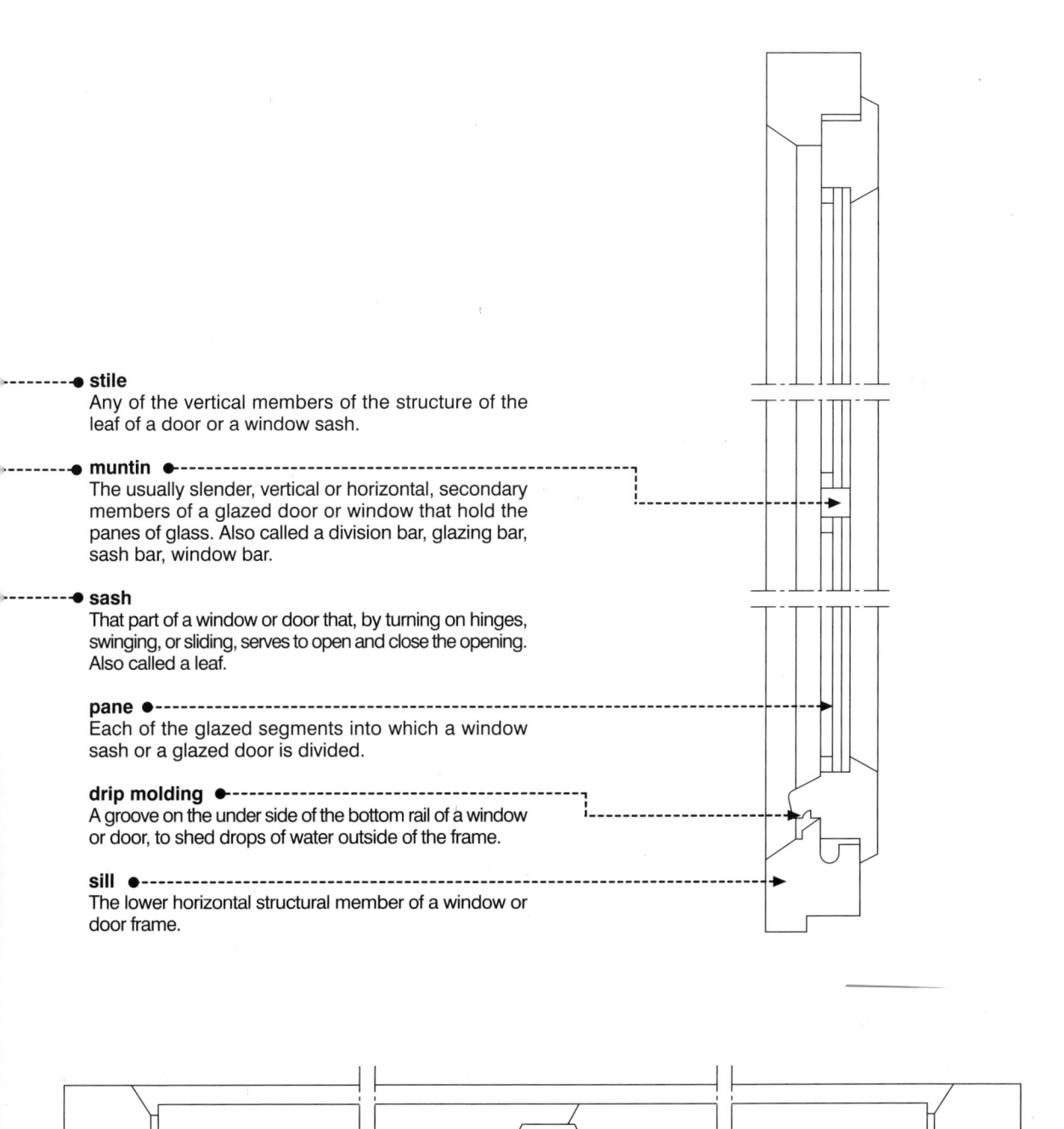

window

Types of window

fixed light
A window or part of one that cannot be moved or opened in any way. Also called a fixed sash.

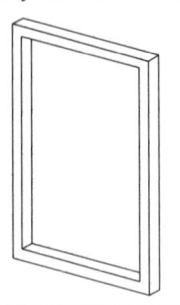

casement window
A window having at least one of its sashes hinged vertically, to swing open inward or outward on the axis of the window jamb.

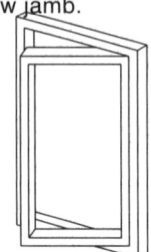

blank window
The ornamental shape of a window, with no real opening, to preserve the unity or symmetry of a façade.

pivoted window
A window that turns on a central, vertical or horizontal, hinge or pivot, as opposed to lateral hinges.

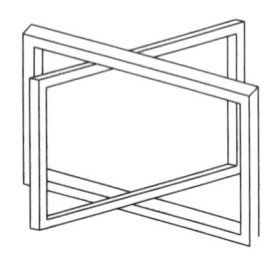

folding casement
A window consisting of several sashes hinged together vertically so as to fold open in a limited space.

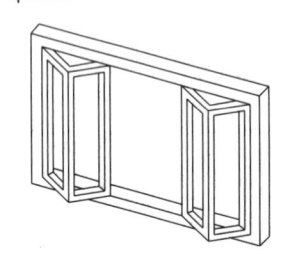

hopper window
A window that opens inward turning on horizontal hinges attached to the bottom rail.

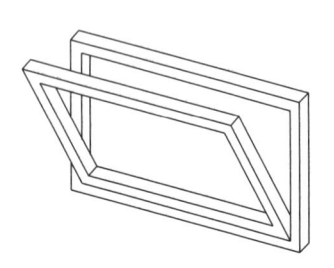

double-hung window
A window with two hung sashes (often counterbalanced for easy opening) that slide vertically to open or close opposite sides of the window frame. Also called a sash window.

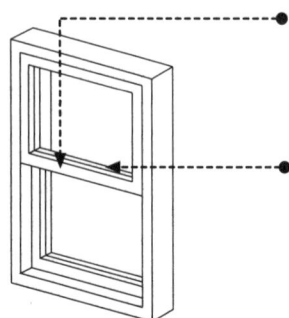

meeting rail
In a double hung window, the horizontal members, or rails, that meet in the centre when the window is closed.

parting bead
In a double-hung window, a long, thin strip of material attached to the jambs of the frame, to separate the sashes to slide past each other. Also called a parting strip, parting stop.

single-hung window
A window with two sashes, only one of which is movable.

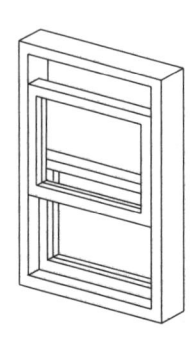

window

drop window
A sliding window in which the sash drops vertically into a box beneath the sill leaving the opening completely free.

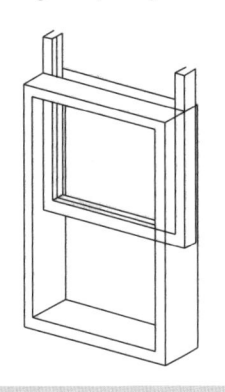

double hung
A window with two sashes that slide vertically to close one or another part of the opening; usually a chord on a pulley connects the sashes counterbalancing their weight, making them lighter to move.

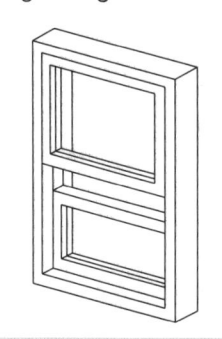

hopper light
A window sash hinged along the bottom so that it tips open inward, and the ventilation enters over the top of the sash.

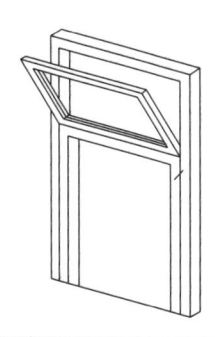

jalousie window
A window consisting of parallel overlapping louvers that pivot simultaneously, so that the upper edge folds closed inward and the lower edge outward.

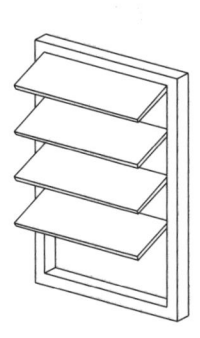

projected window
A window with one or more rotating sashes that turn inward or outward.

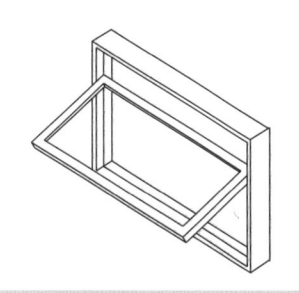

horizontally sliding window
A window with two or more sashes that slide sideways on rails or in parallel horizontal grooves in the window frame.

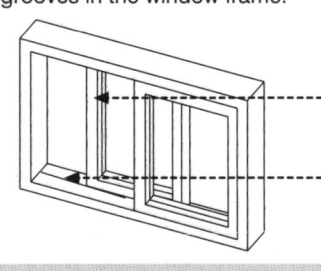

- **sliding sash**
A window or door sash that slides open sideways on rails or grooves in the frame.

- **stop bead**
A slender strip of wood attached to the frame for a door or window sash to close against.

awning window
A window with one or more sashes hinged horizontally along the top rail; the bottom swings outward controlled by a mechanical or hand operated stay.

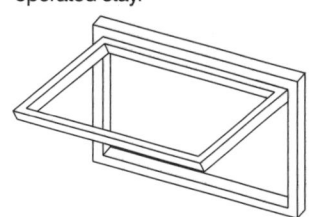

window

gable window
1. A window in or just under a gable. 2. A gable-shaped window.

bay window
A window or set of windows enclosing a roofed gallery, balcony or similar space projecting outward from the façade of a building.

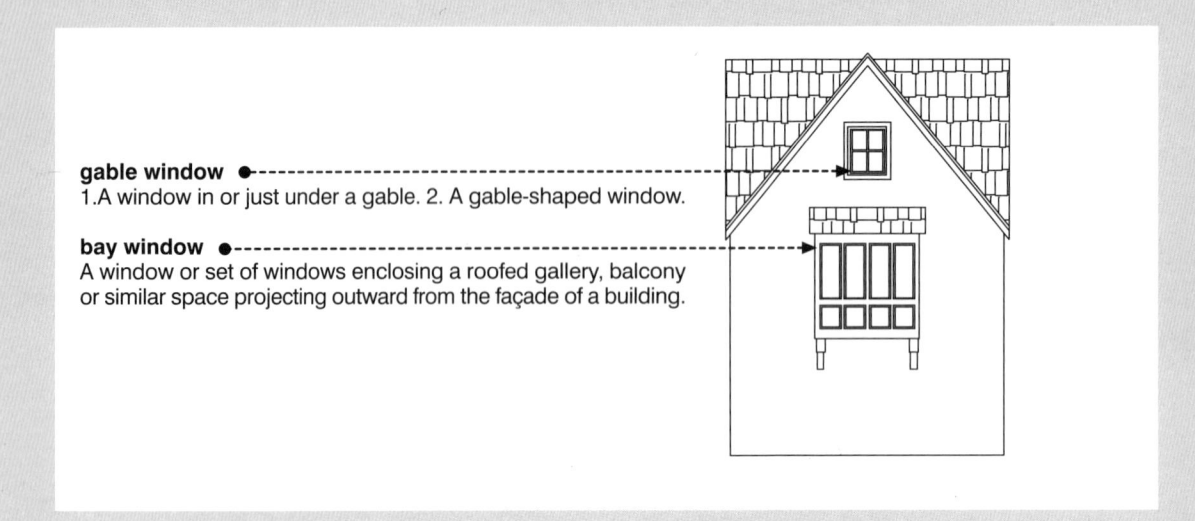

bow window
A bay window with a round front.

cant window
A polygonal bay window, the corners of which are visibly wider than 90º. Also called a cant bay window.

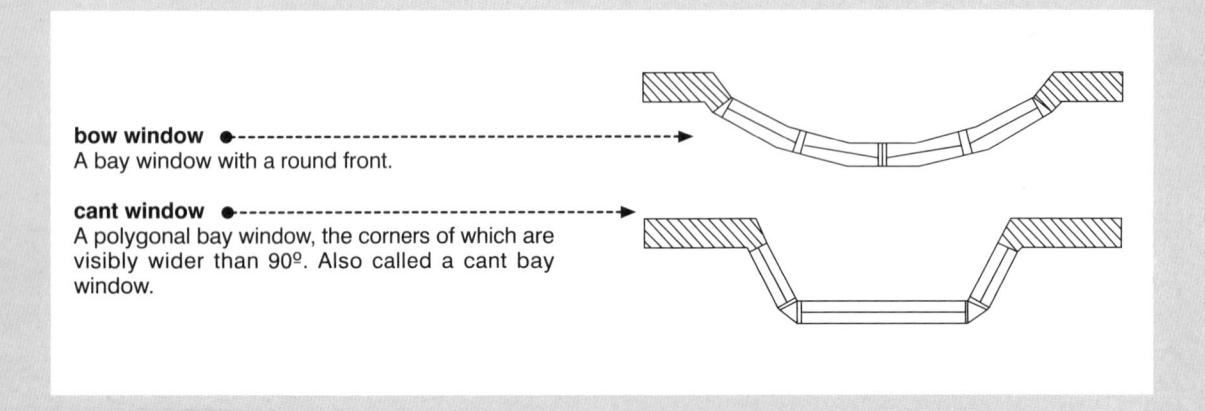

ribbon window
A horizontal series of windows running all the way across a façade, interrupted only by the necessary mullions.

mullion
A vertical member that divides a door or window frame into separate parts.

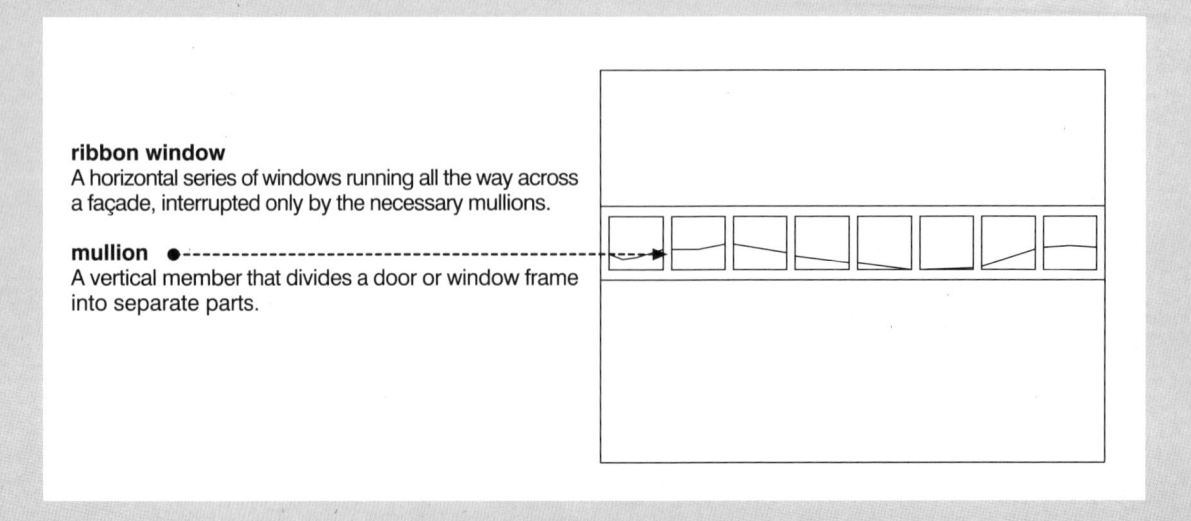

window

Accessory elements of windows

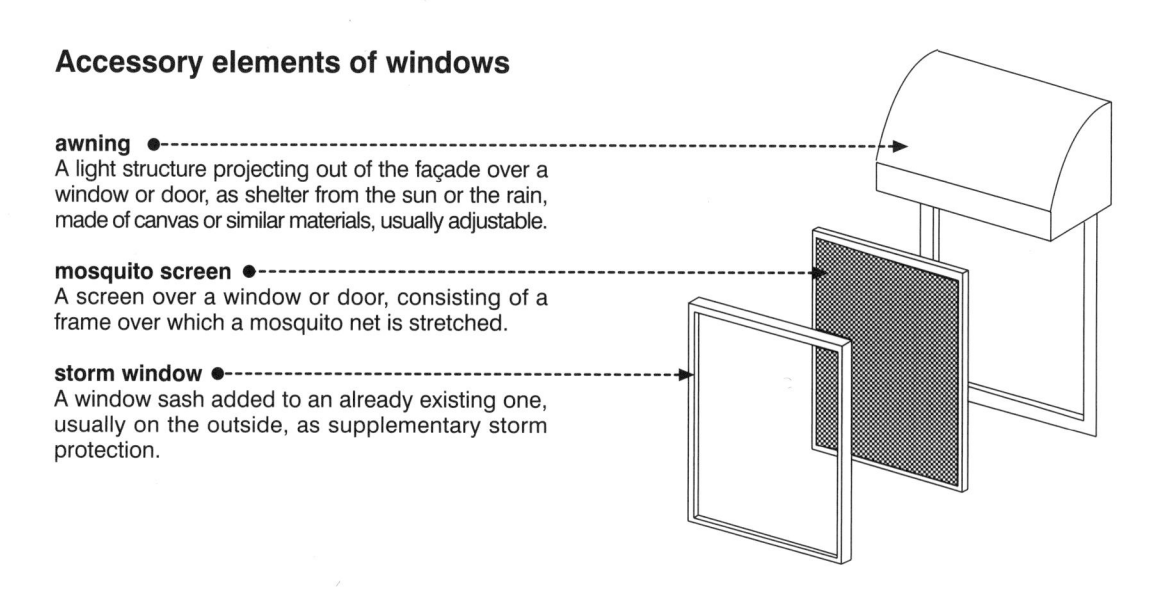

awning
A light structure projecting out of the façade over a window or door, as shelter from the sun or the rain, made of canvas or similar materials, usually adjustable.

mosquito screen
A screen over a window or door, consisting of a frame over which a mosquito net is stretched.

storm window
A window sash added to an already existing one, usually on the outside, as supplementary storm protection.

lattice
A net-like structure of wood, concrete or metal strips, rods or bars, often diagonally disposed, used as an ornamental screen, for ventilation or in gardening.

reinforced concrete lattice

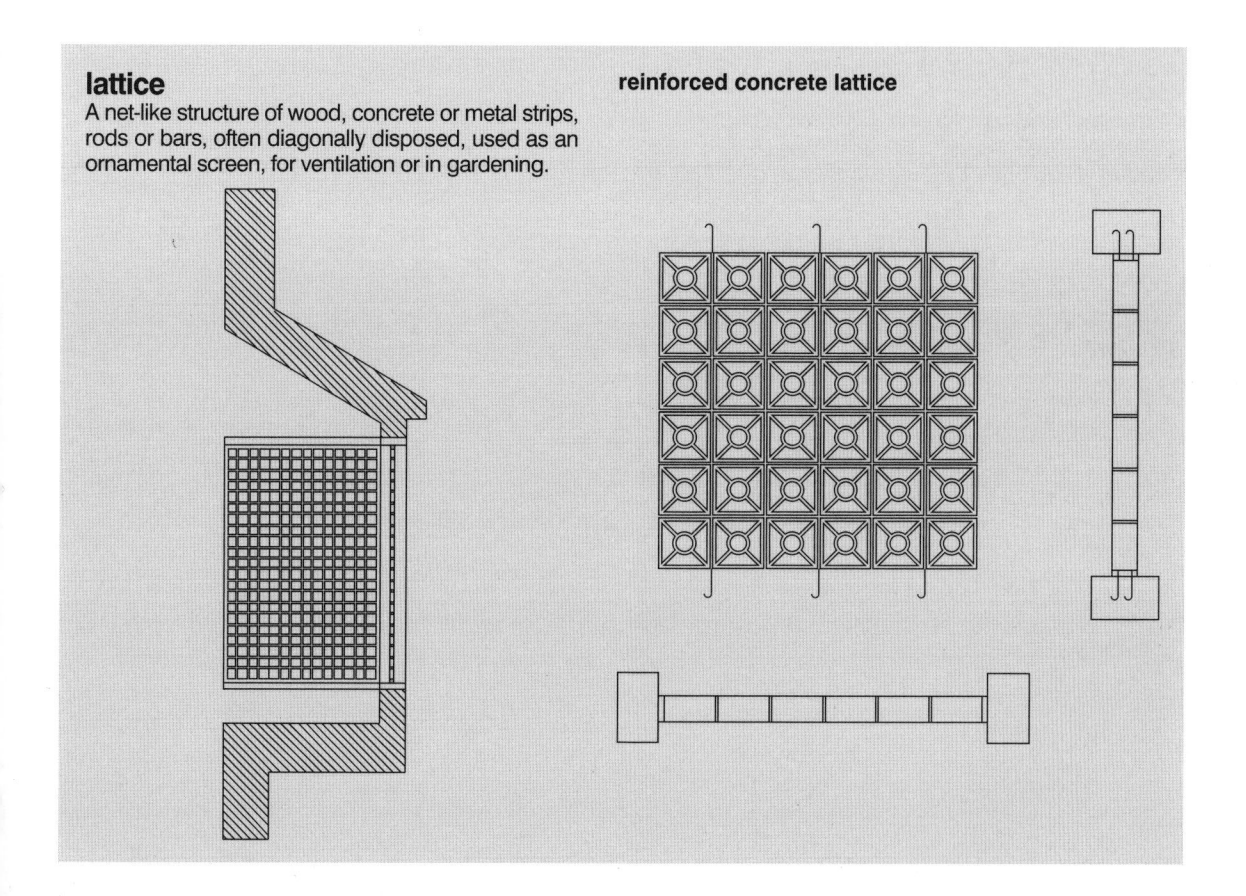

nonbearing partition

An interior wall that supports no other load than its own weight, built to separate a space in two. Also called a non-load bearing partition.

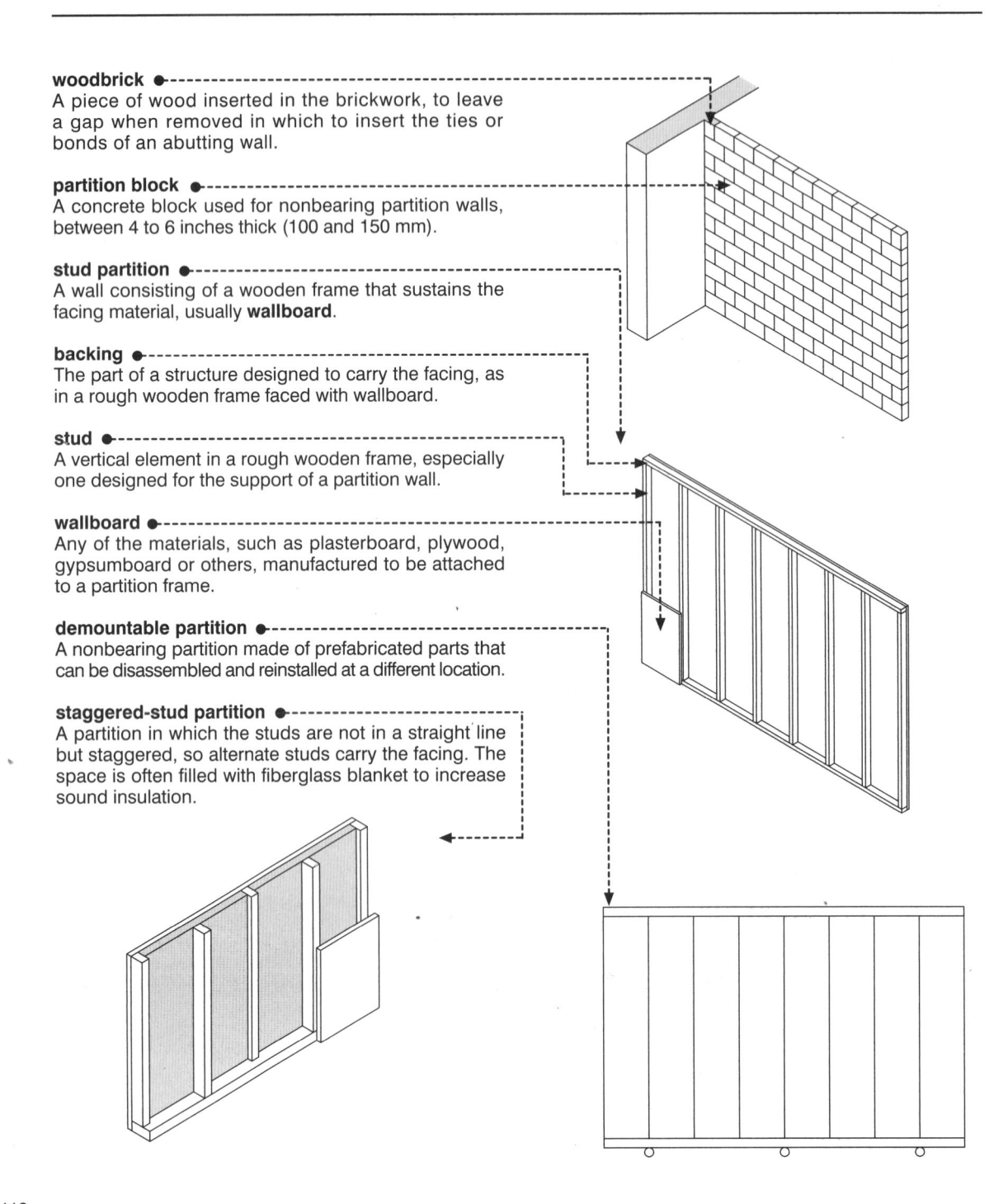

woodbrick
A piece of wood inserted in the brickwork, to leave a gap when removed in which to insert the ties or bonds of an abutting wall.

partition block
A concrete block used for nonbearing partition walls, between 4 to 6 inches thick (100 and 150 mm).

stud partition
A wall consisting of a wooden frame that sustains the facing material, usually **wallboard**.

backing
The part of a structure designed to carry the facing, as in a rough wooden frame faced with wallboard.

stud
A vertical element in a rough wooden frame, especially one designed for the support of a partition wall.

wallboard
Any of the materials, such as plasterboard, plywood, gypsumboard or others, manufactured to be attached to a partition frame.

demountable partition
A nonbearing partition made of prefabricated parts that can be disassembled and reinstalled at a different location.

staggered-stud partition
A partition in which the studs are not in a straight line but staggered, so alternate studs carry the facing. The space is often filled with fiberglass blanket to increase sound insulation.

nonbearing partition

double core hollow brick

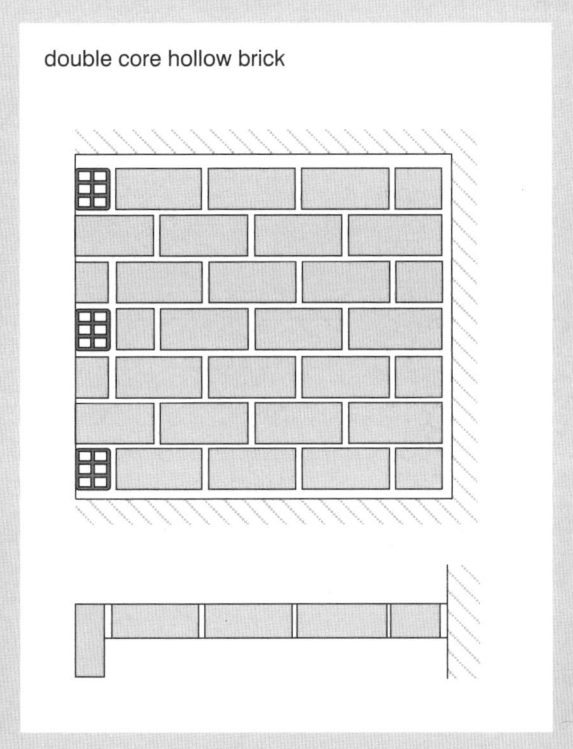

single core hollow brick

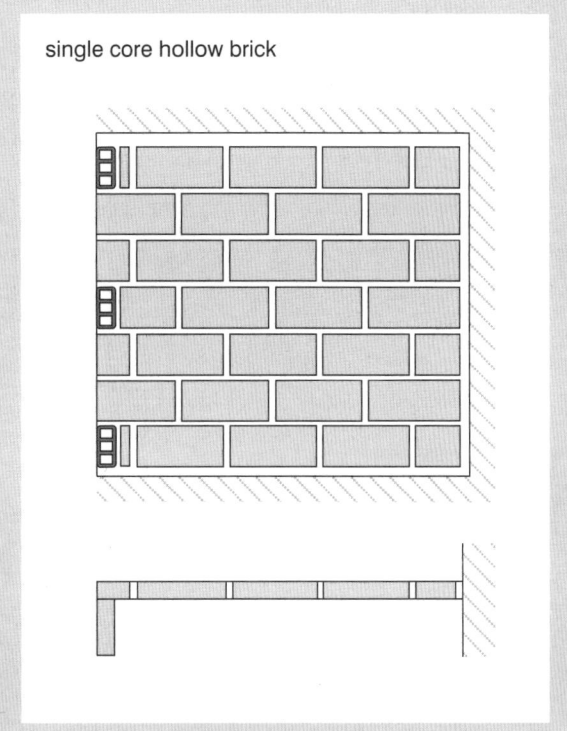

Plaster partition made of solid prefabricated units.

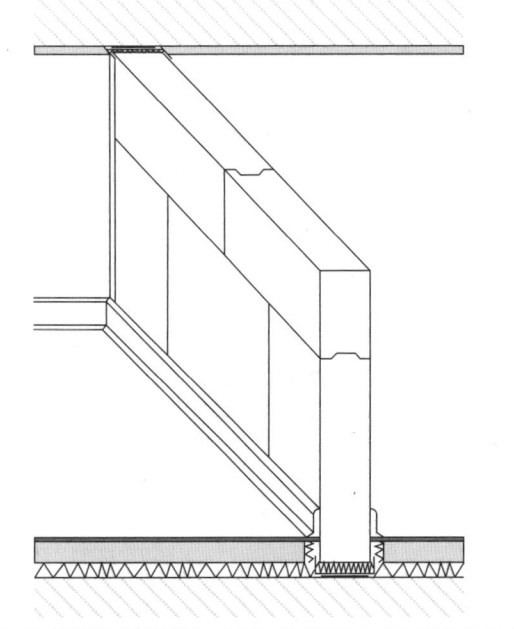

Hollow core prefabricated separating wall; an insulating core sandwiched between two layers of plasterboard or drywall

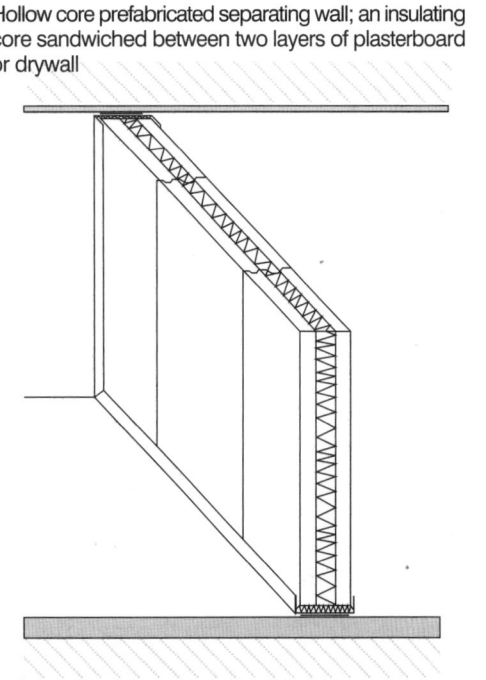

nonbearing partition

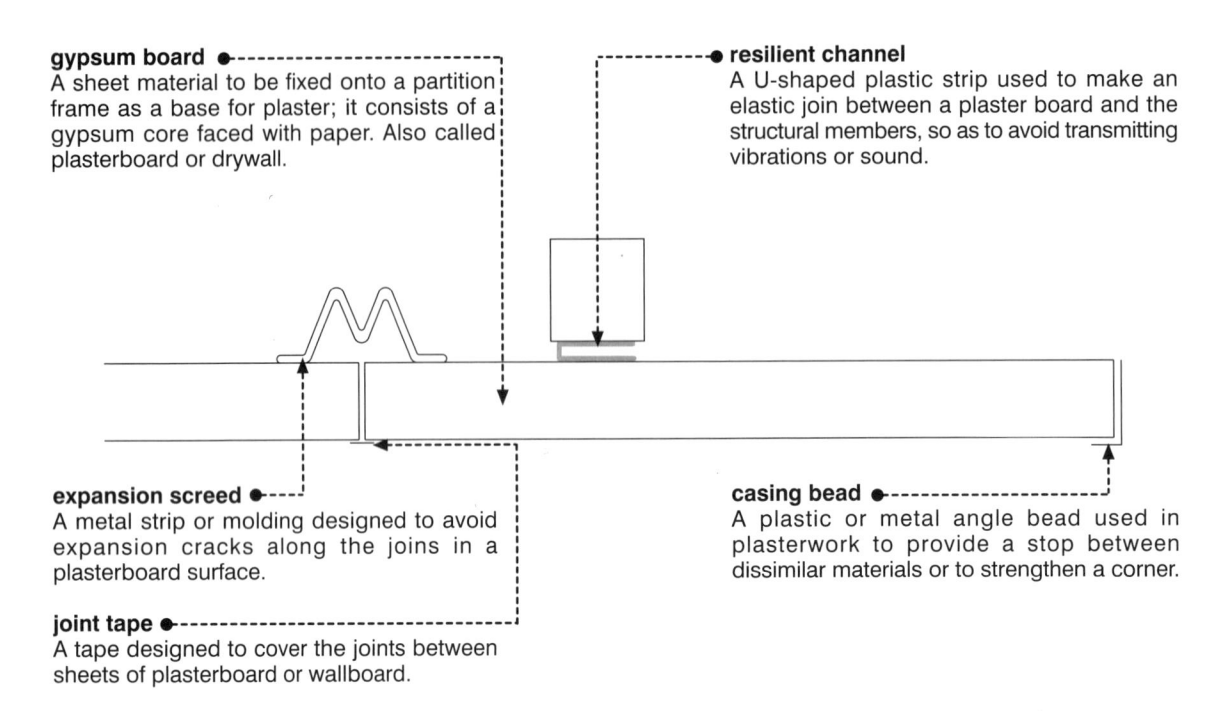

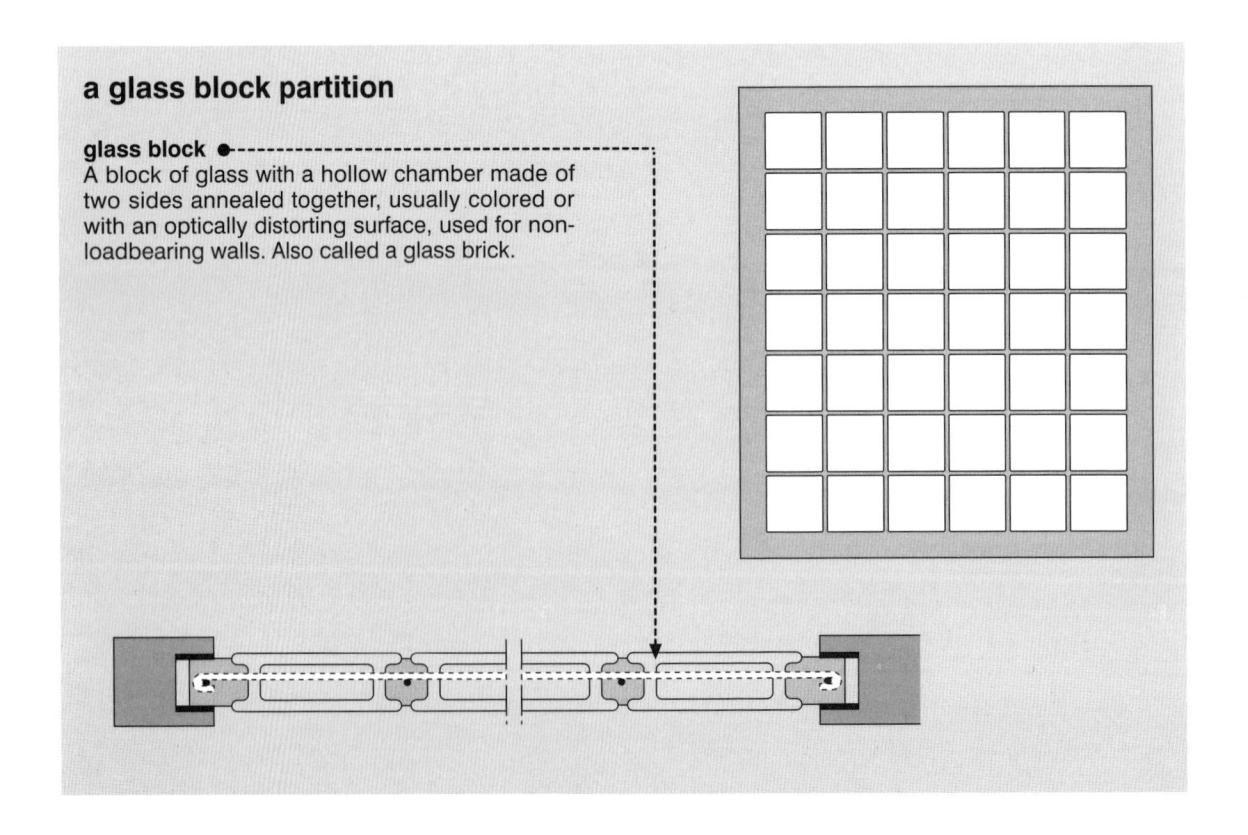

gypsum board
A sheet material to be fixed onto a partition frame as a base for plaster; it consists of a gypsum core faced with paper. Also called plasterboard or drywall.

resilient channel
A U-shaped plastic strip used to make an elastic join between a plaster board and the structural members, so as to avoid transmitting vibrations or sound.

expansion screed
A metal strip or molding designed to avoid expansion cracks along the joins in a plasterboard surface.

casing bead
A plastic or metal angle bead used in plasterwork to provide a stop between dissimilar materials or to strengthen a corner.

joint tape
A tape designed to cover the joints between sheets of plasterboard or wallboard.

a glass block partition

glass block
A block of glass with a hollow chamber made of two sides annealed together, usually colored or with an optically distorting surface, used for non-loadbearing walls. Also called a glass brick.

façade

façade wall
A wall that is exposed to the weather, it is often the main item that defines an interior space which it shelters. Also called external wall or façade.

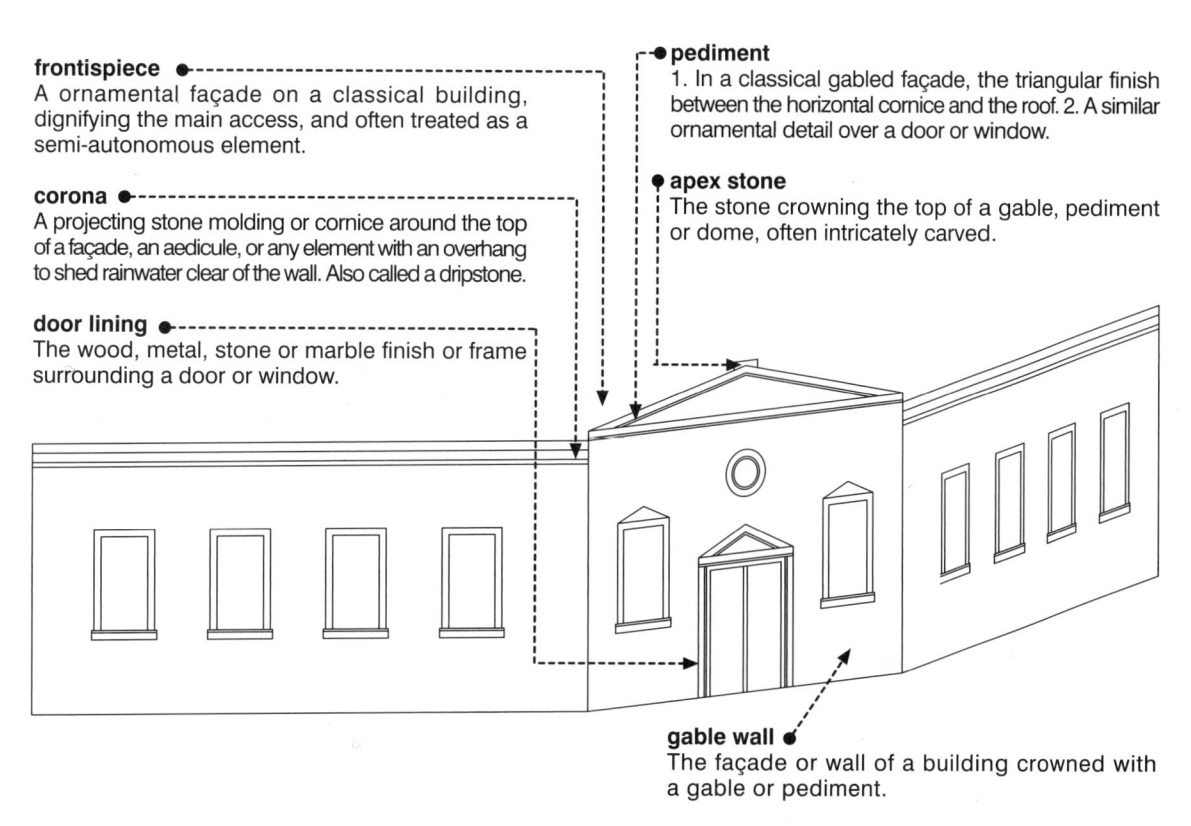

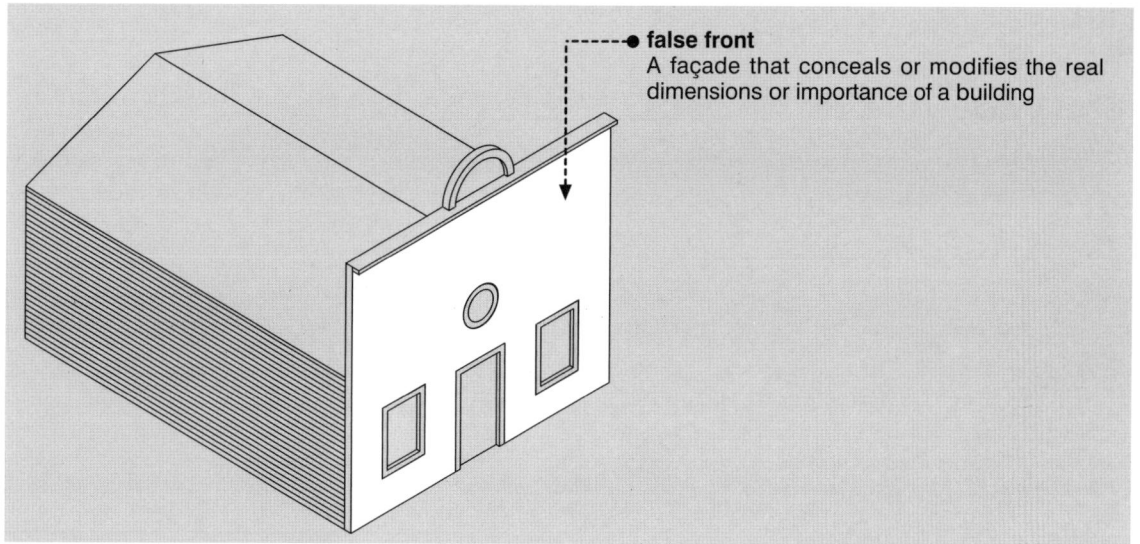

frontispiece
A ornamental façade on a classical building, dignifying the main access, and often treated as a semi-autonomous element.

corona
A projecting stone molding or cornice around the top of a façade, an aedicule, or any element with an overhang to shed rainwater clear of the wall. Also called a dripstone.

door lining
The wood, metal, stone or marble finish or frame surrounding a door or window.

pediment
1. In a classical gabled façade, the triangular finish between the horizontal cornice and the roof. 2. A similar ornamental detail over a door or window.

apex stone
The stone crowning the top of a gable, pediment or dome, often intricately carved.

gable wall
The façade or wall of a building crowned with a gable or pediment.

false front
A façade that conceals or modifies the real dimensions or importance of a building

façade

dressed stone
Stone that has been squared ready for building purposes. Also called ashlar.

through stone
A stone that bonds one side of the wall to the other, through the whole thickness of the wall, also called a bondstone.

cornerstone
A stone used on the corner of a building, with two adjacent dressed sides and usually of a different color, size or texture to other adjacent elements. Also called a quoin, coign or coin.

padstone
A large stone built into a wall to support and distribute a concentrated load. Also called a pad.

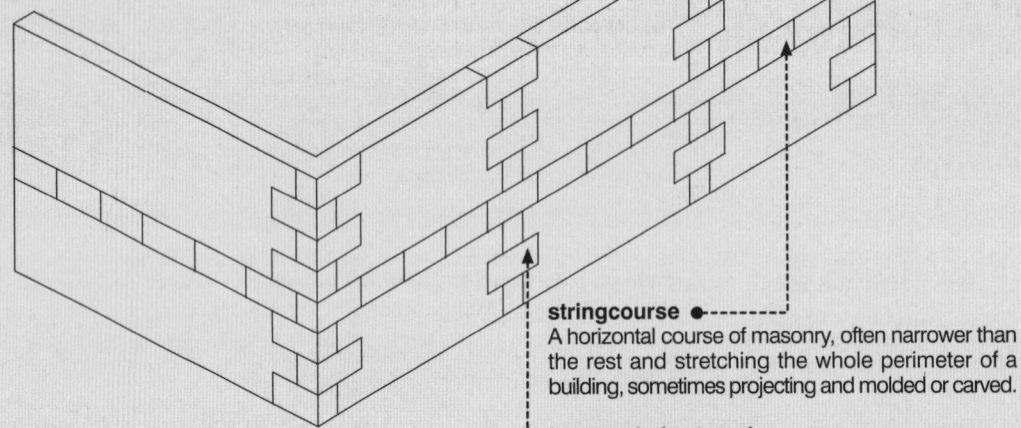

stringcourse
A horizontal course of masonry, often narrower than the rest and stretching the whole perimeter of a building, sometimes projecting and molded or carved.

long-and-short work
A vertical pillar of masonry, usually reinforcing a corner but also bonding the middle of a wall, consisting of large bondstones alternately in a vertical position or capped horizontally.

rustication
Stonework in which the joints between the stones are sharply and deeply beveled so each faced stone seems to project.

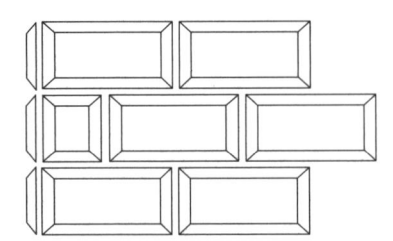

rustic work
Stonework in which the joints between the stones are stressed by rough deep chamfering and the projecting face is picked or hacked.

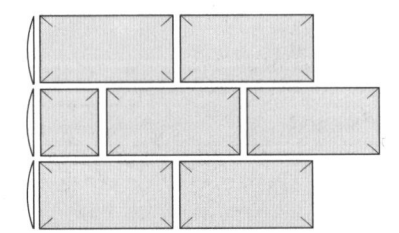

façade

Cyclopean
Descriptive of stonework in which large flat-faced stones, uncut or of irregular geometry, are fitted together without mortar in a manner reminiscent of prehistoric construction.

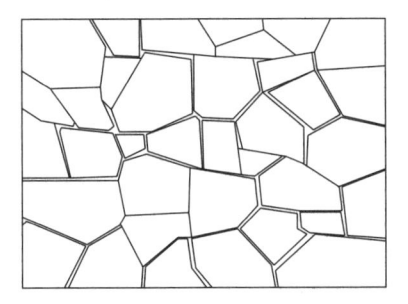

random rubble
Descriptive of stonework executed roughly with stones of different sizes resulting in a regular shape to which the random order of the material is submitted.

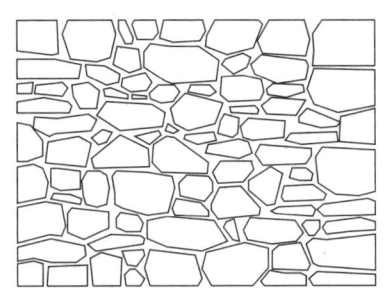

squared rubble
Descriptive of random rubble stonework consisting of different sizes of squared stones randomly combined in courses not exceeding 12 inches in height. Also called block-in-course.

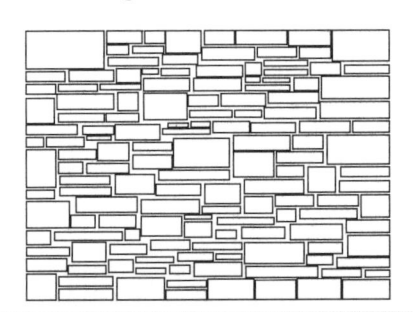

random ashlar
Descriptive of stonework consisting of ashlar stone of different sizes assembled randomly.

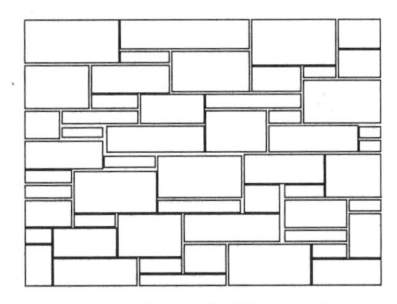

coursed ashlar
Descriptive of stonework in which ashlar stone of different sizes is assembled in leveled courses and the gaps filled with mortar or smaller stones.

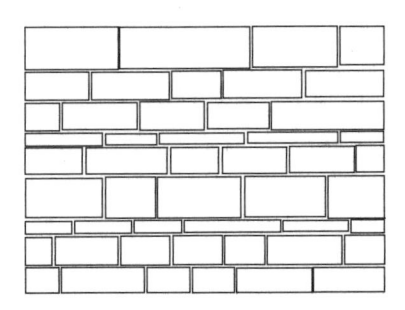

ashlar masonry
A type of masonry which makes use of rectangular blocks of ceramic, concrete or stone, usually bigger than bricks, bonded with mortar.

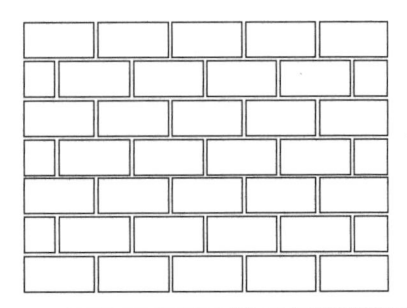

façade

course
A horizontal series or row of masonry units, bricks or tiles laid next to each other in or upon a wall.

bond course
A course of masonry that links or bonds the face of a wall with the inner courses, or the two opposite faces of a bearing wall.

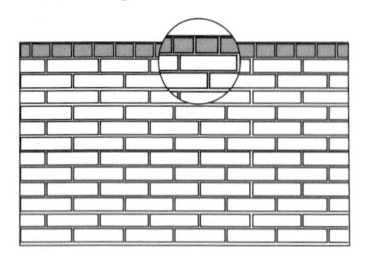

header course
A course of masonry consisting of headers, i.e., masonry units laid horizontally with the short side showing. Also called a heading course.

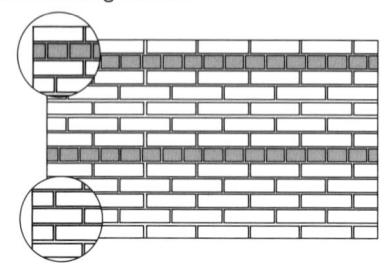

stretcher course
A course of masonry consisting of stretchers, i.e. masonry units laid horizontally with the long side showing. Also called a stretching course.

stack bond
A bricklaying method in which the masonry units are laid in a stack, with all the vertical joints aligned. Also identical elements in veneer masonry, bonded so the vertical and horizontal joints are aligned.

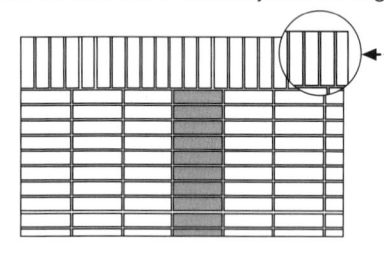

soldier course
A course of masonry or bricks laid vertically, standing on end, often at the top of a wall.

Flemish diagonal bond
A bricklaying method in which a course of alternate headers and stretchers is followed by a course of stretchers, producing a diagonal pattern. Also called a Flemish cross bond.

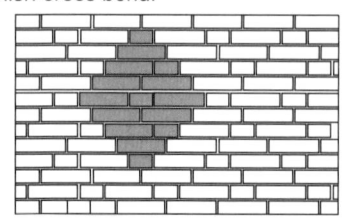

Flemish bond
A bricklaying method with alternate headers and stretchers in every course, with each header centered upon or under the stretcher respectively below or above it.

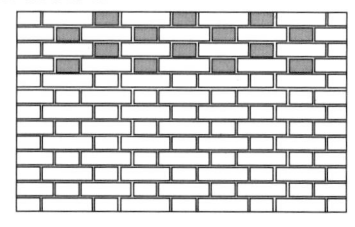

122

façade

bond
Any of the various ways in which the bricks or other constituents of a wall are assembled so as to overlap, increasing the resistance of the construction while enhancing its appearance.

American bond
A bricklaying method alternating five or six courses of stretchers with a course of headers.

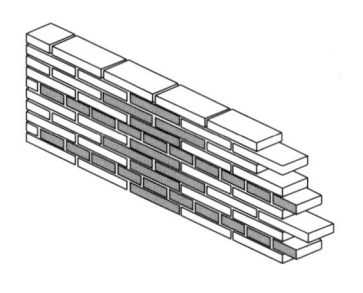

in-and-out bond
A bricklaying method which alternates headers and stretchers so that each stretcher (usually two side by side) has a bonding header across the top.

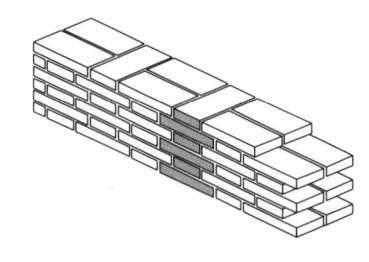

English bond
A bricklaying method in which every second course of stretchers is crossed with a course of headers.

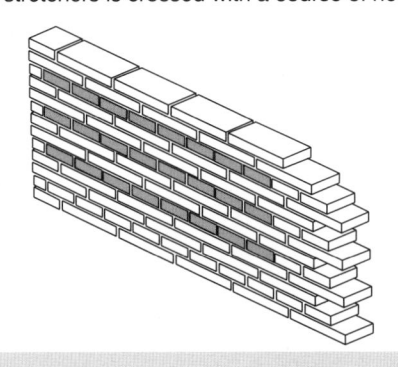

stretcher bond
A method of wall building in which the masonry units are laid lengthwise, so that the vertical joints fall in the middle of the brick or stone below it. Also called a running or stretching bond.

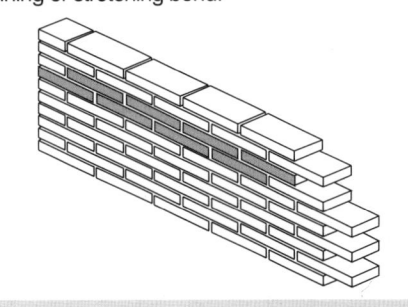

header bond
A wall building method in which masonry units are laid with the short side to the face of the wall, and the vertical joints in the middle of the brick or stone below it. Also called a heading bond.

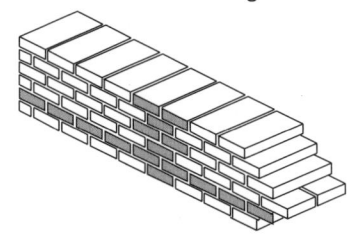

English cross bond
A variant of the English bond in which each course of stretchers is displaced half the length of a stretcher. Also called Dutch bond.

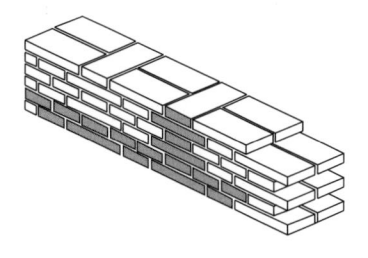

façade

troweled joint (USA)
Descriptive of a joint that has had excess mortar removed and has been finished with a trowel; also called trowelled joint (GB).

flush joint
A mortar joint that has been finished flush (i.e. level) with the wall face.

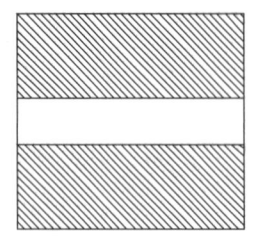

raked joint
A joint from which the excess mortar has been removed when still soft with a square edged tool, so as to underline the characteristics of the material of which the wall is made.

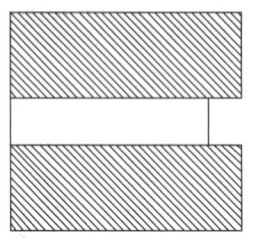

V-joint
A V-shaped joint executed with a pointed trowel or a specially shaped tool.

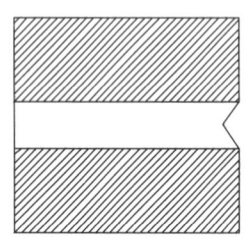

concave joint
A gently recessed finish of the mortar joint between masonry units achieved with a special curved tool; it offers a good resistance to weather factors.

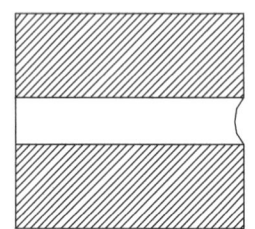

weathered joint
A mortar joint that has been pressed down from the upper masonry edge, resulting in a sloped surface that sheds the rainwater outward.

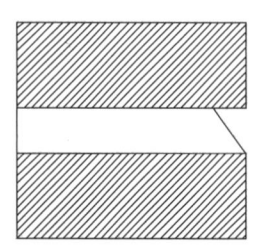

struck joint
A mortar joint that has been pressed up from the lower masonry edge resulting in a sloped surface that will shed the rain onto the edge of the masonry below.

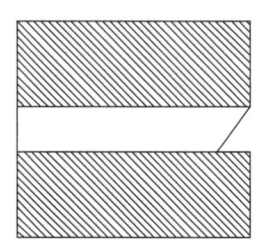

façade

clapboard
A type of weatherproofing for exterior walls characteristic of wood frame buildings, consisting of boards placed one above the other horizontally and facing out, so that they overlap and shed rainwater onto the board below.

clapboard
A type of weatherproofing for exterior walls characteristic of wood frame buildings, consisting of boards placed one above the other horizontally and facing out, so that they overlap and shed rainwater onto the board below; the upper edge is thinner to improve the drip. Also called bevel siding or lap siding.

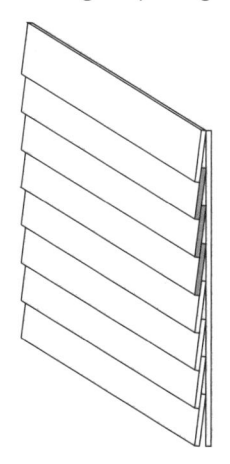

colonial siding
A type of exterior siding characteristic of the early American style, consisting of wide square-edged clapboards.

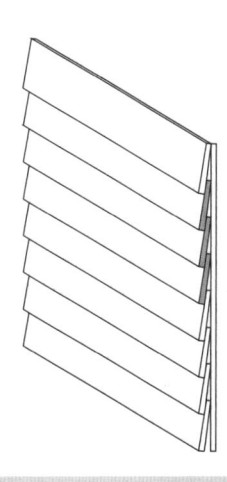

drop siding
A type of weatherproof siding consisting of wooden boards, aluminum or vinyl strips, tongue-and-grooved one over the other shedding the rain outward. Also called novelty siding.

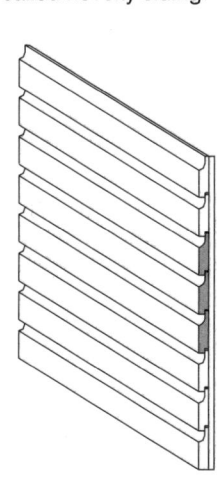

rabbeted
A type of clapboard siding for which the boards have a rabbeted lower edge to fit over the top of the board below, shedding the rain over it and outward.

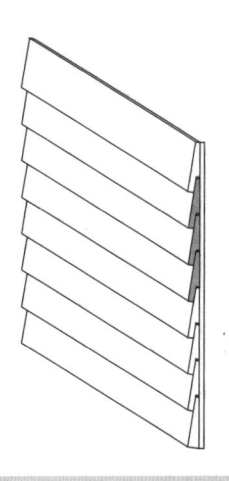

façade

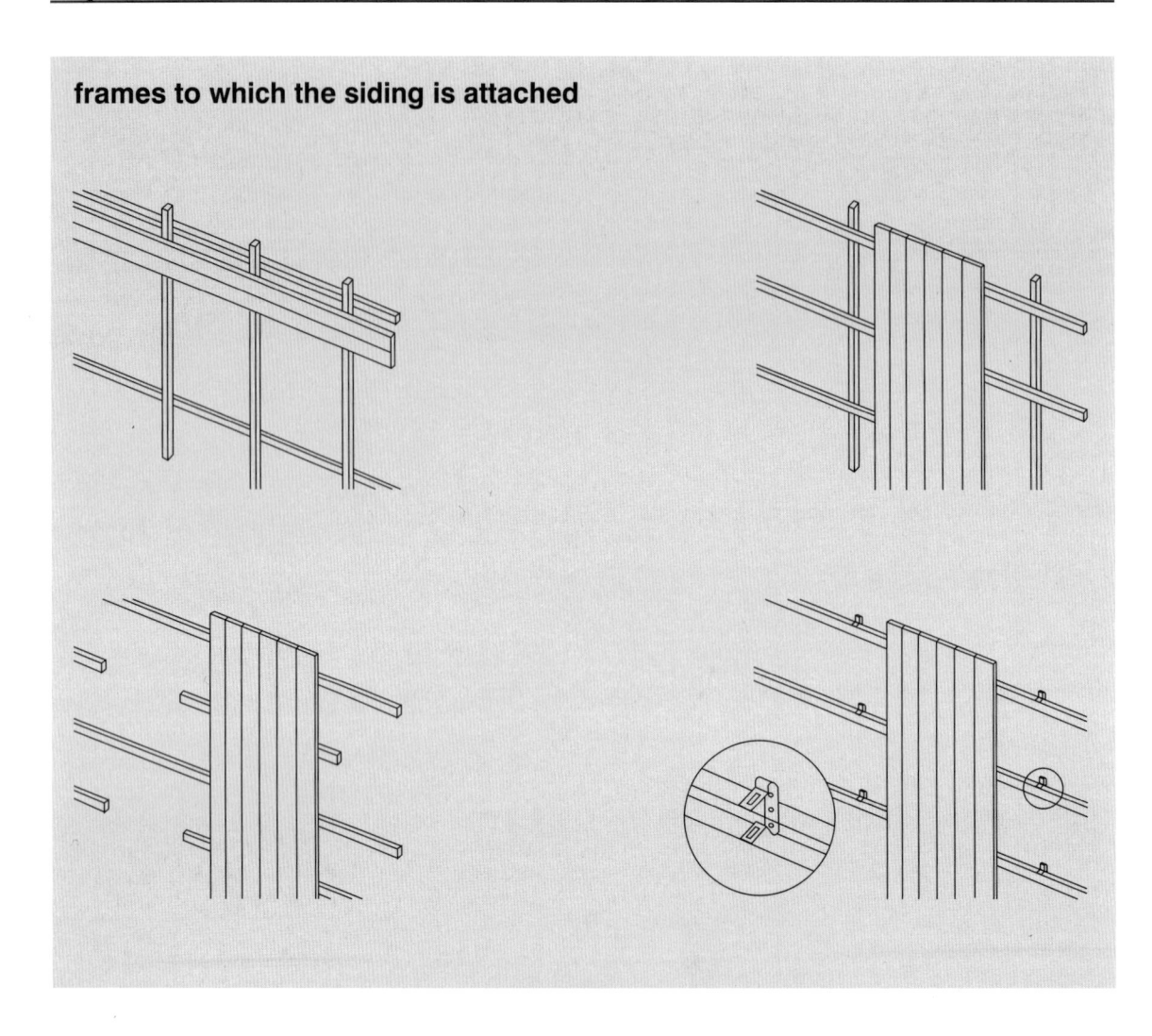

frames to which the siding is attached

anchoring systems for wooden wall siding

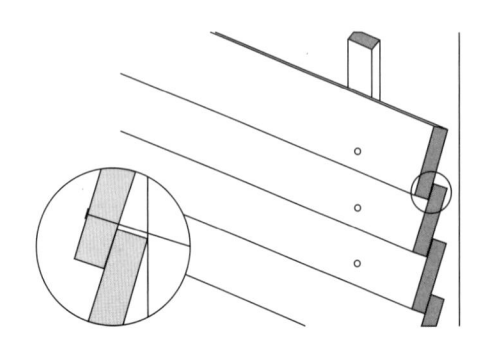

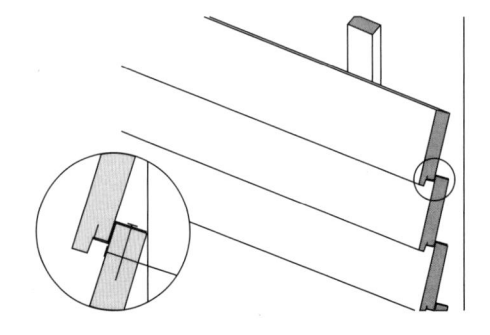

façade

board and batten
A wall cladding method for wood-frame houses consisting of closely spaced vertical boards, with closely spaced narrow wooden strips (battens) covering the joints.

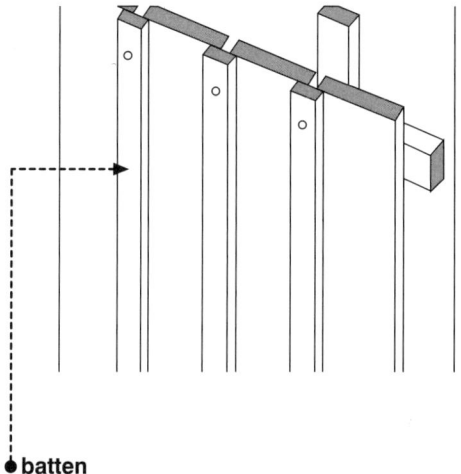

batten
A thin wooden strip used for various purposes, such as added support or anchoring of elements, or to cover the joints in vertically attached wooden wall-cladding (board-and-batten).

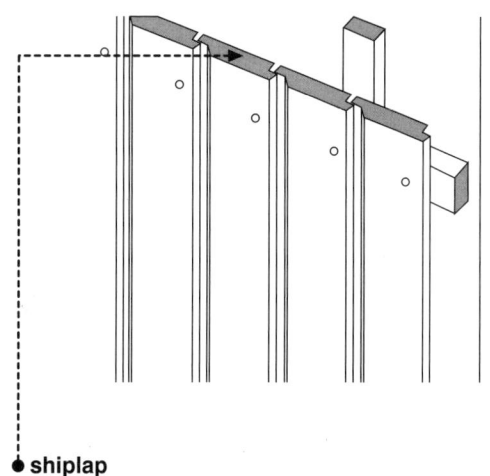

shiplap
A siding of wooden boards with rabbeted edges so that the joints overlap.

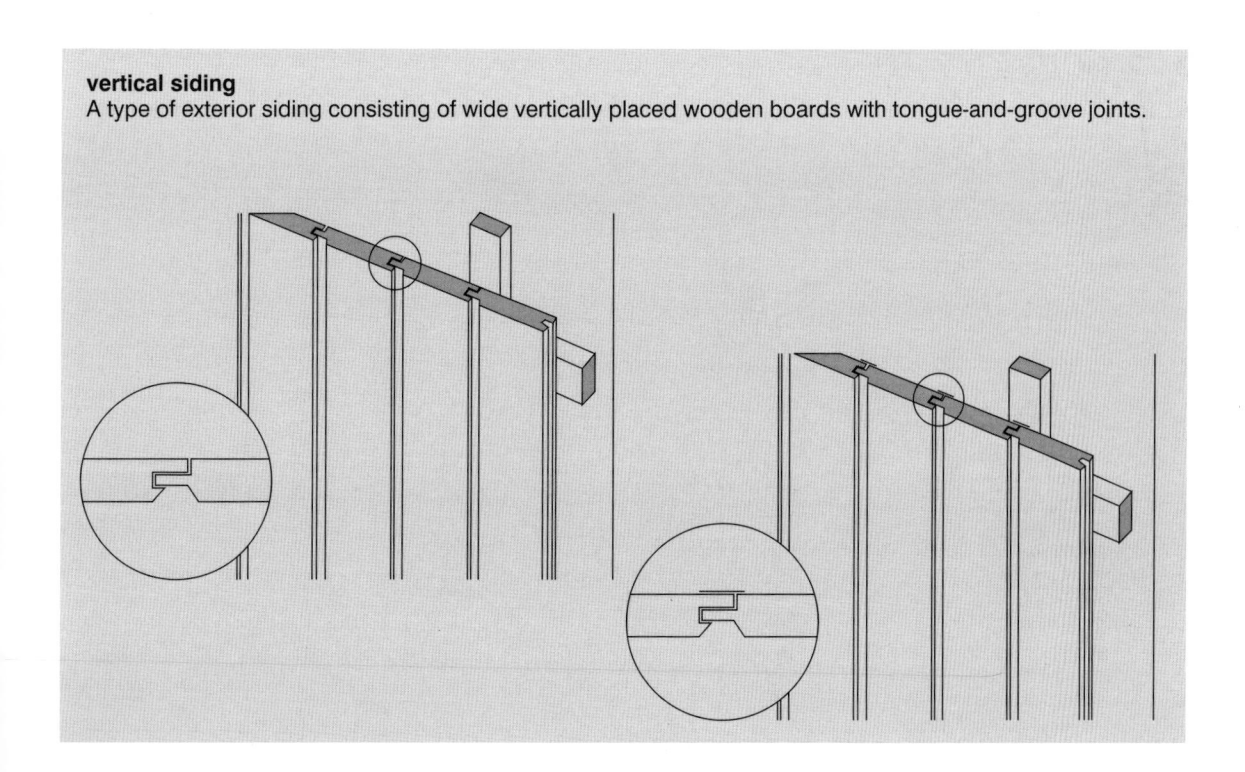

vertical siding
A type of exterior siding consisting of wide vertically placed wooden boards with tongue-and-groove joints.

façade

curtain wall
1. A nonbearing exterior wall that is independent of the building's structural frame of beams or girders. 2. In medieval fortifications, a stretch of wall closing the space between two towers.

unit system
A method of enclosing or dividing a space by means of ready-made wall units to be assembled on site.

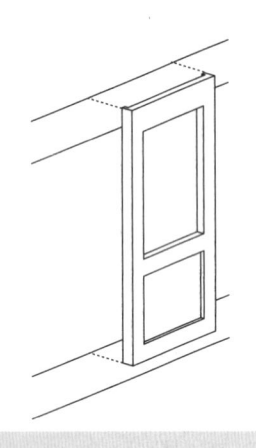

column-cover-and-spandrel system
System of closing a façade in which the prefabricated units, both clear and opaque, are attached to the spandrel beams.

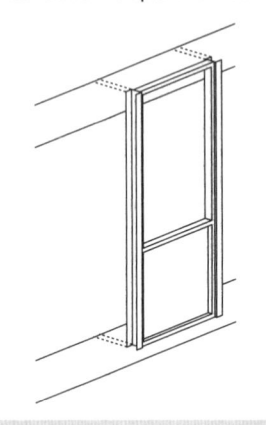

unit-and-mullion system
A curtain wall system consisting of ready made wall panels designed to be fixed to the vertical members of the support structure.

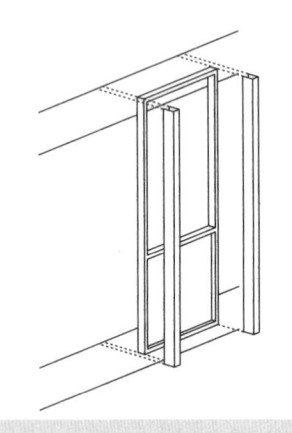

stick system
A curtain wall in which the opaque and the transparent elements are fixed separately onto an auxiliary frame of horizontal and vertical members.

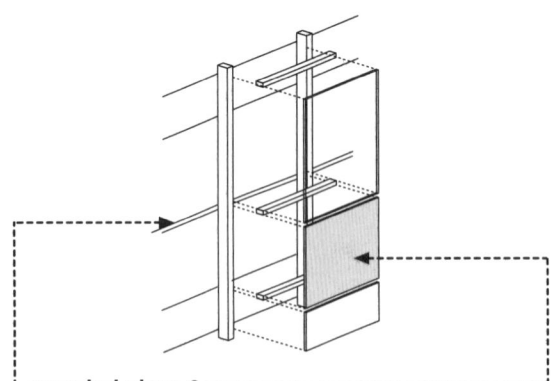

panel system
A method of enclosing or dividing a space by means of ready-made wall panels, complete with doors and windows, to be assembled on site.

spandrel glass
An opaque glass used on curtain walls or windows to conceal structural elements visible from the outside, such as spandrel beams.

backup wall
That part of a curtain wall behind the exterior facing, the fire-proof core of the wall.

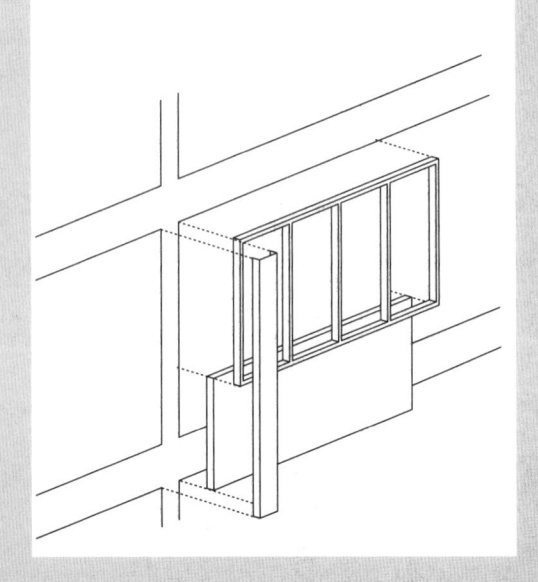

façade

glass façade

butt-joint glazing
A glazing method in which sheets of glass are joined along the abutting edge by means of a structural silicone sealant.

glass mullion system
A glazing system in which sheets of tempered glass are hung from special anchors with a structural silicone adhesive or with sheet metal connectors.

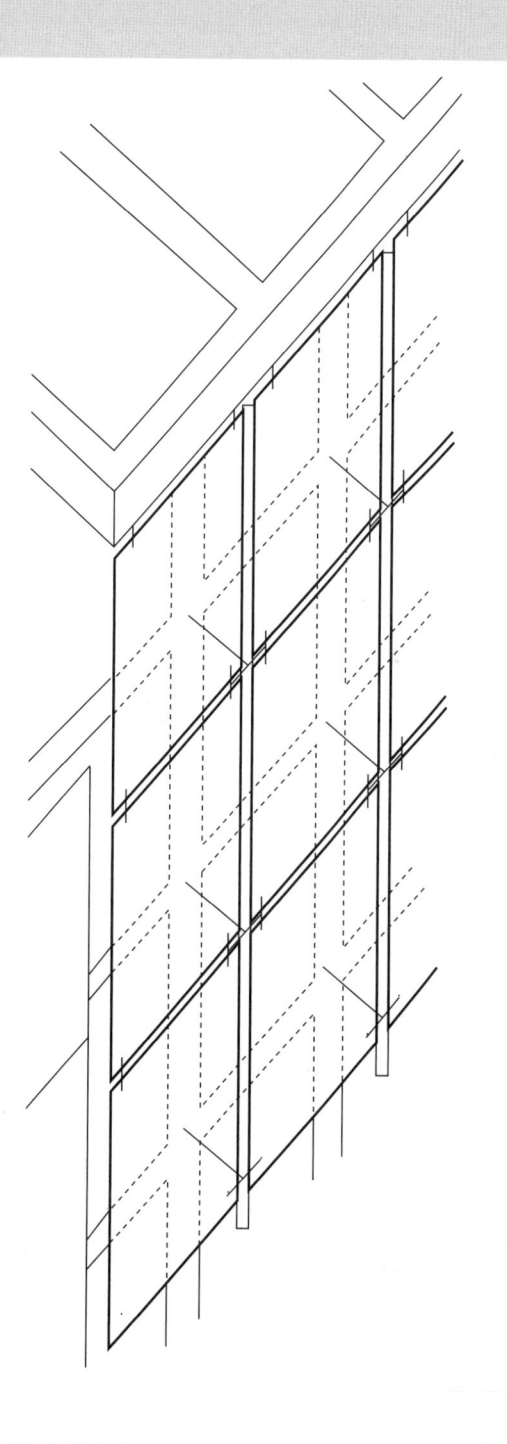

façade

backing
The non-visible inner side of a wall, or the rough material of which that side is built or reinforced.

veneer
A non-structural exterior facing applied as an ornamental element, for insulation, or for protection.

brick veneer
A type of wall veneer, or facing, consisting of bricks.

texture 1 - 11 siding
A large sheet of plywood or vinyl board used for exterior siding, usually having a series of parallel grooves to imitate clapboards; prone to rapid deterioration if not treated with weather resistant paints.

brick facing
A non-structural exterior or interior facing of brick, applied as a finish, for insulation, or protection.

case
To cover an element or a building material with another, as a reinforcement or decoration.

ashlaring
A type of finish or facing consisting in a non structural layer of ashlar stone.

gypsum sheathing
A wallboard consisting of a water and fireproof gypsum core between sheets of water repellent paper, totaling a final thickness of about 1/2 inch, used as a base for exterior veneering.

fiberboard sheathing (USA)
A sheathing material compacted of wood or vegetable fibers with a binding substance; sometimes waterproofed with asphalt, its performance depends on the fibers and binders used; also called fibreboard sheathing (G.B.).

adhered veneer
A thin (max. 3.2 cm) adhesion-type veneer, often ceramic, attached to the wall or the backing with special adhesive mortars.

ceramic mosaic tile
Small pieces of glazed or unglazed ceramic or porcelain, usually square, which generally come pre-assembled on paper sheets or plastic mesh to facilitate the installation.

architectural terra cotta
A clay masonry unit used as a wall's ceramic facing or ornamental finish, glazed or unglazed, possibly made by hand, often more elongated than a conventional brick.

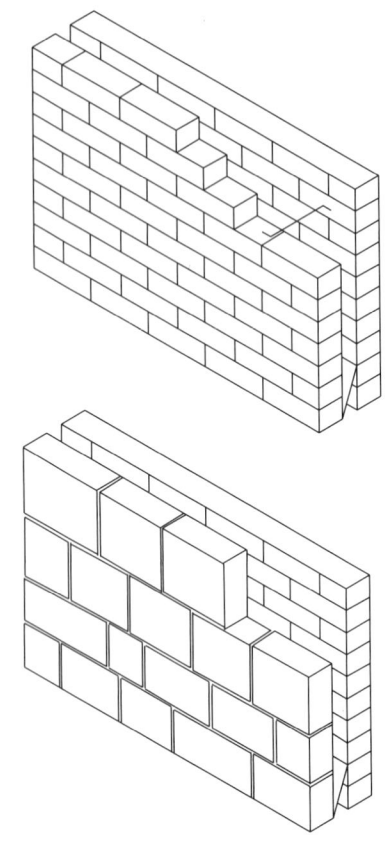

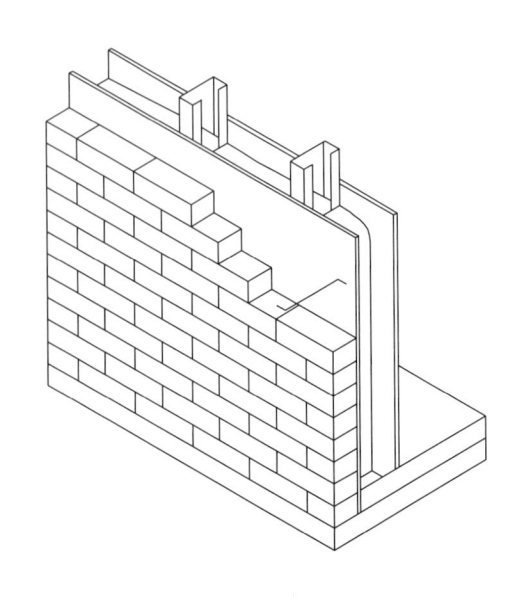

façade

gypsum plaster
A base-coat plaster consisting of ground calcined gypsum to which water is added to start the setting process; the setting speed is controlled with various additives.

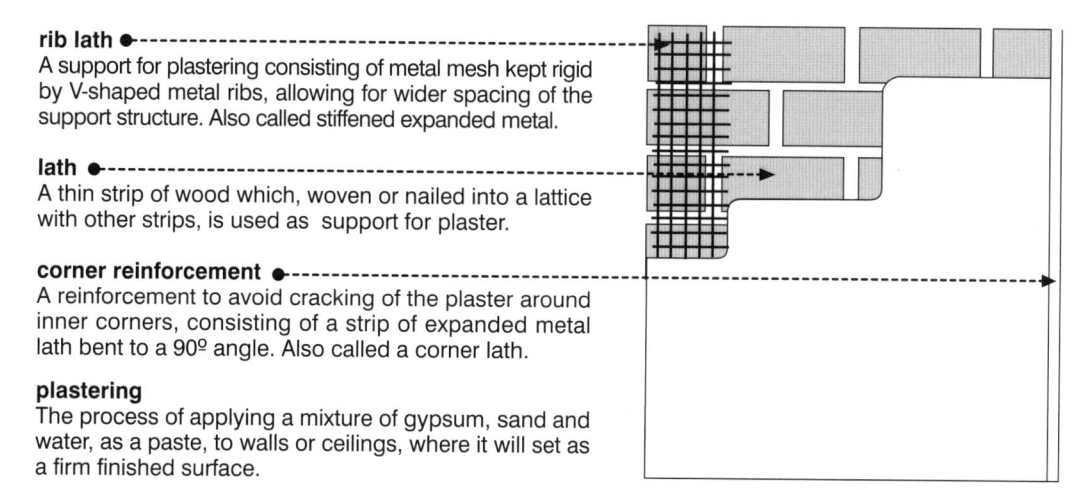

rib lath
A support for plastering consisting of metal mesh kept rigid by V-shaped metal ribs, allowing for wider spacing of the support structure. Also called stiffened expanded metal.

lath
A thin strip of wood which, woven or nailed into a lattice with other strips, is used as support for plaster.

corner reinforcement
A reinforcement to avoid cracking of the plaster around inner corners, consisting of a strip of expanded metal lath bent to a 90º angle. Also called a corner lath.

plastering
The process of applying a mixture of gypsum, sand and water, as a paste, to walls or ceilings, where it will set as a firm finished surface.

plaster of Paris
Finely ground calcined gypsum which is mixed with water to a plastic state that hardens quickly; it is used mainly in statuary, ornamental moldings and, medically, for the immobilization of broken limbs.

paper-backed lath
A lath for plastering, possibly of expanded metal, that has a perforated paper backing.

finish coat
In plastering, the final coat in which a smooth finish is achieved, also called fining coat or setting coat.

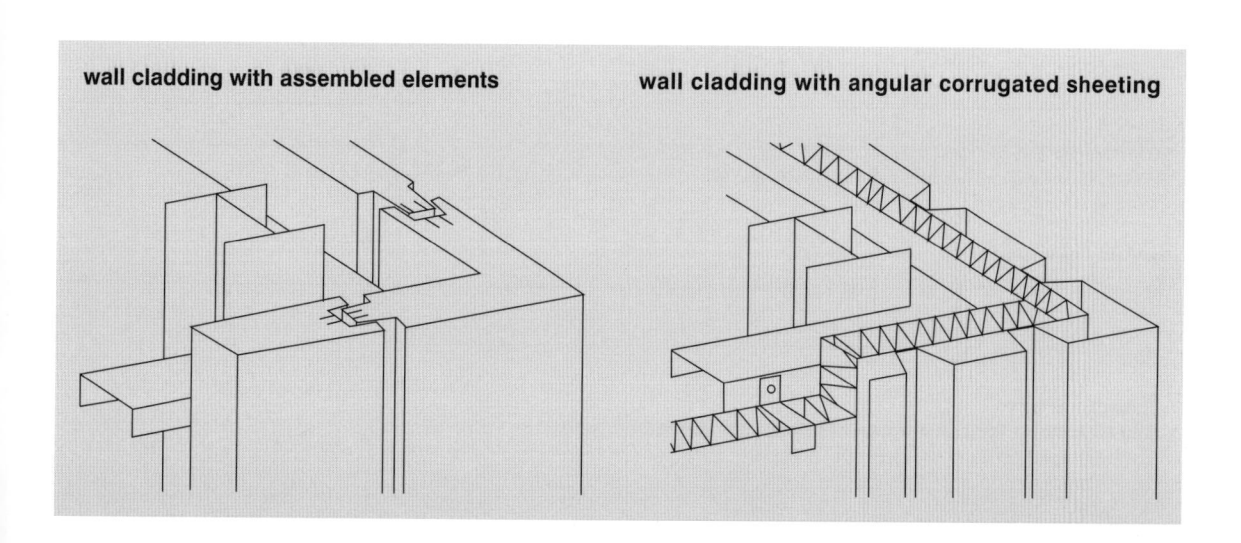

wall cladding with assembled elements

wall cladding with angular corrugated sheeting

finish floor

The surface that results from placing a layer of finish-material over the subfloor; the finished surface one walks upon.

resilient flooring
A flooring or paving material that recovers its form after being compressed or warped, particularly suited for installation in physical exercise or dance spaces.

flooring
A material used as the finish layer of a floor, referred especially to a non-textile material such as floor-tiles.

rubber tile
A flooring material composed of natural or synthetic rubber combined with mineral particles like asbestos, clay, or fibrous talc.

vinyl tile
An elastic flooring material composed of an elastic binder such as vinyl chloride, with plasticizers, pigments and mineral fillers.

mastic
A viscous substance used as a joint sealer or an impermeable film.

underlayment
A layer of material spread on the subfloor to achieve an even surface for the flooring to rest upon.

subfloor
A structural load-bearing surface supported directly by the joists and beams, as a base to which the finish flooring will be attached. Also called blind floor, counterfloor, or rough floor.

brick pavement
A type of overbaked, slightly warped but very hard bricks used for rustic paving purposes.

subgrade
The leveled surface of the ground, ready for the subflooring, such as a concrete slab, to be put in place.

finish floor

raised flooring system
A flooring system in which large removable elements, supported on pedestals or stringers, leave a hollow space underneath; used when a complex cable system needs to be accessible.

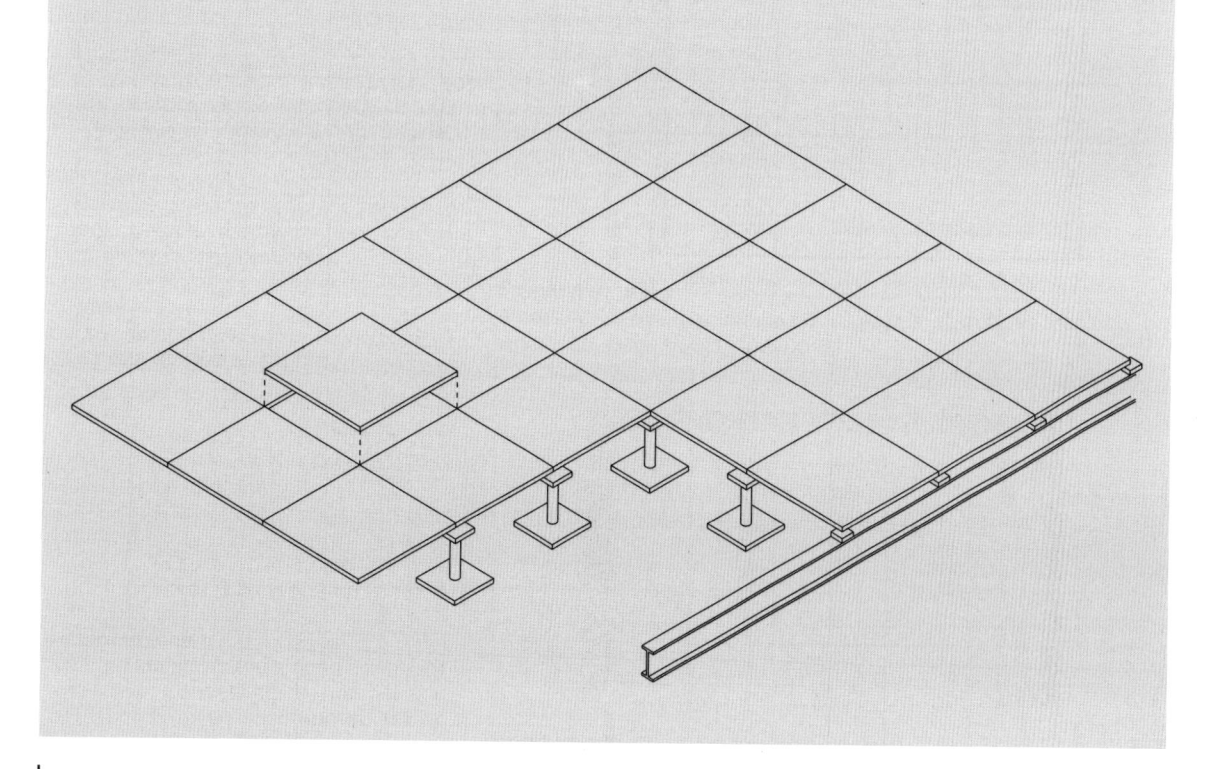

• baseboard
A flat strip of wood or other washable material attached to the base of the interior walls to protect them from wear and conceal the joint of the walls and the floor. Also called mopboard, scrubboard, skirting board, washboard.

• base molding (USA)
A molding used to conceal the joint between a baseboard and the wall. Also called base cap or base moulding (G.B.).

base shoe
A molding (U.S.A.) or moulding (G.B.) used to conceal the joint between the floor and the baseboard. Also called base shoe molding, floor molding, shoe molding (U.S.A.), or base shoe moulding, floor moulding, or shoe moulding (G.B.).

finish floor

thick-set process
A floor-tiling method in which the tiles are laid on a layer of mortar between 3/4" and 1 1/2" thick (20 to 40 mm), that has been spread with the precise level or slope required.

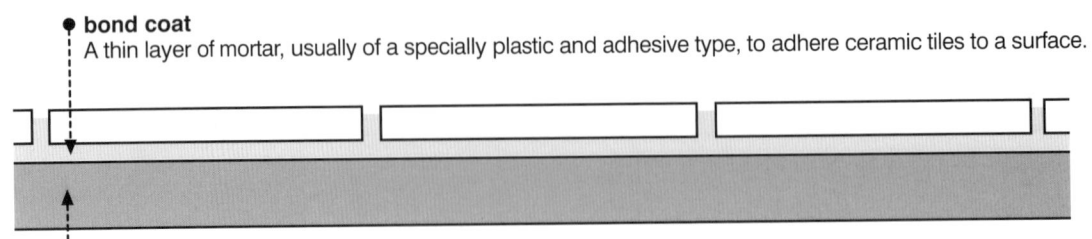

bond coat
A thin layer of mortar, usually of a specially plastic and adhesive type, to adhere ceramic tiles to a surface.

portland cement mortar
A mixture of portland cement, sand, and water. Added lime increases the plasticity, other admixtures change its properties in a variety of ways.

thin-bed process
A floor tiling method in which the tiles are laid on a thin layer of special adhesive mortar, epoxy mortar or an organic adhesive, between 1/32" and 1/8" thick (0,8 to 3,22 mm), attaching them to an already leveled and set subfloor such as a concrete slab.

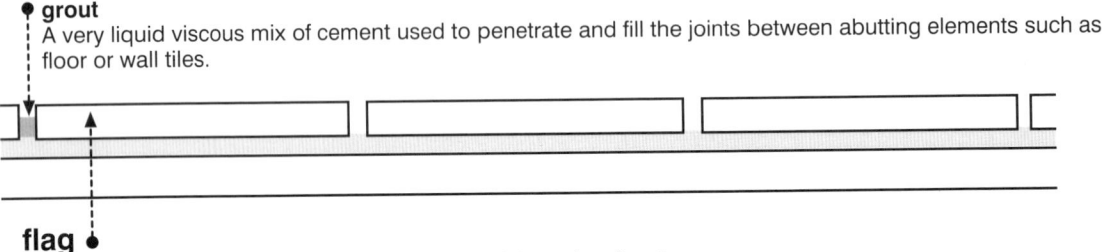

grout
A very liquid viscous mix of cement used to penetrate and fill the joints between abutting elements such as floor or wall tiles.

flag
A small plaque of ceramic, stone, or other material used as flooring.

glazed wall tile
A glazed wall tile used on surfaces undergoing little friction.

asphalt tile
A floor tile made of asbestos fibers, sandstone particles, mineral pigments and an asphalt or resinous binder, designed to be laid on a wood or concrete subfloor.

ceramic tile
A glazed tile used to clad walls or floors where little friction is expected.

cork tile
A tile made of granulated cork bound with synthetic resins; its surface is usually protected by a resistant varnish or a film of vinyl chloride.

slat block
A flooring tile consisting of several wooden elements joined to form a pattern.

cocofiber slab
A flooring material made of coconut fibers.

finish floor

terrazzo
A very hardy paving tile made of a mixture of mortar or cement with stone fragments and mineral pigments; when polished it produces a mosaic-like impression.

standard terrazzo
A type of terrazzo in which relatively small stones are predominant.

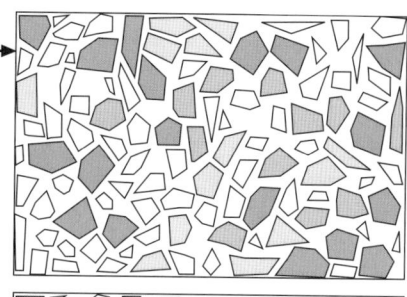

berliner
A type of terrazzo paving tiles in which pieces of marble are hand-placed producing a pattern, and the gaps are filled in with smaller pieces. Also called Palladiana.

rustic terrazzo
Terrazzo which presents a rough finish; the cast is washed before it sets, and is left unpolished.

Venetian terrazzo
A type of polished terrazzo in which large stones are predominant, surrounded by little ones to fill in the gaps.

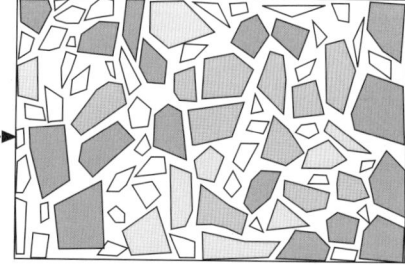

thin-set terrazzo
A finish layer of terrazzo spread directly over a subfloor of concrete, wood or metal.

underbed
A layer of weak cement and sand mortar over which the finish layer of terrazzo will be applied.

monolithic terrazzo
A layer of terrazzo applied in situ directly over a still fresh base of concrete, to produce a seamless terrazzo finish. Contraction cracks tend to appear.

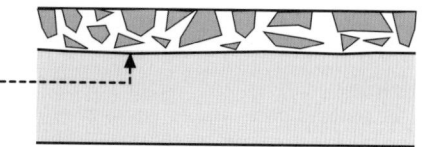

resinous matrix
One of the components of terrazzo, together with other resins or adhesives and stone fragments of various sizes. The resulting material is very resistant to abrasion and chemicals.

bonding agent
A chemical substance used to adhere or improve the adherence of a material to a substrate, such as previously set concrete to a new layer, or terrazzo to a subfloor.

sand-cushion terrazzo
A terrazzo floor having a layer of sand between it and the subfloor, to avoid cracks appearing if structural movements are foreseeable.

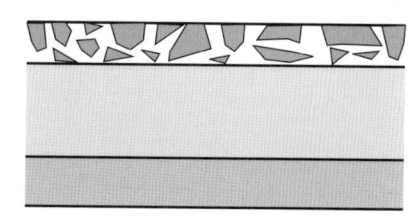

white portland cement
A type of portland cement made of components poor in iron, resulting in a whitish color suitable for terrazzo or staining with colors; light reflective, it is often used for roadworks, etc...

finish floor

wood flooring
A flooring method consisting of wooden boards, laid in parallel rows and fitted closely, usually tongue-and-groove.

plank flooring
A flooring method consisting of tongue-and-groove fitted planks laid directly over the beams or floor battens.

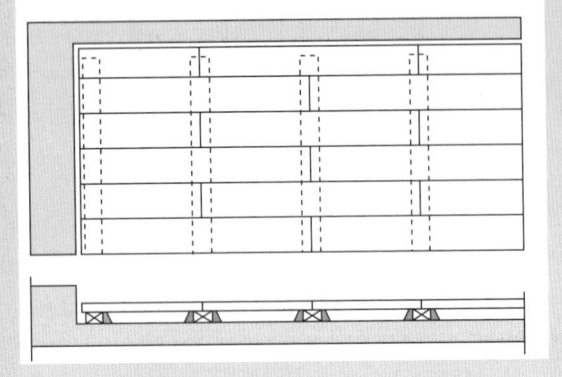

strip flooring
A fine hardwood flooring, usually oak or mahogany, consisting of narrow tongue-and-groove fitted boards or strips up to 4 inches wide, matched side-and-end.

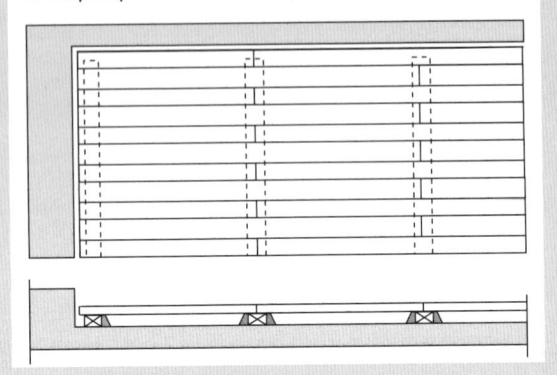

parquet
A wooden flooring supported by floor battens and consisting of short strips fitted together in different directions to create simple geometrical patterns.

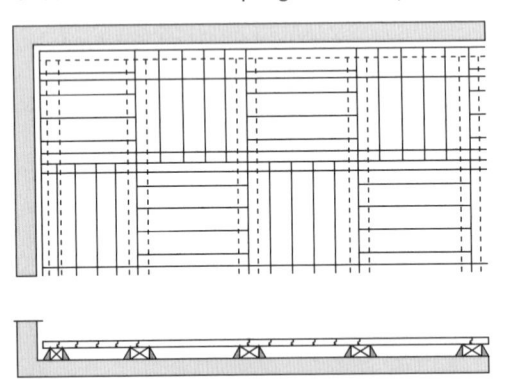

block flooring
A flooring method consisting of attaching wooden blocks directly onto the subfloor with an adhesive.

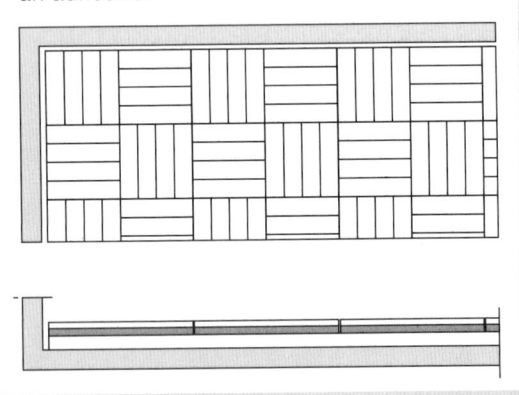

parquetry
A decorative flooring method consisting in joining different colored strips of wood, to form geometrical patterns which may be very intricate.

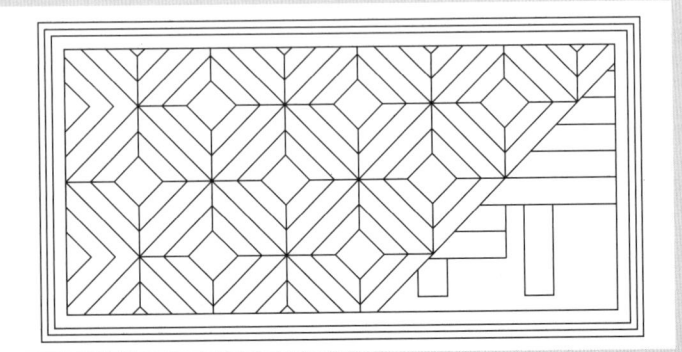

finish floor

solid block flooring
A floor which consists of solid blocks of wood joined with an adhesive.

block paving
A floor consisting of blocks of wood laid with the end-grain upwards and joined with an adhesive.

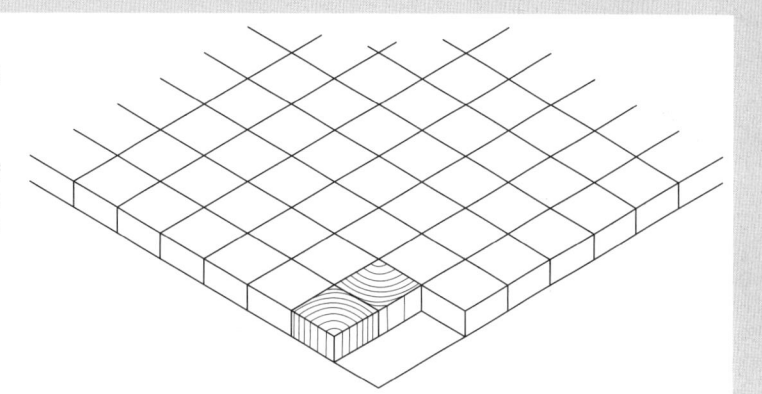

herringbone matching
A symmetrical pattern in which the wooden boards are placed with the grain alternately in a different direction, producing a zigzag effect.

book matching
A method of placing boards or veneer cut from the same flitch alternately facing a different way up, so the grains mirror each other across the joint producing symmetrical patterns.

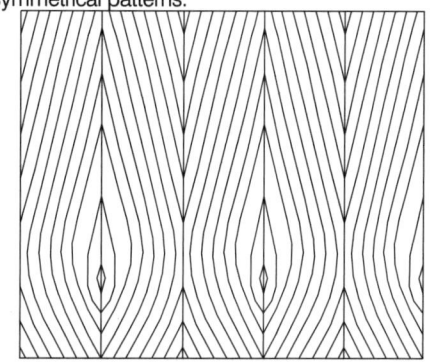

diamond matching
A wood veneer method consisting of matching 4 sheets so the grain is diagonally disposed around a center, creating a rhomboid pattern.

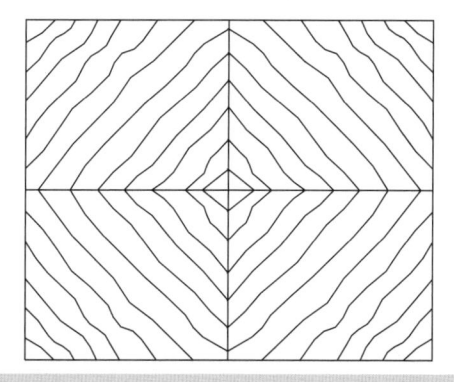

random matching
A wood floor consisting of boards or strips in which the pattern of the woodgrain is distributed randomly or with no apparent purpose.

finish floor

carpet
A thick flexible flooring of woven textile yarn or knotted pile, used to improve the appearance and warmth of a space.

tufted carpet
A non-woven carpet in which the pile has been inserted into the fabric and is held with an adhesive from the other side.

loop pile
A carpet in which the pile consists of a dense texture of looped or curled threads.

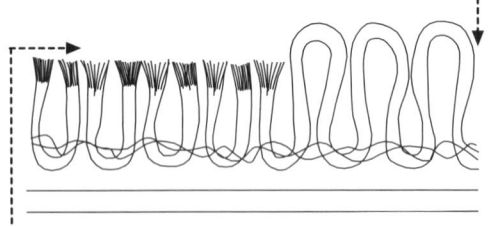

cut pile
A type of carpet in which the pile results from cutting the looped threads that have been inserted or knotted into the fabric.

flocked carpet
A carpet with a short pile that has been blown or projected electro-statically onto an adhesive surface, producing a suede-like effect.

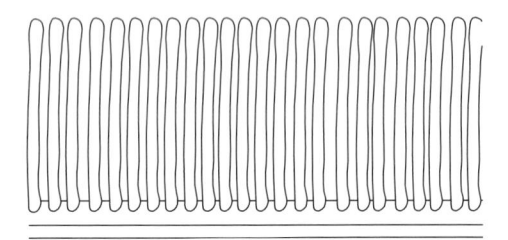

carpet underlay
A material combining the properties of foam rubber or hair felt with jute, to produce a padding layer between the carpet and the floor, adding insulation to the carpet and reducing the abrasive effect of the floor.

fusion-bonded carpet
A carpet manufactured by implanting the pile into a hot vinyl surface.

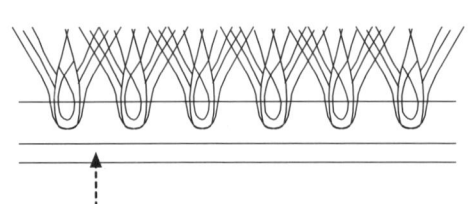

backing
The supporting fabric of a carpet, to which the pile is attached by means of knots, weaving, knitting, gluing, or inserting into a plastic material while it is hot.

knitted carpet
A carpet in which the warp, the weft and the pile are intertwined or knitted together in three different gauges of needlework.

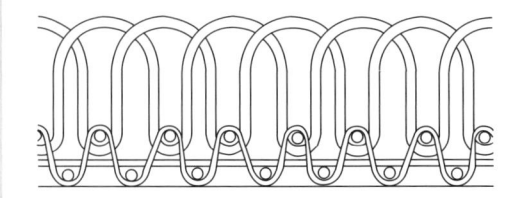

finish floor

stitched pile carpet, f
Carpet manufactured by fixing the pile tufts into an adhesive or woven backing, stitchng it in with a special needle.

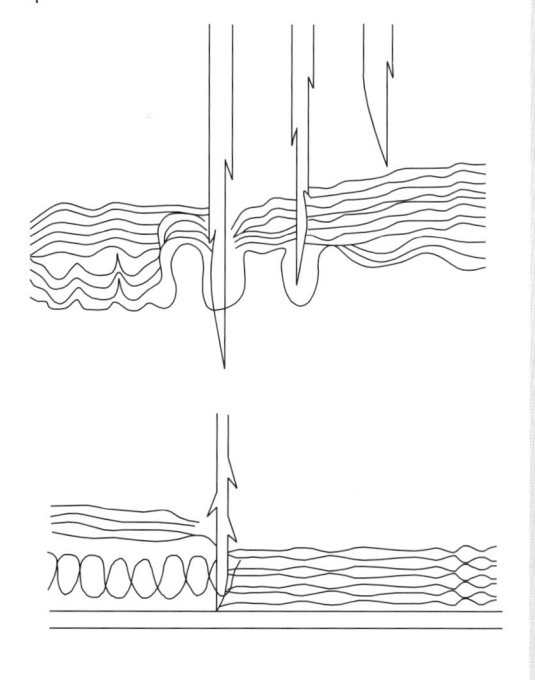

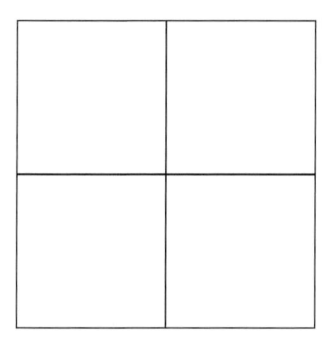

woven carpet, f
Carpet manufactured on a loom, by inserting and knotting tufts of pile into a woven textile fabric, by hand or mechanically.

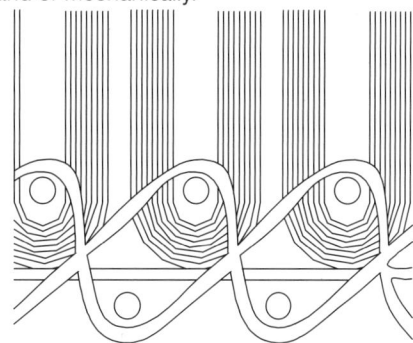

pile, m
Tufts of yarn inserted into a carpet's backing material to form the surface texture; the pile may be cut or in loops.

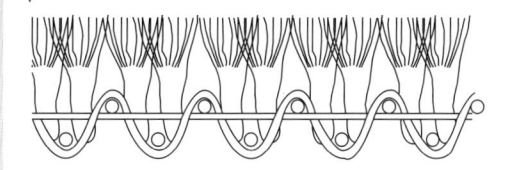

carpet tile, f
Carpet supplied in squares the approximate size of a paving tile.

pile density, f
Weight of the pile per unit of surface of carpet, expressed in grams (of pile) per square meter (of carpet).

pile weight, m
Average weight of a capet's pile, measured in grams per square meter of carpet.

ceiling

Any of the different finishes for the upper interior enclosure of a space or chamber.

---

cove ceiling
A ceiling that curves down to meet the walls, along a concave surrounding perimeter.

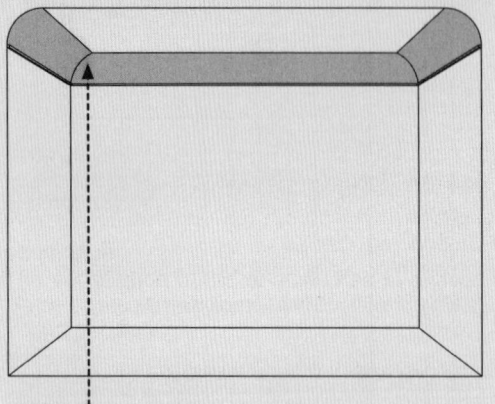

cove
A concave surface or molding, used frequently to finish the line where the ceiling and the walls meet.

beam ceiling
A ceiling in which the beams supporting the next floor are left exposed.

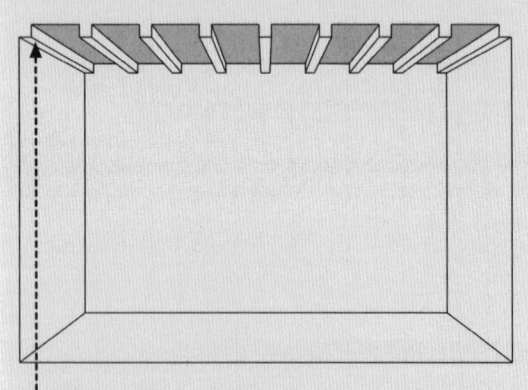

ceiling joist
Any of the small beams that support a ceiling, or which a ceiling is suspended from, usually connected to the main joists that support the floor above.

plafond
A ceiling, flat or arched, that is finished in a specifically decorative manner.

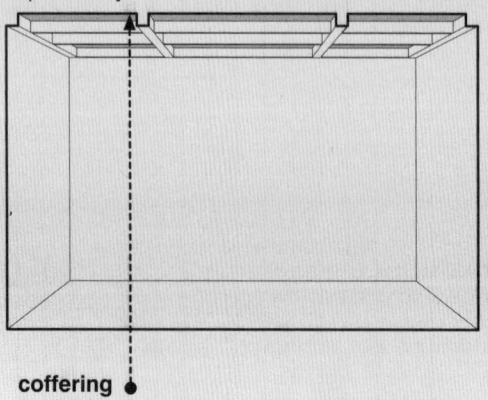

coffering
A highly ornamental ceiling with deep-set caissons, or coffers, surrounded by a network of moldings, creating a repetitive overall geometrical pattern.

Pavilion ceiling
A ceiling having the shape of a pyramid or truncated pyramid.

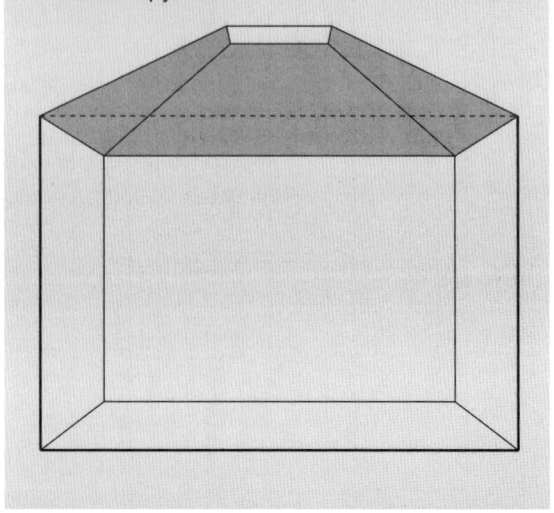

ceiling

false ceiling
A ceiling used to create a space for unsightly plumbing or electrical ducts, or to change the proportions of a room. Often suspended from the floor slab or structural elements overhead, and not bearing on the walls. Also called suspended or dropped ceiling.

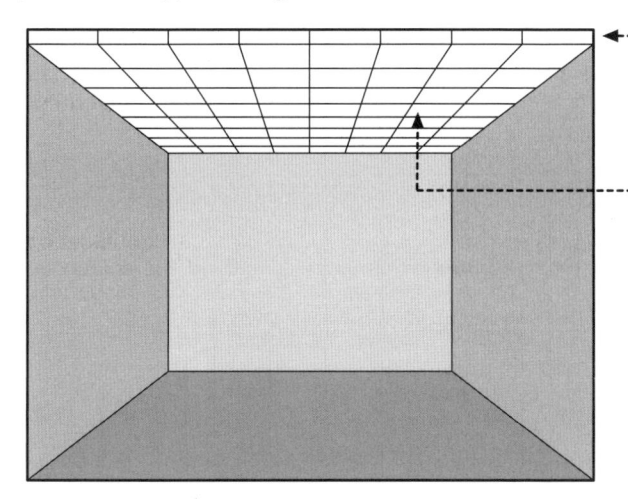

luminous ceiling
A ceiling made exclusively of translucent material, usually separate elements held in a suspended structure, evenly shedding the light from above.

area source
A light source of indefinite width and length such as a luminous ceiling or a window through which a space is illuminated.

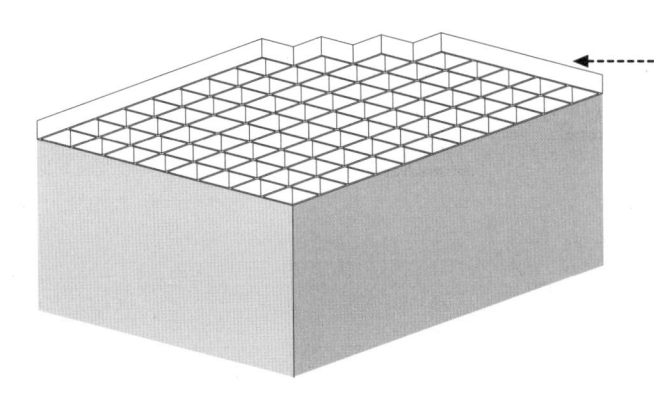

louvered ceiling
A suspended ceiling consisting of a multicellular network of louvers, used to conceal the light sources installed above it.

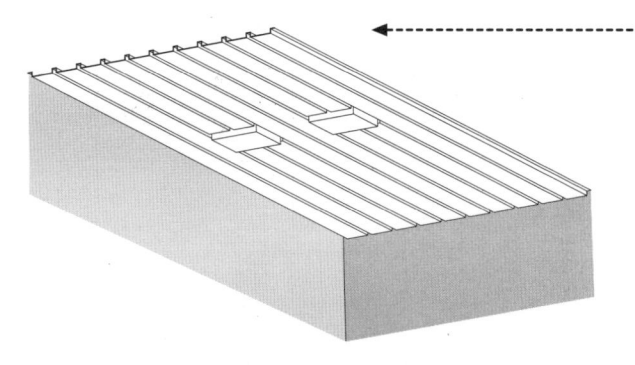

linear metal ceiling
A suspended ceiling system consisting of lightweight ribbed metal sheets, usually holding light-source frames and air-conditioning ducts.

ceiling

suspended ceiling
A ceiling used to create a space for unsightly plumbing or electrical ducts, or to change the proportions of a room. Often suspended from the floor slab or structural elements overhead, and not bearing on the walls. Also called a dropped ceiling or false ceiling.

acoustical ceiling
A suspended ceiling made of a sound absorbing material.

acoustic decking
A type of corrugated metal decking in which the corrugations are packed with glass wool; used as soundproof ceiling elements.

plenum
The space between a suspended ceiling and the structure supporting the floor above.

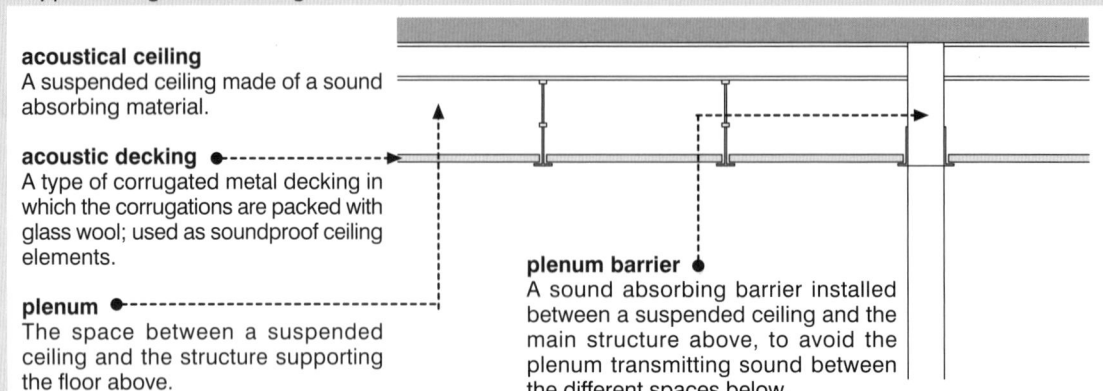

plenum barrier
A sound absorbing barrier installed between a suspended ceiling and the main structure above, to avoid the plenum transmitting sound between the different spaces below.

integrated ceiling
A suspended ceiling system that includes the air conditioning outlets and the light sources, which are integrated into the supporting grid.

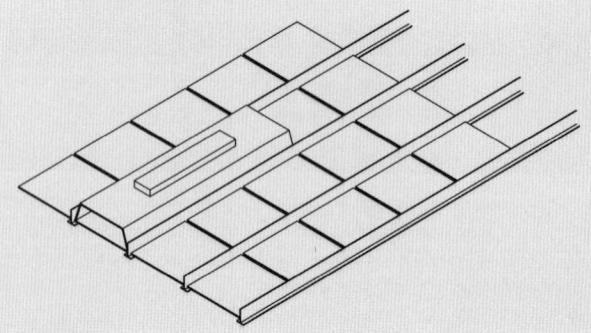

concealed grid ceiling
A suspended acoustical ceiling that conceals the metallic framework supporting the separate sheets.

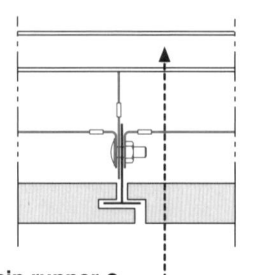

recessed grid ceiling
A suspended acoustical ceiling in which the supporting grid made of inverted T strips is recessed into the rabbeted edges of the individual sheets.

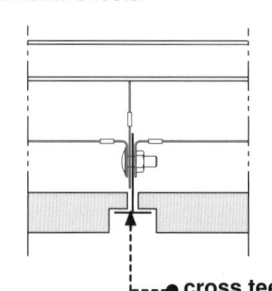

exposed grid ceiling
A suspended ceiling in which nothing conceals the inverted-T grid supporting the soundproof sheets.

main runner
The main supporting element of a suspended ceiling grid, usually a 1 1/2 inch (3,8 cm) inverted-T iron, hung from the main structure supporting the floor above.

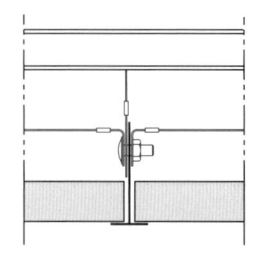

cross tee
The lightweight inverted T-irons between the main runners, used as secondary members of the support grid of a suspended ceiling.

thermal insulation

Any material manufactured and used for its high level of resistance to heat flow or its low thermal conductivity.

thatch
A roof covering technique whereby bundles of reeds, palm leaves in tropical countries, or straw, are attached to a steep pitched roof to shed the rainwater and provide thermal insulation.

reflective insulation
A thermally insulating material with a high level of heat reflectivity and a low level of radiant heat emission, thereby reducing thermal conduction through air spaces.

structural insulating roof deck
An insulating board made of wood shavings and portland cement, suitable to go directly over the unconcealed roof joists; comparatively strong, it can support the placement of a light concrete roof deck.

batt insulation
A flexible, blanket-like material used for thermal and acoustic insulation; made of rock or glass fibers, it may be faced with paper and have a vapor barrier; often used where flexibility is required, as in frame construction.

fiberglass (USA)
Glass fibers of molten glass pulled into fine shreds and bunched into a wool-like mass of various densities, used for insulation; or spun into filaments of diameters from 10 to 30 ym., and used to make insulating textiles or reinforce other materials; also called fibreglass (G.B.).

glass wool
Glass filaments spun into a wool-like yarn used for thermal and acoustic insulation, and for the reinforcement of other materials.

mineral wool
A material consisting of light inorganic fibers processed from molten rock, glass or slag, used as acoustic and thermal insulation, and to reinforce other materials.

thermal barrier
An element of low thermal conductivity placed between parts of a building where heat flow needs to be prevented or reduced. Also called a thermal break.

double glazing
The installation of two or more sheets of glass over an opening, with an air space or a void between them, to prevent thermal and acoustic transmission, while allowing the passage of light.

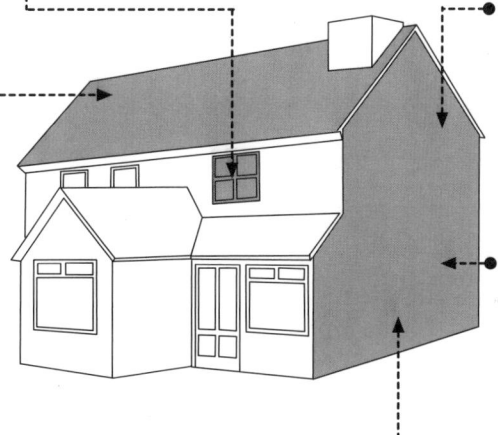

rigid board insulation
An insulating material manufactured as a rigid board capable of standing upright, and is also fire and damp proof.

polyurethane foam
A polyurethane foam, manufactured as nodules or as boards of bubble-like cells, used as thermal insulation.

extruded polystyrene
A polystyrene foam with a high thermal insulation value due to its structure of hollow bubble-like cells.

foam glass
A thermal insulation material manufactured by foaming molten glass, then molded into boards or blocks of sealed bubbles, with a density of 9 to 10 lb per cu ft (14.4 to 16 kg per cu m). Also called expanded or cellular glass.

plastic foam
An insulating material consisting of plastic that has been chemically, mechanically or thermally expanded and lightened by introducing bubbles of air or gas into its structure. Also called cellular plastic.

molded polystyrene (USA)
A polystyrene foam used for acoustic insulation because of its open cell structure; also called moulded polystyrene (G.B.).

foamed-in-place insulation
A plastic thermal insulation foam, for which the ingredients and the foaming agent are mixed immediately prior to being poured into the cavities ready for this purpose, or sprayed onto the walls.

loose-fill insulation
A thermal insulation material manufactured in loose granules, flakes, or fibers, so as to be poured manually, or otherwise, into the cavities or onto the appropriate surfaces.

damp proofing

waterproofing
A treatment for mortar or concrete, either as an admixture or a surface coating, to impede the passage or absorption of water or vapor. Also called waterproofing.

sweating
The process by which humidity from the air will condense upon any surface below dewpoint temperature, such as windowpanes or walls.

condensation
The transformation of vapor into liquid because the temperature drops below a given level, specific to each liquid.

surface condensation
The condensation of liquid on cold glass or when damp air comes into contact with surfaces below the dewpoint, i.e., the temperature at which the air becomes saturated.

damp course
A horizontal layer of a watertight material, such as dense limestone or metal, laid upon the lower course of a masonry wall to prevent damp ascending through the brickwork by capillary action. Also called damp check or damp proof course.

vapor retarder (USA)
A membrane covering the outside of the insulation around a cold water pipe, to prevent the damp from soaking the insulation and reaching the pipe. Also called vapour barrier (G.B.).

aluminum foil
A very thin aluminum sheeting, less than 0.006" thick (0.15 mm), normally used as part of an acoustic insulation system or as a vapor barrier.

pargeting (USA)
A thin layer of mortar with added dampproofing ingredients applied on the outside of masonry walls of basements, near the foundations, below grade. Also called pargetting (G.B.), pargework or parging.

cement-lime mortar
A mortar made with cement, sand and water, plus lime, to add plasticity and dampproofness to the mix.

damp proofing

cold-process roofing
A series of roofing systems consisting of asphalt felt or similar asphalt sheeting rolled on and sealed with asphalt mastic applied cold.

roofing felt
A waterproofing material consisting in asphalt saturated felt sheet, dressed with another more resistant layer of asphalt with mineral fibers or organic stabilizers; the side exposed may be coated with aluminum sheet or other solar protection; it is usually retailed in rolls. Also called asphalt prepared roofing, asphaltic felt, prepared roofing, roll roofing, rolled roofing, rolled strip roofing, roofing felt, sanded bituminous felt, saturated felt, self finished roofing felt.

protected membrane roof
A waterproof membrane that also provides insulation from extreme temperatures by means of a rigid insulation board coated by a layer of gravel.

polyethylene
A plastic of low cost, suitable for use as cold water tubing and low temperature air conditioning ducts, it is mainly employed in membrane waterproofing. Also called polythene.

EPDM
A synthetic rubber, manufactured in waterproof sheets for roofing purposes.

fluid-applied roofing
A waterproof roofing system consisting of several coats of elastomeric material, producing a seamless membrane perfectly adapted to the surface and to any structural movements that might occur. Also called liquid roofing.

asphalt
A dark bituminous substance, with a plastic consistence varying from runny to tough, when it is hot or cold respectively; it is used for paving roads and as a waterproofing material on roofs.

coal tar
A dark brown substance obtained from coke-oven tar, hard when cold but soft above 65º C (about 150º F); used as a waterproofing agent on roofs.

bitumen
A semisolid combination of hydrocarbons derived from petroleum or coal; it is usually emulsified with a solvent or heated to a liquid state for use.

glazing tape
A resilient adhesive material manufactured as a tape or strip, used to make a waterproof seal between a pane of glass and the frame.

joint sealant
Any of the materials designed to fill the joints in a building, so as to create, when dry or cured, a flexible weatherproof seal.

compression gasket
A strip molding of extruded synthetic rubber designed to be fixed to a window-frame; firmly compressed by the pane of glass, it creates a waterproof seal.

sound

A sensation perceived when the ear captures vibrations that the air, or any other suitable environment, transmits as waves of oscillating pressure.

acoustics
The combined characteristics of an auditorium or other space liable to condition the perception of sound within that space. 2.The branch of physics that studies sound and sound waves, their generation, source, effects and transmission through different mediums.

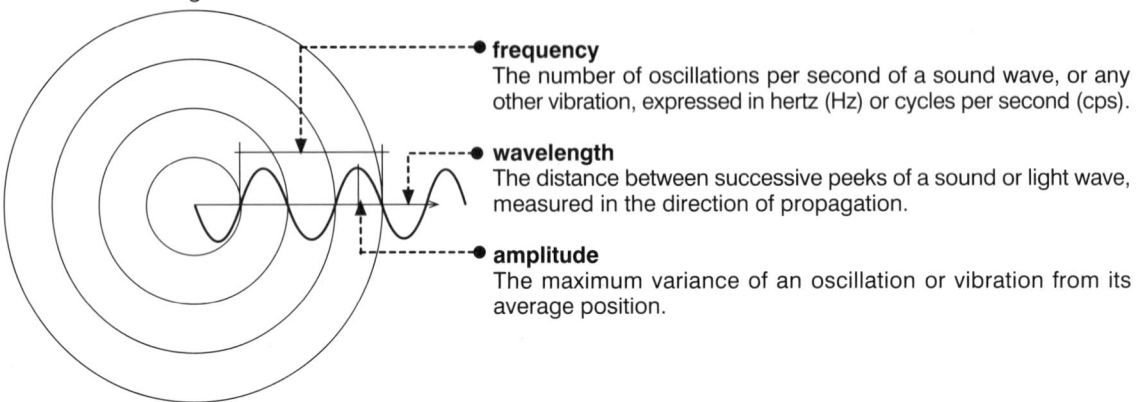

frequency
The number of oscillations per second of a sound wave, or any other vibration, expressed in hertz (Hz) or cycles per second (cps).

wavelength
The distance between successive peeks of a sound or light wave, measured in the direction of propagation.

amplitude
The maximum variance of an oscillation or vibration from its average position.

audio frequency
Any frequency of the oscillation of a sound wave audible for the human ear, generally between 15 and 20,000 Hz.

altitude
A quality of auditory sensation said to vary from high to low according to the high or low frequency of the sound wave.

speed of sound
The speed of sound depends on the medium it is propagating through; in air it travels at 0.340 Km/second (1087 feet); through water at 1,4 Km/second (4500 feet); through steel, at 5,5 Km/second (18.000 feet).

sound intensity
The average rate at which sound energy is transmitted through a given medium in a given direction; expressed in waves per unit of surface area.

loudness
The subjective response to a sound, not only due to the acoustic pressure, but also to the frequency and the shape of the sound wave creating the stimulus.

decibel
A unit in which measures of acoustical intensity are expressed; the symbol is dB.

sound intensity level
The acoustic intensity, expressed in decibels, equal to ten times the decimal logarithm of the quotient between the intensity of a given sound and the sound intensity established as the reference.

sound-power level
The level of sound power averaged over a period of time, the level used as reference being (10 to the minus twelfth power) watts.

transmission loss
The decibels of acoustic intensity that a given sound looses on its way through a given medium.

sound

reverberation
The persistence of a sound within a closed space after the emission of sound has ceased.

reverberation time
The reverberation of a given enclosed space measured in the length of time needed for a given sound pressure to fall 60 dB below the level it had when emitted.

resonance
The state of a system the vibration of which is abnormally increased by an external stimulus of a frequency nearly identical to that originally existing in the system.

sympathetic vibration
The vibration induced into a body by the proximity of an independent vibration source or other vibrating body.

sone
A unit of measure of loudness, or the apparent intensity of sound, the reference level of which is 40 dB with a frequency of 1000 Hz.

sound level meter
An instrument designed to measure the level of acoustic pressure; it has a microphone, an amplifier and a series of filters that assess the sound's different frequencies.

room acoustics
The characteristics of a given space that determine the intelligibility of speech and the perceptual fidelity of sound within it.

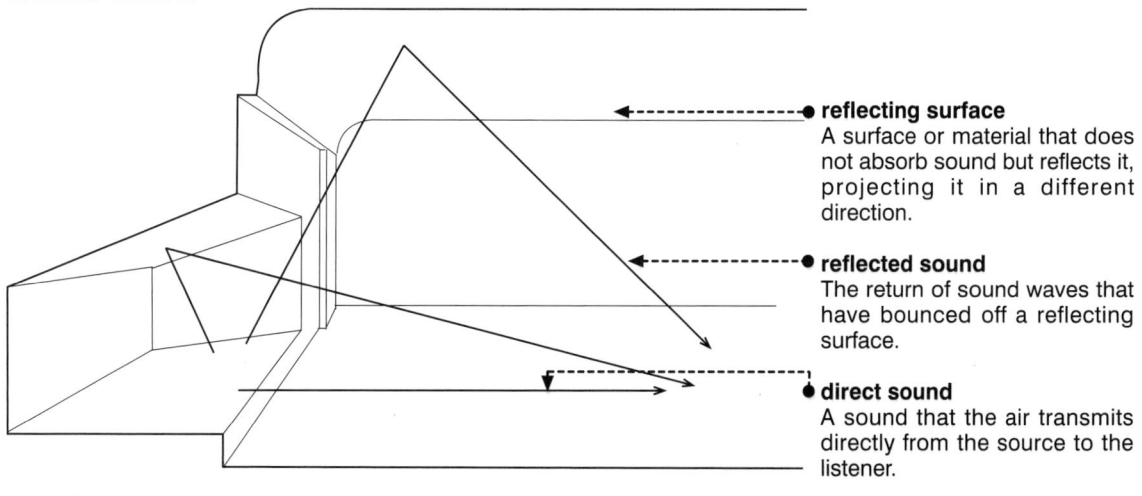

reflecting surface
A surface or material that does not absorb sound but reflects it, projecting it in a different direction.

reflected sound
The return of sound waves that have bounced off a reflecting surface.

direct sound
A sound that the air transmits directly from the source to the listener.

acoustics
The conjunction of physical characteristics of an auditorium or gathering space that condition the perception of the spoken or performed acoustic events liable to take place there.

acoustical analysis
The analysis of a building's use, type of construction, situation and orientation, plus possible sources of noise, as well as the ideal acoustic environment for each habitable unit.

acoustical design
The finishing and furnishing plan of an enclosed space aimed to improve its acoustic quality.

acoustic insulation
The operations undertaken to prevent sound escaping from an enclosed space to affect the surrounding environment, such as installing sound absorbent materials on the floor, ceiling and walls.

sound

sound insulation
The means and materials used to reduce sound transmission between parts of a building, or between the interior and the exterior. Also called sound isolation.

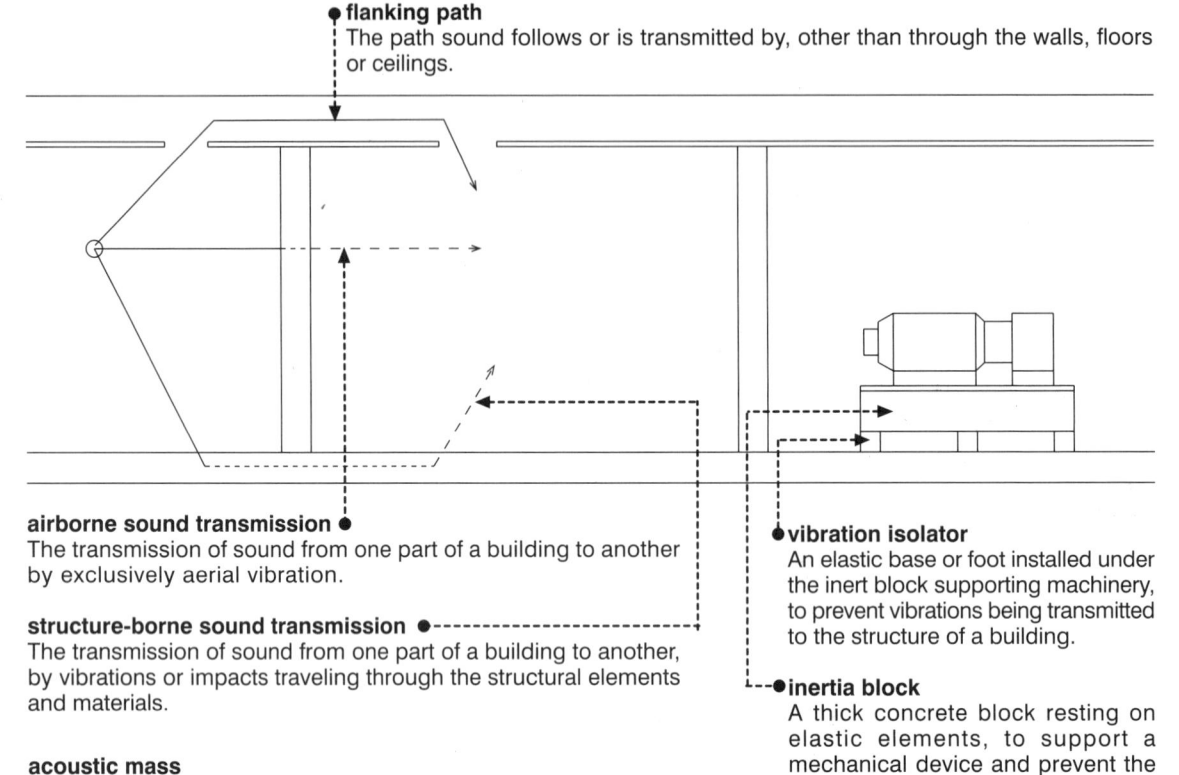

flanking path
The path sound follows or is transmitted by, other than through the walls, floors or ceilings.

airborne sound transmission
The transmission of sound from one part of a building to another by exclusively aerial vibration.

structure-borne sound transmission
The transmission of sound from one part of a building to another, by vibrations or impacts traveling through the structural elements and materials.

acoustic mass
The resistance of an object to transmit sound according to its weight and density, opposed to the inertia and elasticity of its sound transmitting environment.

soundproof
Said of materials that impede the transmission of sound.

discontinuous construction
The constructive strategies to interrupt the continuous structural links carrying sound to different parts of a building.

noise
Any sound that interferes with what people are listening to, or disturbs silence.

background noise
The fairly regular unidentifiable but characteristic sound coming from a variety of indoor and outdoor sources, other than what one is listening to. Also called ambient sound.

white noise
A homogenous noise with a continuous flat spectrum and a similar power per unit-frequency in all wave lengths. Also called white sound.

impact noise
Noises generated by impacts transmitted by the building's structure, such as footsteps or closing doors.

vibration isolator
An elastic base or foot installed under the inert block supporting machinery, to prevent vibrations being transmitted to the structure of a building.

inertia block
A thick concrete block resting on elastic elements, to support a mechanical device and prevent the transmission of vibrations to the structure of the building.

building typology

typology
Within a given field, the systematic classification of types according to their characteristics.

building
A habitable structure or construction of a more or less permanent nature, as opposed to ones that are movable or designed for a purpose other than their occupancy.

low-rise building
A building of two or three floors, usually without an elevator.

high-rise building
A building with a considerable number of floors, equipped with elevators; generally built in a densely populated area where the cost of land is high.

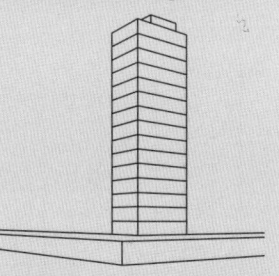

edifice
A building characterized by size and symbolic or ornamental importance.

skyscraper
A building of extraordinary height and number of floors.

mid-rise building
A building having roughly between 5 and 10 floors, generally equipped with elevators.

block
A group of buildings, of similar or different types, usually occupying a roughly rectangular piece of urban land surrounded by streets.

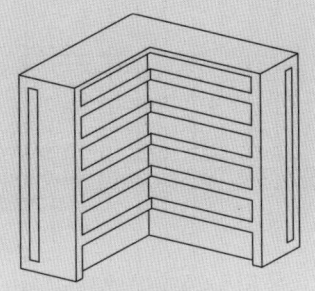

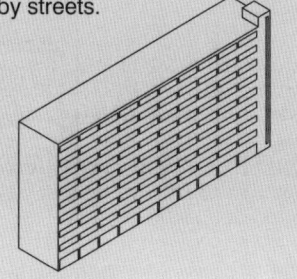

L-shaped building
A building having two wings that meet forming a 90 degree angle.

loft building
A building with several floors of undivided interior space, formerly used for industrial activities.

base
The visible and differentiated lower part of a building's outer walls, having a more massive platform-like character for the building to rise from. Also called plinth.

building typology

temple
A building designed for the system of worship of a deity or deities.

church
A building especially designed for the cult and ceremonies of the Christian religion.

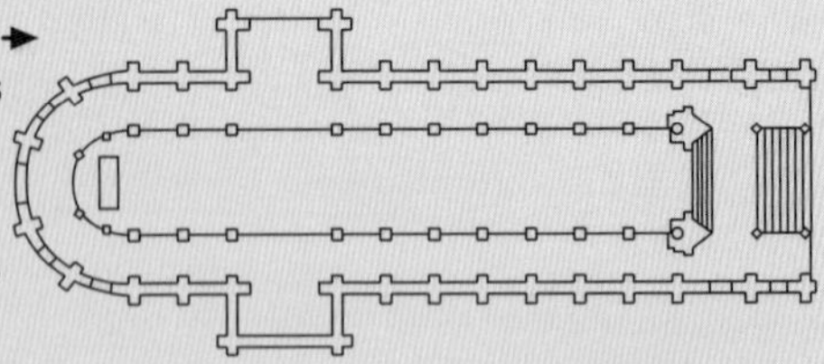

mosque
A religious building or temple dedicated to the Muslim faith.

synagogue
A building dedicated to the teaching and cult of the Jewish religion.

abbey
A building or set of buildings distributed in a manner such as to be inhabited by a religious order under the rule of an abbot or abbess.

rotunda
A building with a circular floor-plan surmounted by a dome.
2. A spacious circular space within a building, with a dome ceiling.

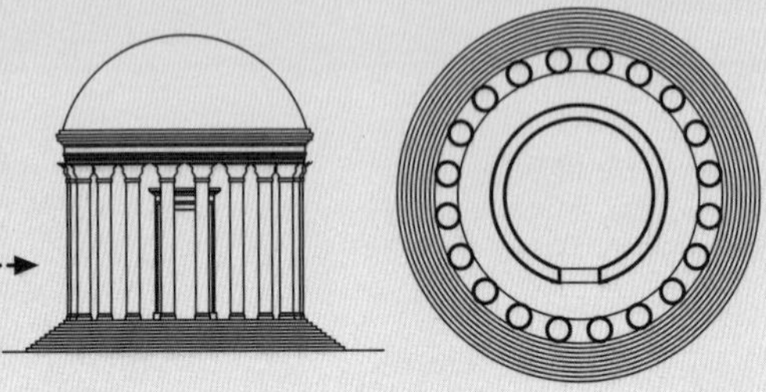

residential building
A building consisting of independent living spaces that share public areas like stairs, elevators, corridors and lobbies. Also called apartment house.

apartment building
A building consisting of compact temporary dwelling units that share public areas like stairs, elevators, corridors, lobbies, and sometimes dining rooms. Also called apartment house.

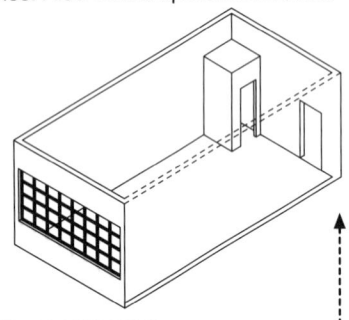

studio apartment
Apartment consisting of a single space to accommodate the functions of dining room, living room, and bedroom, with a kitchenette and separate bathroom. Also called a bed-sit, bed-sitter, efficiency apartment or studio.

condominium
A type of real estate ownership within a multifamily dwelling, in which each proprietor owns 100% of his private apartment and a share of the public facilities such as corridors, lobbies, garden, plumbing installation, etc.

cooperative apartment building
A building owned by a non-profit corporation of stockholders, who lease portions of the building as tenants, and whose periodic payments cover maintenance costs. Also called a residential cooperative.

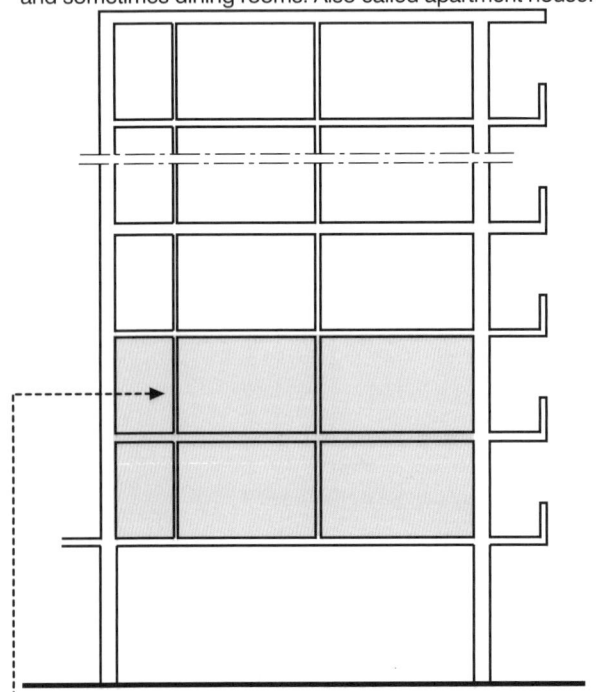

duplex apartment
In an apartment building, a dwelling unit occupying two levels with private access between them. Also called duplex or maisonette.

150

building typology

house
A building used as a place of residence or abode.

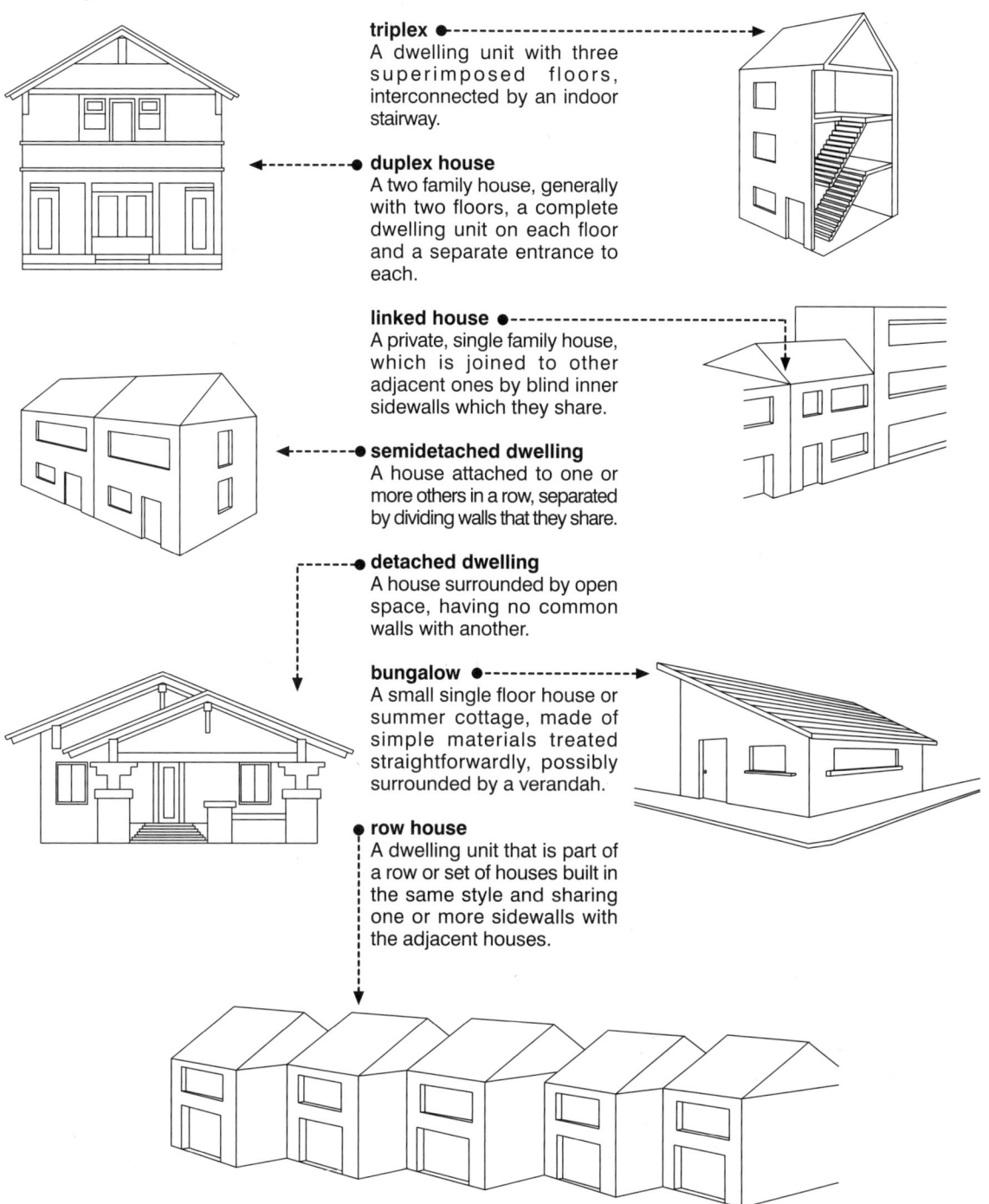

triplex
A dwelling unit with three superimposed floors, interconnected by an indoor stairway.

duplex house
A two family house, generally with two floors, a complete dwelling unit on each floor and a separate entrance to each.

linked house
A private, single family house, which is joined to other adjacent ones by blind inner sidewalls which they share.

semidetached dwelling
A house attached to one or more others in a row, separated by dividing walls that they share.

detached dwelling
A house surrounded by open space, having no common walls with another.

bungalow
A small single floor house or summer cottage, made of simple materials treated straightforwardly, possibly surrounded by a verandah.

row house
A dwelling unit that is part of a row or set of houses built in the same style and sharing one or more sidewalls with the adjacent houses.

building typology

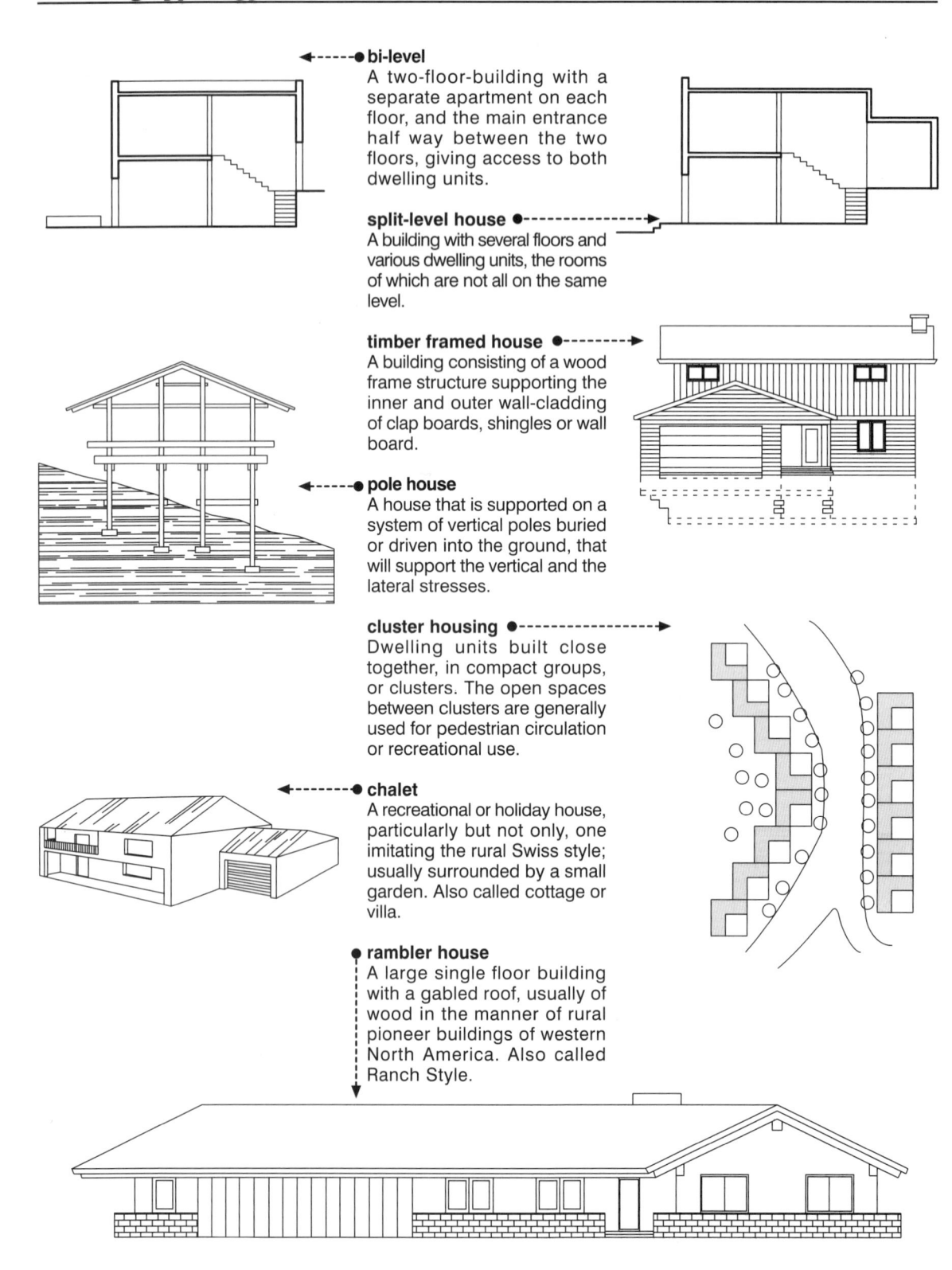

bi-level
A two-floor-building with a separate apartment on each floor, and the main entrance half way between the two floors, giving access to both dwelling units.

split-level house
A building with several floors and various dwelling units, the rooms of which are not all on the same level.

timber framed house
A building consisting of a wood frame structure supporting the inner and outer wall-cladding of clap boards, shingles or wall board.

pole house
A house that is supported on a system of vertical poles buried or driven into the ground, that will support the vertical and the lateral stresses.

cluster housing
Dwelling units built close together, in compact groups, or clusters. The open spaces between clusters are generally used for pedestrian circulation or recreational use.

chalet
A recreational or holiday house, particularly but not only, one imitating the rural Swiss style; usually surrounded by a small garden. Also called cottage or villa.

rambler house
A large single floor building with a gabled roof, usually of wood in the manner of rural pioneer buildings of western North America. Also called Ranch Style.

building typology

igloo
A dome shaped building made of ice blocks, though other shapes and materials (wood, skins and earth) may be used. Also called iglu.

tepee
A North American Plains Indian tent, consisting of a series of wooden poles standing around a circular floor plan, with the ends crossing high up in the centre; the resulting conical volume is covered with animal hides with a ventilation hole left open at the apex. Also called teepee.

trullo
A rural dwelling unit characteristic of southern Italy, made of dry stone walls around a circular floor plan divided into several spaces, covered by a domed corbel-vaulted roof.

yurt
A circular tent with walls built of posts and a conical roof supported by poles, covered with animal hides or textiles; used by Mongolian nomads in Central Asia.

wigwam
A North American Indian tent, consisting of a domed frame of wooden poles covered with animal hides or tree bark, enclosing a circular floor plan.

hogan
A hut typical of the Navajo Indians, with inward slanting walls made of poles and a wood supported sloped roof, all sealed with clay, sods, or tepe.

cabin, hut
A rustic, single space habitation made of materials readily available in the immediate environment.

building typology

theater (USA)
A closed building or an open space designed specifically for the performance of theatrical events; also called theatre (G.B.).

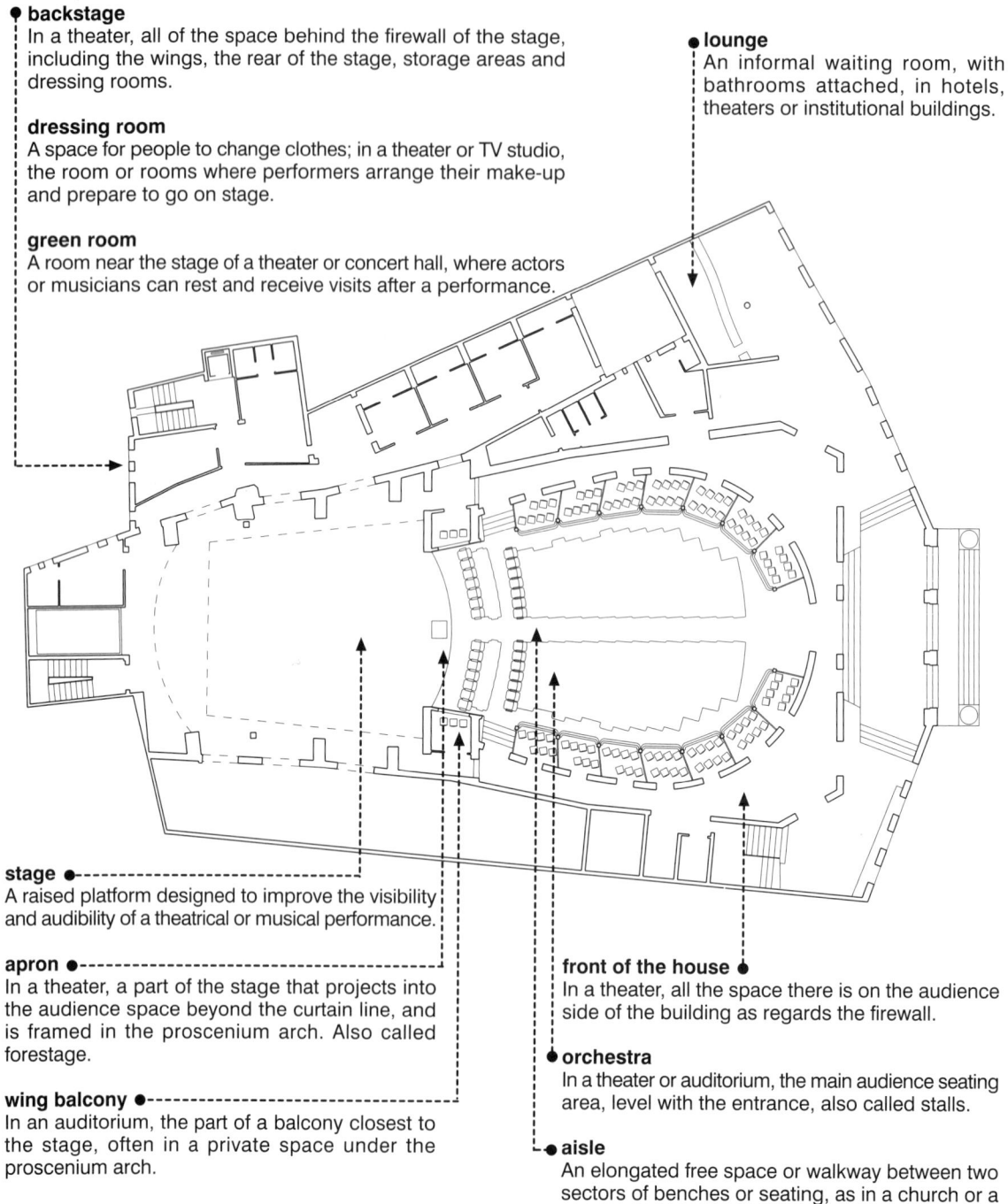

- **backstage**
  In a theater, all of the space behind the firewall of the stage, including the wings, the rear of the stage, storage areas and dressing rooms.

- **dressing room**
  A space for people to change clothes; in a theater or TV studio, the room or rooms where performers arrange their make-up and prepare to go on stage.

- **green room**
  A room near the stage of a theater or concert hall, where actors or musicians can rest and receive visits after a performance.

- **lounge**
  An informal waiting room, with bathrooms attached, in hotels, theaters or institutional buildings.

- **stage**
  A raised platform designed to improve the visibility and audibility of a theatrical or musical performance.

- **apron**
  In a theater, a part of the stage that projects into the audience space beyond the curtain line, and is framed in the proscenium arch. Also called forestage.

- **wing balcony**
  In an auditorium, the part of a balcony closest to the stage, often in a private space under the proscenium arch.

- **front of the house**
  In a theater, all the space there is on the audience side of the building as regards the firewall.

- **orchestra**
  In a theater or auditorium, the main audience seating area, level with the entrance, also called stalls.

- **aisle**
  An elongated free space or walkway between two sectors of benches or seating, as in a church or a theater.

building typology

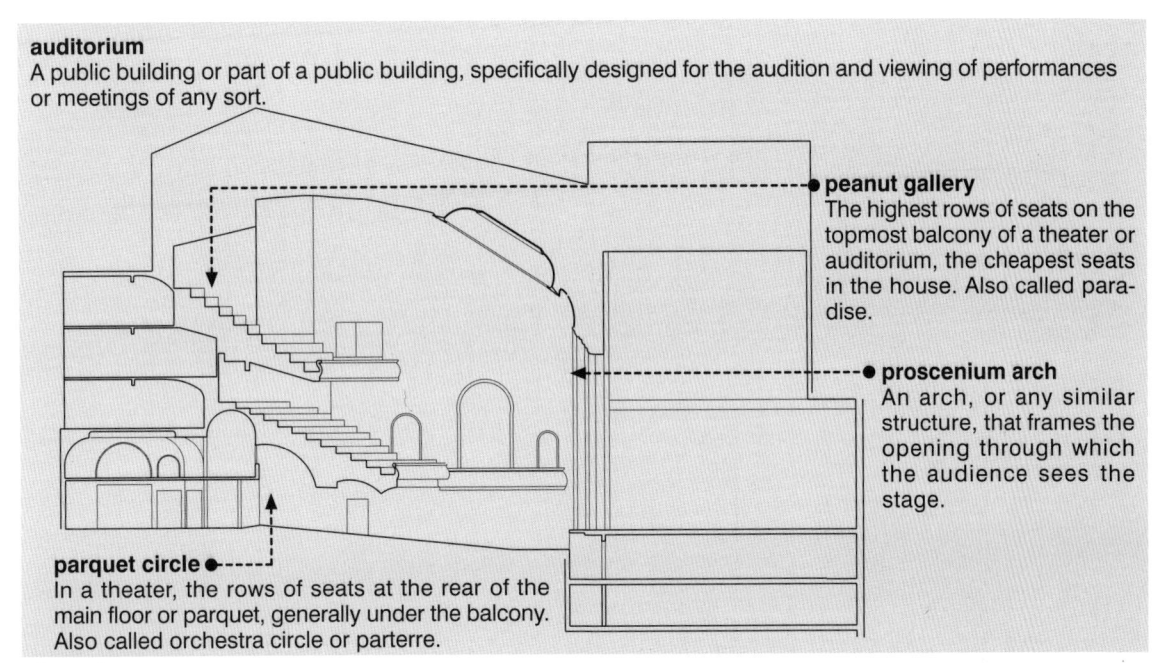

auditorium
A public building or part of a public building, specifically designed for the audition and viewing of performances or meetings of any sort.

peanut gallery
The highest rows of seats on the topmost balcony of a theater or auditorium, the cheapest seats in the house. Also called paradise.

proscenium arch
An arch, or any similar structure, that frames the opening through which the audience sees the stage.

parquet circle
In a theater, the rows of seats at the rear of the main floor or parquet, generally under the balcony. Also called orchestra circle or parterre.

stagehouse
In a theater, all of the building on the stage side of the proscenium wall, including the areas housing the stage machinery, dressing rooms and storage areas.

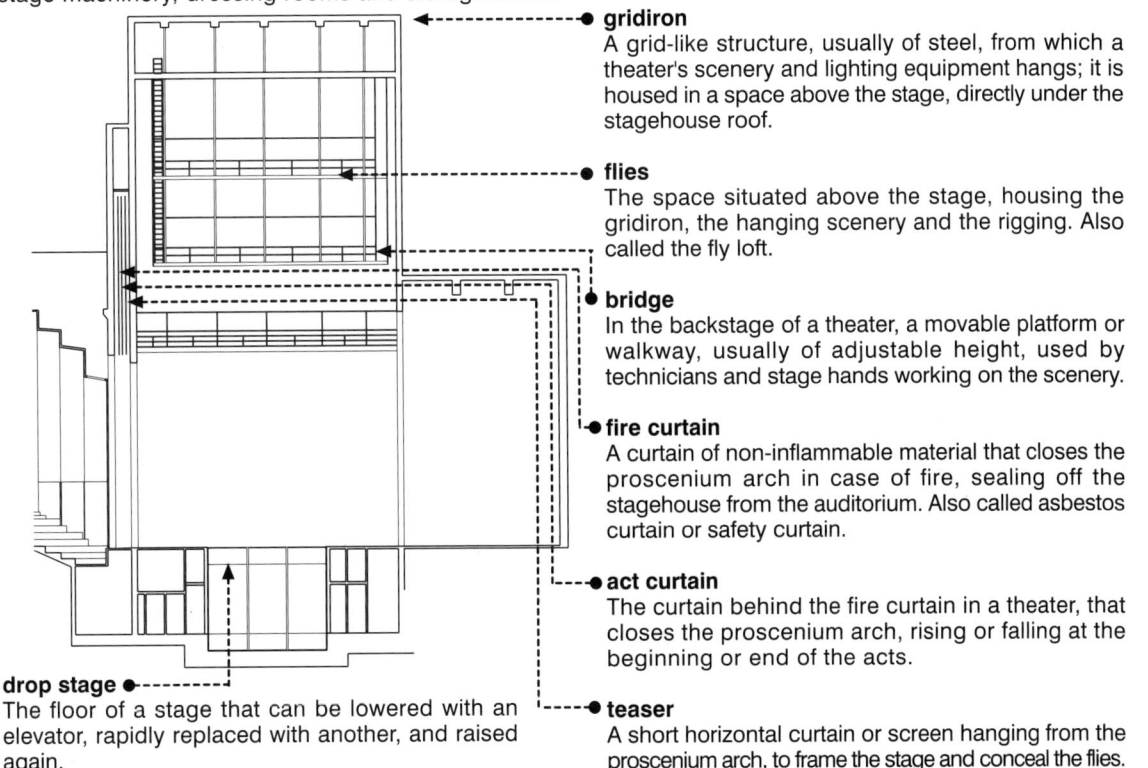

gridiron
A grid-like structure, usually of steel, from which a theater's scenery and lighting equipment hangs; it is housed in a space above the stage, directly under the stagehouse roof.

flies
The space situated above the stage, housing the gridiron, the hanging scenery and the rigging. Also called the fly loft.

bridge
In the backstage of a theater, a movable platform or walkway, usually of adjustable height, used by technicians and stage hands working on the scenery.

fire curtain
A curtain of non-inflammable material that closes the proscenium arch in case of fire, sealing off the stagehouse from the auditorium. Also called asbestos curtain or safety curtain.

act curtain
The curtain behind the fire curtain in a theater, that closes the proscenium arch, rising or falling at the beginning or end of the acts.

drop stage
The floor of a stage that can be lowered with an elevator, rapidly replaced with another, and raised again.

teaser
A short horizontal curtain or screen hanging from the proscenium arch, to frame the stage and conceal the flies.

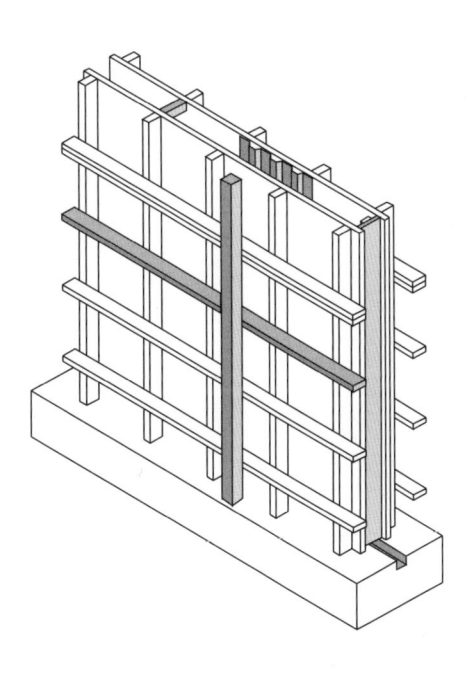

construction

Wood
Metal
Concrete
Brick
Block
Nail
Screw
Bolt
Tool

wood

A hard, fibrous material of which the trunk and branches of trees are constituted;
its workability makes it highly usable in construction.

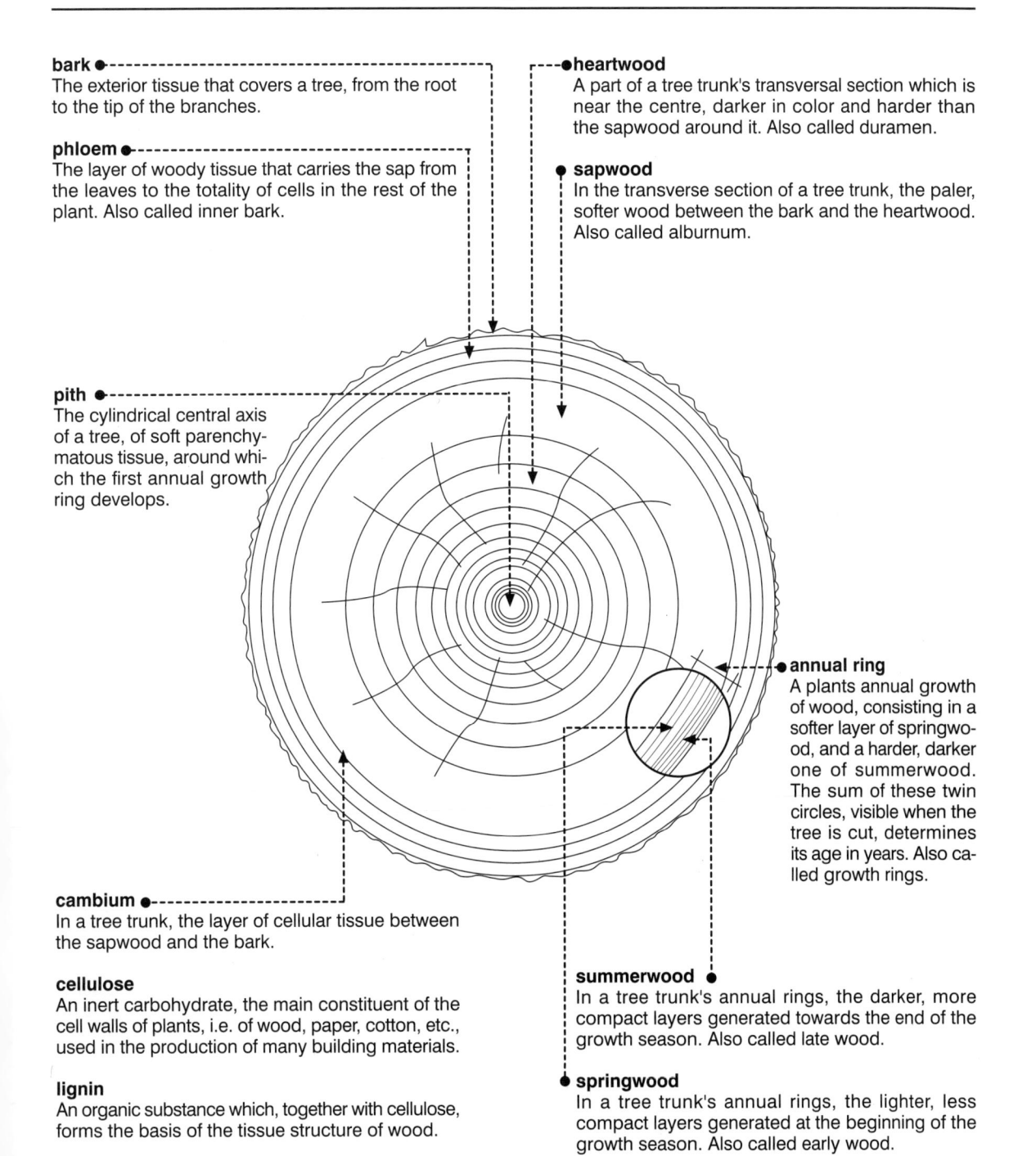

bark
The exterior tissue that covers a tree, from the root to the tip of the branches.

phloem
The layer of woody tissue that carries the sap from the leaves to the totality of cells in the rest of the plant. Also called inner bark.

pith
The cylindrical central axis of a tree, of soft parenchymatous tissue, around which the first annual growth ring develops.

heartwood
A part of a tree trunk's transversal section which is near the centre, darker in color and harder than the sapwood around it. Also called duramen.

sapwood
In the transverse section of a tree trunk, the paler, softer wood between the bark and the heartwood. Also called alburnum.

annual ring
A plants annual growth of wood, consisting in a softer layer of springwood, and a harder, darker one of summerwood. The sum of these twin circles, visible when the tree is cut, determines its age in years. Also called growth rings.

cambium
In a tree trunk, the layer of cellular tissue between the sapwood and the bark.

cellulose
An inert carbohydrate, the main constituent of the cell walls of plants, i.e. of wood, paper, cotton, etc., used in the production of many building materials.

lignin
An organic substance which, together with cellulose, forms the basis of the tissue structure of wood.

summerwood
In a tree trunk's annual rings, the darker, more compact layers generated towards the end of the growth season. Also called late wood.

springwood
In a tree trunk's annual rings, the lighter, less compact layers generated at the beginning of the growth season. Also called early wood.

wood

fiber (USA)
Each of the elongated cells which constitute the supporting structure of the body of plants. Also called fibre (GB).

coarse-grained
Descriptive of wood having a wide space between the annual rings due to its rapid growth; usually of a softer consistency. Also called open grained, wide grained or wide ringed.

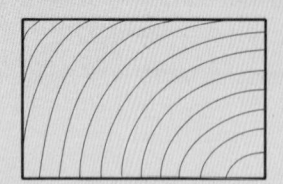

narrow-ringed
Descriptive of wood the annual rings of which are very close, indicating slow growth. Also called close grained, fine grained, close grown, or slow grown.

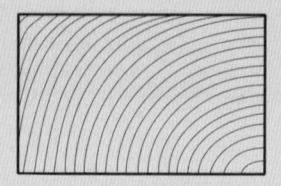

coarse texture
Descriptive of wood with an open cell structure, which requires filling to achieve a sealed finish. Also called coarse grain, or open grain.

fine textured
Descriptive of wood with an even texture of tightly spaced cells or pores. Also called fine grained, or fine grown.

sound knot
A knot that has the same consistence as the rest of the wood around it.

intergrown knot
A knot whose growth rings are interwoven with the rest of the wood.

dead knot
A knot without fibrous connections to the rest of the wood, and may easily fall out; encased knot or loose knot.

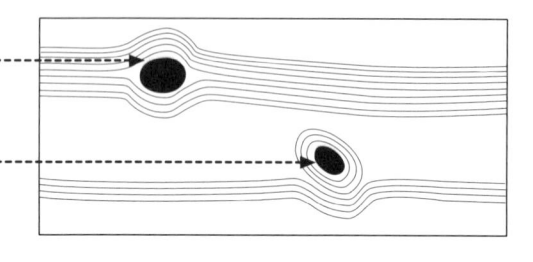

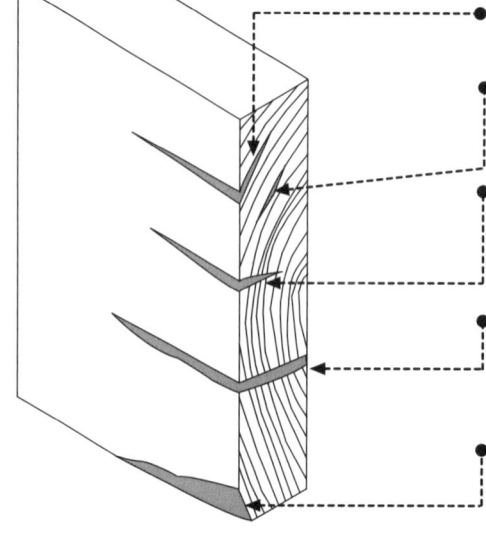

ring shake
A crack occurring between the wood's annual rings.

pitch pocket
A cavity between the annual rings of a soft wood, containing liquid or dry resin; also called resin pocket.

check
Small cracks running along the grain and across the rings, affecting wood due to contraction in the drying process; see heart shake, starshake.

split
A crack along the grain and across the rings, affecting the whole thickness of the wood, due to contraction in the drying process; also heart shake, starshake.

wane
A missing strip of wood along the profile or edge of a piece of lumber, often due to splitting of the rings when sawing.

wood

warp
Distortion of an object's orthogonal shape. In lumber, alterations of the original straight edges and flat planes, usually due to uneven moisture or inadequate drying processes.

cup
A concave distortion of the transversal section of a piece of lumber, regarding the previously straight edge there was between the corners.

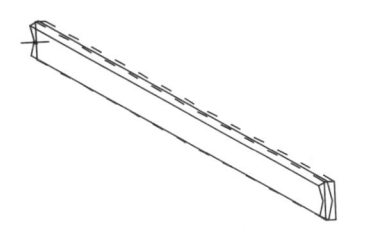

crook
Curvature of the longitudinal edges of a piece of lumber, as compared with a straight line drawn between its opposite ends.

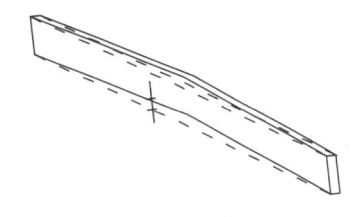

bow
The longitudinal curvature of a piece of lumber, a rod, a bar, or other originally straight element.

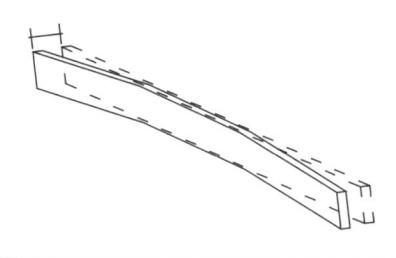

twist
The curvature of a piece of lumber resulting from a bend of its edges in opposite directions.

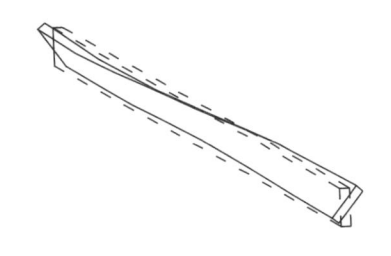

shrinkage
The decrease in volume of a piece of wood during the process of drying. The reduction in length is slight along the grain, but as much as 6% is usual for the transversal shrinkage of boards.

longitudinal shrinkage
The shrinkage of a piece of wood that occurs in a direction parallel to the grain, and amounts to roughly 2% of the radial shrinkage.

tangential shrinkage
The shrinkage of a piece of wood that occurs in a direction that is tangential to its annual growth rings.

radial shrinkage
The shrinkage of a piece of wood that occurs in a direction perpendicular to the grain, across the annual growth rings.

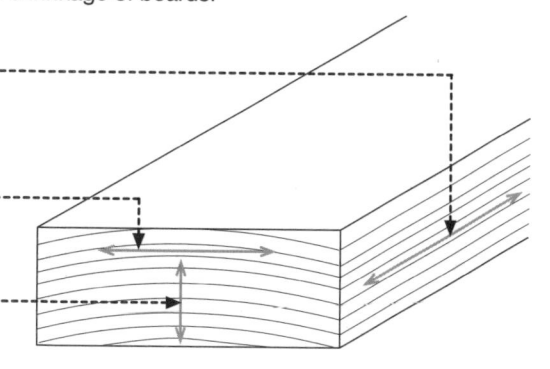

wood

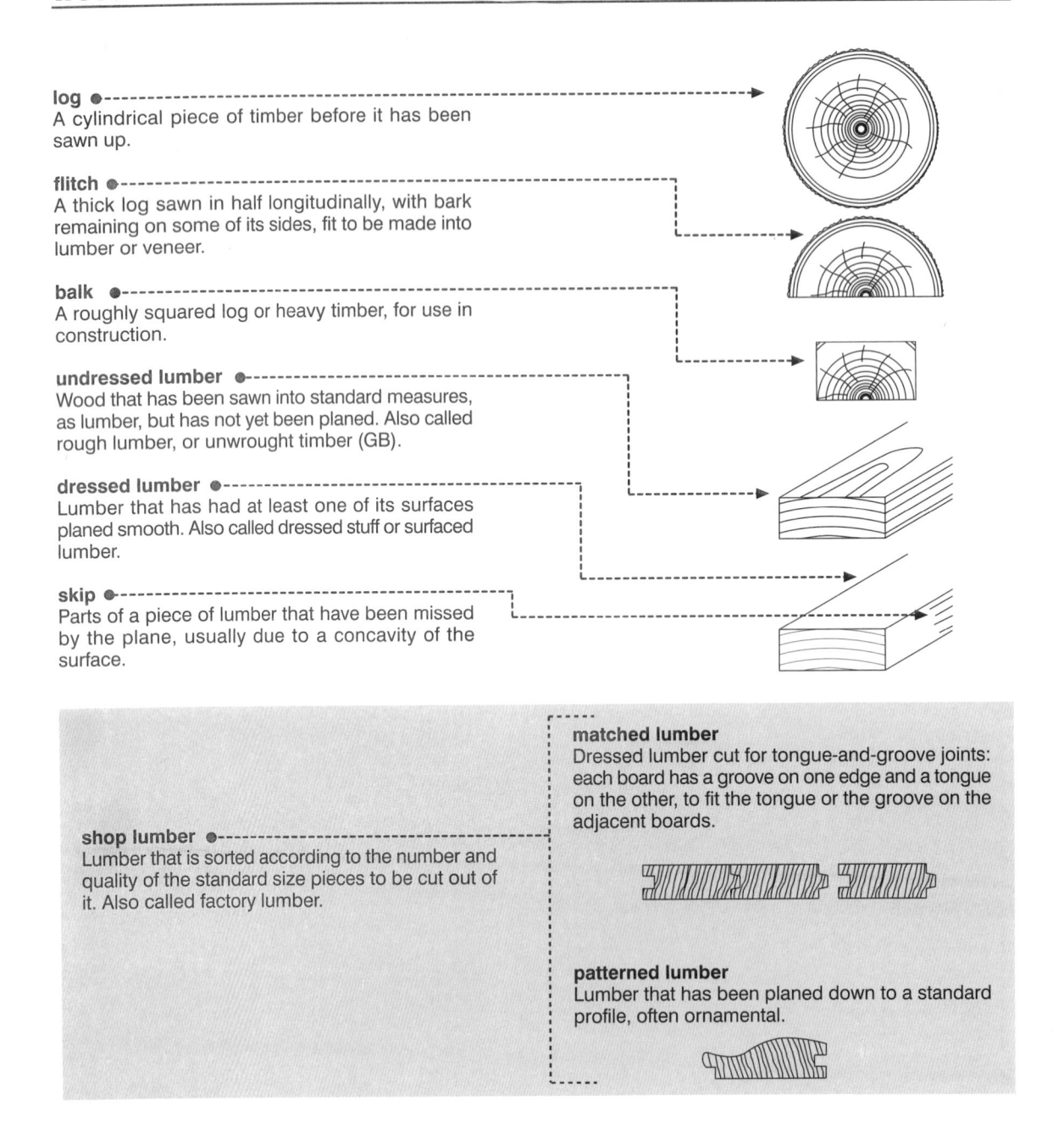

log
A cylindrical piece of timber before it has been sawn up.

flitch
A thick log sawn in half longitudinally, with bark remaining on some of its sides, fit to be made into lumber or veneer.

balk
A roughly squared log or heavy timber, for use in construction.

undressed lumber
Wood that has been sawn into standard measures, as lumber, but has not yet been planed. Also called rough lumber, or unwrought timber (GB).

dressed lumber
Lumber that has had at least one of its surfaces planed smooth. Also called dressed stuff or surfaced lumber.

skip
Parts of a piece of lumber that have been missed by the plane, usually due to a concavity of the surface.

shop lumber
Lumber that is sorted according to the number and quality of the standard size pieces to be cut out of it. Also called factory lumber.

matched lumber
Dressed lumber cut for tongue-and-groove joints: each board has a groove on one edge and a tongue on the other, to fit the tongue or the groove on the adjacent boards.

patterned lumber
Lumber that has been planed down to a standard profile, often ornamental.

appearance lumber
Lumber selected as a finish material, and graded according to its natural characteristics or defects.

wood

dressed size
A timber's dimensions after it has been sawn and planed, approx. 3/8 in.(0.95 cm) in thickness, and 1/2 in. (1.27 cm) in width less than its undressed size.

board measure
A unit of measure for lumber, the board foot in the USA; in countries with the ISO system, the board meter is customary.

board foot
A lumber measuring unit of cubic content, having a volume equal to an area of 1 square foot that is 1 inch thick.

- **yard lumber**
  Lumber up to 5 inches thick (12,5 cm), produced for regular use in construction.

- **dimension lumber**
  Lumber cut to standard dimensions for construction purposes, generally between 2 and 5 inches (5.1 to 12.7 cm) thick, and 5 to 12 inches (12.7 to 30.5 cm) across. Also called dimension stuff.

  light framing wood
  Lumber cut for the needs of structures not requiring great strength, from 2 to 4 in. thick, and more than 4 in. wide.

  decking
  Thick lumber cut to standard measures over 4 in. wide, graded according to its capacity to bridge wide spans between joists without bending.

  joists and planks
  Structural timber square-sawn to standard measures between 2 and 4 in. thick and 8 in. wide, graded according to its resistance to bending.

- **structural lumber**
  Lumber cut to rectangular or square cross sections and graded according to its load bearing strength for the needs of frame construction : (1) Beams and stringers: 5 x 8 in. or more. (2) Joists and planks: 2 to 5 in. thick x 4 in. wide. (3) Posts and timbers: 5 in. x 5 in. or more. Also called framing lumber.

  beams and stringers
  Heavy structural timber graded according to its capacity to bear transverse loads, spanning the gap between frame posts without bending.

  posts and timbers
  Structural timber with an approx. square section of 2 in., selected to bear axial loads and used as a vertical member in frame construction.

board
A piece of wood less than 2 in. (5 cm) thick and between 4 and 12 in. (10 to 30 cm) wide; called a plank when over 2 inches thick.

plank
A long, square-sawn piece of timber, usually no less than 8 in. (20 cm) wide, and between 2 and 4 in. (5 to 10 cm) thick for softwood and 1 in. (2,5 cm) for hardwood.

floorboard
A board or plank used to finish the walking surface of a room (approx 1 inch thick); also called a flooring board.

163

wood

grain
1. The natural distribution of fibers in wood or the strata in stone, indicative of the easiest cleavage direction. 2. The surface pattern of a piece of wood after sawing, due to the wood's annual growth rings and knots; the pattern's characteristics usually identify the type of wood.

plain-sawn
Said of wood sawn so the angle of intersection between the annual rings and the wide face is under 45º. Also called bastard sawn, flat grained, flat sawn, or slash sawn.

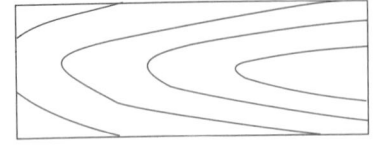

edge-grained
Said of wood sawn so the angle of intersection between the wide face and the annual rings is 45º or more. Also called comb grained, quarter sawn, rift grained, vertical grained.

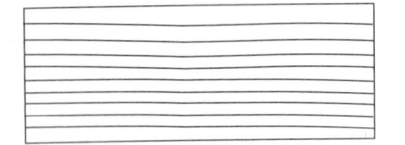

cross grain
In wood, an irregular grain not parallel to the long dimension of the piece, that goes across the face.

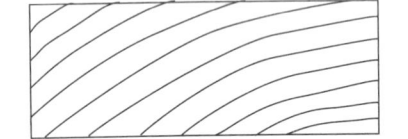

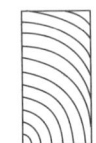

end grain
The grain of a piece of wood where it has been cut across the direction of the grain, exposing the annual rings,

slope of grain
The average angle between the grain of a piece of lumber and a line parallel to its length; in structural timber it must be below 12º, to avoid cleavage.

diagonal grain
A defect in lumber due to the wood grain being at an excessive angle to the long dimension of the piece; it is often caused by careless sawing.

mixed-grain lumber
A random mixture of plain-sawn and edge-grained lumber.

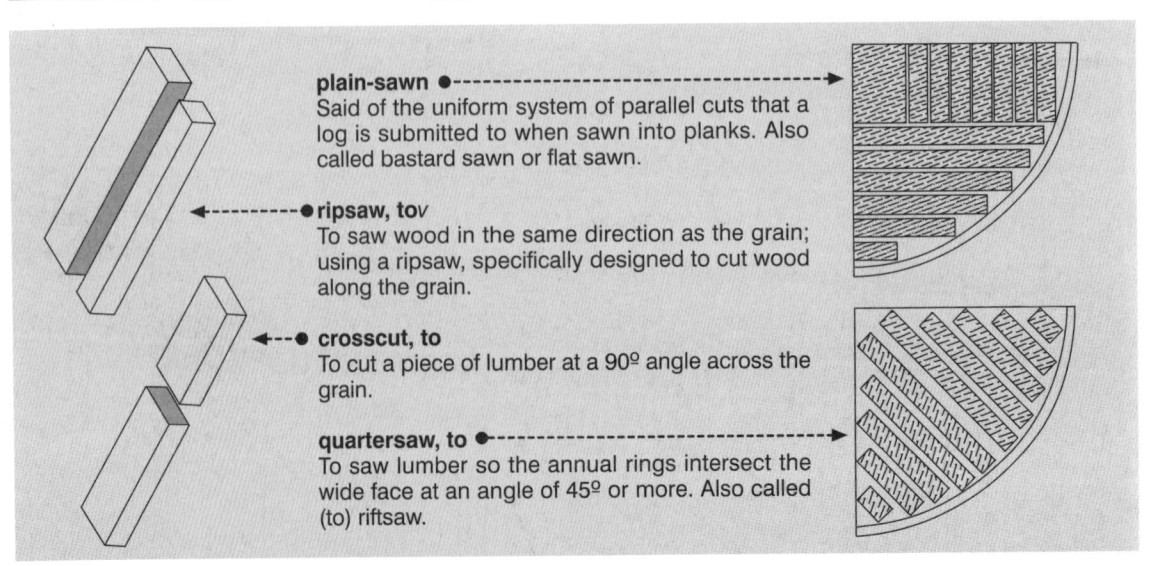

plain-sawn
Said of the uniform system of parallel cuts that a log is submitted to when sawn into planks. Also called bastard sawn or flat sawn.

ripsaw, to
To saw wood in the same direction as the grain; using a ripsaw, specifically designed to cut wood along the grain.

crosscut, to
To cut a piece of lumber at a 90º angle across the grain.

quartersaw, to
To saw lumber so the annual rings intersect the wide face at an angle of 45º or more. Also called (to) riftsaw.

wood

hardboard
A building material manufactured in dense sheets made of compressed wood fiber, widely used for durable interior paneling or siding.

tempered hardboard
A building material manufactured in sheets of compressed wood fiber with a drying oil or oxidizing resin to increase hardness, and water resistance, used for durable paneling or siding.

fiberboard (USA)
A building material manufactured in sheets of compressed wood fibers and glue, used for paneling or siding. Its performance depends on the type of fibers and glue employed. Also called fibreboard (GB).

plywood
A manufactured structural wood made of glued layers of veneer, superimposed so the wood fibers of each ply go in different directions, usually 90º angles.

core
The central layer, or ply, of a plywood board.

waferboard
A sheathing material made of wood chips of varying sizes randomly distributed, compacted at high temperature and pressure with a watertight glue.

OSB, (oriented strandboard)
A composition board made of 3 or 5 layers of long fibered veneer compacted with a waterproof glue, the two outer faces of which have the grain oriented in the sense of the long dimension of the board.

composite panel
A type of hardboard made of two outer sheets of veneer glued to a core of chipboard or particle board, often used in thermal insulation.

particle board (USA)
A type of composition board made of wood particles compacted with a binder; made in densities from 25 to 50 lb per cu ft; often faced with veneer, it is used in furniture construction. Also called core board (U.S.A.), or chipboard (GB).

parallel strand lumber
A type of structural wood manufactured by compacting long fibered lumber with a water resistant binder under high pressure and temperature.

laminated veneer lumber
A strong structural timber consisting of several layers of wood under 2 in. thick (5 cm) joined under pressure with an adhesive; according to the goal sought for, strength, length or width the boards may be joined in various ways.

wood

woodwork
The tasks carried out by a carpenter or a joiner, involving the wooden parts of a structure or an object.

face-nail
A nail which is driven into the surface of the wood perpendicularly to the fibers.

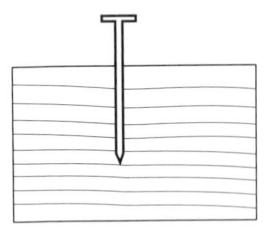

end-nail
A nail driven into the end grain of the wood, in the direction of the fiber.

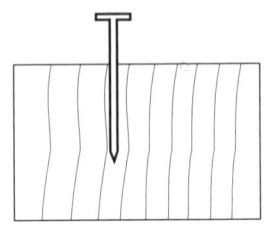

set, to
To drive a nail into the wood so that the head is left level or beneath the surface of the wood.

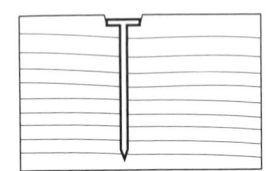

blind-nail
A nail introduced in such a way that it is invisible on the surface of the work. Also called secret nail.

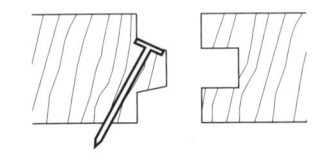

inlay
A shaped piece of a material embedded flush into the surface of another for decorative purposes. Also called marquetry.

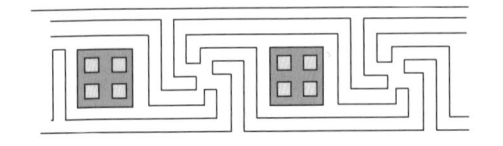

chisel, to
To shape or carve a design into the surface of a hard material such as wood, stone or metal. Also called to engrave.

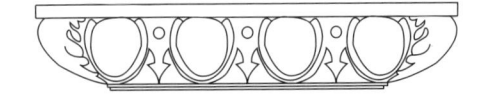

wood

joint
Any of the many ways used to connect or join two pieces of wood.

end joint
Any of the ways of joining two wooden elements end to end, to increase their length.

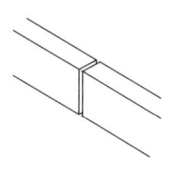

angle joint
A joint between two pieces of lumber achieving a change in direction, such as a dovetail joint, or a mortise-and-tenon joint.

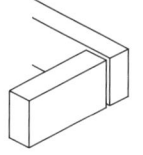

cross-lap joint
The joint between two wooden members that cross each other; half of each member is removed so that the two fit together and make up the thickness of the original piece.

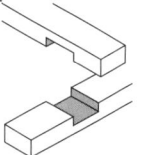

miter joint (USA)
A joint between two members, usually at a 90º angle to each other, in which the end of each is cut at half the angle the members are to meet at; also called mitre joint (G.B.).

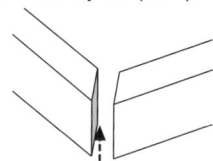

miter (USA)
The oblique cut at the end of a piece of wood that is to be joined to another with a cut in the opposite direction, to change the direction of the piece in an angle equal to double the angle of the miter; also called mitre (G.B.).

rabbet joint
A joint formed by fitting together the ends of rabbeted boards or planks; usually an edge joint.

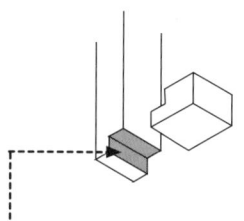

rabbet
A rectangular recess cut out of the edge of a piece of wood to receive another to which it will be fixed or against which it will close. Also called rebate.

edge joint
The joint between the thin edges of two wooden boards or planks, in the direction of the grain.

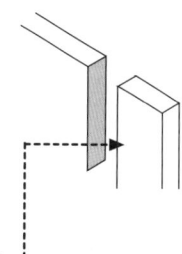

edge
The sharp border of a squared off element such as a brick or a wooden board; the intersection of two plains. Also called arris.

half-lap joint
A joint between two pieces of wood in which the thickness of the joint area of each piece is reduced by half, so that they overlap when fitted together. Also called a halved joint or halving joint.

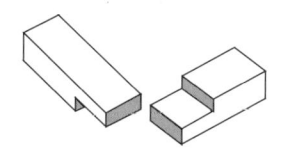

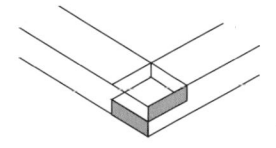

mitered halving (USA)
A joint between two wooden members having overlapping rabbeted ends of which one half is mitered. Called a mitred halving in GB.

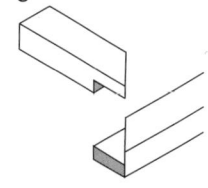

wood

mortise-and-tenon joint
A joint between two members formed be a tenon, or prolongation of one member, being fitted into a mortise, or cavity carved out of the other member.

tenon
In a mortise-and-tenon joint, the projecting end of one member, cut to fit a corresponding cavity (mortise) in the other member.

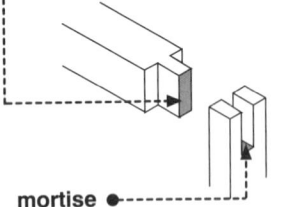

mortise
A rectangular cavity in a wooden element, carved to receive a projecting object such as the tenon of another wooden element, or the bolt of a lock.

barefaced tenon
A tenon that fits into an open mortise, and is visible from the other side. Also called bareface tenon.

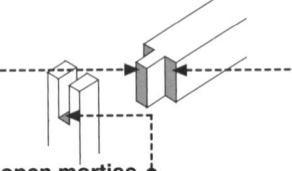

shoulder
In a mortise-and-tenon joint, the thick part of the member from which the tenon projects.

open mortise
A mortise with three open sides; also called slot mortise or slip mortise.

stub tenon
A tenon cut to fit into a blind mortise.

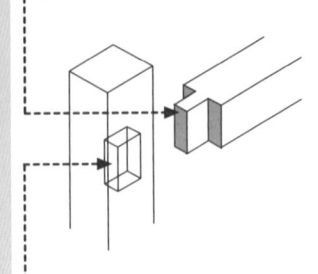

blind mortise
In a mortise joint, a mortise shallower than the wood is thick, thereby concealing the head of the tenon.

chase mortise
A stub mortise with a sloped side allowing the tenon to be put in sideways; used when a lack of space imposes.

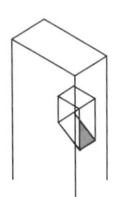

undercut tenon
A tenon in which the shoulder is cut at an angle to the face, making the fit more rigid.

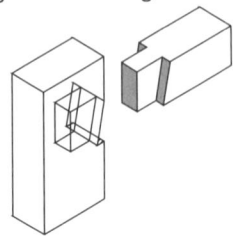

tusk
A beveled transition between a tenon and the rest of the member, adding strength to the tenon.

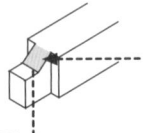

chamfer
An oblique surface that results from beveling an edge or corner, usually at a 45° angle. Also called a bevel or cant.

haunched tenon
A tenon part of which is narrower than the wooden member it projects from.

root
The portion of the tenon in the plane of the shoulders.

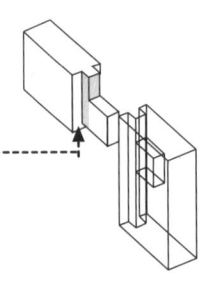

bridle joint
A joint in which the tenoned member has two lateral tenons that fit into two cavities in the sides of the mortised member.

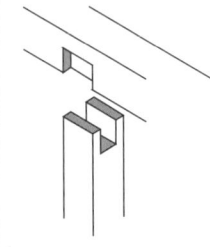

wood

dovetail joint
A joint formed by two or more interlocking dovetails, i.e., tenons that are wider at the end than at the base.

dovetail
A tenon that is wider at the end than at the base, shaped like a dove's tail.

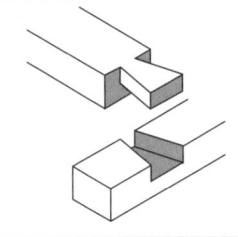

common dovetail
A corner dovetail, showing the end grain on both sides. Also called box dovetail or through dovetail.

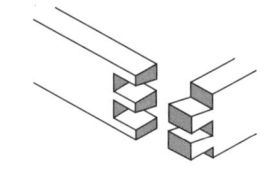

secret dovetail
A dovetail joint in which the pegs of one member do not pass through the whole thickness of the other, remaining concealed from that side; also called half-blind dovetail, lapped dovetail, miter dovetail.

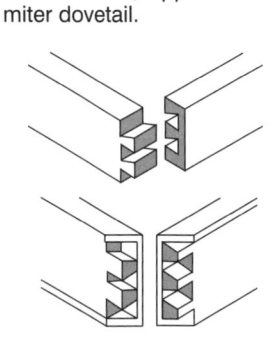

wedge
A small piece of wood, metal, or other material, one end of which is thicker than the other, so as to be driven between two elements until they are tight.

butterfly
A double dovetail wedge or butterfly, wider at both ends than in the middle, used to join the edges of two boards.

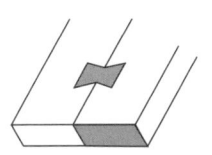

foxtail wedge
A small wedge knocked into the split end of a tenon in a mortise or a bolt in a hole, splaying the end and making it secure. Also called fox tenon or fox wedge.

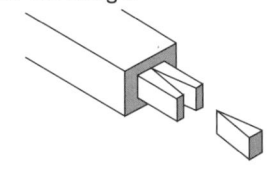

housed joint
A joint between two members in which the end of one is inserted into a corresponding trench or housing carved in the other. Also called a dado joint.

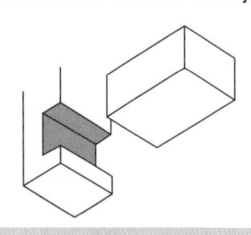

square splice
A joint used to unite the ends of two pieces of timber so as to resist tension; the overlapping ends have a combined mortise and ridge that interlock, sometimes reinforced with a fishplate.

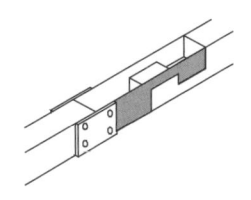

scarf joint
A joint used to unite the ends of two pieces of timber so as to resist tension; the overlapping ends are beveled and have trenches and ridges that interlock, sometimes reinforced with a fishplate.

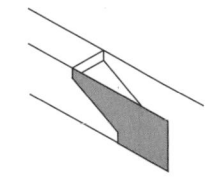

finger joint
A joint between the abutting ends of two members, sawn to create a zigzag pattern, like interlocking fingers.

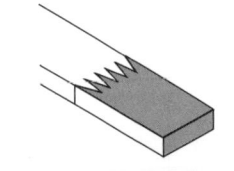

metal

Any of the elementary substances characterized by opacity, ductility, and conductivity; when freshly fractured they have a particular luster, being solid under normal conditions (except for mercury).

galvanic series
The list that places metals in order of nobility or resistance to galvanic corrosion. The further apart they are on the list, the more susceptible the less noble of the two is to corrosion when in contact with the other.

gold
A metallic element characterized by its yellow color, malleability, conductivity and freedom from corrosion. It represents and symbolizes wealth. It has catalytic properties. Symbol: Au.

silver
A white, ductile metallic element used for making mirrors, coins and ornaments. Symbol: Ag.

stainless steel
A tough steel alloy of great resistance to corrosion and oxidization, containing from 4 to 25% of chromium, often with nickel added.

bronze
A copper and tin alloy, or any alloy with enough copper to alter the properties of elements like aluminum or magnesium.

copper
A malleable and ductile reddish metal with high tensile strength, a good electricity and heat conductor, used for water pipes, roofing and electrical wiring. Symbol: Cu.

brass
Any alloy of copper and zinc, with other elements in minor proportions.

nickel
A silvery white metal, hard, ductile and malleable, used in steel or cast iron alloys and in electroplating of metal products against corrosion, such as galvanized wire. Symbol: Ni.

lead
A heavy, soft and malleable metal, workable, with a low melting point and a high thermal expansion coefficient; used in sheets for insulation purposes and as the base soldering alloys. Symbol: Pb.

iron
A strong but ductile and malleable metal, liable to rust, found in nature combined with other elements, and used to make steel or pig iron. Symbol: Fe.

cadmium
A ductile and malleable metal, of a bluish white color similar to tin, found in nature together with zinc, used in plating and in making alloys. Symbol: Cd.

aluminum (USA)
A light, very malleable, non-magnetic, silver-white metal, conducting heat and electricity, used in alloys as an anti-corrosive and as surface color. Used in building alloyed with other elements that give it greater rigidity. Also called Aluminium (GB). Symbol: Al.

zinc
A soft, bluish metal, easily oxidized under exposure, used to galvanize iron and steel, and as an alloy. Symbol; Zn.

magnesium
A light, silvery-white metal (64% of the weight of aluminum) used in various alloys.

metal

• steel
A ferrous alloy with a carbon content between 0,02 and 1,7%, malleable, extremely resistant, hard, and elastic. Different elements give the alloy other specific properties.

carbon steel
Steel having no specified minimum of alloying elements; an increased proportion of carbon reduces its malleability and weldability, but increases its resistance.

carbon
An element with allotropic properties found in many natural alloys; in its pure state it constitutes diamonds or graphite. It is the main element in coal and petroleum. Symbol: C.

mild steel
Steel containing between 0.15 and 0.25% of carbon; almost pure iron, it is very ductile and rust resistant, used in tanks, boilers and enamelware; also called soft steel or low steel.

medium steel
Steel containing between 0.25 and 0.50% of carbon; not a very hard steel, it cannot be called soft.

hard steel
Steel with a high carbon content, between 0.45 and 0.85%, thereby acquiring great hardness and resilience, though loosing malleability.

spring steel
Steel with a very high carbon content, between 0.85 and 1.80%; hard and resilient, brittleness appears in the upper range.

alloy steel
Steel to which, besides carbon, other alloying metals such as chromium, molybdenum or nickel have been added, in quantities greater than a specified minimum, to achieve certain physical, mechanical or chemical properties.

alloy
A composite of two or more metals, intimately mixed by fusion or electro-deposition, usually to alter the original properties of the metals in some desirable way.

high-strength low-alloy steel
Steel with less than 2% alloyed metals, composed to seek mechanical properties and resistance to atmospheric corrosion better than that offered by conventional steel alloys.

weathering steel
A very resistant steel that develops a coat of rust which adheres to the main object when exposed to the weather, and protects it from further corrosion.

stainless steel
A tough steel alloy of great resistance to corrosion and oxidization, containing from 4 to 25% of chromium, often with nickel added.

cast steel
Steel that is cast in a desired shape by pouring it, molten, into a mold.

cold-drawn steel
Steel the elastic limit of which has been increased by a specific process of manufacture.

structural steel
Steel laminated and formed at high temperatures, to manufacture load-bearing structural members, such as beams, angles, bars, sheets, etc.

metal

Structural steel members

structural tee
A standard, structural, hot rolled steel member with a cross section shaped like an inverted letter T, its height is equal to the flanges total width; the inner face of the flange is sloped some 2%. The height and thickness are expressed in mm.

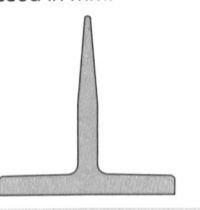

unequal leg angle
A steel structural member, the cross section of which forms a 90º angle; its unequal sides are designated with the letters L and D, followed by the corresponding dimensions.

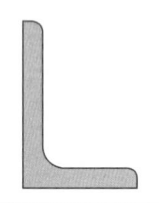

wide flange
A standard structural element the cross section of which is H shaped and the flanges are wider than an I beam; the inner sides of the web have a slight inclination compared to the web's normal angle. The inner angle between the web and the flanges is rounded.

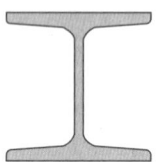

S-shape
A standard, structural, hot rolled steel member with a cross section shaped like a letter I, its category defined by a numerically indicated size with a prefix S. The web is higher than the flanges total width; the inner face of the flange is sloped some 14%.

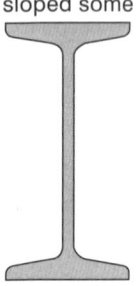

wide flange
A standard structural element the cross section of which is H shaped and the flanges are wider than an I beam; the inner angle between the web and the flanges is rounded.

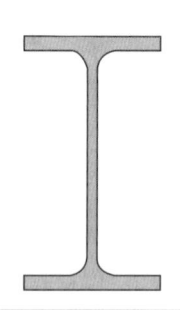

Zee
A hot-rolled structural member shaped like a letter Z, the web being vertical and the flanges, each in an opposite direction at a roughly 90º angle.

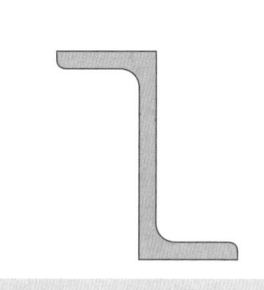

miscellaneous channel
A hot-rolled structural member shaped like a letter C, and defined by the letter C engraved before the size of the member. The inner corners between the flanges and the web are canted.

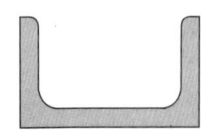

American standard channel
A hot-rolled structural member shaped like a letter C, and defined by the letter C engraved before the size of the member. The inner corners between the flanges and the web are canted, and constitute an 8º slope.

equal leg angle
A steel structural member, the cross section of which forms a 90º angle with equal sides.

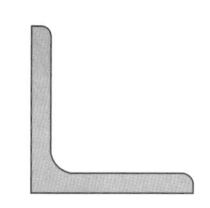

metal

seams in metal sheeting

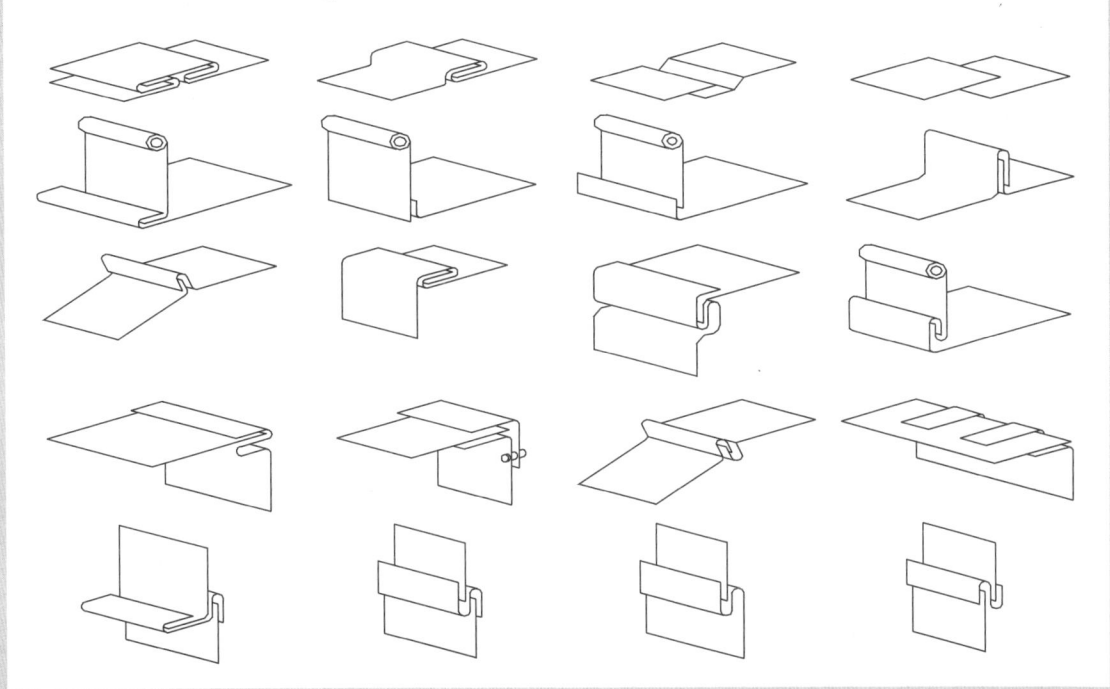

batten seam
A seam between pieces of metal sheeting, which are folded upward on the sides of a wooden strip, or batten, also covered with a folded metal strip.

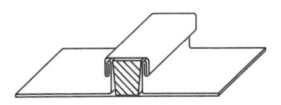

lock seam
A joint or seam between two sheets of metal roofing, which consists in folding both edges upward together; both together are then folded down against each other, and finally folded down flat, so the seam folds over itself like and interlocking hook.

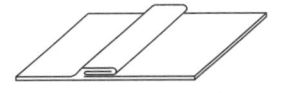

standing seam joint
A type of seam between adjacent sheets of metal roofing which consists in folding the edge of both sheets upward together and then re-folding the fold back down upon itself.

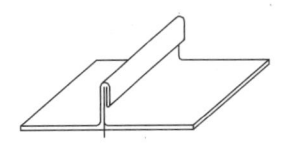

roll joint
A seam or joint between adjacent pieces of sheet metal, consisting in rolling the edges together and then flattening the joint. Also called a roll seam.

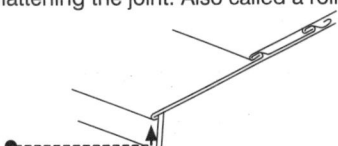

bead
In metal roofing or flashing, the result of folding the edge of the metal sheet, or shaping it into a roll, to add rigidity to the sheet, especially at the edge of the roof.

metal

arc welding
A system of joining metal parts by fusion, the necessary temperature being applied by an electric arc, often with the added use of filler metal and pressure.

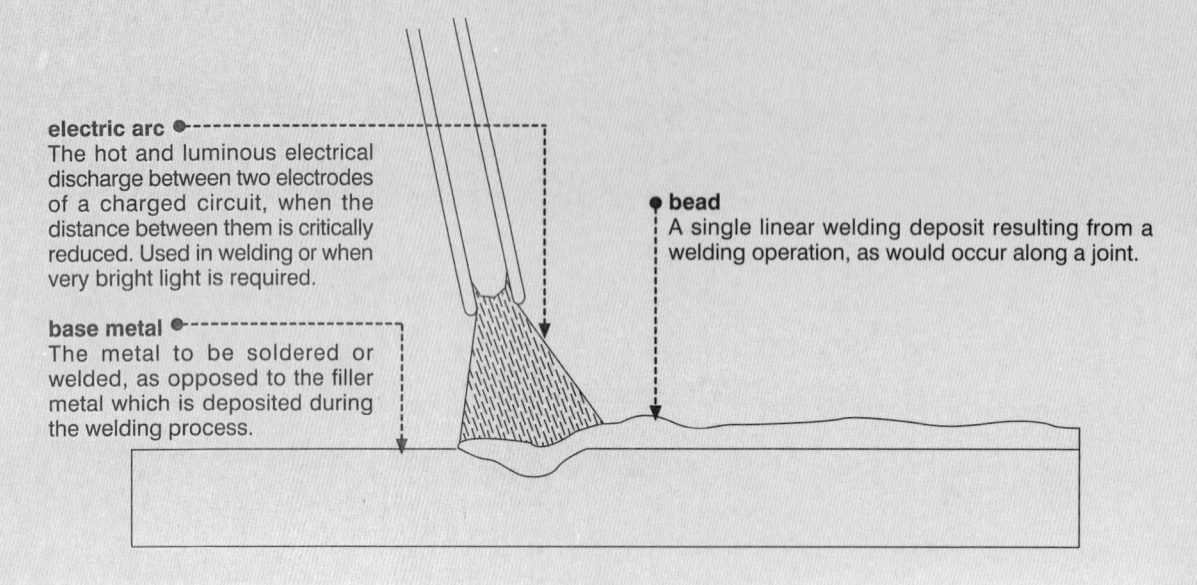

electric arc
The hot and luminous electrical discharge between two electrodes of a charged circuit, when the distance between them is critically reduced. Used in welding or when very bright light is required.

base metal
The metal to be soldered or welded, as opposed to the filler metal which is deposited during the welding process.

bead
A single linear welding deposit resulting from a welding operation, as would occur along a joint.

double-bevel weld
A welding operation in which the edge of one of the members is beveled on both sides.

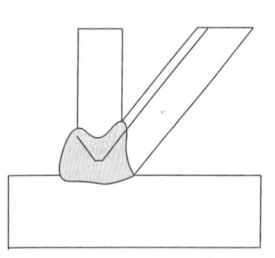

single-vee weld
A welding operation in which the edges of both members of the joint have been beveled.

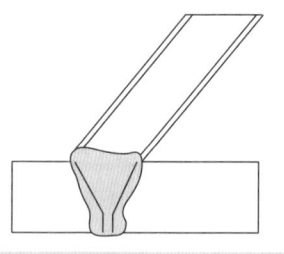

double-vee weld
A welding operation in which the edges of both members have been beveled from both sides.

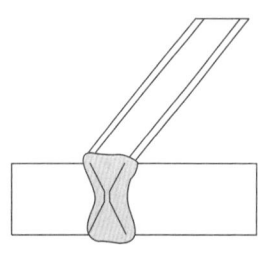

single-bevel butt weld
A welding operation in which only one of the edges of the members of the joint has been beveled.

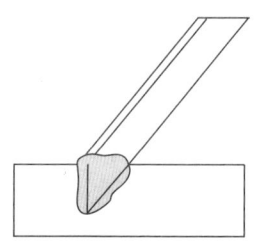

concrete

A building material composed mainly of concrete mortar, i.e., a mixture of portland cement, sand or gravel, and water.

mixing water
The water used to mix concrete, cement mortar or sand-cement grout, over and above the water already contained in the aggregate, sand or gravel.

cement
A pulverized material or mixture of materials (clay and limestone) that is the main binding ingredient in the manufactured mortar or concrete.

white cement
A cement made of pure crushed limestone. Its properties are similar to regular cement but of a higher grade.

slag cement
A binding agent composed basically of pulverized blast-furnace slag and hydrated lime.

hydraulic cement
A special type of cement which hardens under water, where the water makes the constituents of the cement set.

'natural cement
A cement resulting from the fine pulverization of argillaceous limestone, calcined at a temperature just sufficient to eliminate the carbon dioxide.

aggregate
An inert granular material like clean natural sand, gravel, crushed stone, vermiculite, or others, to mix with water and cement, making mortar or concrete.

sand
A hard and inert material used for the preparation of concrete or mortar, sifted by a 4,76 mm sieve. Also called fine aggregate.

coarse aggregate
A coarse natural or manufactured aggregate (crushed rock), passing a 3 in. (76 mm) sieve and retained by a nº 4 (4.76 mm). Also called gravel.

graded aggregate
An aggregate consisting of different sizes of gravel, the smaller grades almost completely fill the cavities between the larger grades, thereby needing a minimal quantity of cement to bind the mix.

particle-size distribution
A sieve analysis of the percentages of different size particles in a soil or aggregate sample for its potential uses in concrete.

uniform grading
An aggregate composed of an even distribution of all pan fractions, with no predominance of any grade or grade group.

expanded clay
Clay which has been expanded to many times its original volume by internal gas formation, during baking; used as a lightweight aggregate.

expanded slate
A lightweight aggregate formed in a similar way to expanded clay, expanding the original volume (exfoliation) by baking, used for lightweight concrete.

perlite
A siliceous volcanic rock expanded by heat (exfoliation) up to 20 times its natural volume, making a very good lightweight aggregate for lightweight concrete, for gypsum wallboard or as loose thermal insulation.

vermiculite
A natural mica expanded by heat (exfoliated) forming a good lightweight aggregate mixed with other materials or as loose-fill thermal insulation.

concrete

portland cement
A hydraulic cement obtained by calcinating a mixture of limestone and clay in an oven, and grinding the result to a fine powder.

white portland cement
A type of portland cement made of components poor in iron, resulting in a whitish color suitable for terrazzo or staining with colors; light reflective, it is often used for roadworks, etc...

air-entraining portland cement
Portland cement to which an air entraining agent has been added.

low heat portland cement
Also called cement type IV, it is a variant of portland cement's normal composition, that generates much less heat during the setting process; also called moderate portland cement.

high early strength portland cement
A type of portland cement rich in tricalcium silicate which allows for a shorter setting time and greater resistance; often used in dam construction and retaining walls.

ordinary portland cement
A good portland cement (type 1) regularly used in construction, where no special properties are necessary.

sulfate resisting portland cement
A portland cement low in tricalcium aluminate, thus less susceptible to the action of sulfates present in the soil or in the water the soil contains.

consistency
Degree of firmness or tendency of a freshly mixed mortar, grout or concrete, to slump, as measured with an Abrams cone (slump test) for concrete, or with a vibration table in the case or mortar or grout.

wet mix
A concrete mix that has an excess of water revealed by the tendency of the Abrams cone to slump and water to separate.

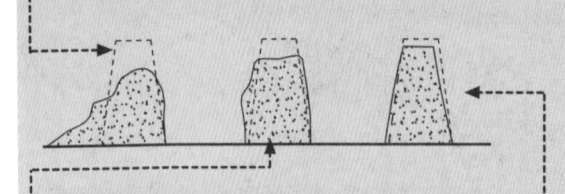

plastic mix
A concrete or cement mix an Abrams cone of which will deform in all directions without breaking up, but will adapt readily to a cast.

dry mix
A concrete or cement mix that contains insufficient water in relation to the other components; the Abrams cone hardly slumps showing a lack of plasticity out tendency to crumble.

Abrams' slump test
The procedure used to determine the consistency and plasticity of a fresh concrete mix by measuring its tendency to maintain or loose (slump) a given shape determined by an Abrams' cone.

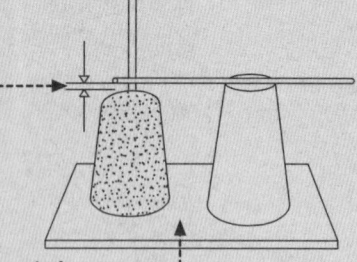

Abrams' slump cone
A mold in the form of a truncated cone, measuring 20 cm (8 inches) across the base and 10 cm (4 inches) across the top, used to make samples of fresh concrete for slump tests.

slump
A measure of a fresh mix of mortar, stucco or concrete's consistency, equal to the decrease in height of the molded mass after removal of the slump cone.

concrete

cast-in-place concrete
Concrete mixed on site or transported their in its plastic state and deposited or cast in its permanent location in the structure, as opposed to precast concrete elements. Also called cast-in-situ concrete or in situ concrete.

pumped concrete
Concrete that is transported in its plastic state by means of a hose or pipe, impelled by a pump to its final location within the work site.

agitator truck
A vehicle with a rotating drum, to convey freshly mixed concrete to a destination without plasticity loss. Also called agitating truck or agitating lorry (GB).

truck mixer
A truck with a rotating drum in which the ingredients for concrete are placed and mixed in transit to the work site.

pump
A mechanical device designed to transport or impel fluids or semi-fluids through a hose, by means of pressure, suction or both; used to raise water to a higher level, or remove residual or seepage water from a work site.

concrete pump
A mechanical device that mixes the ingredients of concrete, which it impels through a hose to the place where it has to be poured.

direct dumping
To discharge concrete directly into place from a crane, a mixer, or the bucket; also called direct placement.

buggy
A two or four-wheeled cart to transport small quantities of concrete from the mixer to the form; often motor driven. Also called a concrete cart.

drop chute
A funnel or an open trough that conveys bulk materials, concrete or rubble, by gravity. Made of different materials according to what it is expected to carry.

cement mixer
A motor driven rotating drum in which to mix the ingredients of a given mortar or concrete.

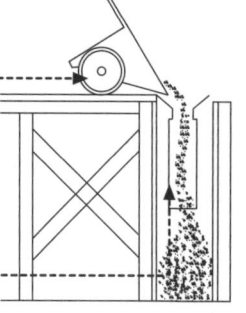

consolidation
The operation that compacts freshly poured concrete or mortar, to eliminate gaps and effectively fill every hollow in the mold; usually by vibration or tamping; also called compaction.

spading
A method of consolidating or compacting freshly poured concrete in a mold, by repeatedly introducing a rod; only viable with small masses of soft, fluid concrete.

vibrator
A mechanical device used to transmit vibrations to the freshly poured concrete, to consolidate it and eliminate hollows and bubbles.

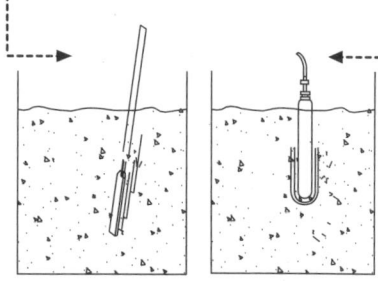

concrete

formwork
A provisional structure, with all the necessary pressure withstanding support elements, built to form and contain the freshly poured concrete.

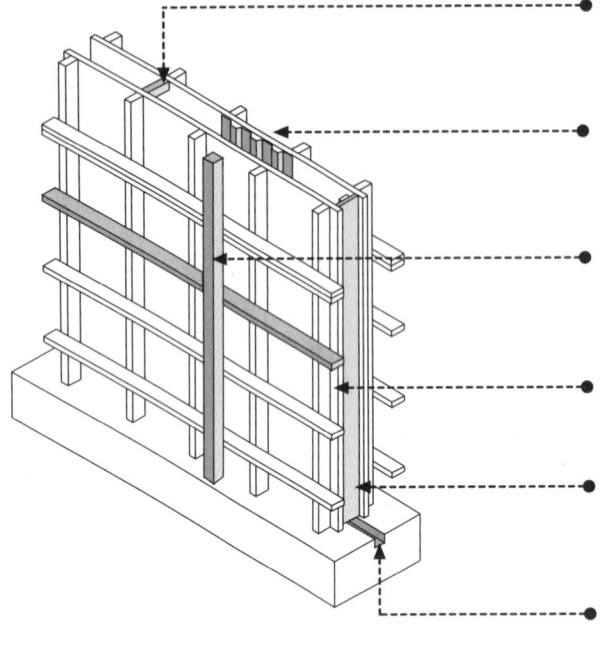

- **spreader**
A short wooden element used to maintain the separation between the walls of the formwork until the concrete is poured.

- **form liner**
A lining on the inside of a concrete form, used to absorb excess water or impose a smooth or patterned finish to the set surface.

- **strongback**
The vertical members of the structure supporting the back of a concrete form, resisting the pressure of the concrete placement; also called a stiffback.

- **ledger**
A horizontal member, of wood or steel, as part of the supporting structure of a concrete form.

- **bulkhead**
A partition to block the end of a concrete form, or keep fresh concrete within a certain part of the form.

- **sinking**
A cavity or cavities let into an already set stretch of cast concrete to serve as links with the next placement.

- **snap tie**
A tie used in concrete formwork, with two incisions near the ends so they can be easily snapped off when the form is removed.

- **cone-nut tie**
A tie rod used in concrete forms, with a nut on the outside and a cone nut on the inside of the form, so it is also a spreader; also called cone bolt.

- **rustication strip**
A strip of material attached to the inside of a concrete form so as engrave its form on the concrete face, often in a pattern imitating stonework.

- **grade strip**
A strip of wood attached to the inside of a concrete form to mark the level the concrete placement is to reach.

- **she-bolt**
A type of tie rod used in concrete formwork consisting of two she-bolts that screw into a threaded bolt sleeve which will remain inside the concrete, reducing the size of the holes visible on the surface.

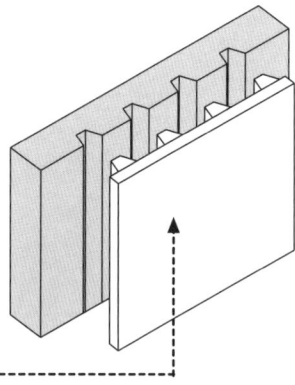

concrete

form
A sheet of wood, metal, plastic or fiber, either smooth or with an ornamental form, texture or relief to be imprinted on the concrete surface.

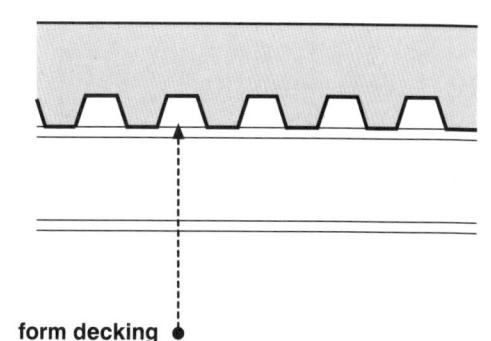

form decking
Light sheets of metal, corrugated, or otherwise stiffened, to bear a freshly poured concrete floor until it sets.

climbing form
A concrete form which is raised as succeeding lifts of concrete harden; usually supported on bolts fixed into the previous lift. It is not the same as a slip form, moved as the concrete is placed.

slip form
A concrete form that is moved upward slowly by mechanical jacks, supported by the already set concrete poured previously.

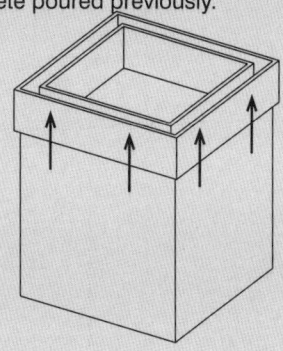

flying form
A type of large, reusable, prefabricated formwork unit, much used in the construction of floor slabs and façades.

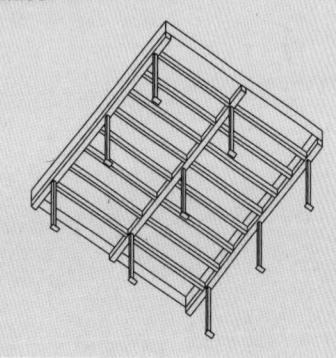

construction joint
The joint between successive placements of concrete, formed so that they will be solidly linked. Also applied to the separation left between parts of a building to allow for shifting.

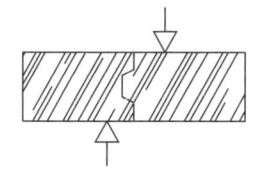

waterstop
A flexible watertight strip or diaphragm introduced in a concrete joint to prevent the passage of water.

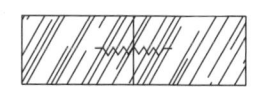

dowel-bar reinforcement
A short steel bar (usually several of them) that penetrate equally into two abutting concrete placements, to ensure the firmness of the joint.

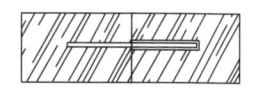

concrete

reinforcement
In reinforced concrete, the network of steel bars that is embedded in the concrete, to add to it an important resistance to traction forces.

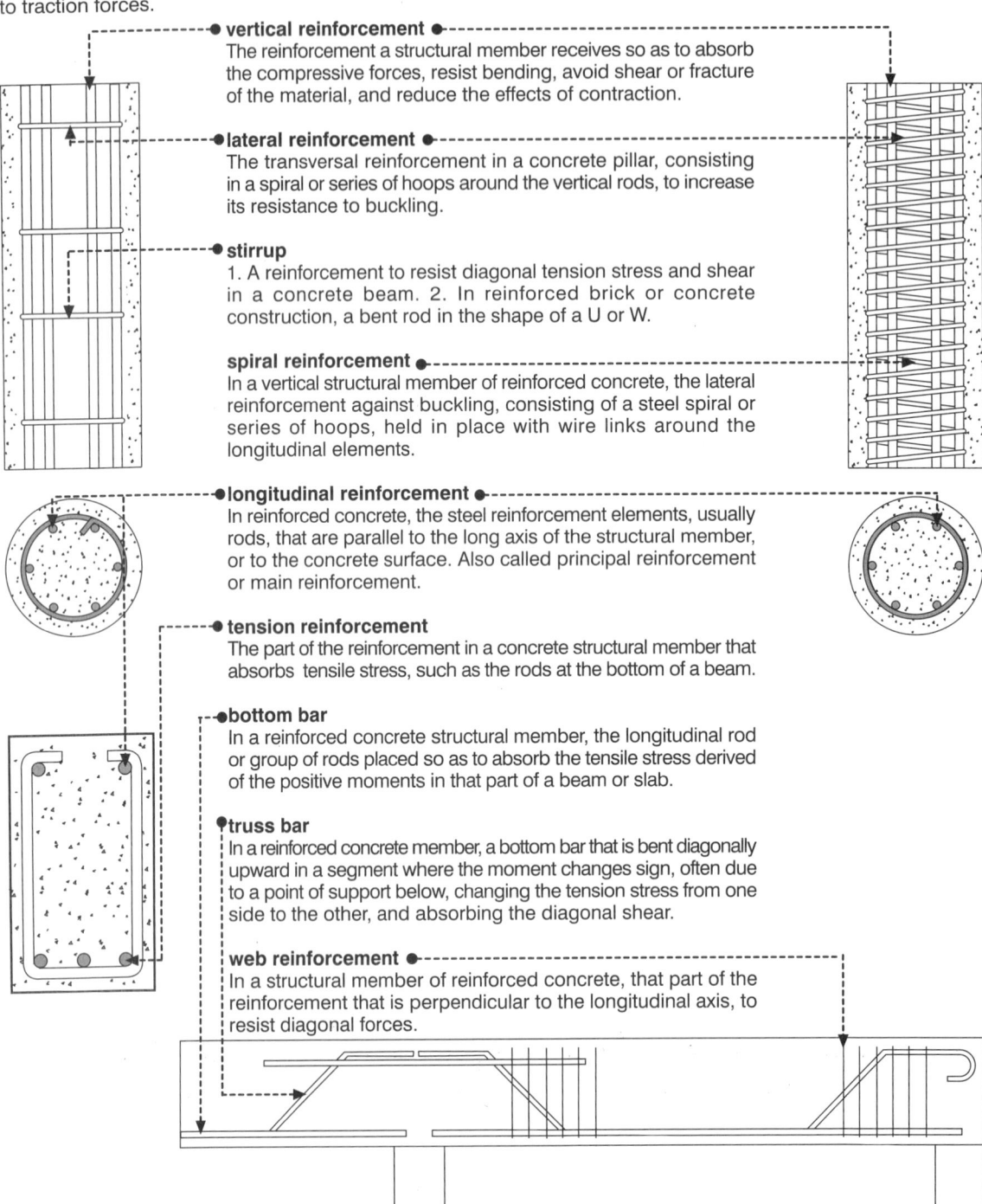

vertical reinforcement
The reinforcement a structural member receives so as to absorb the compressive forces, resist bending, avoid shear or fracture of the material, and reduce the effects of contraction.

lateral reinforcement
The transversal reinforcement in a concrete pillar, consisting in a spiral or series of hoops around the vertical rods, to increase its resistance to buckling.

stirrup
1. A reinforcement to resist diagonal tension stress and shear in a concrete beam. 2. In reinforced brick or concrete construction, a bent rod in the shape of a U or W.

spiral reinforcement
In a vertical structural member of reinforced concrete, the lateral reinforcement against buckling, consisting of a steel spiral or series of hoops, held in place with wire links around the longitudinal elements.

longitudinal reinforcement
In reinforced concrete, the steel reinforcement elements, usually rods, that are parallel to the long axis of the structural member, or to the concrete surface. Also called principal reinforcement or main reinforcement.

tension reinforcement
The part of the reinforcement in a concrete structural member that absorbs tensile stress, such as the rods at the bottom of a beam.

bottom bar
In a reinforced concrete structural member, the longitudinal rod or group of rods placed so as to absorb the tensile stress derived of the positive moments in that part of a beam or slab.

truss bar
In a reinforced concrete member, a bottom bar that is bent diagonally upward in a segment where the moment changes sign, often due to a point of support below, changing the tension stress from one side to the other, and absorbing the diagonal shear.

web reinforcement
In a structural member of reinforced concrete, that part of the reinforcement that is perpendicular to the longitudinal axis, to resist diagonal forces.

concrete

prestressed concrete
Concrete reinforced with internal stresses, to counteract the tensile stress of the service load; this is achieved by tensioning the tendons.

prestress
The application of calculated internal stresses in a concrete structural member, to counteract the specific tensile stress of the service load.

pretension
A system of prestressing reinforced concrete by tensioning the tendons before the concrete is poured.

effective prestress
The prestress finally remaining in the concrete when loss of prestress has occurred, including its own weight but not the subsequent weight applied.

initial prestress
The prestress transmitted to a concrete member when the tendons are first tensioned, before loss of prestress.

partial prestressing
The prestressing of concrete up to nominal levels of stress defined in the specifications of the project.

post-tensioned concrete
A system of prestressing reinforced concrete, tensioning the tendons after the concrete has set.

pre-post-tensioning
A way of manufacturing prestressed concrete in which some of the tendons are pretensioned and others are post-tensioned; also called pre-post-tension.

tendon
In prestressed concrete, a steel cable, bar, rod or wire, which, when submitted to tension, imparts prestress to the concrete.

depressed tendon
In reinforced concrete, a post-tensioning tendon that curves like a suspended cord, not quite parabolic, with some straight segments.

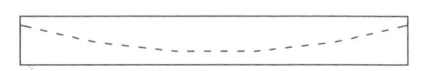

deflected tendon
In reinforced concrete, a tendon following a curve as regards the central axis of the member; also called draped tendon.

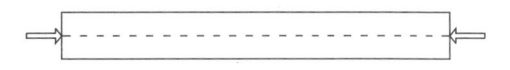

concentric tendon
A tendon in reinforced concrete that coincides with the central axis of the member, so the compression stresses are equally shared out.

harped tendon
In a reinforced concrete member, each of the tendons following a curved course regarding the center of gravity, but sloping differently (like harp strings).

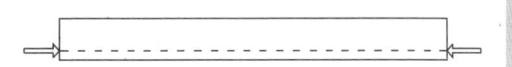

eccentric tendon
In reinforced concrete, a tendon that follows a straight line not coincidental with the longitudinal axis of the member.

brick

A rectangular block of clay used as a walling unit; solid or hollow; molded in a plastic state, dried, and baked in a kiln; usually smaller than 33.75 cm long, 22.5 cm wide, 11.25 cm high; sometimes only sun dried (see adobe brick).

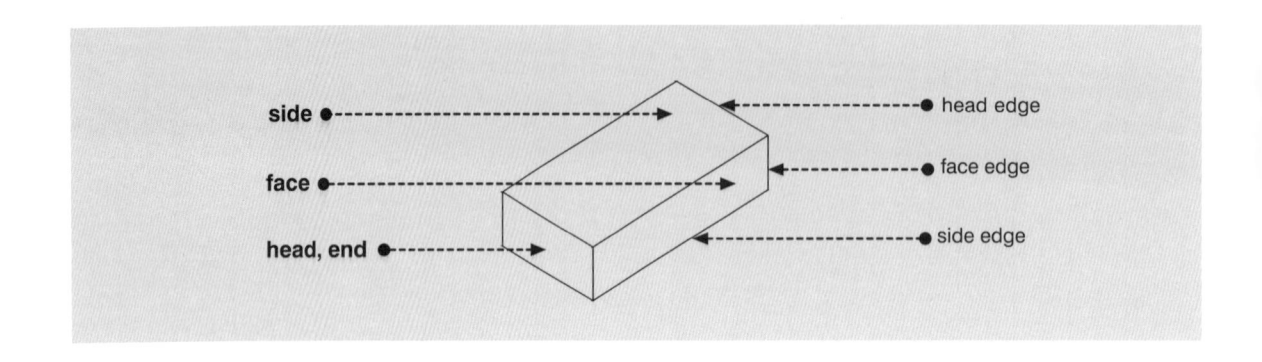

side •
face •
head, end •
• head edge
• face edge
• side edge

soldier •
A masonry unit laid vertically, on its head, with one of its faces showing.

brick on edge (vertical) •
A brick laid vertically on its end or head (or short narrow side), with its side parallel to the wall.

brick on edge (horizontal) •
A brick laid horizontally on its face (long narrow side), its side parallel to the wall.

stretcher •
A masonry unit laid flat on its side with its face parallel to the direction of the face of the wall.

header •
A masonry unit laid flat on its side with its head, or end, showing in the wall face.

rowlock •
A brick laid on its face (long narrow side), with its head (or end) showing perpendicular to the direction of the face of the wall. Also called rolock.

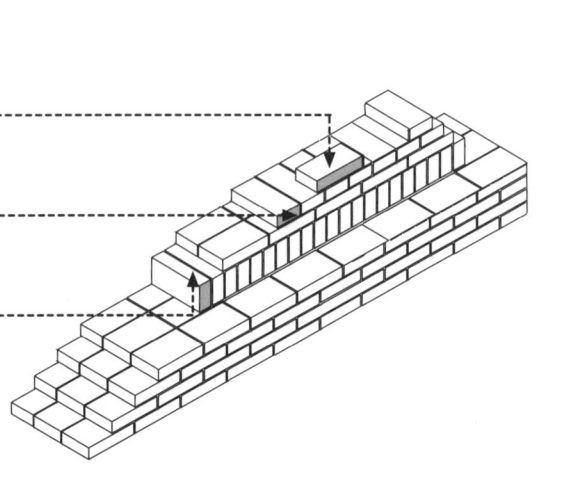

brick

common brick
A rectangular block of clay, or other hard material, used as a walling unit, usually smaller than 33.75 cm long, 22.5 cm wide, 11.25 cm high; sometimes only sun dried (see adobe brick).

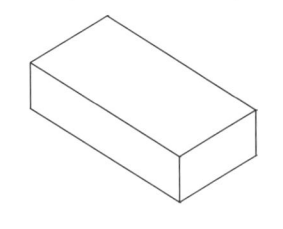

perforated brick
A brick or masonry unit with holes exceeding 25% of its volume passing through it; the holes are large, to improve ease of handling.

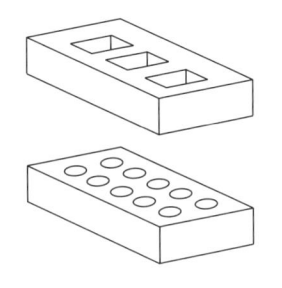

ornamental hollow brick
A hollow clay masonry unit with an ornamental face; its cross sectional solid area is not less than 60% of the area of the corresponding parallel face.

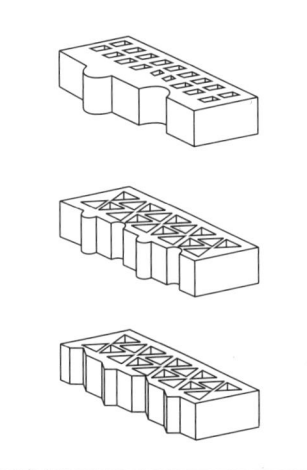

king closer
A rectangular brick from which a corner is removed, cut from diagonal line half way across the width of the brick; used to complete a horizontal course.

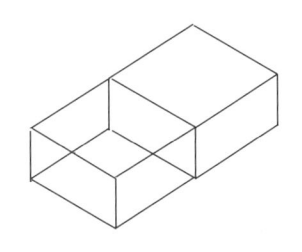

queen closer
A brick cut from head to end to half its normal width but maintaining its length; used to complete a course of brickwork; also called queen closure or narrow brick.

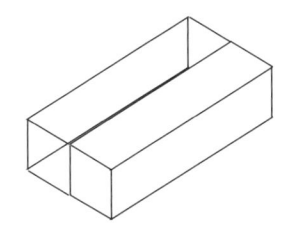

hollow brick
A hollow clay masonry unit, the net cross sectional area of which is not less than 60% of the gross cross sectional area of the same section, in any plane.

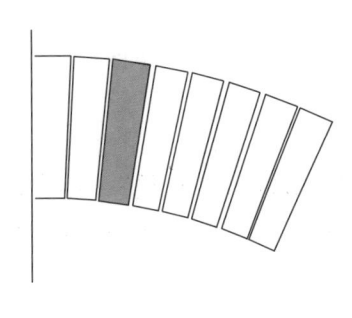

arch brick
A wedge shaped brick, made for arch construction; also called compass brick, featheredge brick, radial brick, radiating brick, radius brick, or voussoir brick.

bull header
A molded clay brick having a rounded edge, used in brick window sills and doorways, or for decorative work; also called bull head, molded brick, or moulded brick.

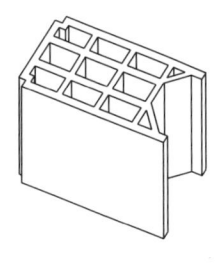

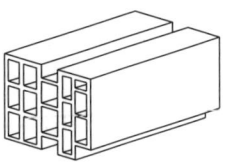

brick

ceramic
The craft of manufacturing objects out of clay or other similar material, from bricks to fine porcelain, burnt at high temperatures in a kiln.

clay
An earthy material composed mainly of hydrated silicates of aluminum; very plastic when wet, it contracts and hardens through calcination.

brickmaking mold (USA)
A mold used in the manufacture of bricks; also called brickmaking mould (G.B.).

green brick
Wet clay that has been shaped in a mold, and is drying before being put in the kiln.

kiln
A type of oven or furnace designed for (1) the firing of bricks, tiles, or other ceramics or (2) drying timber.

brick kiln
A kiln specifically designed for the firing of clay bricks.

firing
The process of firing clay at specific controlled temperatures to achieve a finished product of determined characteristics.

hard-burnt
Said of almost vitrified clay fired at very high temperatures, producing low-absorption bricks with a high compressive resistance.

soft-burned
A ceramic product that has been fired at moderate temperatures, with a relatively absorbent result and low compressive strength.

chuff
A brick that poor firing in the kiln has made useless.

clinker brick
A brick that has been fired too hard, is warped by the temperature and partly vitrified; used for paving.

slop-molding (USA)
A way of manufacturing multicolored bricks, by using clay with a high water content; also called soft mud process or slop moulding (G.B.).

soft-mud brick
A brick molded by hand out of fairly wet clay (20 to 30% humidity); the mold is made wet to prevent the clay from adhering (water struck brick); if the mold is dusted with sand for the same reason, it is a sand struck brick.

'water-struck brick
A brick molded by hand out of fairly wet clay (20 to 30% humidity); the mold is made wet to prevent the clay from adhering.

stiff-mud process
A brick produced by mechanically extruding stiff, but still plastic clay (relative moisture: 15%) through a die or mold, reducing the drying time.

dry-press process
A brick manufacturing process whereby relatively dry clay is used, molded at high pressure.

fire clay
A type of clay that is resistant to high temperatures due to a given content of metal oxides; used to manufacture special bricks to withstand high temperatures, used for fireplace construction.

firebrick
A porous and absorbent brick used to line fireplaces; it resists temperatures due to fireclay's specific composition of metal oxides.

glazed brick
A brick or tile with one ceramic glazed surface; used for hygiene, resistance to corrosion and ornamental quality; also called enameled brick.

vitrified brick
A brick rich in lime and iron oxide, fired at vitrification heat, so fusion closes the surface making it impervious.

concrete block

A hollow walling unit, wider than most masonry units, consisting of portland cement and a variety of aggregates, combined to improve the perfomance; incorrectly called a cement block.

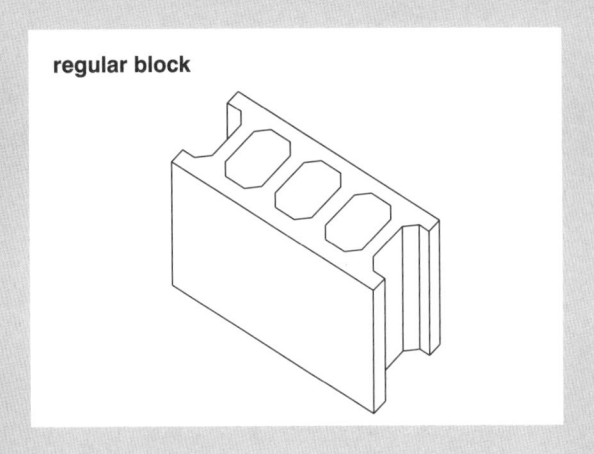

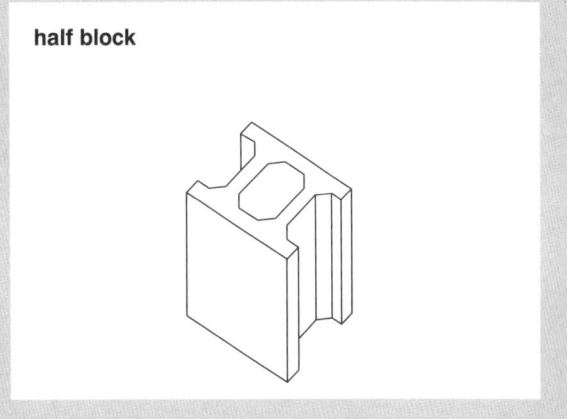

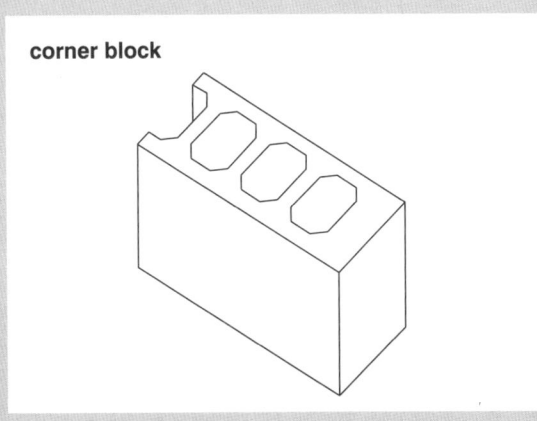

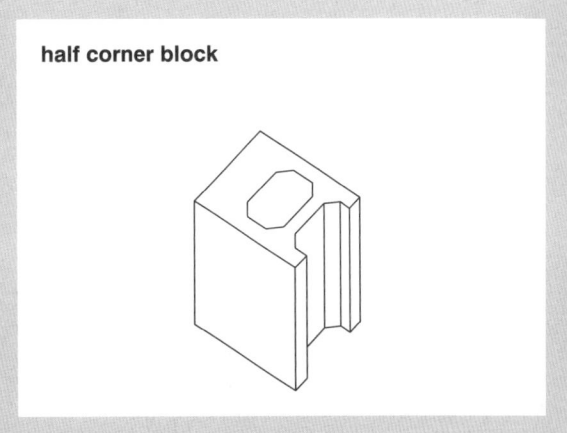

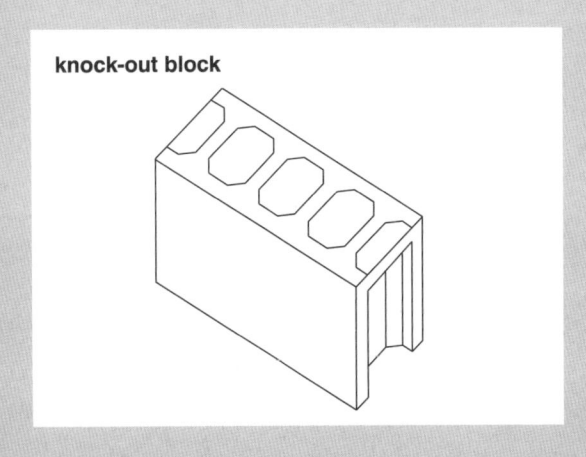

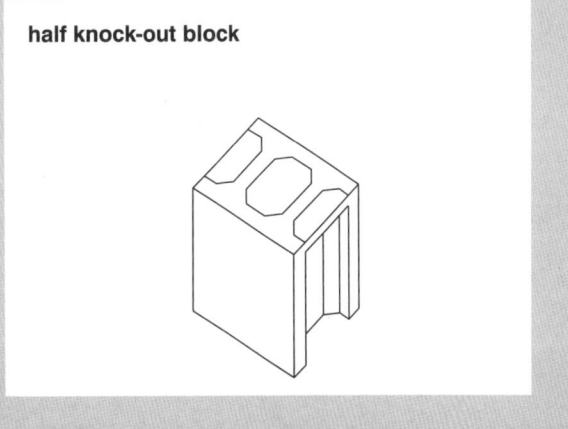

regular block

half block

corner block

half corner block

knock-out block

half knock-out block

concrete block

header block
A hollow walling unit which is shaped to receive the support structure of the building or accomodate the reinforcement bars of the lintel of a door or opening.

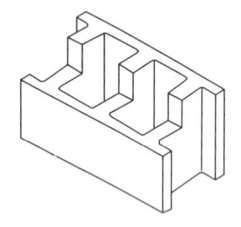

cap block
A concrete masonry unit the upper side of which is solid, used as a first course over the foundations or for lintels.

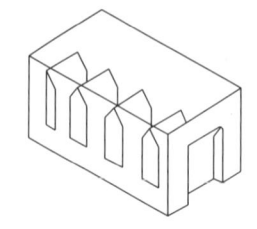

sound-absorbing masonry unit
A concrete masonry unit with a solid upper surface; the side, though, is open and the inside is filled with a sound absorbing material.

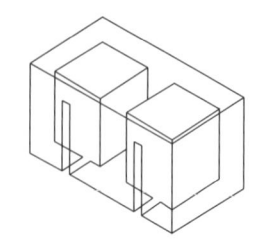

shadow block
A cement block the lateral face of which has an ornamental pattern in relief, that tangent light shows up.

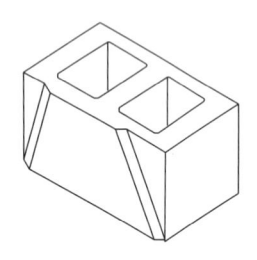

scored block
A concrete masonry unit, one of the lateral faces of which has been scored vertically down the middle.

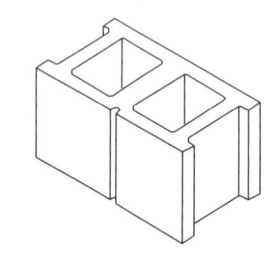

A-block
A hollow concrete masonry unit one end of which is open; there is a web in the middle so two cells are formed when the block is laid in the wall; often used to accommodate a vertical member; also called an open-end block.

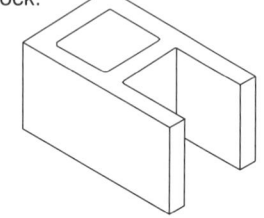

split-face block
A concrete masonry unit, hollow or solid, which is split longitudinally once cured, so as to be laid with the rough texture of the fractured side showing.

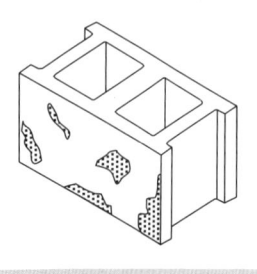

slump block
A concrete masonry unit the base of which is slightly widened due to settling in the curing process; used in wall construction.

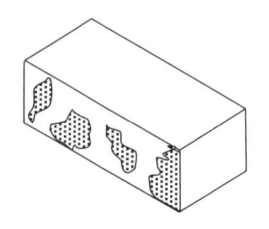

faced block
A concrete masonry unit having one lateral shell faced with ceramic, plastic, or a polished ornamental finish.

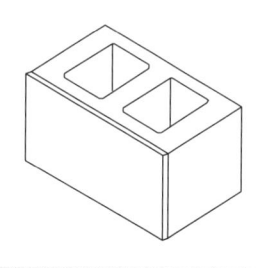

concrete block

bullnose block
A concrete masonry unit with one or more round exterior corners.

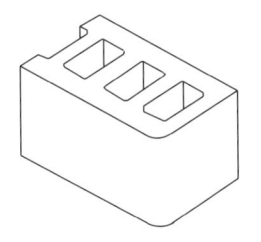

double-corner block
A concrete masonry unit with two smooth heads as well as smooth sides, for use on corners or at the end of walls.

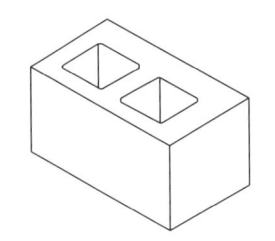

coping block
A concrete masonry unit with a solid top laid as the finishing course on top of a wall; perhaps sloped so as to shed water.

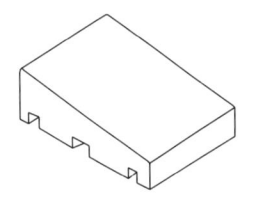

screen block
A hollow concrete masonry unit the inner cores of which describe a pattern; designed to be laid with the ornamental hollows showing, so air can pass but not the sunshine.

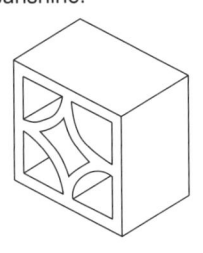

lintel block
A single core, U shaped concrete block, designed to be laid with the open end upward as the lintel of a door or window, and be filled with reinforced concrete.

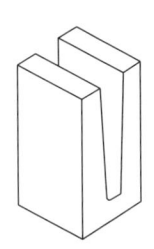

sill block
A concrete masonry unit with a sloped top, often with a drip, used for windowsills.

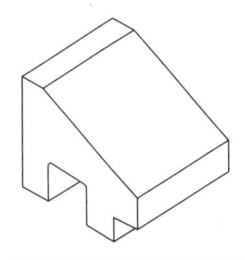

partition block
A concrete block used for nonbearing partition walls, between 4 to 6 inches thick (100 and 150 mm).

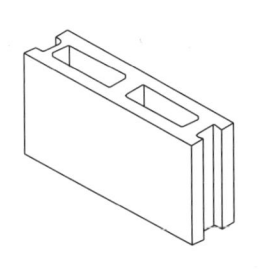

jamb block
A concrete masonry unit, similar to a corner block, with a vertical slot or a rabbeted profile at the end, to receive a door frame; also called a sash block.

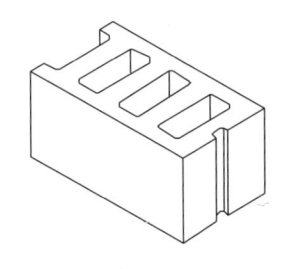

pilaster block
Any of the various masonry units used to construct pilasters.

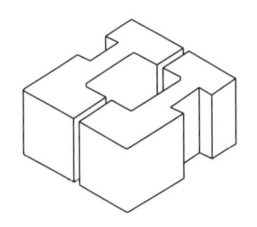

concrete block

diamond faced block

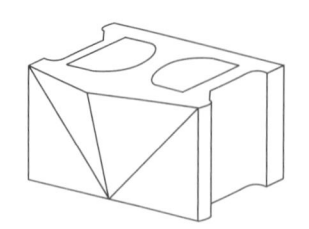

double diamond type block

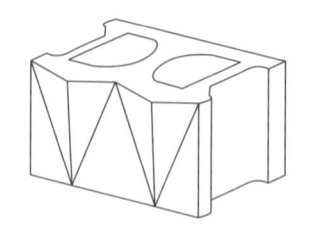

bar type block

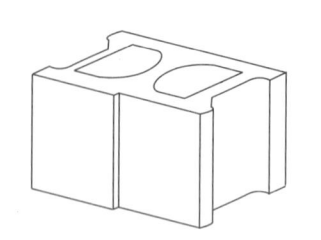

rudolph type block

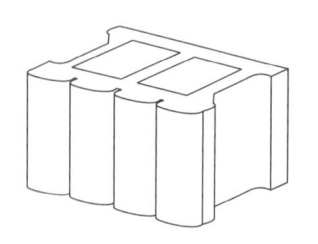

split type block

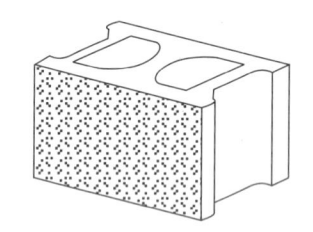

mistral type block

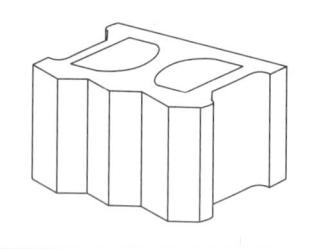

return corner block
A double corner block with a narrow end, used when the masonry units used on a particular stretch of wall are wider than others nearby, but the design specifies that the same rhythm of mortar joints is to be maintained throughout.

corner block
A concrete masonry unit with a smooth head as well as smooth sides, for use on corners or at the end of walls.

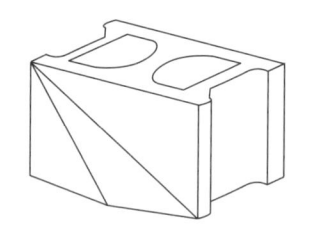

tarraco type block

ger type block

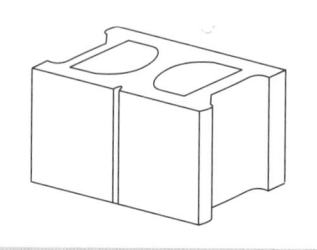

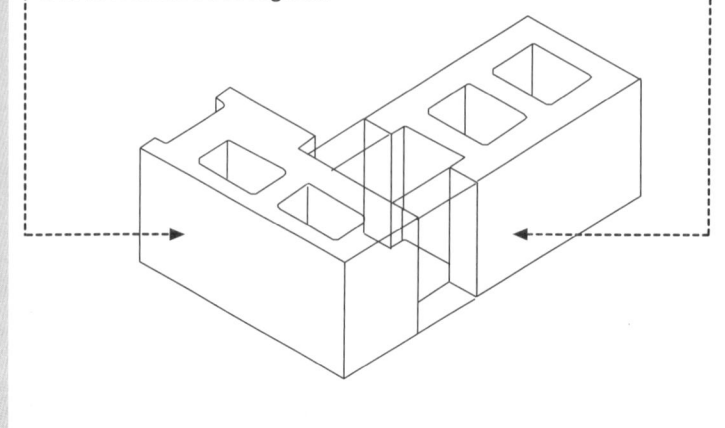

nail

A metal building accessory consisting of a thin shank with a point at one end and a widened head at the other, where it is struck with a hammer and driven into wood or other materials; used to hold two elements together.

box nail
A flat headed nail similar to a regular nail but with a thinner shank.

drive screw
A nail with a helically threaded shank, driven in with a hammer but hard to remove, some sorts requiring a screwdriver; also called a screw nail.

common nail
A nail with a sharp diamond-shaped point, a thin shank and a wide head, for tasks in which the appearance is not of prime importance.

roofing rail
A short, broad headed nail used for roofing, often provided with a watertight washer of a material suited to the type of roofing being used (shingles, roofing felt); the shank is barbed; usually made of a galvanized or rust-free metal.

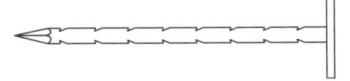

double-headed nail
A nail with two heads on the same shank, one above the other; the upper is driven with the hammer, the lower one presses on the material; easy to extract by pulling the upper head; often used for temporary structures; also called scaffold nail or form nail.

masonry nail
A nail of hardened steel with a short, thick shank, a diamond point and a countersunk head; used for nailing to concrete or masonry.

cut nail
A nail with a blunt square point, and a flat, wedge shaped shank.

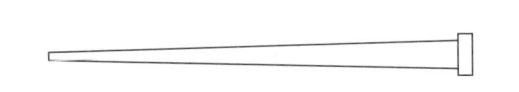

flooring nail
A steel nail with a countersunk head, blunt diamond-shaped point and a mechanically shaped shank, sometimes helically threaded, used in flooring.

nail

tack
A nail, usually made of soft steel, with a large flat head and a relatively short shank tapered to a sharp point; used for installing linoleum and carpet.

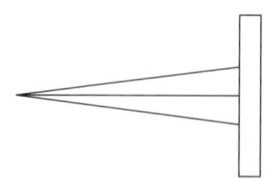

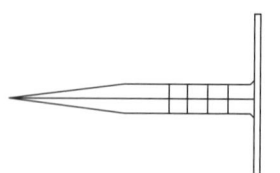

ring-shank nail
A nail the shank of which has ring-like grooves flaring towards the head so it enters easily but grips firmly once it is in.

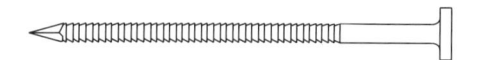

ratchet nail
A strong nail with a countersunk head and ratcheted shank, used on stone walls.

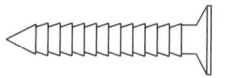

diamond point
A nail point having four diamond-like facets (the most current type).

round point
A nail point with a round, conical shape.

casing nail
A nail with an unusually long, thin shank, small slightly countersunk head, used in finishing work due to its discreet appearance.

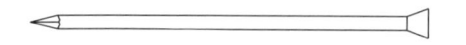

wire nail
A nail manufactured by cutting and forming segments of round wire.

brad
1. A small nail with a countersunk head little wider than the shank, used for finishing. 2. A square-shanked, tapering nail, with a countersunk head, used for finishing.

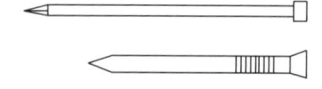

copper clout nail
A flat-headed copper nail, with a tapering, square or round shank, used for exteriors due its resistance to corrosion.

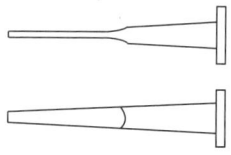

screw

Any threaded fastener or tightener; more usually, a metal building accessory similar to a nail, with a tapering, threaded shank, and a groove in the head to be turned with a screwdriver.

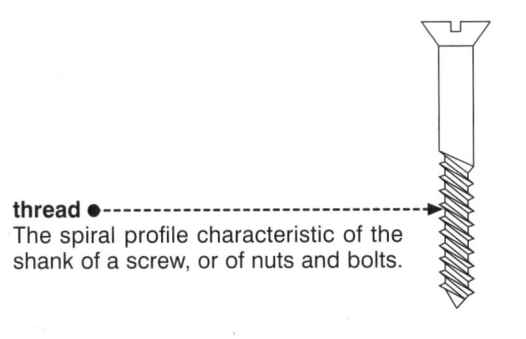

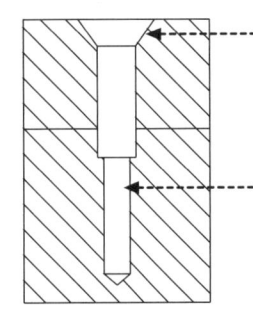

thread
The spiral profile characteristic of the shank of a screw, or of nuts and bolts.

countersink, to
To make a wider conical aperture at the entrance of a screw-hole, to take in the screw's countersunk head.

pilot hole
A hole made to open the way for a nail, a screw, or to guide a wider perforation.

setscrew
1. A headless screw made to hold a detachable doorknob or bulb holder onto a shaft, or to adjust or tighten a mechanical part; also called a grub screw or adjusting screw. 2. The screw in a cramp drawing the two sides together.

machine screw
A threaded bolt with a straight shank and any of the current heads, countersunk, button, square, or hexagonal.

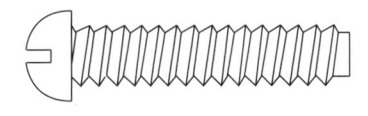

cap screw
A bolt-like screw, threaded along its whole length, with a chamfered end, driven into a hole and made fast without a nut.

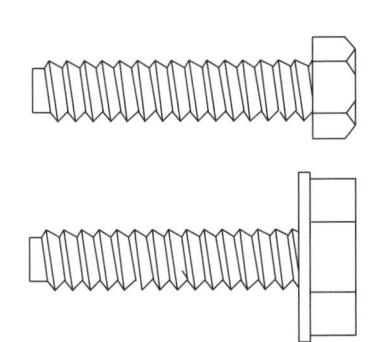

tapping screw
A screw with a coarse threaded, tapered shank, designed to fasten sheet metal or other materials without a tapped hole; also called a sheet metal screw, self-tapping screw or Parker screw.

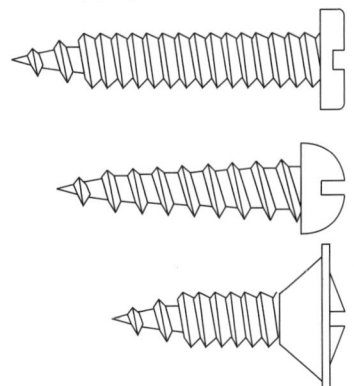

screw

bolt head
The various sorts of widening at the top of a bolt; turning it drives the bolt in, and then tightens the elements the bolt holds.

fillister head
A screw having a cylindrical head, with a rounded top crossed by a groove, and a flat grip underneath.

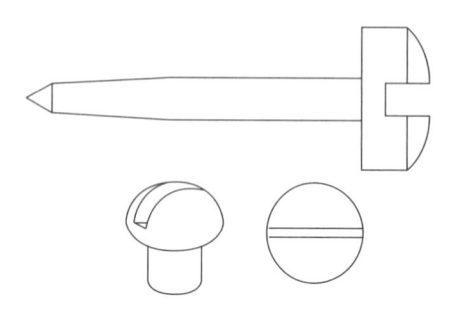

Phillips head
A screw head, flat, countersunk or round, with a special crossed groove, designed to be driven with a Phillips head driver.

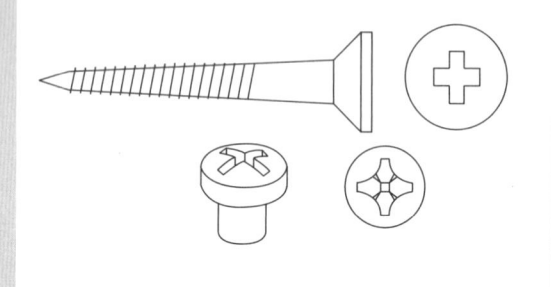

Allen head
A screw head with a hexagonal recession in the center, designed to be turned with an Allen wrench.

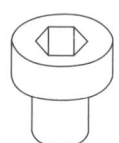

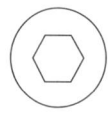

security head
A screw head with a groove designed so that it can only be driven inward.

square head
A square headed screw or bolt, which is turned with a wrench.

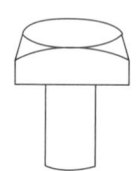

hex-head
A screw or bolt with a hexagonal head, designed to be turned with a wrench.

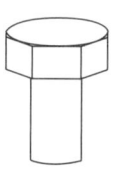

screw

truss head
A screw head with a slightly domed top and a flat grip underneath.

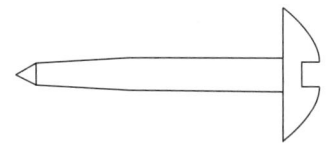

bugle head
A screw head with a flat top and a flared grip underneath, similar but flatter than a countersunk screw.

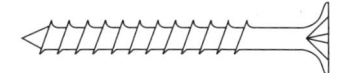

oval head
A screw head with a round head, and a conical grip underneath.

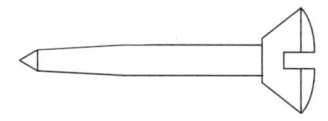

flathead
A screw head with a flat top, designed to come flush with the adjacent surface, with a conical grip underneath, for countersinking.

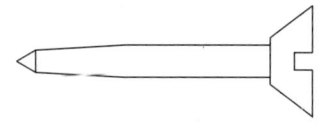

slotted head
A screw or bolt head that is crossed by a straight groove, so it can be turned with a screwdriver.

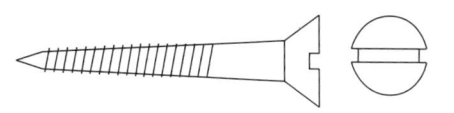

round head
A screw head that has a flat grip underneath with a semi-spherical top.

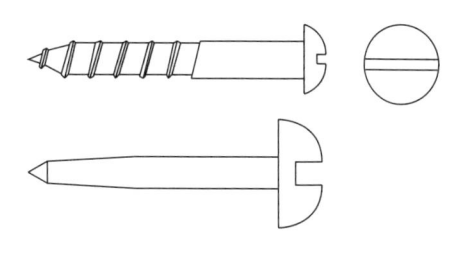

panhead
The head of a rivet or screw, with a cylindrical shape and inward sloping edge.

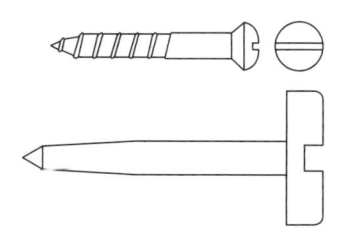

bolt

A straight piece of metal, usually cylindrical, threaded, used to hold elements together, and held in position by a nut on the other side.

Lewis bolt
An eyebolt with a wedge shaped end, fixed into a dovetailed hole in the stone by filling it with concrete or molten lead; used to lift heavy stones.

eyebolt
A bolt with a ring in the place of a head, used to hang or attach heavy objects.

J-bolt
A metal rod that is bent like a letter J; the other end is threaded so as to receive a nut.

U-bolt
A metal rod bent like a letter U; both parallel ends are threaded, to be held by two nuts.

carriage bolt
A round headed bolt with no groove; it has a square neck, that is hammered into the wood and prevents the bolt from turning when the nut is tightened from the opposite end.

machine bolt
A threaded bolt with a straight shank and a square or hexagonal head, which is tightened with a wrench.

bolt

slotted top screw
A relatively small machine bolt with an unusually wide threaded shank.

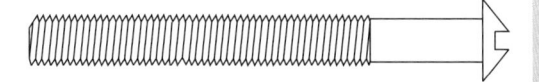

expansion bolt
An anchoring device for concrete, stone or brick, consisting of a bolt in a metal sheath; turning it draws a wedge-shaped nut back into the sheath, which is forced open, tightly holding the bolt in position.

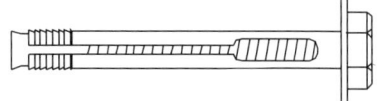

Molly®
A type of expansion bolt, consisting of a sheathed shank with a nut on the end; when it is in the wall and the bolt is turned, the nut is drawn back, forcing the sheathe to grip the hole it is in.

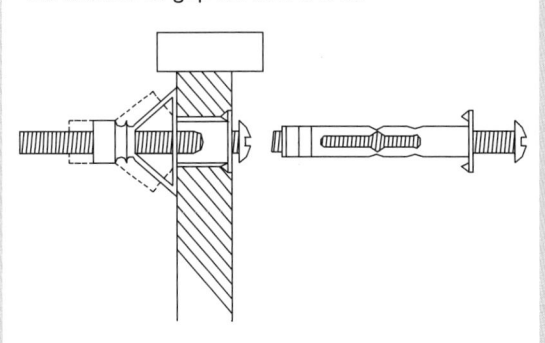

fox bolt
An anchoring device in the form of a bolt with a cleft end, into which a wedge can be driven, forcing the shank open.

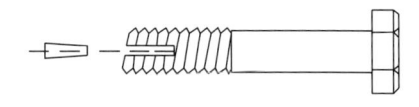

tension-control bolt
A highly resistant bolt with a partly sawn tip, which breaks and drops off when the required tension is reached.

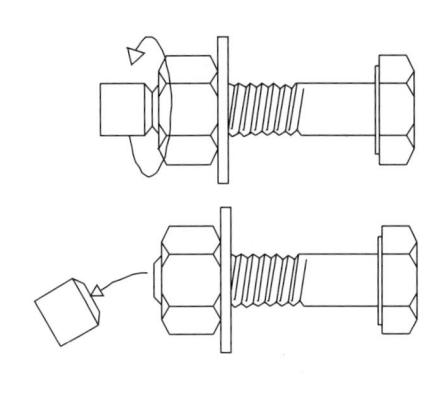

split-ring
A metal connector between two pieces of timber, consisting of a steel ring with grooves that is inserted into a prepared depression between the two timbers; as the bolt is tightened the ring adapts and bites into the wood, holding it in position.

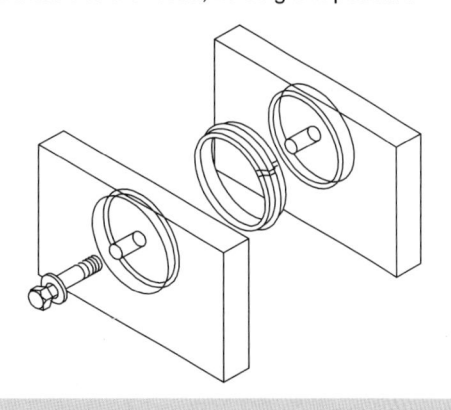

bolt

washer
Any of the ring shaped devices placed between the head of a bolt or screw, and the material surface it is being tightened against, to distribute the pressure, avoid abrasion, or seal an opening. It may be metal, plastic or rubber, wide, narrow, open or closed, serrated, grooved or smooth.

load-indicating washer
A washer having small protuberances that flatten as the bolt is tightened; this is measured with a feeler gauge, indicating the bolt's tension.

wing nut
A nut with two wing-like projections that offer leverage to manipulate it without requiring a tool; also called a thumbnut.

nut
A metal part with a threaded hole in the center, so as to be screwed onto a bolt; the outside is prism shaped so as to be gripped with a wrench.

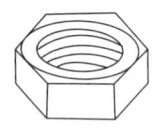

castellated nut
A nut with radial projections around the hole, so a wedge may be driven between them and a groove in the end of the bolt, locking it.

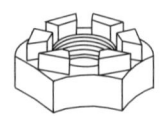

locknut
A nut designed to lock into place when it is tightened so it cannot come loose.

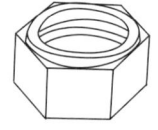

cap nut
A nut with a hexagonal base closed by a flat, ringed, or dome-shaped finish; used to cover and protect the end the bolt.

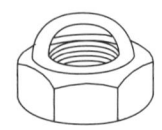

cap
A nut in which the threaded hole is sealed off with a flat or dome shaped cap, to close the end of a tube.

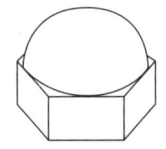

back nut
1. A dish-shaped nut with a grommet, forming a watertight pipe joint. 2. An auxiliary nut used to prevent another from being loosened by vibration.

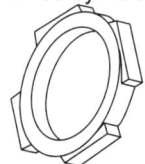

tool

An object or instrument designed specifically to perform a given task or carry out a profession.

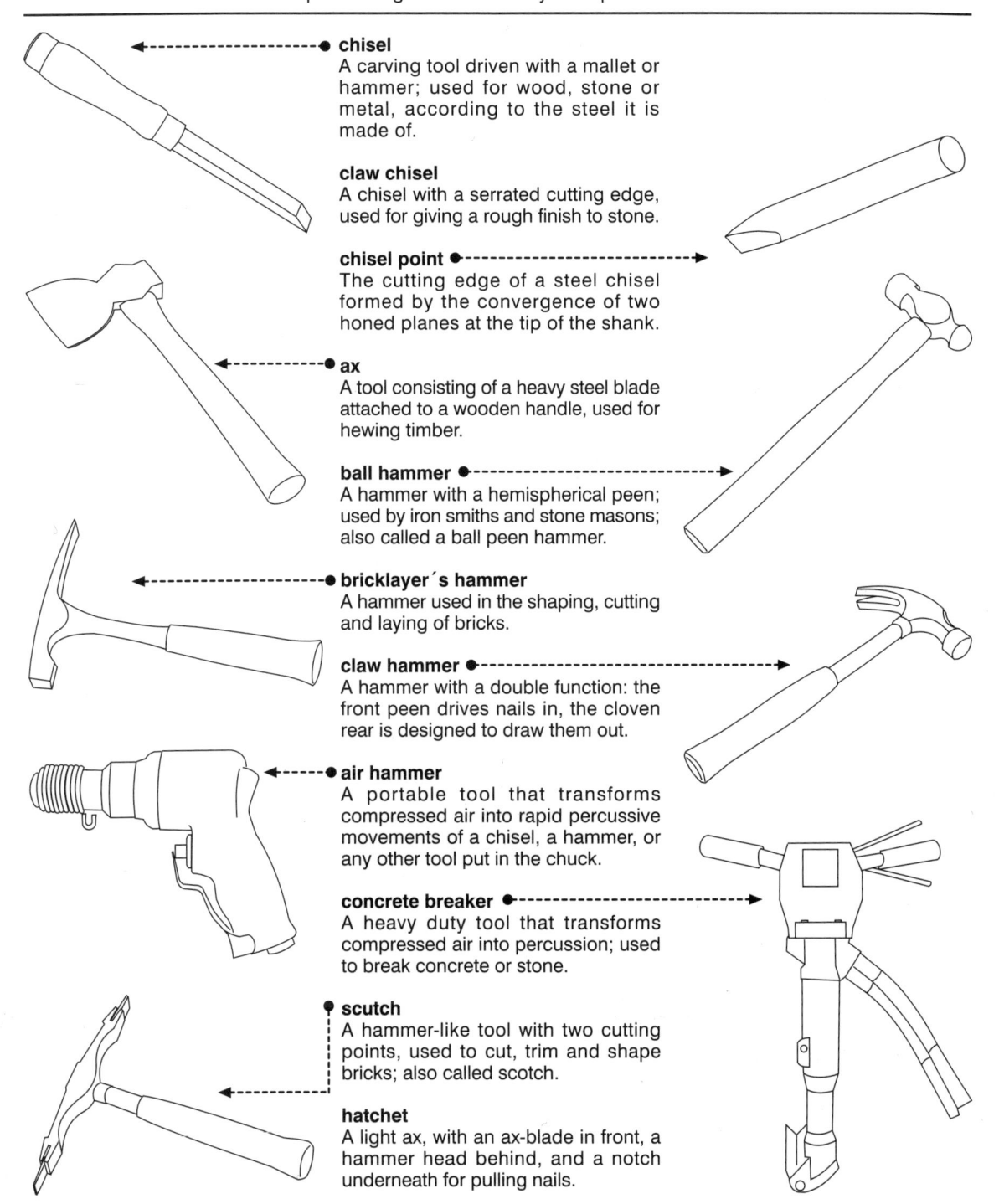

chisel
A carving tool driven with a mallet or hammer; used for wood, stone or metal, according to the steel it is made of.

claw chisel
A chisel with a serrated cutting edge, used for giving a rough finish to stone.

chisel point
The cutting edge of a steel chisel formed by the convergence of two honed planes at the tip of the shank.

ax
A tool consisting of a heavy steel blade attached to a wooden handle, used for hewing timber.

ball hammer
A hammer with a hemispherical peen; used by iron smiths and stone masons; also called a ball peen hammer.

bricklayer´s hammer
A hammer used in the shaping, cutting and laying of bricks.

claw hammer
A hammer with a double function: the front peen drives nails in, the cloven rear is designed to draw them out.

air hammer
A portable tool that transforms compressed air into rapid percussive movements of a chisel, a hammer, or any other tool put in the chuck.

concrete breaker
A heavy duty tool that transforms compressed air into percussion; used to break concrete or stone.

scutch
A hammer-like tool with two cutting points, used to cut, trim and shape bricks; also called scotch.

hatchet
A light ax, with an ax-blade in front, a hammer head behind, and a notch underneath for pulling nails.

tool

floater (USA)
A flat tool with a handle, usually rectangular though the shape and size can vary, used to flatten a surface of fresh mortar or concrete; also called a float (GB).

bull float
A float to which a long articulated handle has been attached.

trowel
A flat hand tool consisting of a usually rectangular sheet of metal with a handle, used to spread and shape plaster or mortar; also to impart a fairly smooth finish surface to a concrete floor.

darby
A wood or metal tool about 10 cm wide by a meter long, used to flatten a fresh concrete surface before the final layer; also called a derby or a derby float.

screed
A geometrically straight piece of wood or metal used to strike off a fresh surface of mortar or concrete, usually guided by screed rails.

edger
A trowel with a bent edge, used to give a rounded corner to an edge or fresh concrete or plaster. Also, tool used to round of the edges of concrete steps and slabs.

mechanical trowel
A machine designed to provide the finish to a concrete surface; it consists of a series of metal or rubber blades that rotate around a central pivot; also called a power trowel.

bricklayer's trowel
Any of various tools having a flat, triangular, oval or square blade with a raised handle, used to deposit and work mortar or plaster.

sieve
A tool consisting of a surface with regularly spaced holes of uniform size, such as woven wire, held by a frame; used for sorting aggregates (sand, gravel) according to particle size.

scarifier
A tool similar to a rake, used to roughen a surface to improve its adherence to another layer of material.

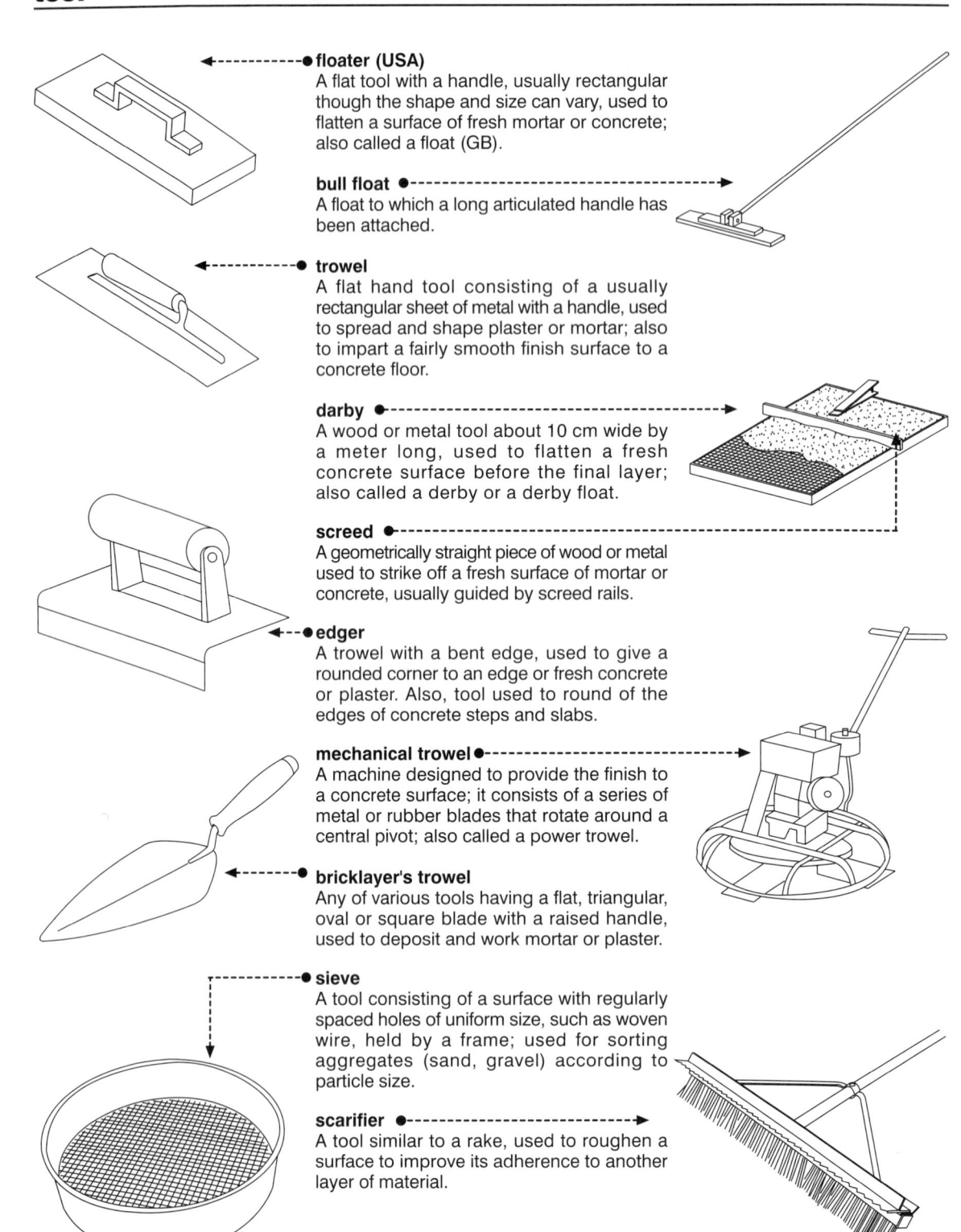

tool

bow saw
A saw consisting of a thin steel blade held taught by bow-like steel frame.

circular saw
A saw consisting of an electrical engine driving a rapidly rotating steel disc with a serrated edge; also called a disk saw.

chain saw
A hand-held mechanical saw that drives an endless chain, which carries the teeth; used for cutting wood.

band saw
A mechanically driven saw consisting of an endless steel band with a serrated edge.

pavement saw
A mechanically driven saw, moved on wheels, with a carbon silicate or diamond blade; used to cut contraction joints in pavements.

auger
A hand held tool, similar to a gimlet but larger, consisting of a steel twist bit crossed by a wooden handle, like a letter T; used for drilling holes in wood.

breast drill
A portable drill, with a hand-driven cogwheel moving the bit, and a butt at the back on which to lean for extra pressure.

drill
An electrically powered portable tool, with interchangeable appliances to perforate or polish wood, metal or stone.

air drill
A heavy duty drill powered by compressed air provided by an external pump; used for breaking up concrete.

crown saw
A wood drill bit, consisting of a wide cylinder with a serrated edge, that cuts a relatively large hole leaving the inner cylinder intact.

drill bit
A cylindrical cutting tool which, rotated by a drill, makes holes in the material it is designed for.

auger bit
A bit with a square tang, to be fitted into a brace and rotated; used to drill holes in wood.

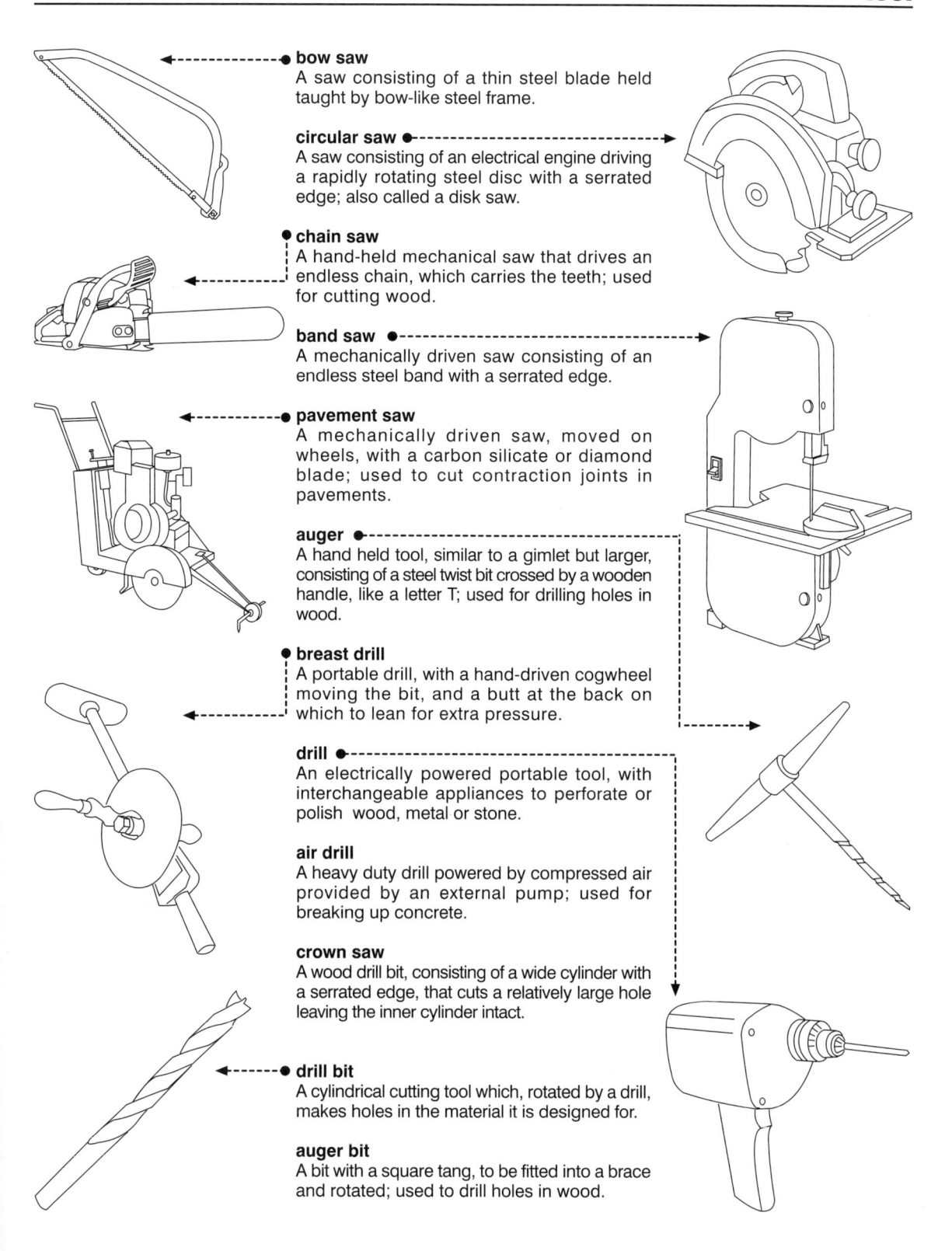

199

tool

aligning punch
A pointed metal tool used to align mating holes prior to bolting.

driftpin
An unthreaded rod, square or round, driven into an existing hole, in substitution for a bolt, or other anchoring device.

awl
A pointed tool used for starting holes in soft or thin wood, or thin sheet metal.

blow torch
A portable tool used by plumbers, electricians and painters, to apply intense heat onto a precise area.

acetylene blowlamp
A type of blow torch that uses acetylene gas and oxygen, producing a flame hot enough for welding and cutting steel.

grinder
A power tool that rotates abrasive appliances at high speed, used to polish or sharpen tools.

stake
A small, relatively portable anvil used for light metal work or sheet metal.

rivet set
A tool used to shape the head of a rivet.

compass plane
A woodworking plane with a concave or convex base plate, to form concave or convex pieces of wood.

mortise chisel
A tool used to cut mortises in wood.

scaffold
Any temporary structure installed to provide workers with walkways, space for their materials and tools, safety barriers, and everything needed to carry out a task one or more levels above the ground; also called staging.

air brush
A light portable tool equipped with a pump, which projects paint, die or other pigments by means of compressed air.

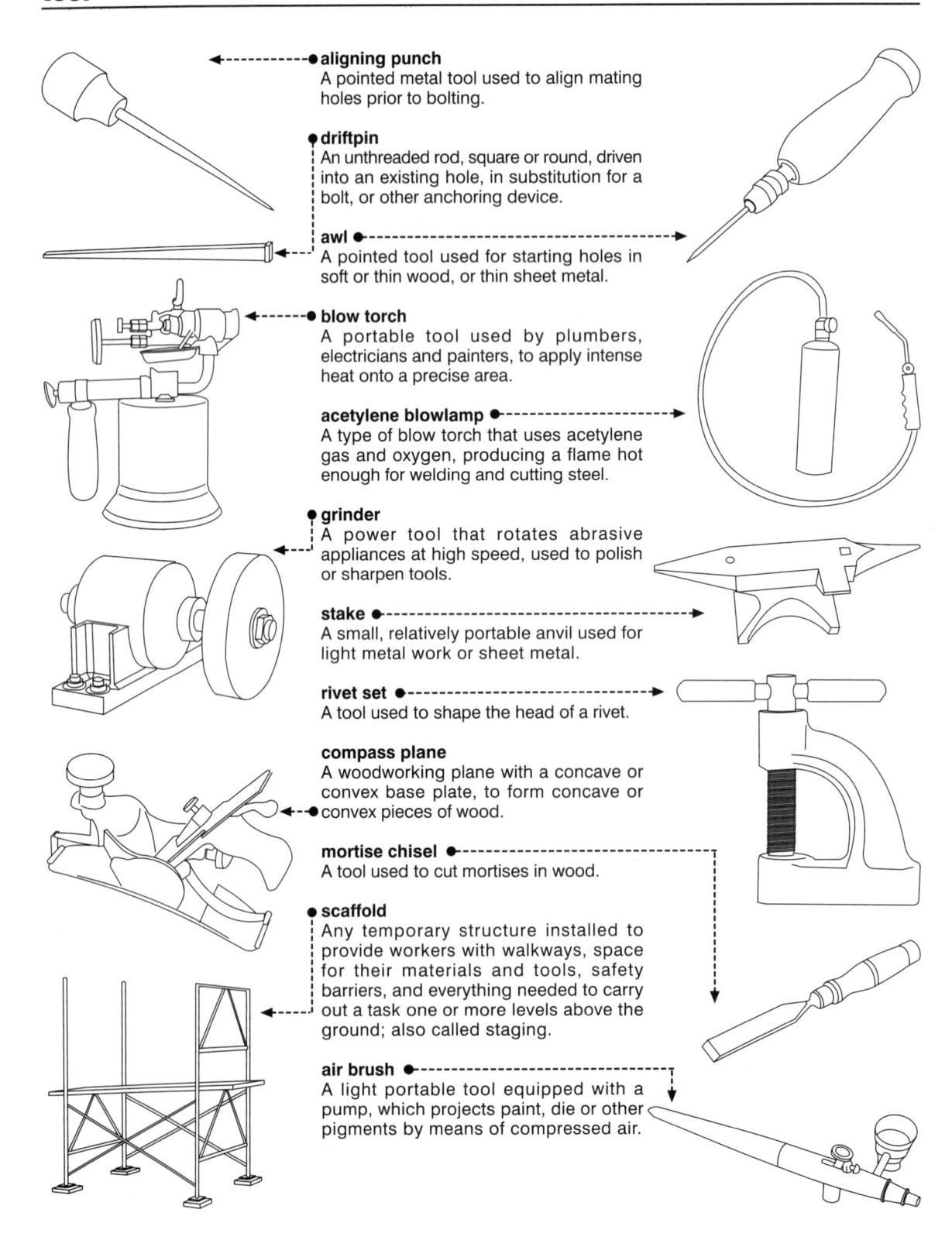

Installations

HVAC
Solar energy
Electricity
light
plumbing
Fire safety

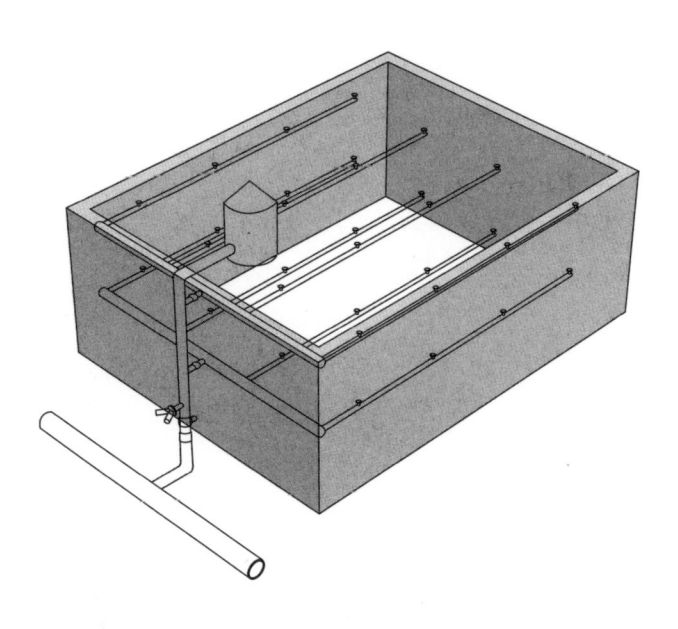

HVAC

An internationally accepted abbreviation standing for "heating, ventilation, and air conditioning".

heat
A non-mechanical energy transfer due to a difference in temperature between two bodies, the warmer transferring heat to the cooler. It causes temperature to rise, accelerates chemical reactions, making substances expand and change state, melting, evaporating, or burning.

heat of condensation
The heat liberated from the mass of a gas at the moment when it condenses into a liquid state, and is at boiling point.

radiant heat
Calorific energy that is transmitted by radiation of electromagnetic waves.

temperature
A measure of the heat that a substance, a body, or the atmosphere contains in relation to a defined value.

ambient temperature
The temperature of the surrounding air.

effective temperature
A temperature representing the human body's perception of heat or cold, which combines the effects of ambient temperature, relative humidity, and air movement; it is equal to the temperature necessary for motionless dry air to produce the same effect.

mean radiant temperature (MRT)
The calculation of the total radiant temperature of the walls, the floor and the ceiling affecting a given point of measurement, taking into account the solid angle of each of them from that point. MRT is equal to the average temperature of all the surfaces, times the angle of incidence upon the reference point, divided by 360.

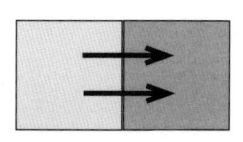

conduction
The process by which heat is transferred between two parts of a stationery system which are in direct contact, caused by a temperature difference between the parts.

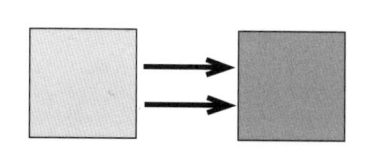

radiation
1. The complete process in which energy is emitted by one body, transmitted through an intervening medium or space, and absorbed by another body. 2. The energy transferred by these processes.

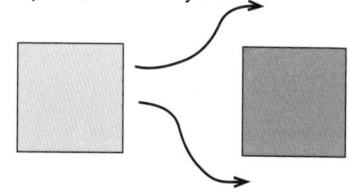

convection
The transmission of heat due to the circulation of the heated parts of a liquid or a gas, moved by mechanical means or induced by a difference in density.

thermal conductivity
A property of a given material, usually represented by the letter k, called k factor, equal to the quantity of heat per unit of time per unit of area, conducted through a plate of unit thickness of the said material, when the two faces of the plate differ by one unit of temperature.

thermal emissivity
The ratio between the rate of radiant heat emission by a body at a given temperature, and the rate of radiant heat emission by a blackbody at the same temperature under identical conditions.

HVAC

chimney
A hollow vertical structure used to conduct outside the smoke and gases resulting from combustion of various materials related to heating, cooking, or other purposes; also called a vent.

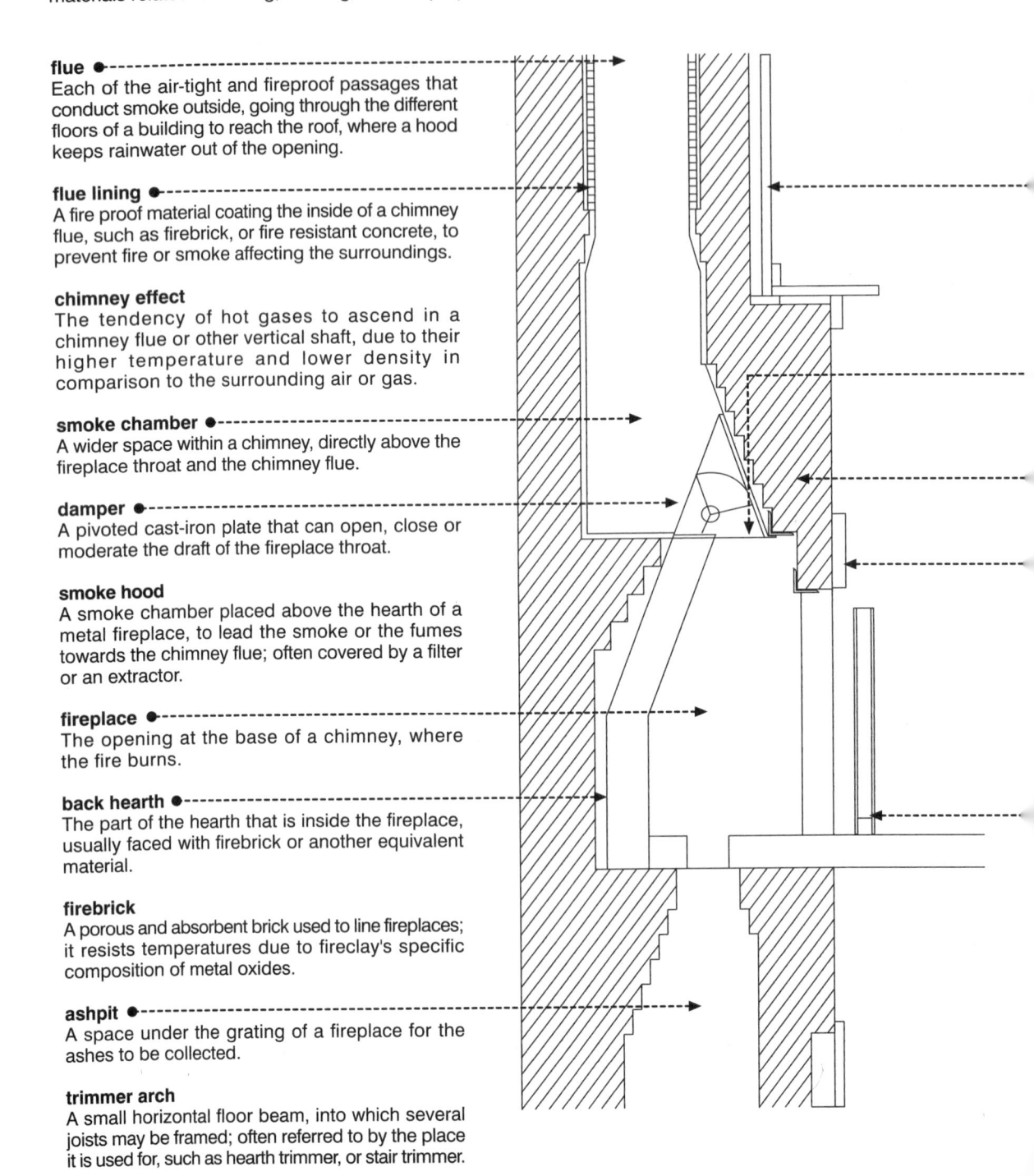

flue
Each of the air-tight and fireproof passages that conduct smoke outside, going through the different floors of a building to reach the roof, where a hood keeps rainwater out of the opening.

flue lining
A fire proof material coating the inside of a chimney flue, such as firebrick, or fire resistant concrete, to prevent fire or smoke affecting the surroundings.

chimney effect
The tendency of hot gases to ascend in a chimney flue or other vertical shaft, due to their higher temperature and lower density in comparison to the surrounding air or gas.

smoke chamber
A wider space within a chimney, directly above the fireplace throat and the chimney flue.

damper
A pivoted cast-iron plate that can open, close or moderate the draft of the fireplace throat.

smoke hood
A smoke chamber placed above the hearth of a metal fireplace, to lead the smoke or the fumes towards the chimney flue; often covered by a filter or an extractor.

fireplace
The opening at the base of a chimney, where the fire burns.

back hearth
The part of the hearth that is inside the fireplace, usually faced with firebrick or another equivalent material.

firebrick
A porous and absorbent brick used to line fireplaces; it resists temperatures due to fireclay's specific composition of metal oxides.

ashpit
A space under the grating of a fireplace for the ashes to be collected.

trimmer arch
A small horizontal floor beam, into which several joists may be framed; often referred to by the place it is used for, such as hearth trimmer, or stair trimmer.

HVAC

space heating
A compact, self contained heater, using electricity or a liquid fuel to supply heat energy to heat the space; often provided with a powerful fan to ensure that the hot air circulates.

stovepipe
A pipe serving as the smoke outlet for a boiler, heater or stove, which it connects to the main chimney flue or directly with the outside.

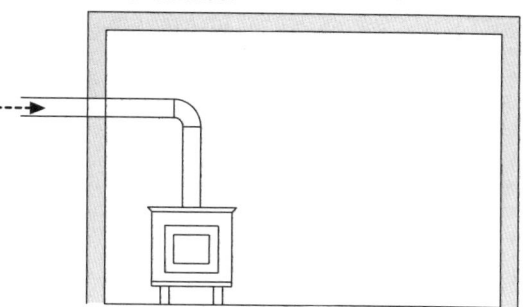

chimney breast
The wall over the fireplace, whether projecting into the room or not, carried on the arch, bar, or mantle.

hood
A projecting cover over a fireplace to prevent smoke escaping.

Franklin stove
A cast iron stove that imitates the features of an open fireplace, but which is freestanding in the room.

throat
A narrow passage at the bottom of a chimney, between the fireplace and the smoke chamber.

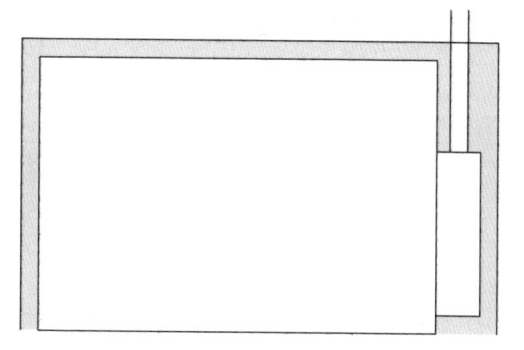

mantel
The structure that supports the masonry over a fireplace opening.

mantelpiece
An ornamental frame around a fireplace opening, concealing the mantel and structure, often surmounted by an overmantel and a shelf.

wall furnace
A self-contained furnace, complete with air grilles, designed to be installed on a wall; the hot air produced circulates by gravity or helped by a blower.

draft
The upward current produced within a chimney due to the low density of the hot gases inside it compared to the colder air outside, helping to fan the fire.

fire screen
A screen sometimes placed in front of the fireplace to prevent sparks from entering the room.

cowl
A device installed a the top of a chimney flue or vertical shaft to increase the draft.

downdraft
A downward current frequently occurring in a chimney, preventing the proper exit of smoke and combustion gases.

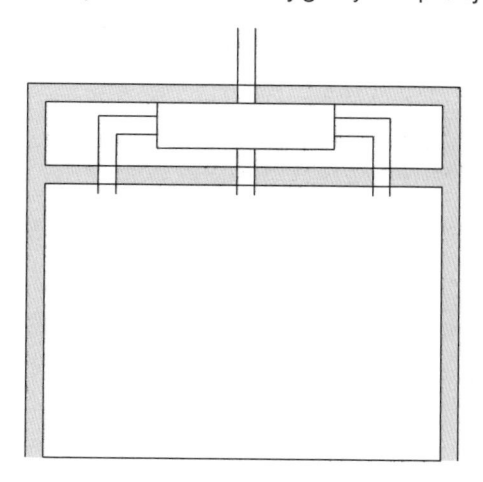

horizontal furnace
A heater designed to be installed horizontally, on a raised shelf with limited space available.

205

HVAC

central heating
A system which distributes the heat from a central source to the whole of a building, along a network of pipes.

radiator
A closely spaced grid of tubes designed to liberate the heat carried by the hot water or steam circulating through it from a central heater.

fin tube
A radiator pipe consisting of horizontal tubes and vertical fins, thereby increasing the transmission of heat to the surrounding air.

convector
A heating device in which radiator-heated air is made to circulate mechanically, by a fan or similar unit.

baseboard heater
A heating convector in which the elements are installed in panels along the baseboard of the walls.

diffuser
An accessory consisting of movable fins, used to convey the hot air in different directions.

return pipe
In a central heating system, the pipe by which the water produced by the condensation of steam is returned to the boiler.

dry return
In a central heating system by steam, the return pipe that carries condensation water and air back to the boiler.

cold-air return
A pipe returning cold air to the source of heat, to be reheated.

condensation pump
A mechanism designed to remove condensation liquid from the return pipes.

combustion air
The air necessary for the combustion of a boiler or furnace to take place.

boiler house
The room where the central mechanisms of a heating system are housed.

thermostat
A device that responds to temperature changes in its vicinity, stopping or starting the heating or refrigeration systems it is connected to.

thermocouple
A mechanism consisting of two junctions of two dissimilar metals in an electric circuit; when the two junctions are at different temperatures, a voltage is generated, permitting the temperature difference to be measured.

safety valve
A valve designed to release the interior pressure of gas or steam when it rises above a specific level, until it returns below the security limit.

furnace
A device designed to generate heat or steam.

gas furnace
A heating furnace that uses the combustion of gas as its energy source.

electric furnace
A heating furnace that generates heat using electricity as the energy source.

HVAC

water heater
An electrical or gas burning device used to heat household water to a temperature between 50º and 60º C (120º - 140º F).

air heater
A heating unit that differs from regular radiators by having a blowing device (a fan or turbine), which permits the orientation of the hot air towards the area that requires heating.

caliduct
A conduit for the conveyance of hot water or air, for heating purposes.

fan
A mechanism designed to rotate a series of radiating blades, the helical disposition of which impels air in a given direction.

blower
An air-impelling mechanism housed in a building's bottom floor, designed to move hot air throughout the heating ducts of the rest of the building.

pump
A mechanical device designed to transport or impel fluids or semi-fluids through a pipe, by means of pressure, suction or both; used to raise water to a higher level, or ensure that the fluid in a circuit does not remain still.

vent
A hollow vertical structure used to conduct outside the smoke and gases resulting from combustion of various materials related to heating, cooking, or other purposes; also called a chimney.

combustible
Said of a material capable of undergoing combustion in air.

heating medium
Any solid, liquid such as water, or gas such as air or steam, used to transmit heat from a source, directly or by means of a heating device, to the surrounding medium being heated.

hot-water heating
A heating system in which heated water is made to move through a circuit of pipes leading to the radiators that heat the different areas of a building.

one-pipe system
A plumbing system that relies on a single pipe for the whole distribution.

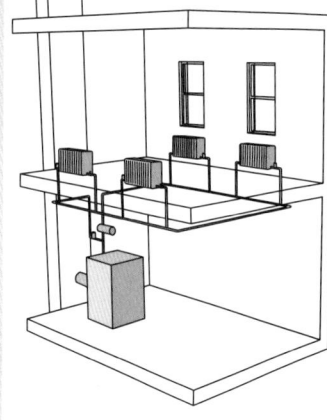

steam heating
The heating system in a building, consisting of a heater that impels steam through the circuit that connects the radiators.

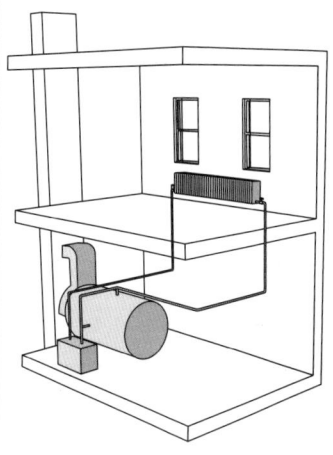

forced warm-air heating
The heating system in a building, consisting of a heater that impels hot air through a circuit of ducts connecting the air diffusers.

ductwork
The network of pipes, shafts, or other means used to convey the hot or cold air in a heating or ventilation system.

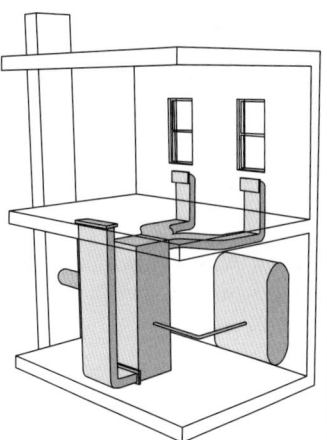

HVAC

two-pipe system
A heating system that works with two pipes; one of them takes the hot water from the boiler to the radiators, and another returns the cold water back to the boiler.

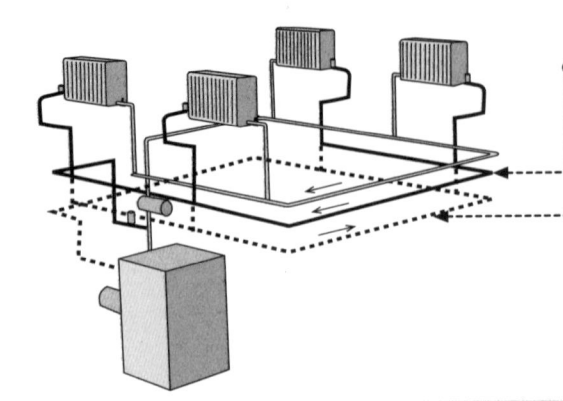

- **direct return**
  A heating system consisting of two pipes, one of which is used for the return from each of the radiators of the circuit, along the shortest route back to the boiler.

- **reverse return**
  A two pipe heating system, in which the length of the pipe conveying the water is equal to the length of the pipe returning it.

perimeter heating
A hot air heating system, with ducts embedded in the floor slab and perimetral walls, registers in or near the floor releasing hot air, registers near the ceiling drawing it back to the furnace.

closed loop system
A perimeter heating system consisting of a single duct, forming a closed circuit, leading hot air to the various outlets throughout the floor.

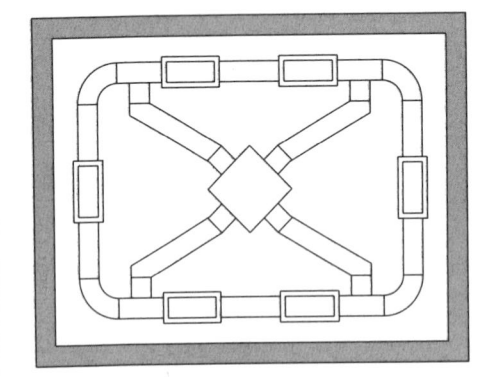

perimeter radial system
A perimeter heating system consisting of a radial duct pattern, branching out from a centrally located furnace, leading hot air to the various outlets throughout the floor.

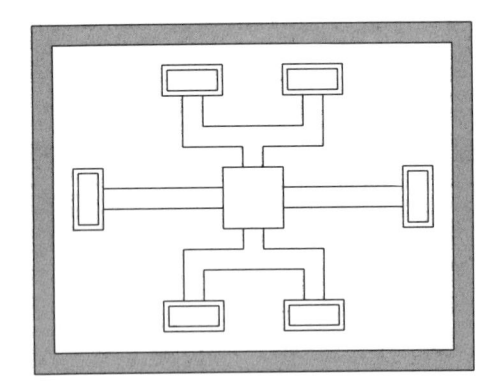

extended plenum system
A duct pattern in a heating system by hot air characterized by having a single main duct from which narrower secondary ducts branch out to each individual register.

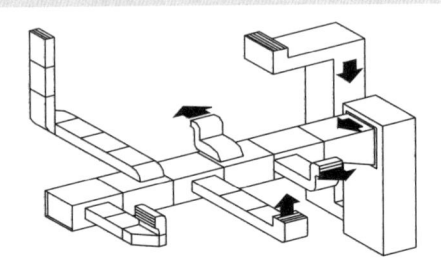

HVAC

air conditioning
The processes through which the properties of the air inside a given space are simultaneously controlled and altered, monitoring its temperature, humidity, hygiene and distribution.

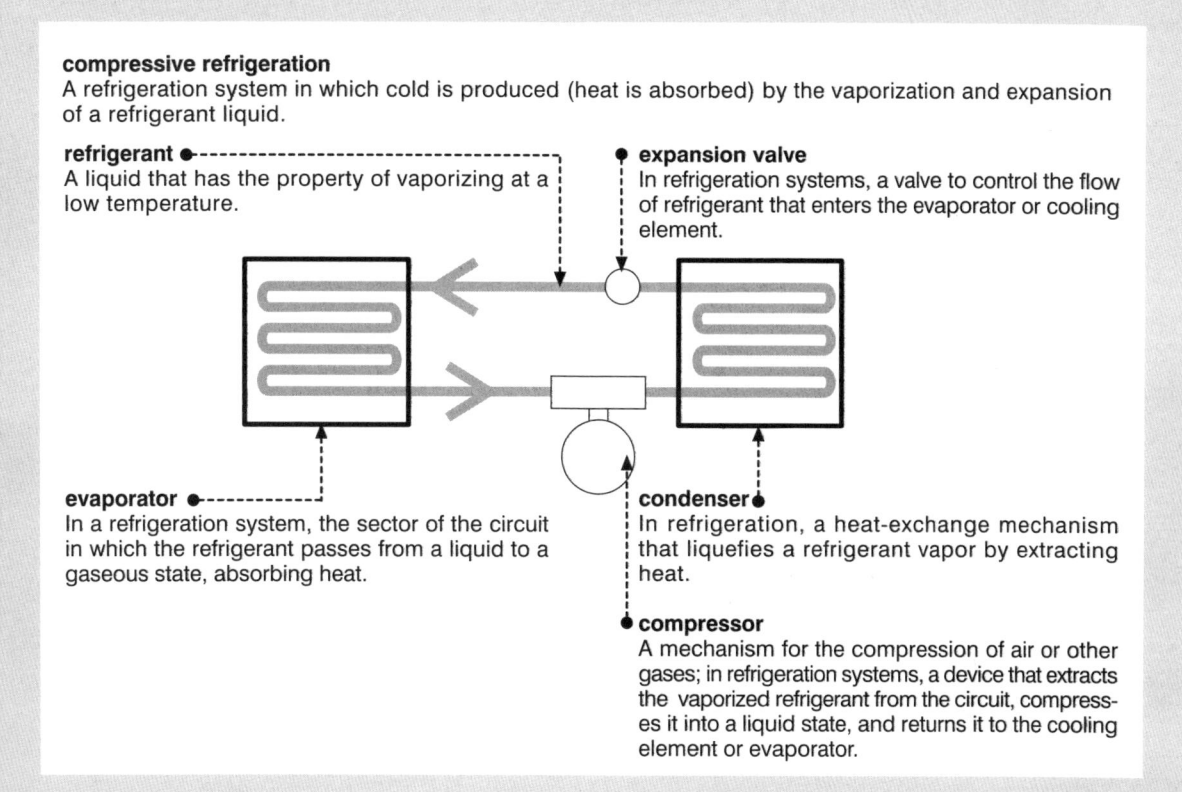

compressive refrigeration
A refrigeration system in which cold is produced (heat is absorbed) by the vaporization and expansion of a refrigerant liquid.

refrigerant
A liquid that has the property of vaporizing at a low temperature.

expansion valve
In refrigeration systems, a valve to control the flow of refrigerant that enters the evaporator or cooling element.

evaporator
In a refrigeration system, the sector of the circuit in which the refrigerant passes from a liquid to a gaseous state, absorbing heat.

condenser
In refrigeration, a heat-exchange mechanism that liquefies a refrigerant vapor by extracting heat.

compressor
A mechanism for the compression of air or other gases; in refrigeration systems, a device that extracts the vaporized refrigerant from the circuit, compresses it into a liquid state, and returns it to the cooling element or evaporator.

absorption refrigeration
A refrigeration process in which the refrigerant gas evolved in the evaporator is not compressed but taken in an absorber, heated and released in a generator.

evaporator

heat exchanger
A device designed for the transmission of heat between two fluids that are physically separated by a barrier.

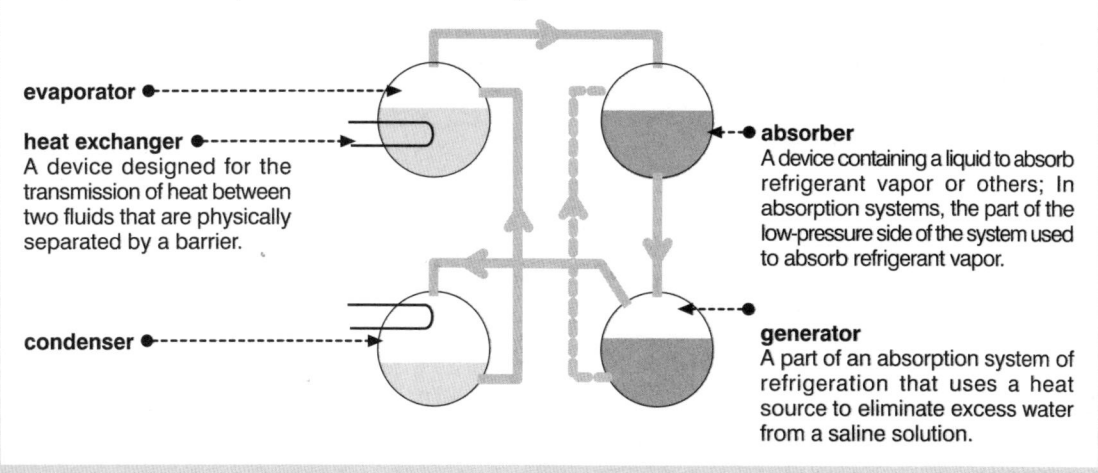

condenser

absorber
A device containing a liquid to absorb refrigerant vapor or others; In absorption systems, the part of the low-pressure side of the system used to absorb refrigerant vapor.

generator
A part of an absorption system of refrigeration that uses a heat source to eliminate excess water from a saline solution.

HVAC

central air conditioning
A system in which the air is conditioned in a centralized unit and mechanically impelled through a network of ducts to the registers in the rest of the building.

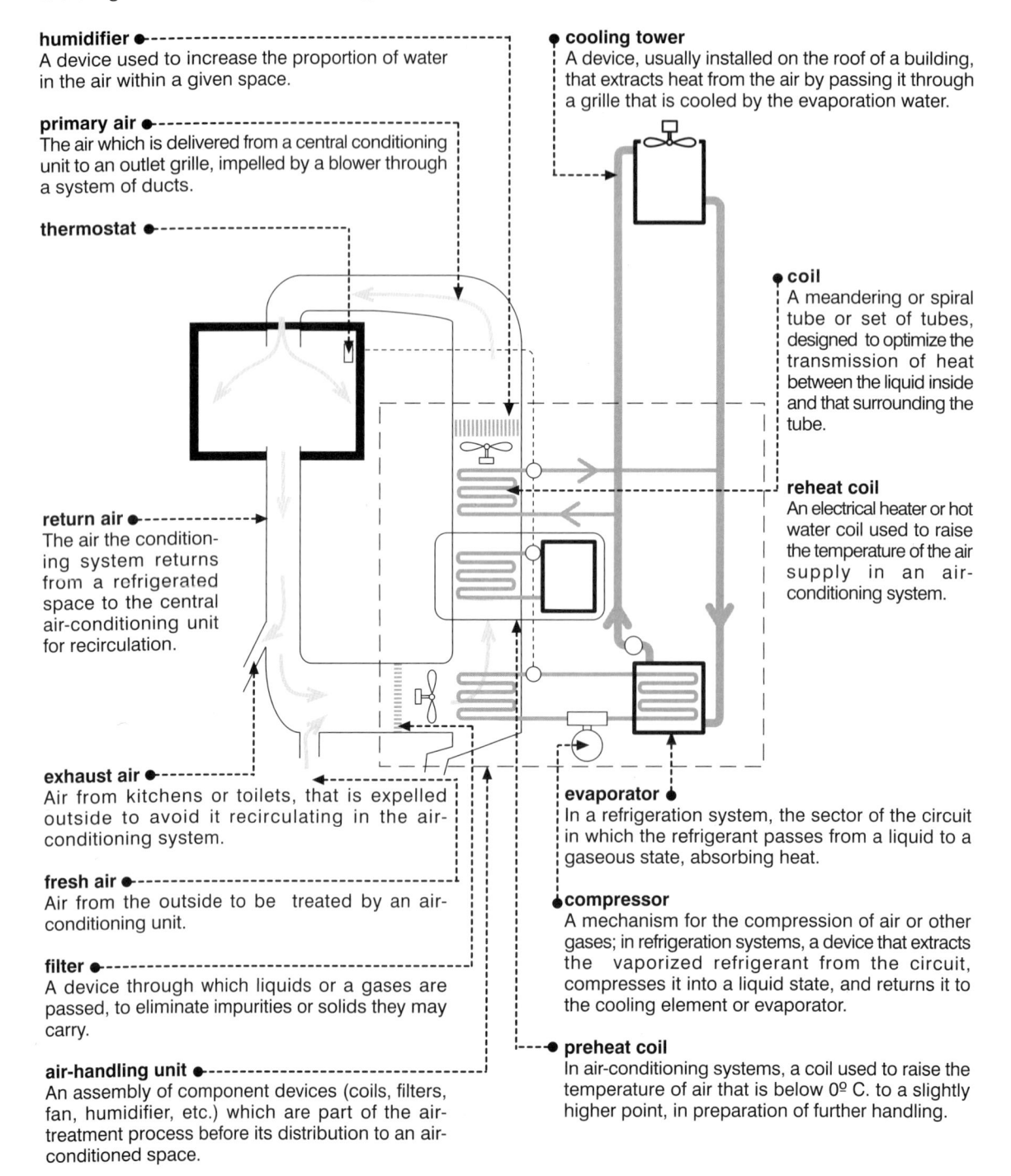

humidifier
A device used to increase the proportion of water in the air within a given space.

primary air
The air which is delivered from a central conditioning unit to an outlet grille, impelled by a blower through a system of ducts.

thermostat

return air
The air the conditioning system returns from a refrigerated space to the central air-conditioning unit for recirculation.

exhaust air
Air from kitchens or toilets, that is expelled outside to avoid it recirculating in the air-conditioning system.

fresh air
Air from the outside to be treated by an air-conditioning unit.

filter
A device through which liquids or a gases are passed, to eliminate impurities or solids they may carry.

air-handling unit
An assembly of component devices (coils, filters, fan, humidifier, etc.) which are part of the air-treatment process before its distribution to an air-conditioned space.

cooling tower
A device, usually installed on the roof of a building, that extracts heat from the air by passing it through a grille that is cooled by the evaporation water.

coil
A meandering or spiral tube or set of tubes, designed to optimize the transmission of heat between the liquid inside and that surrounding the tube.

reheat coil
An electrical heater or hot water coil used to raise the temperature of the air supply in an air-conditioning system.

evaporator
In a refrigeration system, the sector of the circuit in which the refrigerant passes from a liquid to a gaseous state, absorbing heat.

compressor
A mechanism for the compression of air or other gases; in refrigeration systems, a device that extracts the vaporized refrigerant from the circuit, compresses it into a liquid state, and returns it to the cooling element or evaporator.

preheat coil
In air-conditioning systems, a coil used to raise the temperature of air that is below 0º C. to a slightly higher point, in preparation of further handling.

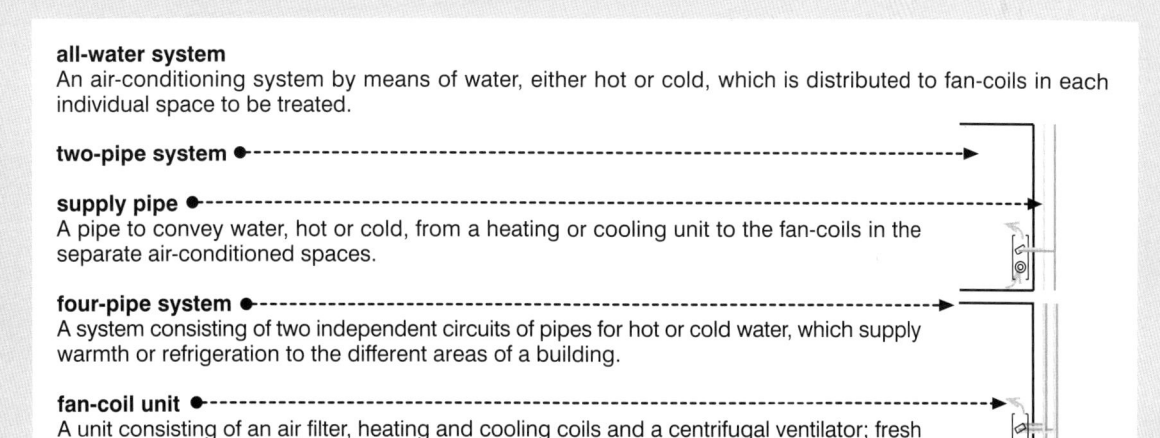

HVAC

all-water system
An air-conditioning system by means of water, either hot or cold, which is distributed to fan-coils in each individual space to be treated.

two-pipe system
supply pipe
A pipe to convey water, hot or cold, from a heating or cooling unit to the fan-coils in the separate air-conditioned spaces.

four-pipe system
A system consisting of two independent circuits of pipes for hot or cold water, which supply warmth or refrigeration to the different areas of a building.

fan-coil unit
A unit consisting of an air filter, heating and cooling coils and a centrifugal ventilator; fresh air comes from a central plant or straight from outside, through an opening at the back of the unit.

all-air system
An air-conditioning system in which central ventilators impel the air to the outlets through the ductwork of the building.

single-duct system
A ventilation system in which the air is impelled through a single duct to the various spaces being air-conditioned.

variable-air-volume system
An air conditioning system in which the volume of air supplied to a given zone is regulated, based on the load in each zone.

constant-air-volume system
An air-conditioning system in which a thermostat regulates the amount of air supplied to a given zone.

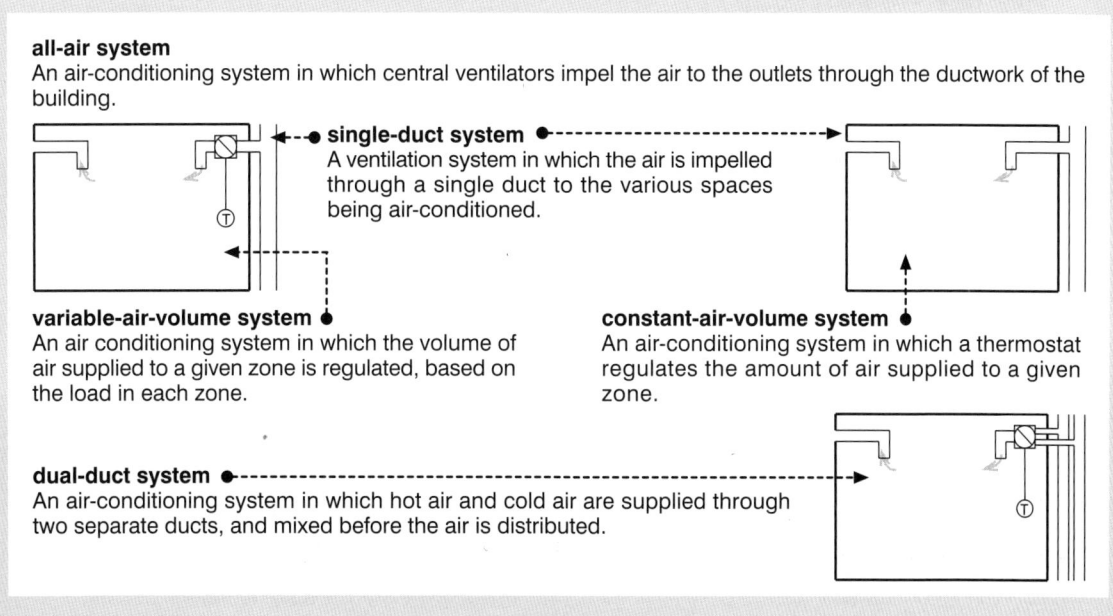

dual-duct system
An air-conditioning system in which hot air and cold air are supplied through two separate ducts, and mixed before the air is distributed.

air-water system
An air-conditioning system in which ducts bring fresh air from a central source, to be mixed with the air of the zone being air-conditioned, and then heated or cooled by a convection unit in situ.

terminal reheat system
An air-conditioning system in which a heating coil regulates the temperature of the air in each supply zone, directly before it is released.

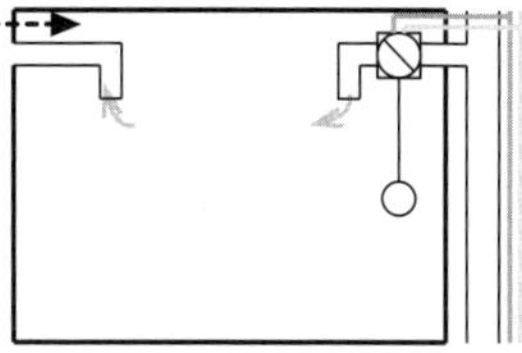

induction unit

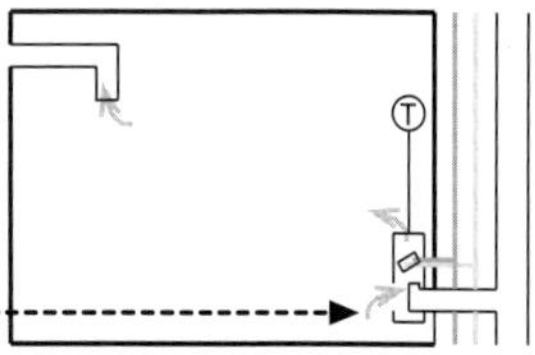

HVAC

ventilation
The process by which the movement and renovation of air in a given space is administered.

natural ventilation
The process of ventilation by means of the air's natural movement or currents.

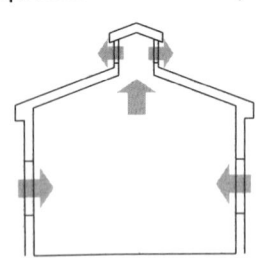

ventilate, to
To provide clean air to renovate the supply available in a given zone.

air change
The substitution of the volume of air in a given space by the same volume of fresh air every given period of time.

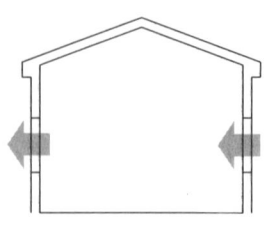

cross ventilation
The circulation of air through windows or other openings at opposite ends of an enclosed space.

fan
A mechanism designed to rotate a series of radiating blades, the helical disposition of which impels air in a given direction.

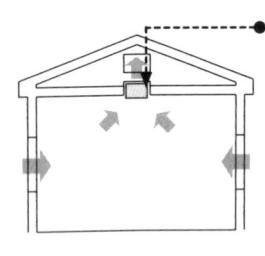

whole-house ventilator
A powerful ventilator that draws out the stale air from the interior of a house and expels it outside through a series of vents generally above the roof.

centrifugal fan
A motor driven ventilator which absorbs the air along the propeller hub, and impels it outward radially.

plenum chamber
In air conditioning systems, an enclosed volume a little above atmospheric pressure (in supply systems) connected to supply ducts, or below atmospheric pressure (in return systems); connected to the return grilles.

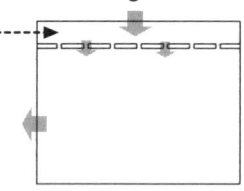

attic ventilator
A mechanical fan installed in the attic of a house, designed to move large quantities of air at a comparatively low speed.

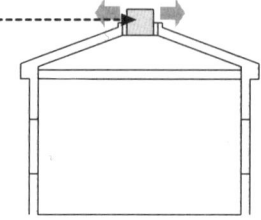

exhaust fan
A ventilator used to absorb air from an interior space and expel it outside.

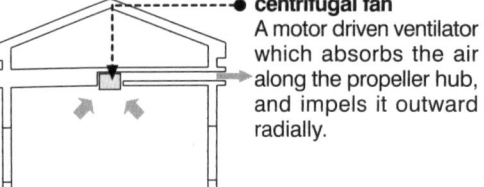

solar energy

Energy which the sun emits, and reaches the earth as radiation.

solar house
A house designed to get the maximum advantage of the solar radiation it receives, as an alternative source of energy, light and heat.

solar orientation
The orientation of a building in accordance with the solar cycle.

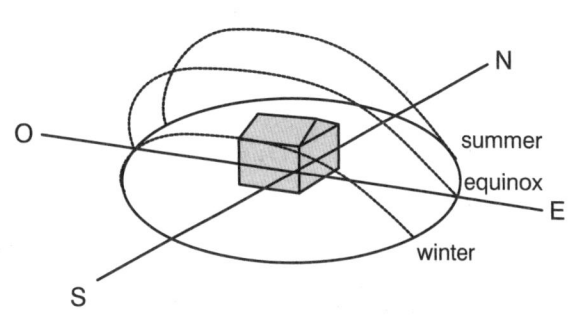

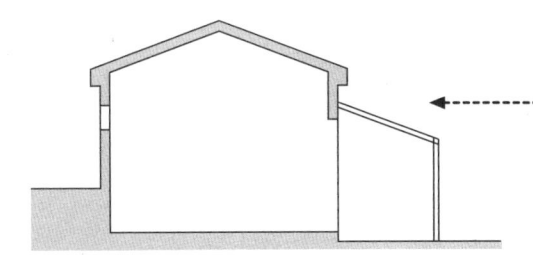

solarium
A sunny room in which glass is predominant, designed specifically for sun bathing and solar therapy; also called sun room, sun porch, sun parlor (U.S.A.) or sun parlour (G.B.).

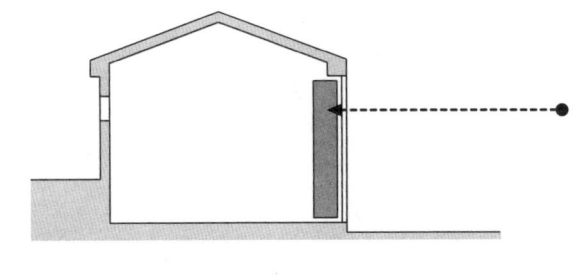

drumwall
A wall of steel drums in front of a large sun window, filled with water, and painted matt black on the side facing the sun, so as to accumulate the solar energy as heat, which it will release into the building slowly, after dark.

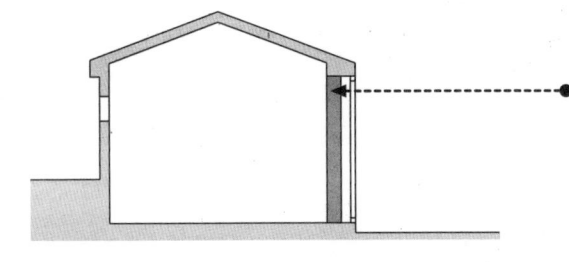

Trombe wall
A solid wall of brickwork or stone in front of a large sun-window, painted matt black so as to absorb the solar energy transformed into heat which it accumulates, and distributes through the house during the night.

solar energy

solar-heating system
A heating system that uses solar radiation as the predominant source of energy.

passive solar-heating
A system in which the solar energy is collected, stored and distributed in the structure mainly by natural convection, conduction or radiation.

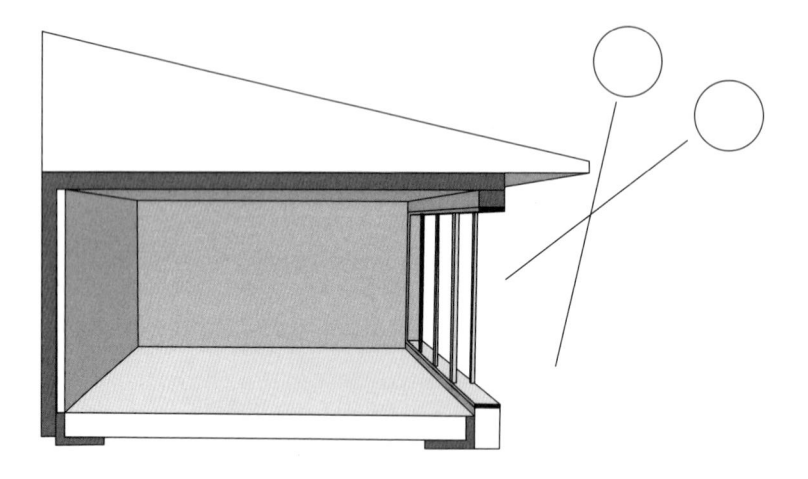

active solar-heating system
A system in which solar energy is collected and transferred mainly by mechanical means (fans, pumps) powered by energy from non-solar sources.

solar collector
A device designed to absorb solar radiation and transform it into heat. Also called collector.

absorbing surface
The surface of a solar collector, usually metallic, painted matt black, which will absorb the maximum and reflect the minimum amount of solar radiation.

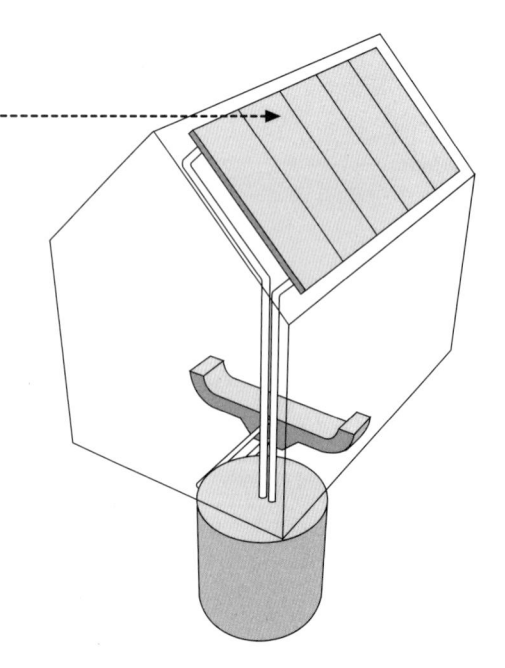

solar energy

sun control
Any of the methods used to control the periodic entrance of heat and light through an opening, consisting in some sort of vertical or horizontal canopies, screens, panels, slats, or louvers, movable mechanically or by hand.

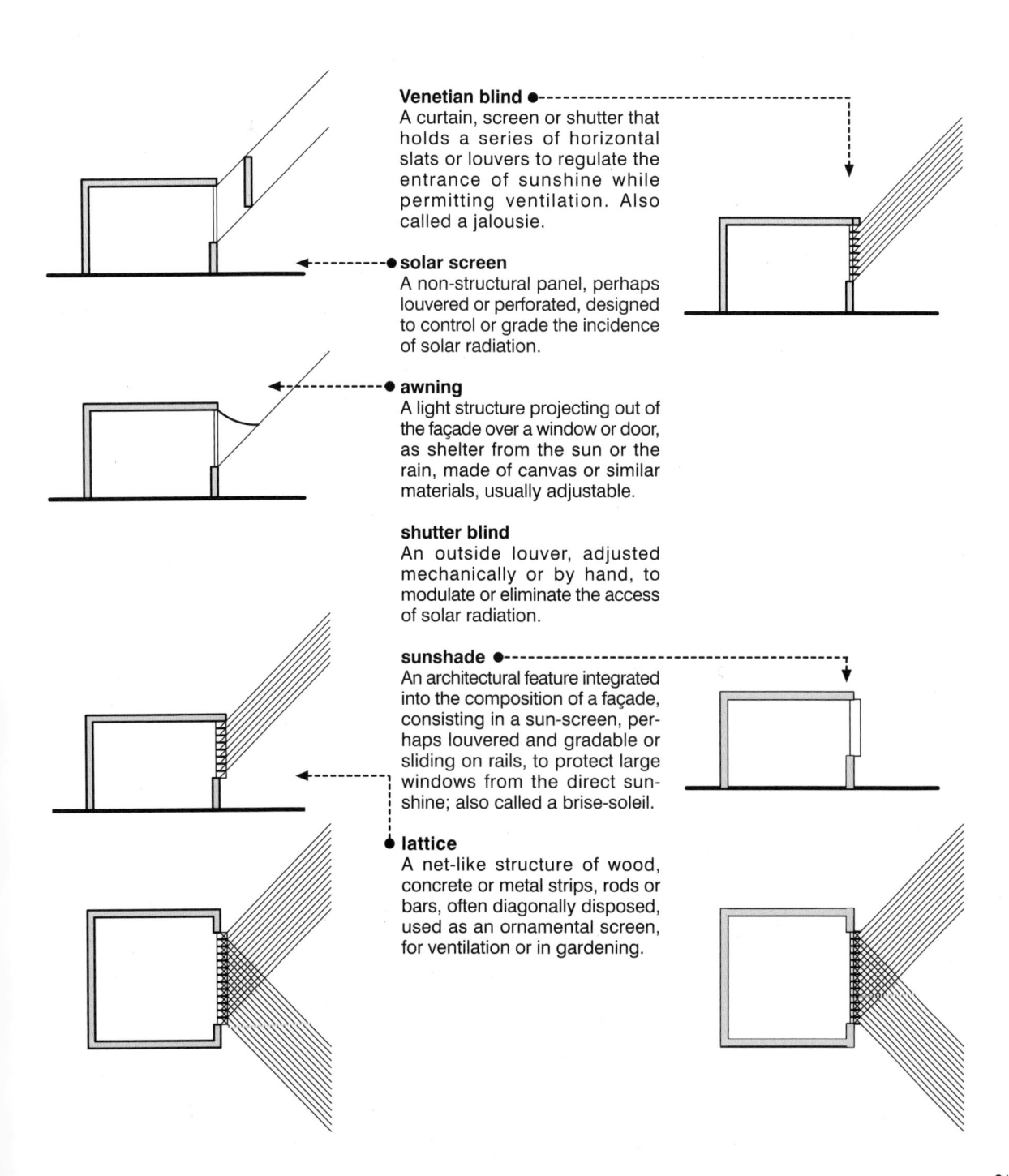

Venetian blind
A curtain, screen or shutter that holds a series of horizontal slats or louvers to regulate the entrance of sunshine while permitting ventilation. Also called a jalousie.

solar screen
A non-structural panel, perhaps louvered or perforated, designed to control or grade the incidence of solar radiation.

awning
A light structure projecting out of the façade over a window or door, as shelter from the sun or the rain, made of canvas or similar materials, usually adjustable.

shutter blind
An outside louver, adjusted mechanically or by hand, to modulate or eliminate the access of solar radiation.

sunshade
An architectural feature integrated into the composition of a façade, consisting in a sun-screen, perhaps louvered and gradable or sliding on rails, to protect large windows from the direct sunshine; also called a brise-soleil.

lattice
A net-like structure of wood, concrete or metal strips, rods or bars, often diagonally disposed, used as an ornamental screen, for ventilation or in gardening.

electricity

A fundamental physical agency caused by the presence and motion of electrons, protons and other charged particles, manifesting itself by phenomena of attraction, repulsion, luminous effects and others.

Ohm´s law
The law stating that the current in an electric circuit is directly proportional to the voltage in the circuit, and inversely proportional to the resistance.

$$I = V / R$$

current
The flow of electricity in a circuit; its unit of measure is the ampere.

amperage
The measure, in amperes, of the current in an electric circuit.

ampere
The international unit of electric current; the current flow of 1 ampere is equal to the electromotive force of 1 volt acting across a resistance of 1 Ohm.

ammeter
A device used to measure the number of amperes of an electric current.

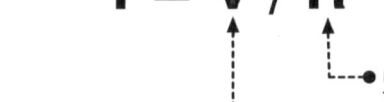

voltage
The measure of the potential difference in an electric circuit, expressed in volts.

volt
The unit of potential difference in an electric circuit, that will cause a current of one ampere to flow through a conductor with a resistance of one ohm. Symbol: V.

resistance
The physical property of a conductor or device whereby an electric current looses power as heat when flowing through it; it is measured in ohms. Symbol: R.

Ohm
The unit of measure of electrical resistance, equal to the resistance in a conductor in which one volt of potential difference produces a current of one ampere. Symbol: Ω

circuit
The continuous electrical path or network of conductors through which an electrical current flows, including the source of electricity.

direct current
An electrical current of constant direction and invariable magnitude, or a magnitude with minimal variations.

anode
1. The positive electrode, that emits positive ions and attracts negative ions in a voltaic cell or similar device.
2. The positive terminal or pole of a battery (opposed to cathode).

cathode
The negative terminal of a battery or source of electric current (opposed to anode); the electrode which emits electrons or gives off negative ions, attracting positive ions in a voltaic cell, X-ray tube or similar device.

electric charge
The quantity of electricity accumulated in a body, measured in coulombs. Charges of the same sign are mutually repellent, opposite charges are mutually attractive.

coulomb
The unit of measure of electrical charge, equal to the charge transferred in one second by a body conducting a constant current of one ampere. Symbol: C.

switch
A device designed to connect, disconnect or redirect an electrical circuit or an electrical current.

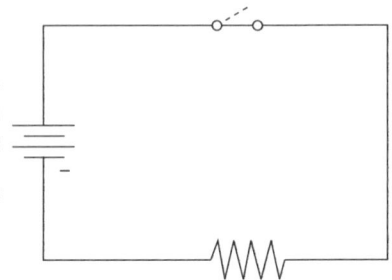

Joule´s law
A law stating that the amount of heat produced by the passage of an electric current through a conductor is directly proportional to the resistance of the circuit and to the square of the current.

electromotive force
The force that causes or tends to cause electricity to flow through a conductor. The difference in potential between the two terminals of an electrical source.

electrical resistivity
The resistance in ohms per unit of length of a given conductor of unit of cross section; also called resistivity, or specific resistance.

conductivity
A measure of a given material's capacity to conduct electricity, equal to the reciprocal of the resistance. Also called specific conductance. Symbol: σ

electric heat
The heat generated by a conductor's resistance to the flow of electric current.

electricity

Electrical supply

high-voltage
That which operates with, generates, or transfers a high difference of potential between the terminals of a conductor.

substation
An auxiliary station along an electrical network, where the supply is changed from constant to alternating current.

line voltage
The tension or voltage of an electrical supply line, measured at the point of arrival.

transformer
A device consisting of two or more coupled windings, used to adapt a supply of electricity from one voltage to another.

step-down transformer
An electrical transformer designed to convert a higher voltage to a lower one.

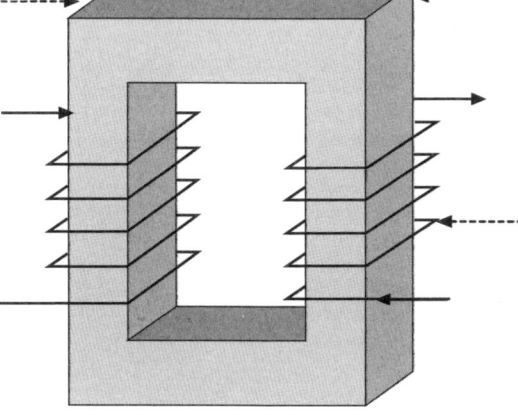

core
Part of a magnetic circuit, usually of laminated iron or steel, enveloped in an insulated conductive coil, intensifying the magnetic field when carrying current; used in devices such as transformers.

coil
A conductor such as copper wire, wound in a spiral, used to create magnetic fields, or adapt an electrical current before connection to a circuit.

electric motor
A device that converts electricity into mechanical energy, or movement.

generator
A device that transforms mechanical energy into electricity.

alternator
A generator that produces alternating current by the turning of a rotor.

dielectric strength
The maximum voltage to which a material can be exposed before it breaks down, usually expressed in volts or kilovolts per unit of thickness.

breakdown voltage
The minimum voltage sufficient to cause the breakdown of an insulator or an electrode.

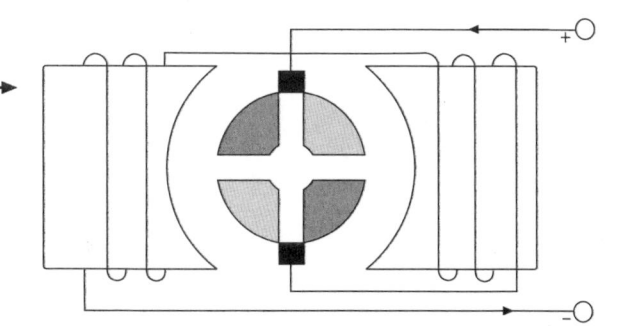

volt-ampere
A unit of electrical measurement equal to the product of one volt times one ampere; in direct current systems it is equivalent to one watt, in alternating current systems it is the unit of apparent power. Symbol VA.

live
Said of a lead or conductor that is connected to a source of electricity, or charged with a potential different from that of earth; also called hot.

dead
Not connected to any source of electrical current. Devoid of electrical potential difference.

electricity

service conductor
The conductors provided and maintained by the company, from the overhead lines to the point of service delivery, or connection to a building.

service entrance conductor
The part of the service conductors from the point of utility company supply, through the wall of the building to the main service switch box.

standby generator
A generator installed to take over if the normal source of electrical power fails, also called an emergency generator.

switchgear room
A room where the transformer, the electricity meters and other auxiliary devices and switches of a building are installed.

uninterruptible power supply
A system designed to circumvent emergency cases, by providing an alternative supply of electric power, such as a generator, when the normal source fails.

line drop
A low voltage level in the conductors of an electric circuit, usually due to their resistance.

fault
A defect of the insulation or of the conductive performance of any component or device in an electric circuit, leading to an interruption of current flow or an unintended path of current flow of abnormal magnitude.

short
An accidental low resistance connection between two different potential points of an electrical circuit, causing abnormally high current flow at that point, often with a dangerous generation of heat.

maximum demand
The maximum load an electrical circuit has to deliver during particular periods of time.

switchgear room

main switchboard
A large control panel or group of panels in an electrical installation, to carry switches, overcurrent, safety devices, buses, fuses, etc. Sometimes closed in a metal container, usually accessible from both front and rear. Also called panel board, panel, or switchgear.

watt-hour meter (U.S.A.)
A meter designed to register the quantity of energy consumed in a period of time; also called watt-hour metre (G.B.).

wattage
The quantity of power needed for an electrical device to be put in operation.

power
The relation between the work performed and the energy consumed or transferred, usually expressed in watts or horse-power.

watt
The unit of measure of electrical power, equal to 1 Joule per second (J/s), also equal to the power dissipated in a circuit in which a potential difference of 1 volt causes a current of 1 ampere to flow. Symbol: W.

kilowatt
A unit of measure of power, equal to 1,000 watts, equivalent of approx. 1.34 horse power. Symbol Kw or kw.

bus
A heavy, rigid, metal electrical conductor, used to transfer or distribute powerful currents from one circuit to another. Also called a busbar.

service equipment
The location of the supply conductors, generally near the entrance, with the main control and means of cutoff, usually a switch, fuses, circuit breakers and other accessories for the whole building.

circuit breaker
An electric overcurrent protection, designed to interrupt the circuit if an abnormally high current should arise; unlike a fuse, it may be repeatedly re-closed and re-used without replacing any components.

fuse
An overcurrent protection consisting of a metal conductor gauged to melt when made to carry a higher current than the electric circuit can safely bear.

cartridge fuse
An electric overcurrent protection (fuse) enclosed in a cylindrical tube, to facilitate its placement or removal from between the terminals it connects.

knife-blade fuse
A type of cartridge fuse with a projecting blade at each end, to fit into the contact jaws of the terminals it connects; used as circuit overcurrent protection.

plug fuse
A fuse mounted in a porcelain container with a threaded metal base similar to a light bulb; the front has a window to inspect the state of the fuse.

service switch
A switch on the switchboard panel to disconnect the supply, except for the emergency supply; exclusively affecting the energy registered by the meter.

electricity

feeder
In a building's electric power distribution net, a group of electric conductors originating at a main center and supplying secondary branch circuit centers.

unit substation
One or more transformers mechanically or electrically connected to the circuits' corresponding switchgear or motor control assemblies.

distribution panel
A large control panel or group of panels in an electrical installation, to carry switches, overcurrent, safety devices, buses, fuses, etc. Sometimes closed in a metal container, usually accessible from both front and rear. Also called panel board, panel, or switchgear.

branch circuit
In an electrical installation, that part of the system that extends beyond the final overcurrent prevention device, or fuse, that protects the circuit, and the outlets and appliances attached to it.

individual circuit
In an electrical circuit, a branch which supplies one single electrical device.

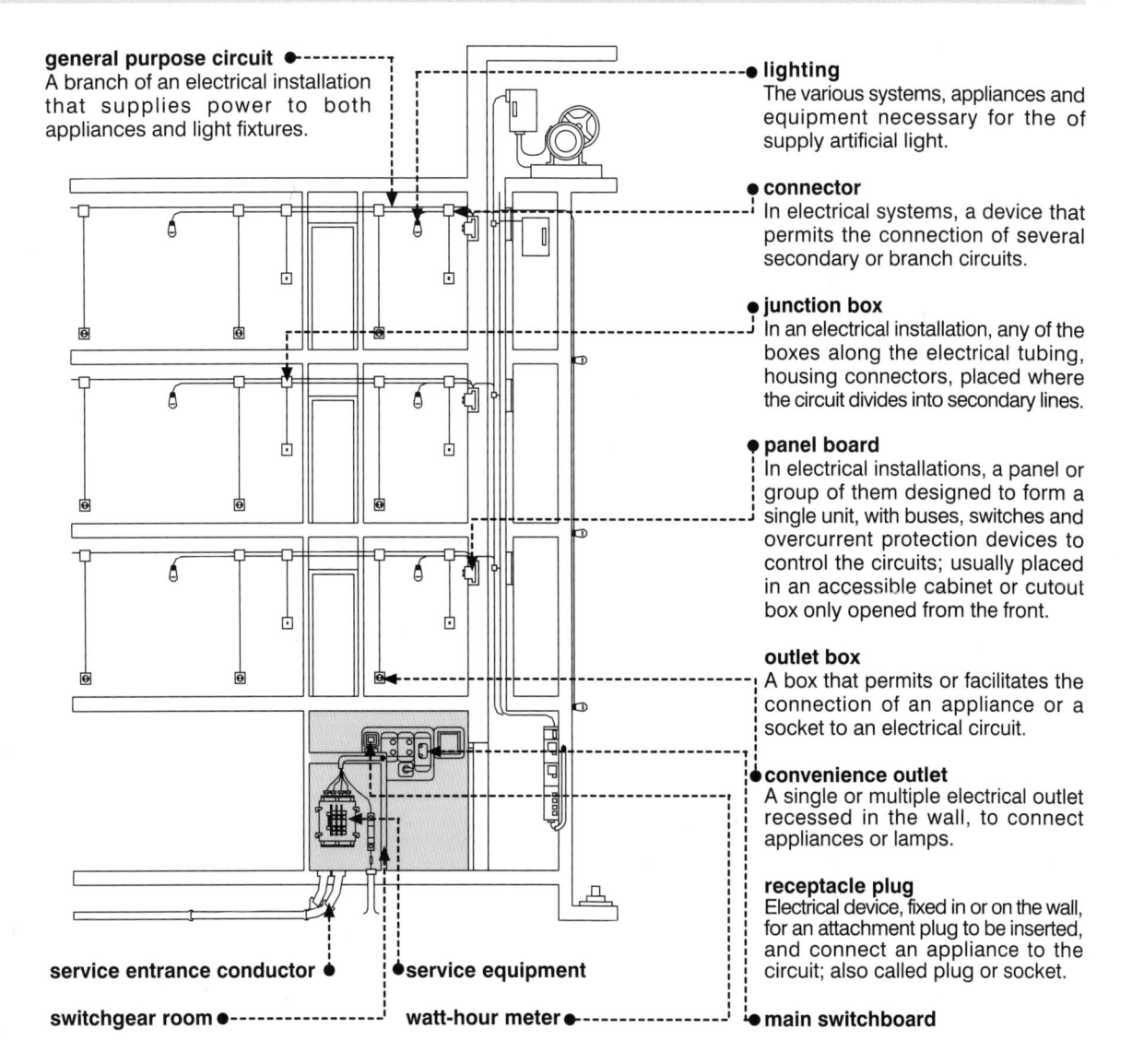

general purpose circuit
A branch of an electrical installation that supplies power to both appliances and light fixtures.

lighting
The various systems, appliances and equipment necessary for the of supply artificial light.

connector
In electrical systems, a device that permits the connection of several secondary or branch circuits.

junction box
In an electrical installation, any of the boxes along the electrical tubing, housing connectors, placed where the circuit divides into secondary lines.

panel board
In electrical installations, a panel or group of them designed to form a single unit, with buses, switches and overcurrent protection devices to control the circuits; usually placed in an accessible cabinet or cutout box only opened from the front.

outlet box
A box that permits or facilitates the connection of an appliance or a socket to an electrical circuit.

convenience outlet
A single or multiple electrical outlet recessed in the wall, to connect appliances or lamps.

receptacle plug
Electrical device, fixed in or on the wall, for an attachment plug to be inserted, and connect an appliance to the circuit; also called plug or socket.

service entrance conductor

service equipment

switchgear room

watt-hour meter

main switchboard

219

electricity

switch
A device designed to connect, disconnect or redirect an electrical circuit or an electrical current.

air switch
A switch by means of which the disconnection of a circuit takes place in the air.

knife switch
A type of switch consisting of a hinged metal lever, that swings down to insert its two sides between two contact jaws, thereby establishing the circuit. No longer permitted nowadays.

float switch
An electrical switch operated by a conductor floating on a liquid, so as to connect or disconnect a circuit when a predetermined level is reached.

ground-fault interrupter
A type of ground fault protection designed to trip at a ground current far below any harmful level, used where the risk of electric shock is high, such as in damp locations.

key switch
A security electrical switch that can only be operated with the use of a key.

mercury-contact switch
An electrical switch consisting of a sealed tube filled with mercury, mounted on a pivot, to provide a silent contact when it is operated.

flush plate
Plastic or metal plate providing a neat protective cover for a flush electrical outlet or switch; with holes to take the appliances, it is attached to the wall with screws or pressure clips.

outlet
Any of the devices along the path of an electrical circuit, such as receptacle plugs, for the connection of an electrical appliance and its portable circuit.

grounding outlet
An electric outlet with a receptacle of the polarity type with an additional contact to connect the grounding conductor of an appliance.

appliance
Any device using electricity or gas as a source of energy to produce light, warmth, air conditioning, refrigeration or any other task, generally of a standard size and form easily connected to the supply.

four-way switch
An electric switch with extra connections so that, in combination with two other switches of that sort, plus the appropriate wiring, a light may be operated from three different points.

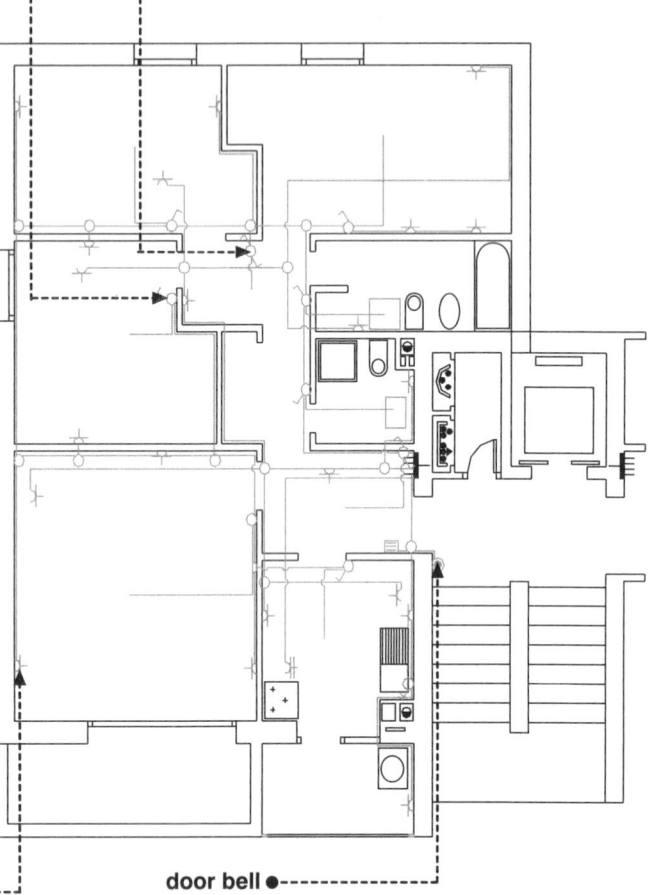

door bell
A device emitting sound when pressed, installed on or next to the main entrance door to a residence, alerting the inhabitants that someone is at the door.

plug
A device designed to connect a portable appliance to the supply when inserted into a receptacle plug; also called an attachment plug.

grounding plug
An attachment plug having the necessary extra terminal to make a connection to the ground wire in the supply circuit.

pigtail
The flexible conductor attached to an electrical appliance, providing its necessary connection to the circuit.

light

The electromagnetic radiation perceptible by the human eye; light travels at a speed of 186,300 miles per second (299,972 Km/s).

luminous intensity
The luminous flux emitted by a point source of light per unit solid angle, expressed in candlepower.

candlepower
The International Standard unit of luminous intensity of a light source, measured in candelas; symbol: cp.

candle
Until recently the accepted unit measure of the luminous intensity of a light source, now quoted in candelas.

candela
The International Standard unit of luminous intensity, close to the formerly accepted "international candle"; equal to a radiant intensity of 1/683 watts per steradian. Also called standard candle.

luminous flux
The rate of transmission of luminous energy, expressed in lumens.

lumen
In the International System, the unit of luminous flux equal to that received on a unit surface, all points of which are equidistant from a point source with an intensity of 1 candela; symbol: lm.

illumination
The luminous flux density incident on a surface or luminous flux per unit area; usually expressed in lumens per square foot, or per square meter, or lux.

lux
In the International System, the unit measure of illumination, equal to 1 lumen per sq. meter; symbol: lx.

luminance
The luminous intensity of a surface in a given direction per unit of projected area of the surface as viewed from that direction; a directional property of luminous radiation.

Lambert
A unit of luminance, equal to 0.32 (1/? candelas per cm); equal to the uniform luminance of a perfectly diffusing surface reflecting light at the rate of 1 lumen per sq. cm. Symbol: L.

Lambert's law
A law stating that the luminous intensity in any direction of a plane surface varies in proportion to the cosine of the angle between that direction and the perpendicular from the point source to the surface.

inverse-square law
A law applied to light or sound sources located far from any reflecting surface: intensity at a given point, as measured on a plane perpendicular to a line between that point and the source, varies inversely with the square of the distance between the point and the source.

221

light

law of reflection
Applied to light, sound or radiant heat incident on a surface: the angle of reflection is equal to the angle of incidence; the incident and reflected rays, and a line perpendicular to the surface at the point of incidence are in one plane.

incidence
The impact of a light ray, or a heat or sound wave upon a surface.

angle of incidence
The angle between a straight line inciding on a plane and a perpendicular line to the plane at the point of incidence.

reflection
The direction change of luminous or acoustic waves incident upon a reflecting surface.

angle of reflection
The angle between a ray reflected off a surface and the normal or perpendicular at the point of incidence.

refraction
The change in direction of a light ray piercing the surface between two refracting media, due to the different speed at which light travels in each.

angle of refraction
The angle between a refracted light ray having pierced the interface of two media, and a normal to the surface at the point of incidence.

absorption coefficient
The ratio between the luminous flux absorbed by a given surface, and the total amount inciding on it.

reflectance
The ratio between the luminous flux reflected off a given surface and the total magnitude inciding on it.

diffusion
The reflection or dispersion of light in all directions when the rays incide upon a rough or irregular surface.

diffuse light
Light rays that are randomly dispersed when inciding on an irregular surface.

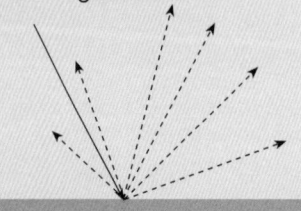

diffraction
The deviation of light rays near the edge of an opaque body, or the bending of sound and light waves around opaque obstacles in their path.

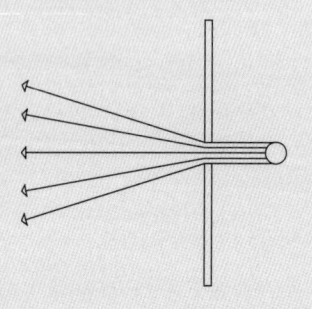

light

lamp
A device designed to produce light or heat from electricity or gas.

lamp bulb
A glass bulb containing a gaseous mixture designed to prevent the tungsten or platinum filament from evaporating when the electric current it carries makes it incandescent; its form is identified by a letter followed by a number indicating its diameter in eighths of an inch; also called bulb.

incandescent lamp
A glass bulb with a tungsten filament that becomes incandescent when resisting an electric current.

incandescence
The emission of visible light by a body, caused by its high temperature.

tungsten
A heavy metal with a high melting point, used in alloys and in the manufacture of electric components; symbol: W.

discharge lamp
Any lamp that produces light due to the phosphors resulting from an electrical discharge through the gases or vapours within the lamps envelope.

fluorescence
Emission of visible light by a substance, such as phosphor, due to its absorption of short wavelength radiation.

phosphor
Any of several substances that exhibit luminescence when struck by light of certain wavelengths, such as ultraviolet.

phosphorescent
Said of substances emitting visible light at temperatures below incandescence due to the absorption of electromagnetic radiation.

phosphor
A substance capable of luminescence, such as fluorescent powder, which absorbs ultraviolet radiation and reemits it as visible light; used as a coating on the inside of electric-discharge lamps.

ballast
A device used to provide the required starting voltage and operating current for fluorescent, mercury or other electric-discharge lamps.

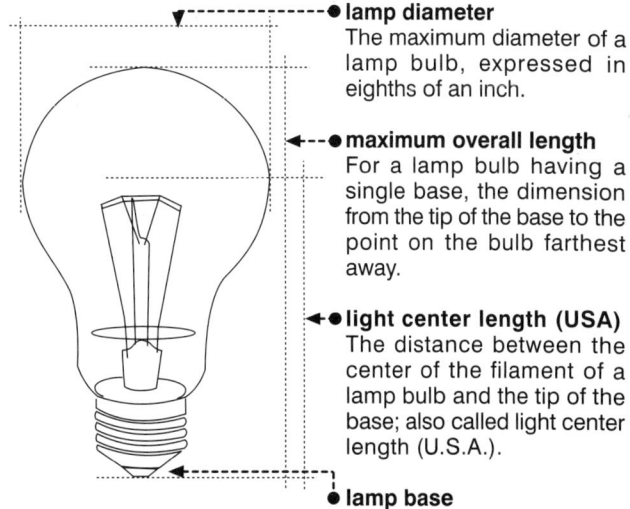

lamp diameter
The maximum diameter of a lamp bulb, expressed in eighths of an inch.

maximum overall length
For a lamp bulb having a single base, the dimension from the tip of the base to the point on the bulb farthest away.

light center length (USA)
The distance between the center of the filament of a lamp bulb and the tip of the base; also called light center length (U.S.A.).

lamp base
The metallic part of a lamp bulb designed to connect it to the socket.

fluorescent lamp
An electric-discharge lamp consisting of a glass tube with an electrode at each end, sending an arc through a gaseous mixture, generating ultraviolet radiation; the inner tube surface is coated with a phosphor which converts enough of the ultraviolet radiation into visible light.

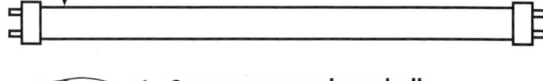

energy-saver lamp bulb
A variety of compact lamp bulb based on the principle of fluorescent lighting, producing many times the amount of light of an incandescent bulb of similar wattage, and offering a very extended useful life.

sodium lamp
A very efficient electric-discharge lamp which produces light by making electric current flow between two electrodes in a transparent envelope or capsule containing sodium vapor; also called a sodium vapor lamp.

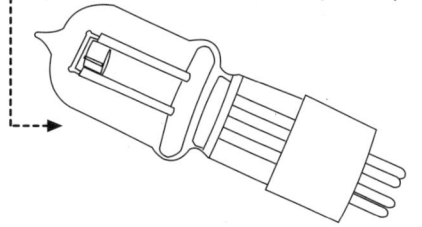

light

light, to; illuminate, to
To provide a space with light or with lighting, by correspondingly natural or artificial means.

reflector
A surface designed or placed so as to reflect light, heat or sound, aiming or distributing it in a desired direction.

elliptical reflector
A reflector with an elliptical surface, tending to make parallel rays converge towards a central area.

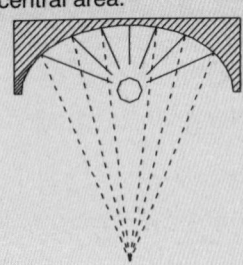

parabolic reflector
A reflector with a paraboloid surface; if a small light source is placed near the focal point of the reflector, the reflected light will be concentrated in a nearly collimated beam parallel to the reflector's axis; the result varies with the position of the light source.

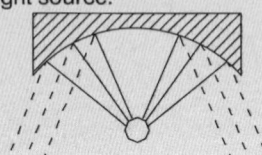

collimate, to
To bring into line, to make parallel, as a reflector with divergent rays of light.

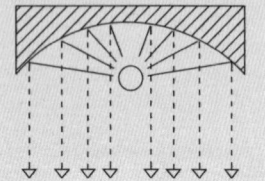

lens
A transparent element of glass or plastic the two surfaces of which are differently curved so as to concentrate, collimate, or disperse the rays of a light source in specific ways.

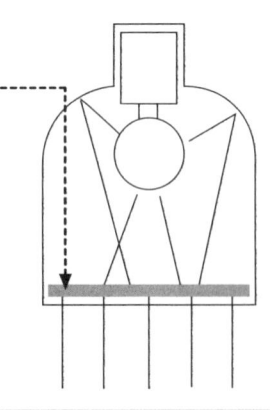

Fresnel lens
A lens the convex paraboloid surface of which has been divided into concentric segments, each of which has the appropriate angle to concentrate the light without the thickness of a traditional lens.

diffuser
Any device, object or surface, reflective or transparent, used to scatter, spread, or filter the light entering a space.

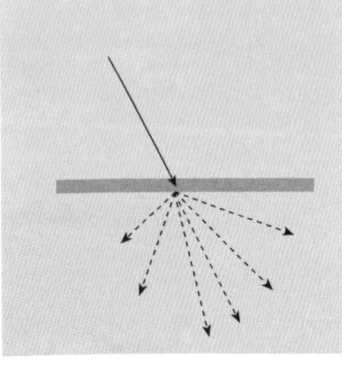

eggcrate
A metal or plastic grid-like device similar to an eggcrate, placed below a light source as a light diffuser.

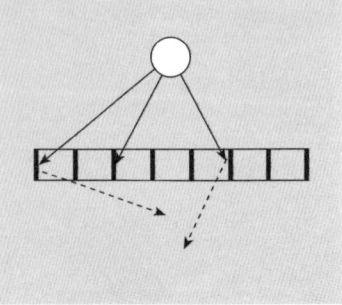

dimmer
A device to vary the intensity of a light source without altering its distribution, by control of the current flow, to determine the output; also dimmer switch or light dimmer.

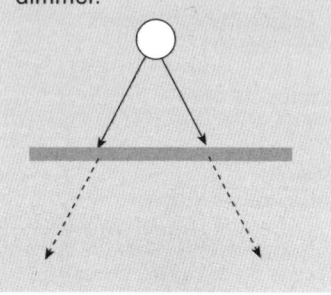

light

artificial light
Light supplied by an artificial source, with a spectral distribution similar to natural light, at a correlated color temperature.

direct lighting
A lighting distribution in which the luminaires shed 90% or 100% of their light directly onto the surfaces to be illuminated, usually downward.

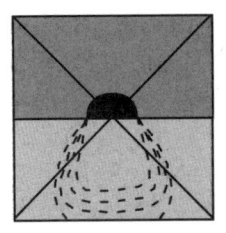

general diffuse lighting
A lighting system that distributes the light evenly in all directions.

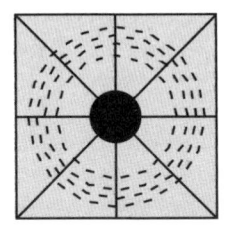

mixed lighting
A lighting system that distributes between 40% and 60% of the light upward and the rest downward.

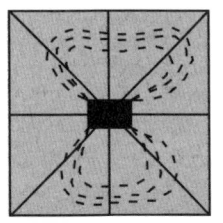

indirect lighting
Lighting in which 90% or 100% of the emitted light is distributed upward, to be reflected by the ceiling or by a reflector.

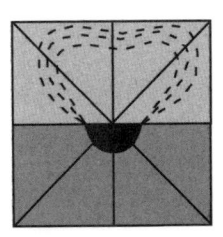

semi-indirect lighting
Lighting in which the luminaires distribute 60% to 90% of the emitted light upward.

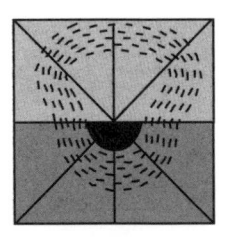

semidirect lighting
Lighting in which the luminaires distribute 60% to 90% of the emitted light downward.

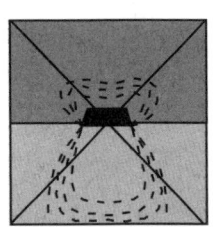

glare
The sensation produced by light of a greater intensity than the eye is adapted to, causing discomfort and a loss of visibility.

direct glare
The glare produced by an excessively bright or insufficiently shielded light source, or by a reflecting area in the visual field.

reflected glare
The glare that is caused by a bright, polished or glossy surface reflecting the light rays into the field of vision of the onlooker; also called indirect glare.

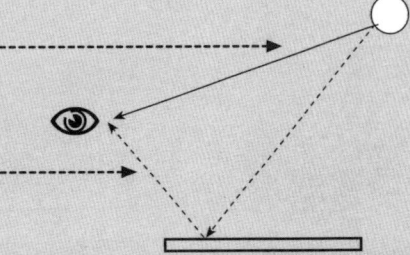

light

cove lighting
Lighting from non visible luminaires situated above a wall molding, ledge or horizontal recess, shedding light toward the ceiling and upper wall, which is reflected back into the room.

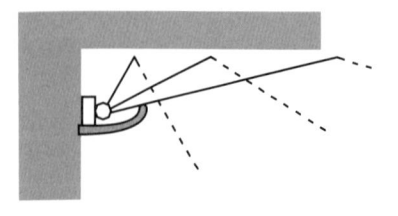

general lighting
Lighting designed to distribute light uniformly in a given space.

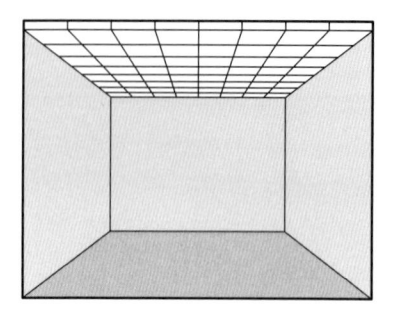

valance lighting
Indirect lighting by a luminaire concealed behind a panel parallel to the wall at the top or sides of a window, shedding light up or down; also called pelmet lighting.

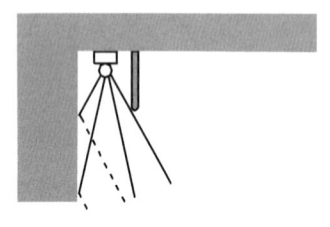

local lighting
Lighting designed to shed all the light on a limited zone leaving the surrounding area virtually unlit.

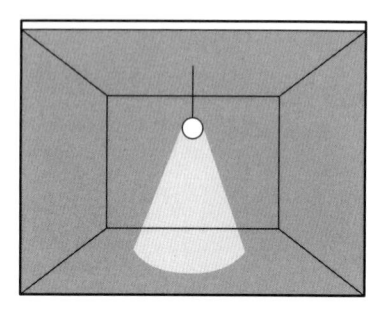

cornice lighting
Lighting from luminaires shielded by a panel parallel to the wall and attached to the ceiling or upper edge of the wall, and distribute light over the wall.

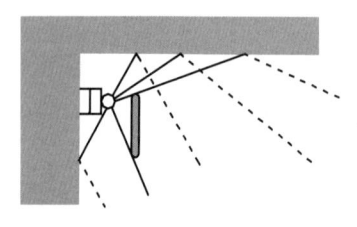

task lighting
Lighting designed to provide very bright light on a work area where tasks requiring it are carried out.

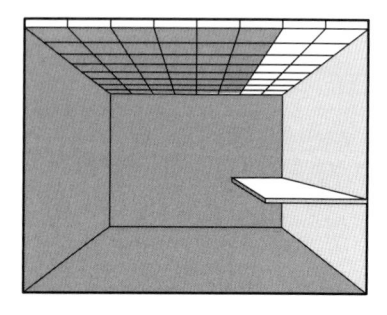

light

luminaire
A lighting appliance that may consist of more than one lamp, together with the necessary elements to protect the lamps, distribute the light, and connect the system to the supply circuit; also called a lighting fixture.

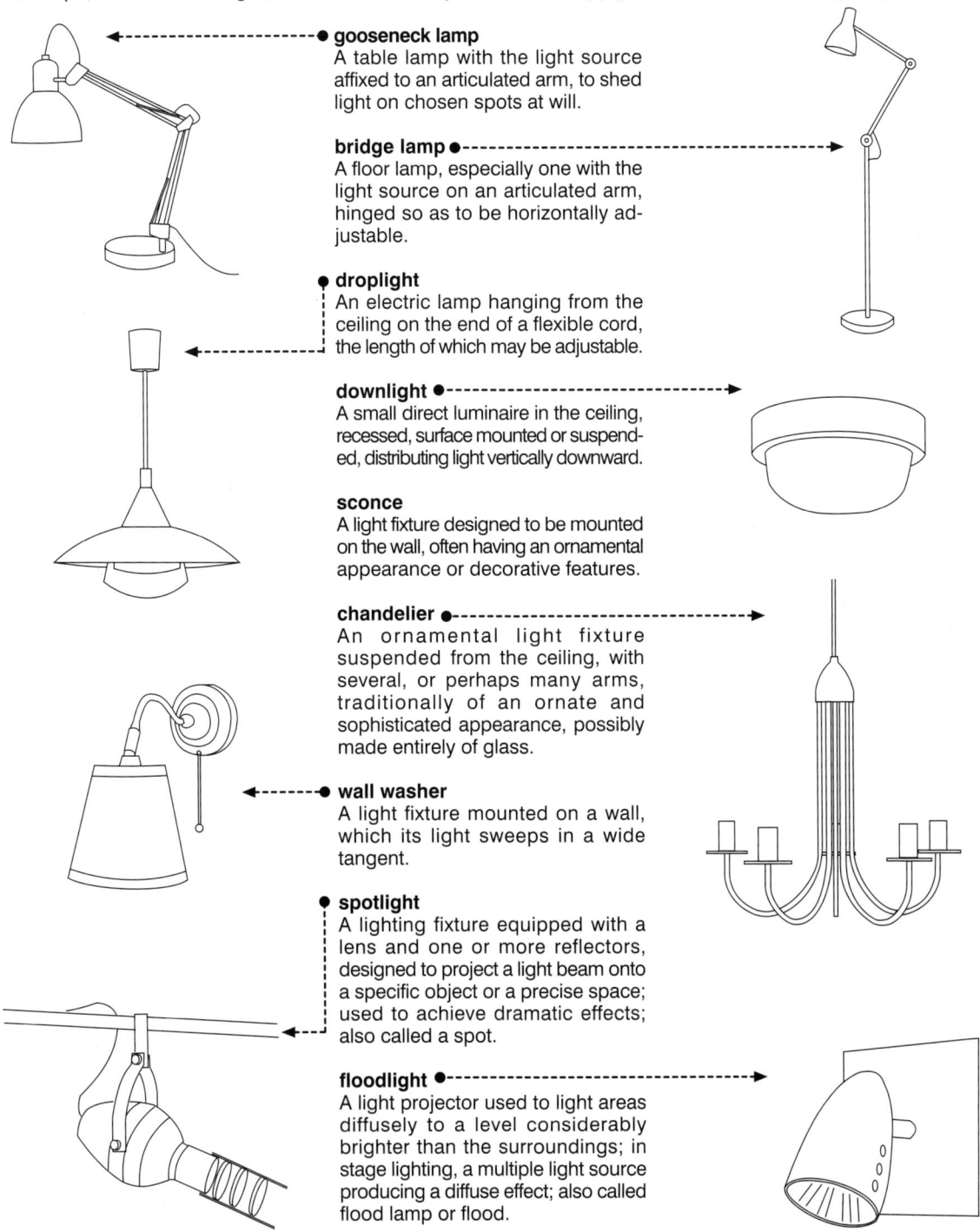

gooseneck lamp
A table lamp with the light source affixed to an articulated arm, to shed light on chosen spots at will.

bridge lamp
A floor lamp, especially one with the light source on an articulated arm, hinged so as to be horizontally adjustable.

droplight
An electric lamp hanging from the ceiling on the end of a flexible cord, the length of which may be adjustable.

downlight
A small direct luminaire in the ceiling, recessed, surface mounted or suspended, distributing light vertically downward.

sconce
A light fixture designed to be mounted on the wall, often having an ornamental appearance or decorative features.

chandelier
An ornamental light fixture suspended from the ceiling, with several, or perhaps many arms, traditionally of an ornate and sophisticated appearance, possibly made entirely of glass.

wall washer
A light fixture mounted on a wall, which its light sweeps in a wide tangent.

spotlight
A lighting fixture equipped with a lens and one or more reflectors, designed to project a light beam onto a specific object or a precise space; used to achieve dramatic effects; also called a spot.

floodlight
A light projector used to light areas diffusely to a level considerably brighter than the surroundings; in stage lighting, a multiple light source producing a diffuse effect; also called flood lamp or flood.

light

lumen method
In lighting design, a procedure used to define the number and type of luminaires required to provide suitable average illumination on a work plane, considering both direct and reflected light; also called the flux method.

room cavity
An imaginary cavity enclosed within the work plane, the lighting plane and that part of the walls between the two horizontal planes mentioned.

room cavity ratio
A number derived from the dimensions and characteristics of a space, which permits an estimation of the relative use of its various zones.

work plane
In a given space, an imaginary plane on which work is generally carried out, which is assumed to be a horizontal plane 30 in. from the floor (76 cm.); used as a guideline during parts of the design process such as lighting design.

floor cavity
An imaginary space enclosed between the walls of a given space, the floor, and a plane situated an established height above it.

point method
Method of calculating the illumination produced by a light source based on Lambert's cosine law; it is not entirely precise as it overlooks the effect of reflected light.

spacing criterion
A formula used to determine the appropriate separation between two light sources to obtain the uniform illumination of a surface; symbol: sc.

$$\text{average maintained illuminance } (E_m) = \frac{\text{initial illuminance} \times CU \times NRF \times RF}{\text{work surface area}}$$

coefficient of utilization (USA)
The ratio of the luminous flux incident on a work plane, to the total luminous flux emitted by a luminaire; also called coefficient of utilisation (G.B.). Symbol: CU

maintenance factor
A factor used to calculate the effective illumination provided by a system after a period of time under given conditions such as temperature and voltage variations and accumulation of dirt on the envelope of the luminaire.

nonrecoverable light loss factor
Maintenance factors that consider the permanent effects of time on the system, such as voltage variations and inevitable deterioration of the fixtures; symbol: NRLLF.

recoverable light loss factor
A factor accounting for aspects of a system that adequate maintenance can address, i.e. removal of dirt from lamps and replacement of exchangeable components. Symbol: RLLF

plumbing

The network of pipes, taps, connectors and other devices which combine to provide the water supply and drainage system of a building.

groundwater
The water present beneath the surface of the ground, mostly the result of surface water seeping down; the water that feeds wells and natural springs.

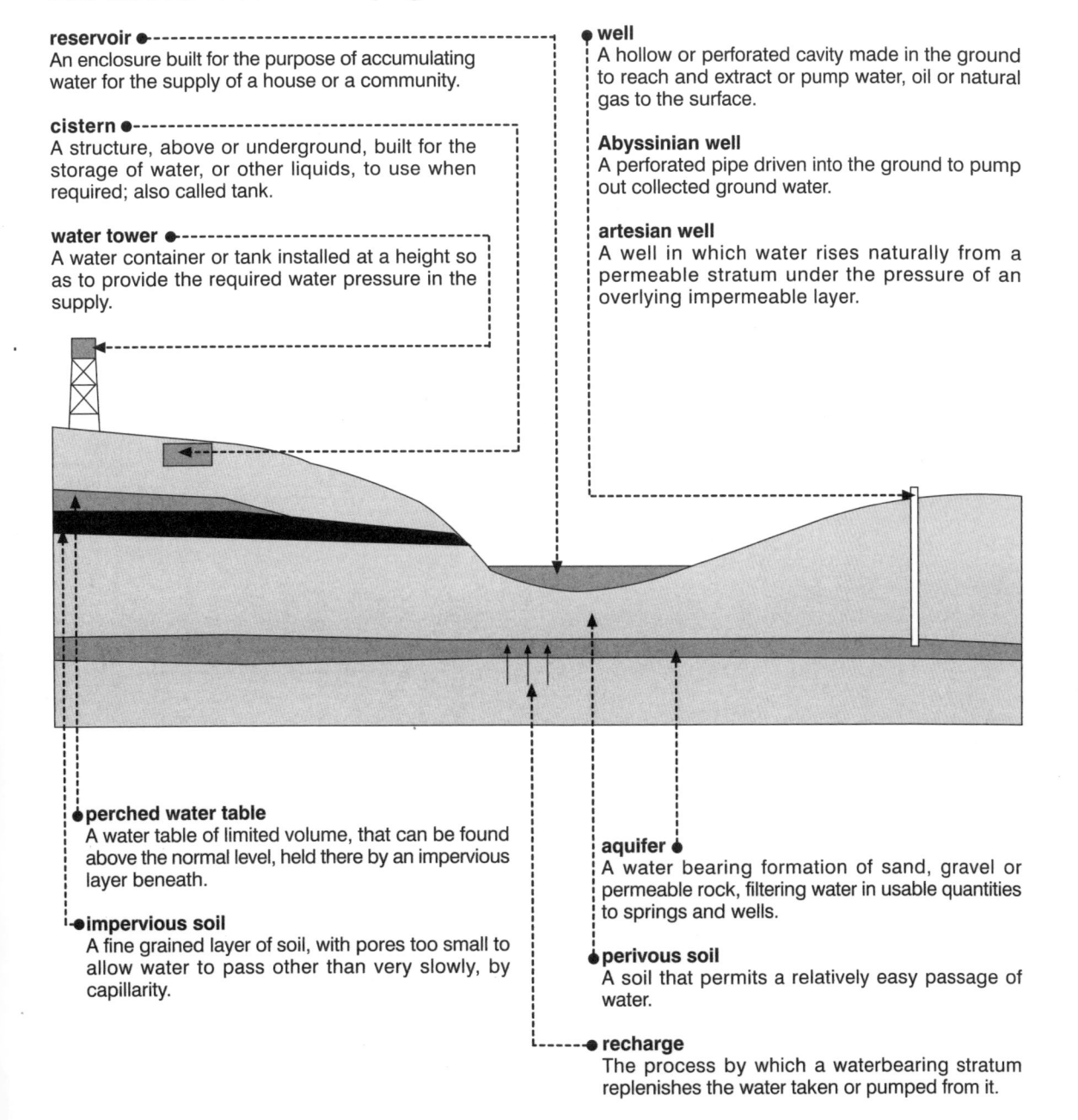

reservoir
An enclosure built for the purpose of accumulating water for the supply of a house or a community.

cistern
A structure, above or underground, built for the storage of water, or other liquids, to use when required; also called tank.

water tower
A water container or tank installed at a height so as to provide the required water pressure in the supply.

well
A hollow or perforated cavity made in the ground to reach and extract or pump water, oil or natural gas to the surface.

Abyssinian well
A perforated pipe driven into the ground to pump out collected ground water.

artesian well
A well in which water rises naturally from a permeable stratum under the pressure of an overlying impermeable layer.

perched water table
A water table of limited volume, that can be found above the normal level, held there by an impervious layer beneath.

impervious soil
A fine grained layer of soil, with pores too small to allow water to pass other than very slowly, by capillarity.

aquifer
A water bearing formation of sand, gravel or permeable rock, filtering water in usable quantities to springs and wells.

pervious soil
A soil that permits a relatively easy passage of water.

recharge
The process by which a waterbearing stratum replenishes the water taken or pumped from it.

plumbing

water supply
The combination of tanks, pipes, and valves by which potable water is made available to a community or a building.

service
The delivery or supply of various utilities of public use, such as potable water, gas, electricity, etc.

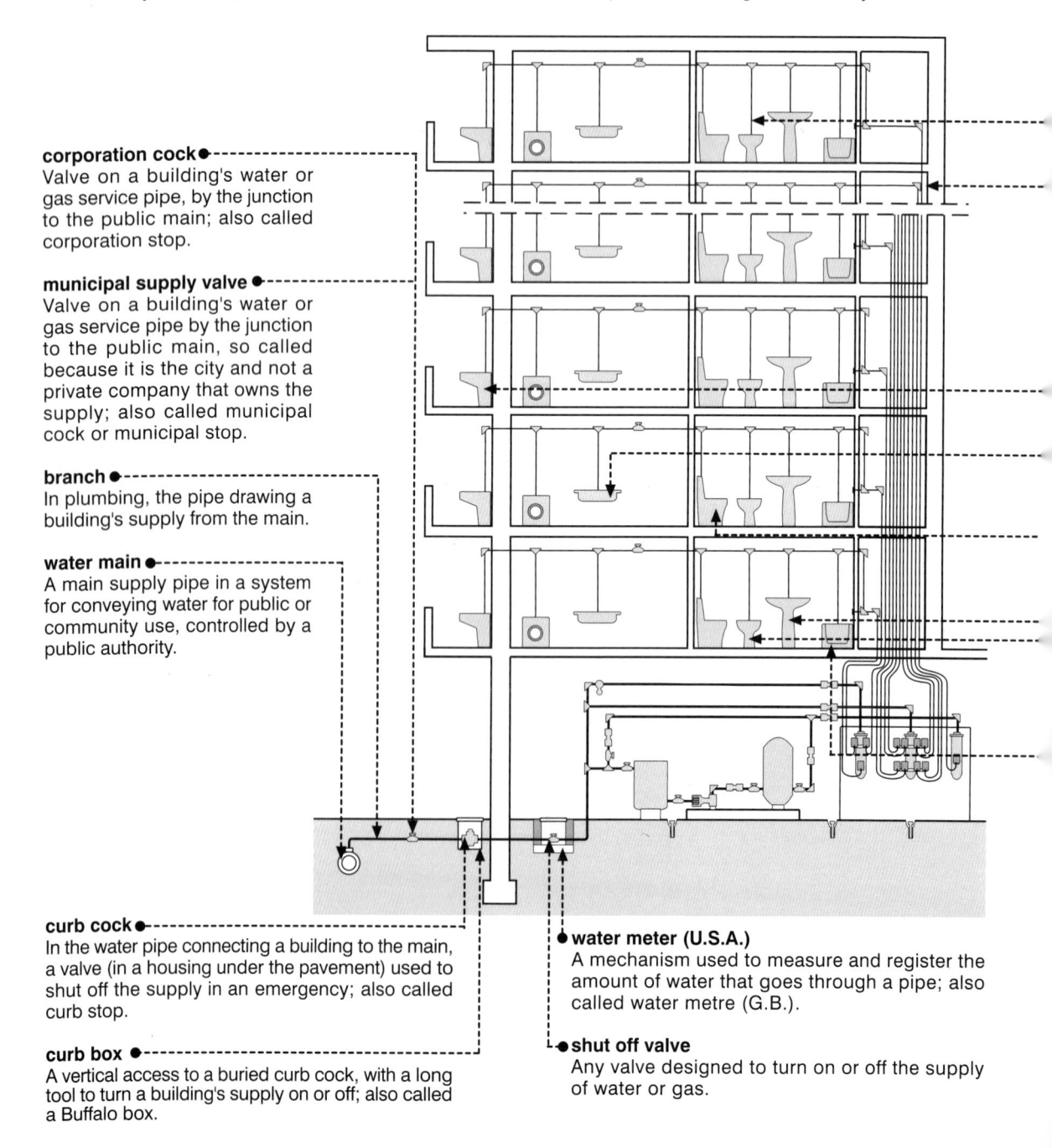

corporation cock
Valve on a building's water or gas service pipe, by the junction to the public main; also called corporation stop.

municipal supply valve
Valve on a building's water or gas service pipe by the junction to the public main, so called because it is the city and not a private company that owns the supply; also called municipal cock or municipal stop.

branch
In plumbing, the pipe drawing a building's supply from the main.

water main
A main supply pipe in a system for conveying water for public or community use, controlled by a public authority.

curb cock
In the water pipe connecting a building to the main, a valve (in a housing under the pavement) used to shut off the supply in an emergency; also called curb stop.

curb box
A vertical access to a buried curb cock, with a long tool to turn a building's supply on or off; also called a Buffalo box.

water meter (U.S.A.)
A mechanism used to measure and register the amount of water that goes through a pipe; also called water metre (G.B.).

shut off valve
Any valve designed to turn on or off the supply of water or gas.

230

plumbing

'water system
The combined network of pipes, valves, taps and other devices that distribute the water supply in a building.

gravity water system
A water system in which the water source is above where the water is to be used, gravity generating the necessary pressure in the building's supply.

pneumatic water supply
A water supply system of a building in which the necessary pressure is maintained by compressed air in a storage tank at the base of the system.

pipe
A cylindrical channel used to convey water or gas throughout a building, or to protect electrical wiring.

riser
A water supply, drainage, gas, or vent pipe that extends vertically more than one floor to service several branches, fixtures or whole apartments.

wet standpipe
In a water system, a vertical distribution pipe that the main supply keeps permanently full of water, at adequate pressure for immediate use.

plumbing fixture
Any of a type of receptacles that use water from a supply system and discharge water-borne wastes into a drainage system connected to it.

laundry tub
A deep, wide sink designed specifically for washing clothes; also called a laundry tray or set tub.

sink
A receptacle, as in a kitchen or laundry, connected to the water and drainage system, used for washing dishes or clothes.

toilet bowl
A plumbing fixture used for defecation and urination, consisting of a large ceramic bowl flushed by a jet of water, connected to the drainage system; also called toilet, watercloset or WC.

wash basin
A receptacle, connected to the water and drainage systems, used for personal hygiene; often made of ceramic or stainless steel; also called a sink.

bidet
A kidney shaped plumbing fixture, usually ceramic, used for intimate hygiene.

bathtub
A long tub accommodating one person for bathing; connected to the water supply and drain; also called bath.

shower
A bathroom fixture designed for water to be sprayed or poured on a bather from above; also called a shower bath.

---

hard water → **water softener**
Water containing a high proportion of mineral salts, calcium sulfates, magnesium carbonates, or others.
A device to filter or chemically remove calcium and magnesium salts present in the water, often by ion exchange.

raw water
Water from any source that requires treatment to make it potable, safe for public use.

→ **water treatment**
Any process through which water is made potable or safe for public use.

plumbing

pipe fitting
A plumbing accessory used to connect water or drainage pipes; available straight, curved, T or Y shaped.

sweep fitting
Any fitting that has a wide radius of curvature.

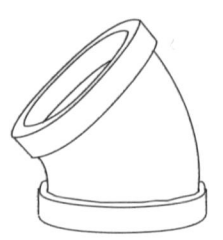

elbow
A pipe fitting having a 90º curve, also called an ell.

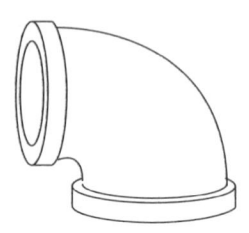

drop elbow
A 90º pipe elbow with lugs on the side to attach it to a wall; also called a drop ell.

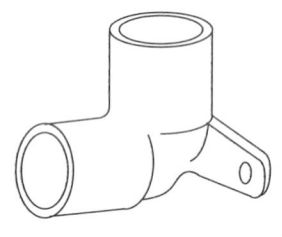

return bend
A pipe fitting that turns 180º.

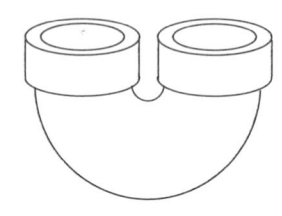

drop tee
A T shaped pipe fitting, with lateral lugs to attach it.

Tee
A pipe fitting shaped like the letter T, allowing three pipes to be connected.

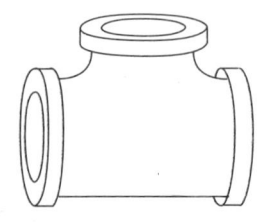

cross
A pipe fitting which permits four pipes to be connected.

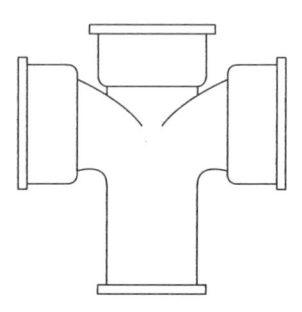

plumbing

Y-pipe
A pipe fitting shaped like a letter Y. Also a fitting with a branch departing at a 45º angle. Also called a wye.

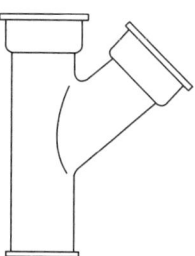

sanitary tee
A Tee fitting for soil pipes, with a curve in the 90º transition, to channel the flow in the direction of the main flow.

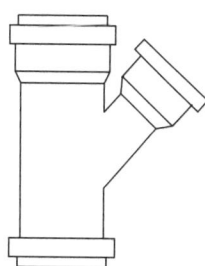

coupling
A short segment of pipe, internally threaded at both ends to join or extend two pipes end to end.

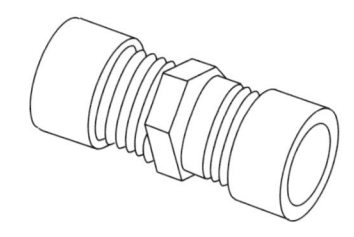

increaser
In plumbing, a tapered coupling to connect a pipes having different diameters.

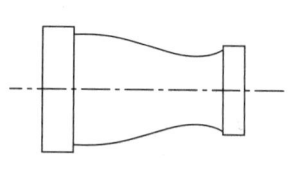

bell-and-spigot joint
A straight connection of two pipes in which the spigot end of one is inserted in the flared-out end of the other; also called bell-and-socket or spigot and socket joint.

- **male connector**
In couplings consisting of two parts, as in pipe fittings, the one having to fit partly or entirely into the other; also called male.

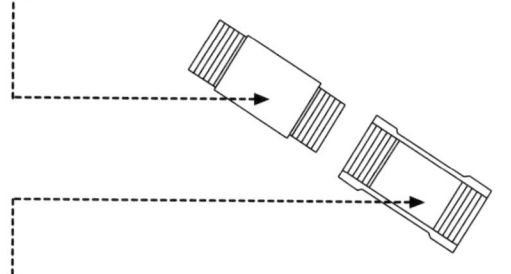

- **female**
In couplings consisting of two interpenetrating parts, as in pipe fittings, the one having partly or entirely to house the other; also called a female connector.

plug
A short threaded pipe fitting with no outlet, used to close the end of a pipe.

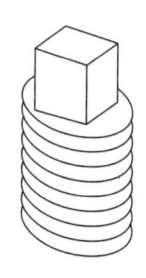

plumbing

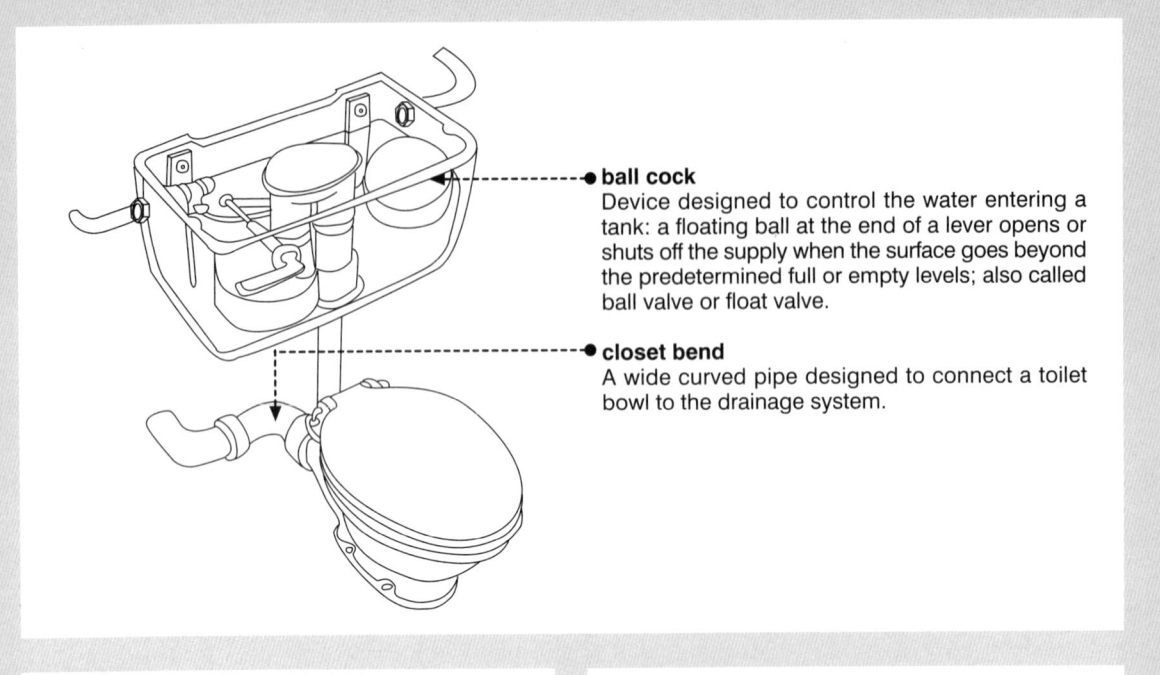

ball cock
Device designed to control the water entering a tank: a floating ball at the end of a lever opens or shuts off the supply when the surface goes beyond the predetermined full or empty levels; also called ball valve or float valve.

closet bend
A wide curved pipe designed to connect a toilet bowl to the drainage system.

wash-down closet
The traditional type of closet in which waste is washed and pushed through the trap seal to the drain by the action of the water released from an overhead tank; no longer produced but still in use.

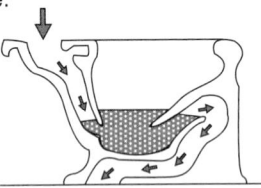

reverse-trap closet
A closet bowl similar to the siphon-jet type but with a somewhat narrower drain outlet.

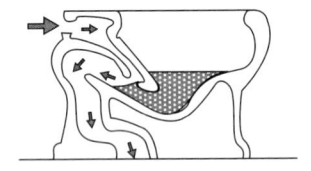

siphon-vortex closet
A water closet similar to the siphon jet type but in which the flush water comes from the rim of the bowl exclusively, creating a whirling motion which contributes to remove the waste.

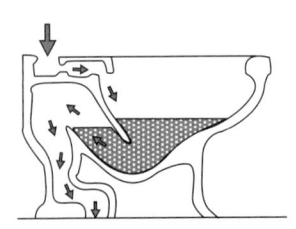

siphon-jet closet
A water closet in which the flush water flows from the rim of the bowl, filling the siphon which drags the waste down the drain with it when it starts to flow.

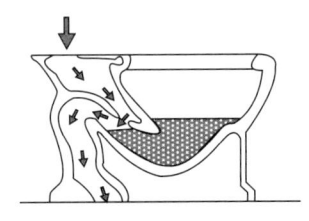

plumbing

tap
A device used to control or shut off the flow of a liquid, especially water or gas, in a pipe; also called a faucet or valve.

angle valve
A valve or tap designed to shut off the passage of water or gas where the exit is at a 90º angle to the rest of the pipe.

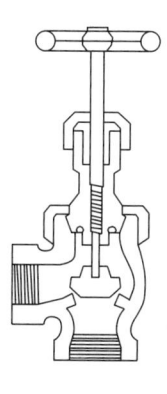

gate valve
A device to control water-flow through a pipe, operated by a wedge-shaped gate, which allows full flow when raised or restricts it when lowered; not adequate for very close fluid control or very tight shutoff; also called full-way valve.

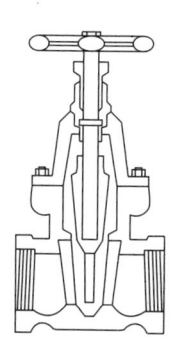

backflow valve
A valve designed to allow the flow of fluids or gases in one direction only, especially in drains; incorrect flow automatically closes the valve; also called backwater valve or check valve.

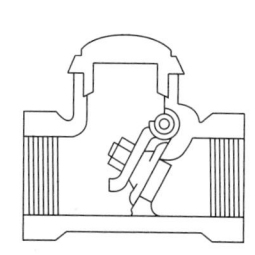

globe valve
A valve in which a movable spindle is tightened into a fixed seat, restricting the flow of water; the spindle has a washer to ensure the fit; the device is usually encased in a characteristic globular housing.

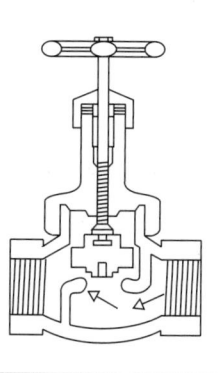

tap, faucet
A device used to control the passage of liquid through a pipe, by tightening a valve.

mixing faucet
A water outlet to mix hot and cold, regulated automatically or by hand, in proportions ; also called blender, blending valve, mixer tap, mixing tap.

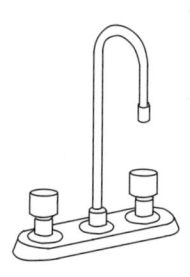

mixer faucet
A water outlet designed to mix hot and cold water by manipulating one single control; also called mixer tap.

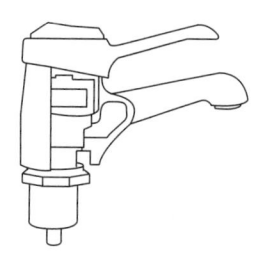

anti-scald faucet
A water outlet valve equipped with a thermostat to blend hot and cold water at a prefixed temperature, in spite of pressure variations in the two pipes; also called anti-scald tap.

plumbing

drainage system
The combined network of pipes, valves and other devices that lead liquid-borne waste and/or storm water out of a building and into the public sewers.

fixture drain
The pipe connecting the trap seal of a plumbing fixture to the drainage system.

waste pipe
Drain pipe that collects water-borne waste other than fecal matter from a building's plumbing fixtures.

indirect waste pipe
Drainage pipes that are not connected directly to the building's main drainage system, but lead the waste to it through a trapped receptacle.

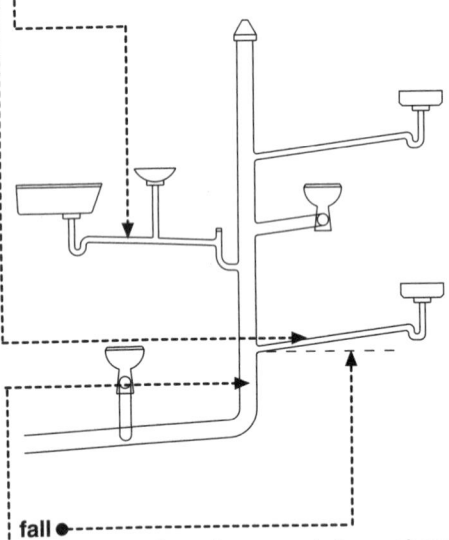

fall
The slope of a pipe, conduit or channel, expressed in inches per foot, centimeters per meter or in percent.

stack
Any vertical pipe, such as a soil pipe, waste pipe, vent or leader stack, or similar pipes collectively.

soil stack
A vertical soil pipe that conveys the discharge from the toilet fixtures.

soil pipe
A pipe carrying the discharge from water closets, with or without the waste from other fixtures; also called soil line.

storm sewer
A pipe taking rain water from a building to the storm sewer system or combined drainage system; also called a building storm sewer or house storm sewer.

storm sewer
A drain to convey rainwater, subsurface water, street wash, cooling water or similar discharges, but not sewage or industrial waste, to a disposal point.

combined sewer
A pipe that conveys waterborne waste and soil, together with storm water.

sanitary sewer
A sewer conveying household waterborne waste together with fecal matter from water closets, to which storm water is not added intentionally.

roughing-in
Installing the concealed part of a plumbing system to the point of connection to the fixtures.

sewage
Waterborne waste containing human fecal matter from a water closet.

building drain
The pipe conveying the discharge of a building's storm water, sewage pipes and soil stacks to the public drainage system; also called a house drain or main drain.

sewer
A public conduit taking liquid waste from one building, or a neighborhood, to a local sewage treatment plant; also called public sewer; see building sewer.

box culvert
A buried water conveying conduit made of concrete, square in cross section.

sanitary sewer
A sewer to convey waterborne waste containing fecal matter from water closets, and not stormwater.

main drain trap
A running trap (a curved depression in a pipe remaining permanently full of water) at a building's outlet to the public sewer, to prevent odors passing from the sewer to the plumbing of the building; also called building trap or house trap.

building sewer
That part of a drain system that joins the end of the building drain to the public or private sewer, or other sewage disposal system.

plumbing

vent system
A network of pipes to ventilate the building sewer, connecting the soil stack, waste stack and soil pipes with the exterior, to prevent siphonage breaking the trap seals or accumulations of sewer gas.

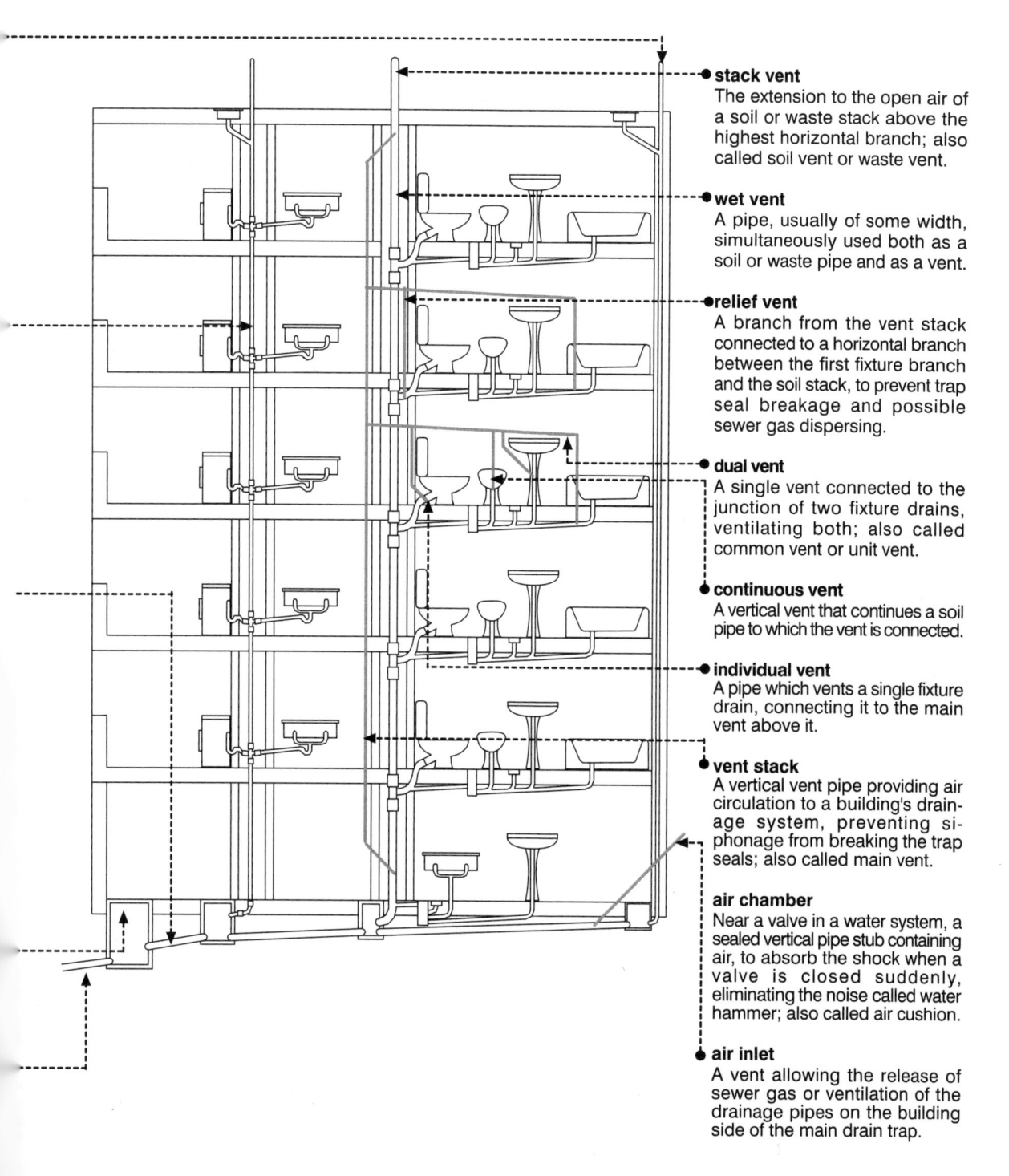

stack vent
The extension to the open air of a soil or waste stack above the highest horizontal branch; also called soil vent or waste vent.

wet vent
A pipe, usually of some width, simultaneously used both as a soil or waste pipe and as a vent.

relief vent
A branch from the vent stack connected to a horizontal branch between the first fixture branch and the soil stack, to prevent trap seal breakage and possible sewer gas dispersing.

dual vent
A single vent connected to the junction of two fixture drains, ventilating both; also called common vent or unit vent.

continuous vent
A vertical vent that continues a soil pipe to which the vent is connected.

individual vent
A pipe which vents a single fixture drain, connecting it to the main vent above it.

vent stack
A vertical vent pipe providing air circulation to a building's drainage system, preventing siphonage from breaking the trap seals; also called main vent.

air chamber
Near a valve in a water system, a sealed vertical pipe stub containing air, to absorb the shock when a valve is closed suddenly, eliminating the noise called water hammer; also called air cushion.

air inlet
A vent allowing the release of sewer gas or ventilation of the drainage pipes on the building side of the main drain trap.

plumbing

sewage treatment plant
A system which is the destination of sanitary sewage, where the offensive or dangerous organic and bacterial content of the waste is reduced.

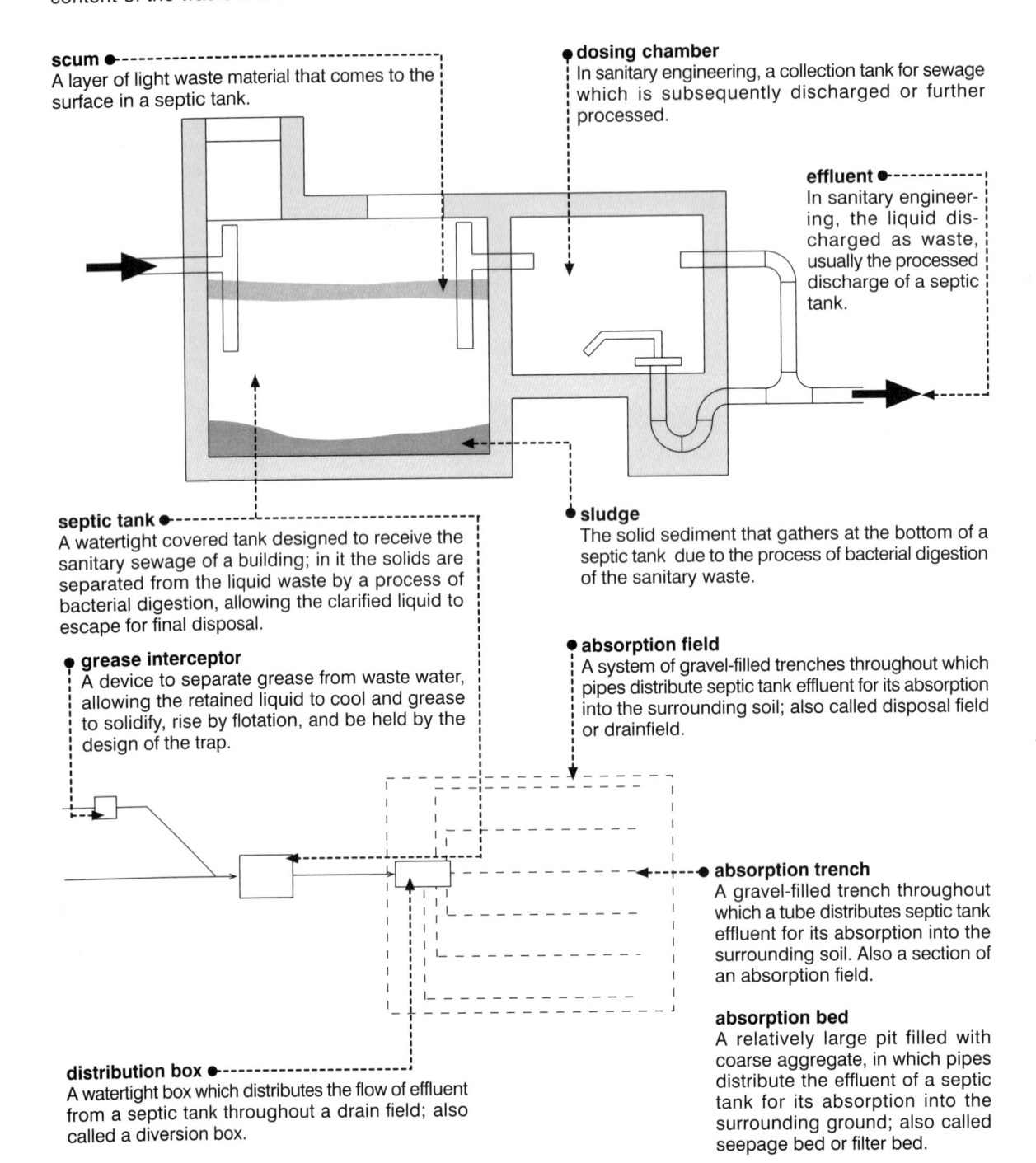

scum
A layer of light waste material that comes to the surface in a septic tank.

dosing chamber
In sanitary engineering, a collection tank for sewage which is subsequently discharged or further processed.

effluent
In sanitary engineering, the liquid discharged as waste, usually the processed discharge of a septic tank.

septic tank
A watertight covered tank designed to receive the sanitary sewage of a building; in it the solids are separated from the liquid waste by a process of bacterial digestion, allowing the clarified liquid to escape for final disposal.

sludge
The solid sediment that gathers at the bottom of a septic tank due to the process of bacterial digestion of the sanitary waste.

grease interceptor
A device to separate grease from waste water, allowing the retained liquid to cool and grease to solidify, rise by flotation, and be held by the design of the trap.

absorption field
A system of gravel-filled trenches throughout which pipes distribute septic tank effluent for its absorption into the surrounding soil; also called disposal field or drainfield.

absorption trench
A gravel-filled trench throughout which a tube distributes septic tank effluent for its absorption into the surrounding soil. Also a section of an absorption field.

absorption bed
A relatively large pit filled with coarse aggregate, in which pipes distribute the effluent of a septic tank for its absorption into the surrounding ground; also called seepage bed or filter bed.

distribution box
A watertight box which distributes the flow of effluent from a septic tank throughout a drain field; also called a diversion box.

plumbing

serial distribution
A pattern of absorption trenches designed so that the absorption field is completely utilized before the effluent passes on to the next.

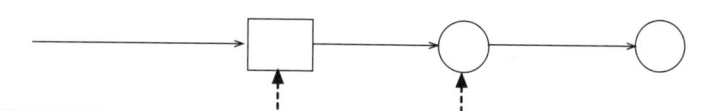

septic tank
A watertight covered tank designed to receive the sanitary sewage of a building; in it the solids are separated from the liquid waste by a process of bacterial digestion, allowing the clarified liquid to escape for final disposal.

seepage pit
A covered pit with a perforated or open jointed concrete lining, to allow septic tank effluent to seep or leach into the surrounding soil.

sand filter
A bed of fine sand that is laid over a graded gravel, used to remove impurities from a water supply or a septic tank effluent.

subsurface sand filter
From the topsoil down, a wide bed with a series of perforated pipes surrounded by clean coarse aggregate; an intermediate layer of filter sand; at the bottom is a layer of coarse aggregate around the system of underdrains to carry away the filtered sewage.

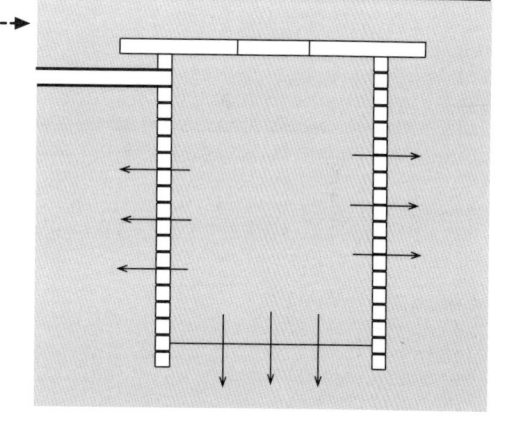

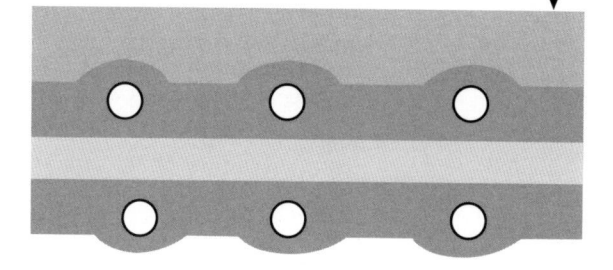

cesspool
A covered excavation in the ground, lined so that the liquid component of organic waterborne waste or domestic sewage can seep through into the ground, retaining the solids; a method of disposal no longer permitted. Also called cesspit.

plumbing

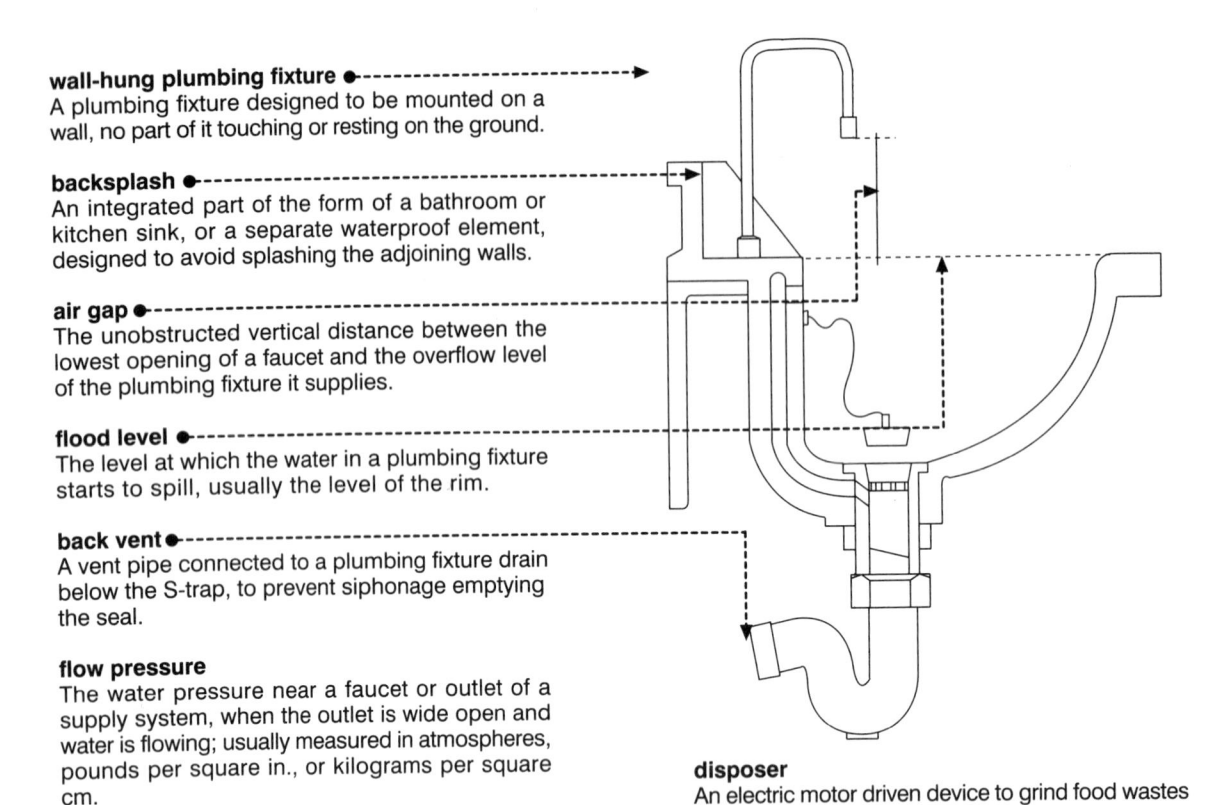

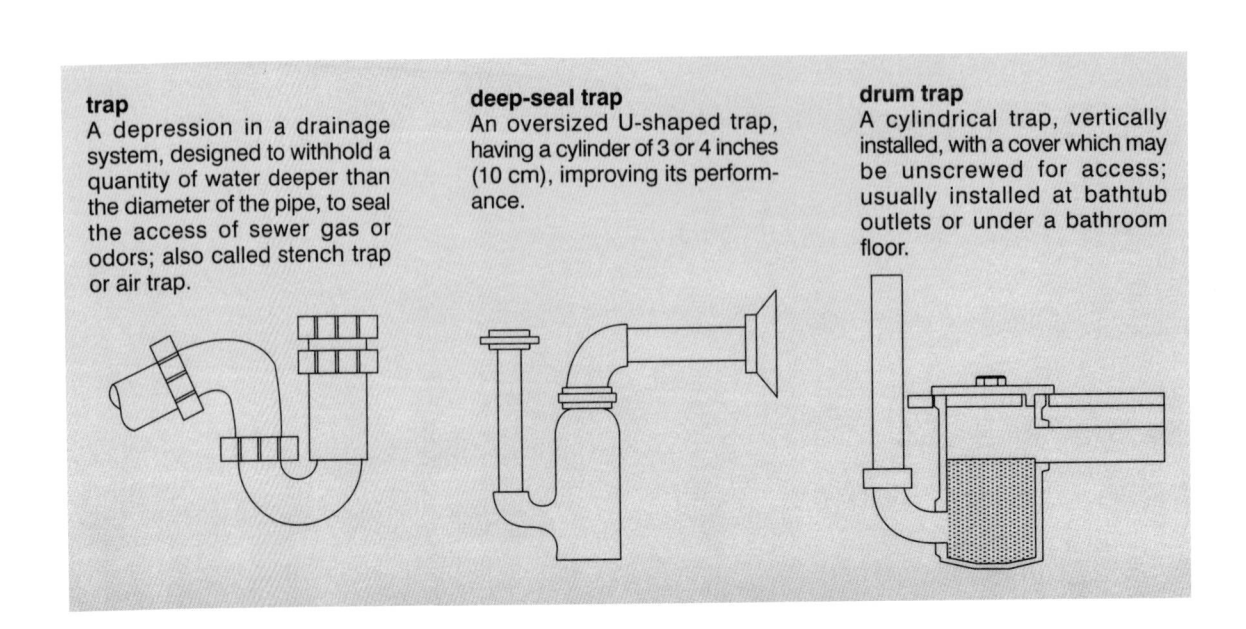

wall-hung plumbing fixture
A plumbing fixture designed to be mounted on a wall, no part of it touching or resting on the ground.

backsplash
An integrated part of the form of a bathroom or kitchen sink, or a separate waterproof element, designed to avoid splashing the adjoining walls.

air gap
The unobstructed vertical distance between the lowest opening of a faucet and the overflow level of the plumbing fixture it supplies.

flood level
The level at which the water in a plumbing fixture starts to spill, usually the level of the rim.

back vent
A vent pipe connected to a plumbing fixture drain below the S-trap, to prevent siphonage emptying the seal.

flow pressure
The water pressure near a faucet or outlet of a supply system, when the outlet is wide open and water is flowing; usually measured in atmospheres, pounds per square in., or kilograms per square cm.

disposer
An electric motor driven device to grind food wastes and dispose of them through the plumbing drains; may not require a grease trap in a residence.

trap
A depression in a drainage system, designed to withhold a quantity of water deeper than the diameter of the pipe, to seal the access of sewer gas or odors; also called stench trap or air trap.

deep-seal trap
An oversized U-shaped trap, having a cylinder of 3 or 4 inches (10 cm), improving its performance.

drum trap
A cylindrical trap, vertically installed, with a cover which may be unscrewed for access; usually installed at bathtub outlets or under a bathroom floor.

fire safety

The combination of measures adopted to prevent fire or to reduce its effects in case it should occur.

fire area
In a building, any area surrounded by fire walls or fire-resistant construction within which a fire would be confined.

fire separation
A floor or wall with an officially approved fire-rating and adequately protected openings, estimated capable of preventing the spread of fire.

occupancy separation
A vertical or horizontal separation between zones dedicated to different activities, graded in accordance to consequent safety hazards, complying with a typified building code.

fire wall
An interior or exterior wall having a grade of fire resistance and structural stability high enough to prevent a fire spreading, as required by code; it should reach from the lowest level to about 3 feet above the roof; all openings are protected by self-closing fire-doors or fire-shutters.

protected opening
An opening in a wall or floor, i.e., a window or door, provided with the required fire protection.

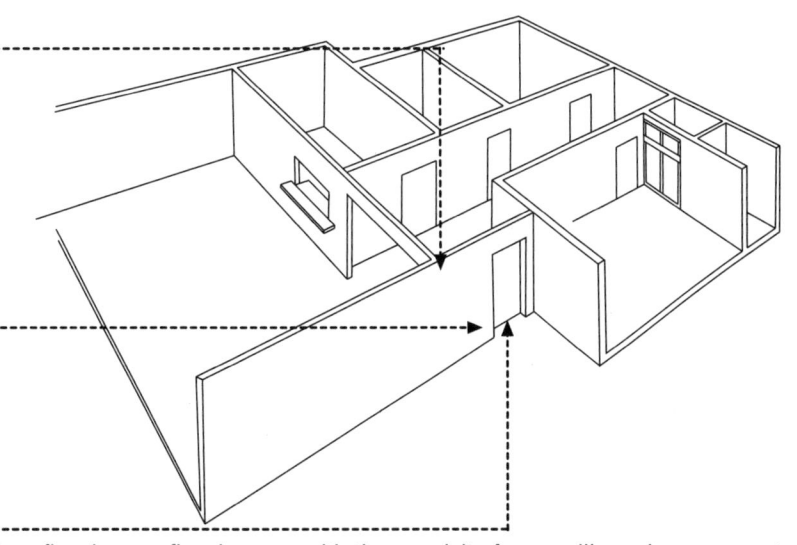

fire assembly
The total assembly of a fire window, fire door or fire damper, with the requisite frame, sill, anchorages and hardware to perform the task during a fire.

class A element
An element having a 3 hour estimated resistance to fire; used to protect the openings in a fire wall or class-A openings.

class B element
An element having a 1 or ½ hour estimated resistance to fire; used to protect class-B openings, fire exits and passageways.

class C element
An element having a ¾ hour estimated resistance to fire; used to protect class-C openings.

class D element
An element having a 1½ hour estimated resistance to fire; used to protect outer walls and exposed areas.

class E element
An element having a ¾ hour estimated resistance to fire; used to protect outer walls and moderately exposed areas.

fire-resistance rating
The time, measured in hours, during which a material or a structure can perform its task in a building while resisting or confining a fire, according to established norms or the result of standard tests.

fire safety

exit
A way out, separated from the rest of the building by walls, floors, doors or other fire rated elements, providing the building's occupants with a relatively protected escape path to an escape stair.

exit corridor
A corridor enclosed between fire resistant walls, leading to a fire tower or other protected means of leaving the building in the event of fire.

horizontal exit door
A means of passage from one part of a building into another or from one building to another, through a fire door and a separation wall with specified fire resistance ratings.

exit door
A fire-protected means of passage equipped with a panic exit device, to a fire tower, fire escape, vertical exit or corridor leading to the street.

area of refuge
The safety area established around the zone where an evacuation has been effected because of fire or smoke.

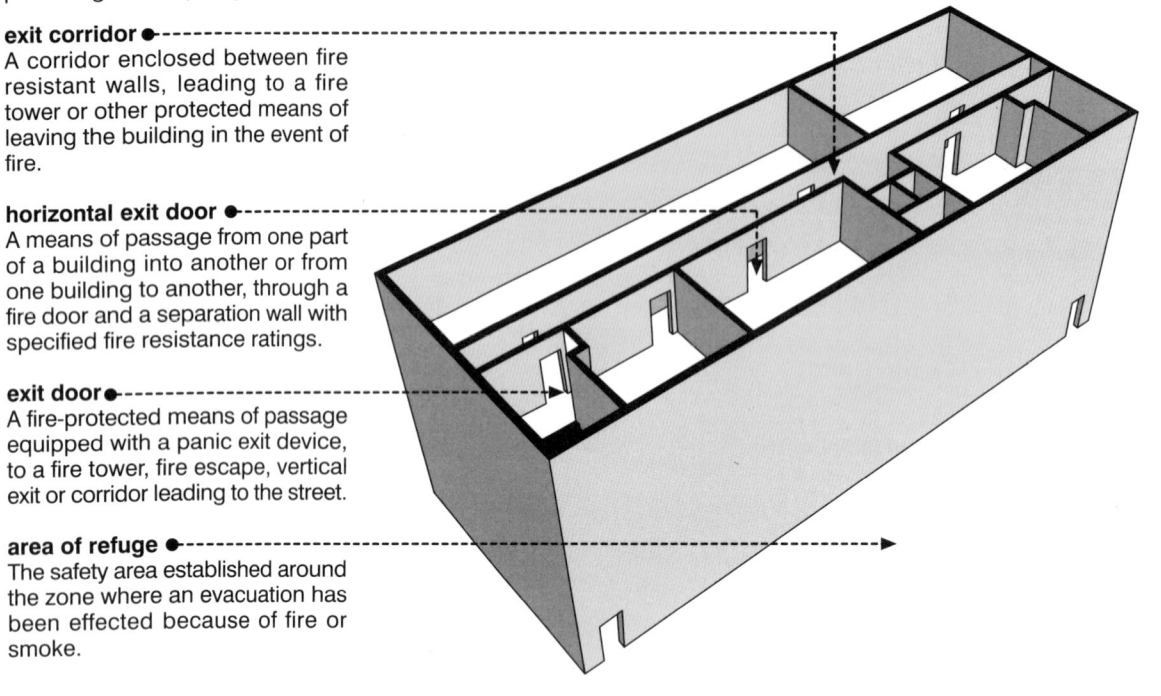

exit discharge
That portion of a means of egress between the end of the exit at the exterior of the building and the ground level.

fire escape
A fire resistant stairway affixed to the outside of a building, connecting the different floors which it provides with a safe exit to the street in case of fire.

fire door
A door, together with all its hardware, which is graded fire resistant according to established norms and tests; usually equipped with a panic exit device.

emergency lighting
A lighting system designed to provide the necessary illumination for the evacuation of a building to take place safely when the normal power supply fails.

exit light
A luminous sign indicating the way to the nearest emergency exit.

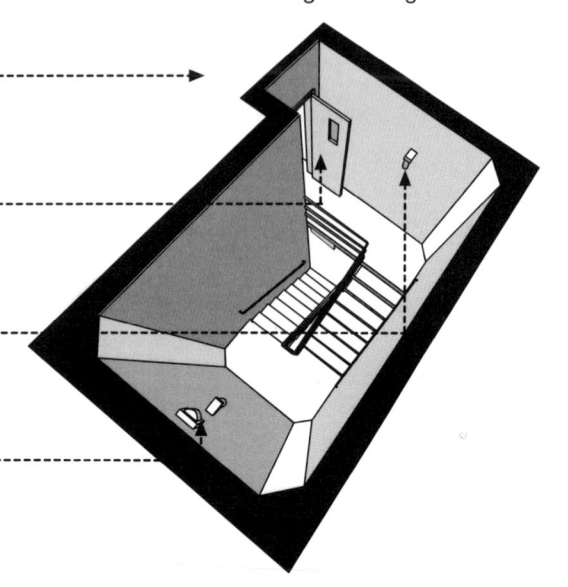

fire safety

automatic fire-extinguishing system
A device that detects a fire and automatically releases a fire-extinguishing agent over it.

sprinkler system
The installation of a network of pipes concealed in the ceiling, connected to the water supply, with spaced sprinklers that will be activated if a given temperature is reached.

sprinkler head
Any of the outlets of a sprinkler system, designed to spray water under pressure into the area below when a set temperature indicating fire is reached, that triggers the release mechanism.

standpipe
A vertical pipe or reserve tank in a water supply system, especially for emergency use and fire fighting.

siamese connection
A wye connection, installed close to the ground on the outside of the wall of a building, providing two inlet firehose connections to the standpipes and the building's fire fighting sprinkler system.

fire hydrant
A public water supply outlet with several connections, situated at intervals along the street, for the exclusive use of fire department personnel attending an emergency; also called hydrant or fire plug.

fire hose
An wide gauge high-pressure flexible hose which, connected to a hydrant, supplies firemen the water they need.

fire pump
A pump especially designed for use in fire fighting, providing the high water pressure necessary for the task; as it is rarely used it must be periodically tested to ensure that it is in operative condition.

fire-detection system
A system of interconnected sensors and equipment designed to detect the presence of fire or a dangerously high temperature which triggers off an alarm signal.

fire-alarm system
A device designed to activate an alarm signal automatically when triggered by a fire detection system.

fire extinguisher
A portable device for the immediate control of an incipient fire; it consists of a canister containing a fire extinguishing agent; different sorts combat different types of fire.

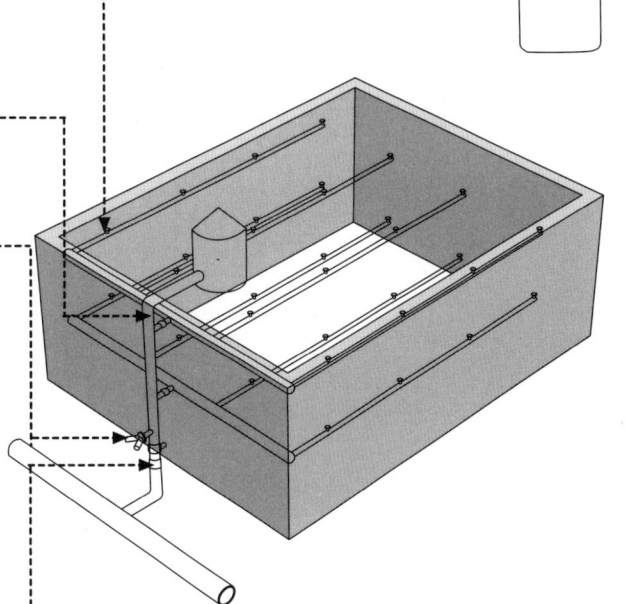

preaction system
A sprinkler system in which the water pressure is supplied by a valve activated by a more sensitive fire detector than the sort installed on the sprinkler heads; up until that moment no water is present in the piping.

deluge system
A sprinkler system in which the sprinkler heads are permanently open, and the flow is controlled by a valve activated by a heat, smoke or flame detector.

wet-pipe system
A system that permanently contains a sufficient water pressure to supply an immediate discharge through the sprinklers when fire is detected.

dry-pipe system
A sprinkler system in which the pipes contain air or nitrogen under pressure, which is released when fire is detected and the sprinklers open; that triggers the water valve open. Used where there is danger of freezing.

Geometry

Euclidean geometry
Drawing
Topographic Survey

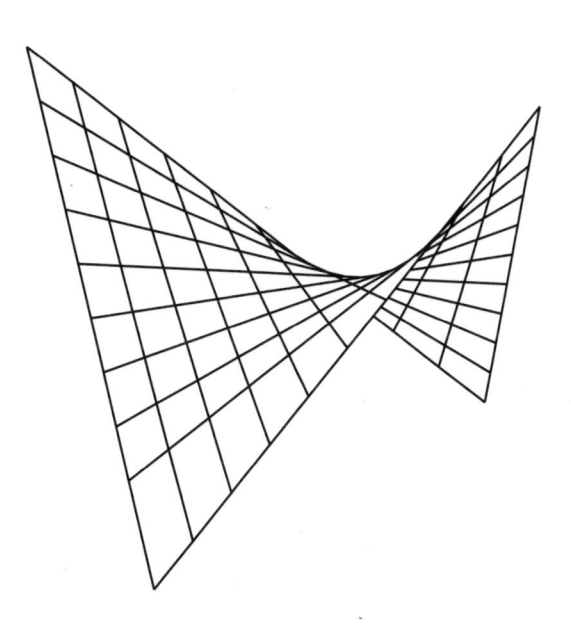

Euclidean geometry

Geometry based on the postulates of Euclid, especially the postulate that only one line can be drawn through a given point parallel to a given line.

plane geometry
The branch of geometry that studies figures whose parts all lie in one plane.

point
Geometrical concept having position but no extension, as the intersection of two lines.

parallel
Said of two or more straight lines that lie in the same plane but never meet however far they extend

surface
Any two-dimensional figure, or that part or aspect of a body considered without depth, on the plane.

angle
The space between two straight lines diverging from the same point; measured in radians or in degrees, minutes and seconds.

right angle
An angle of 90°, formed by the intersection of two perpendicular lines.

acute angle
Any angle of less than 90°

vertex
The point of intersection of the sides of an angle.

obtuse angle
An angle of more than 90°

triangle
A polygon with three sides.

acute triangle
A triangle with three acute angles.

scalene triangle
A triangle in which all three sides are of different lengths.

isosceles triangle
A triangle two of whose sides are equal.

obtuse triangle
A triangle having one obtuse angle.

Euclidean geometry

Pythagorean theorem
The theorem stating that the square of the hypotenuse of a right triangle is equal to the sum of the other two sides.

right triangle
A triangle having one 90º angle.

hypotenuse
The side opposite the right angle of a right triangle.

base
The side on which it is supposed that geometrical figures rest and from which their height is measured.

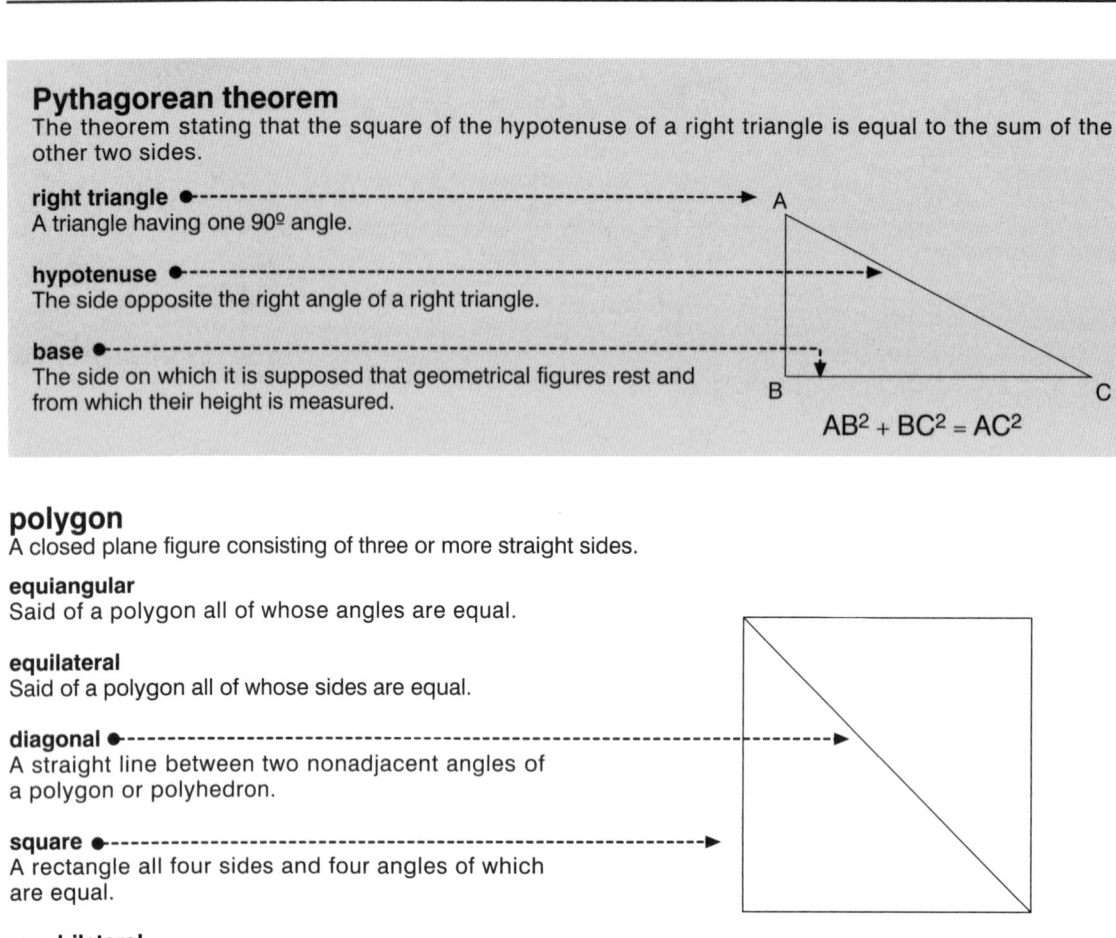

$$AB^2 + BC^2 = AC^2$$

polygon
A closed plane figure consisting of three or more straight sides.

equiangular
Said of a polygon all of whose angles are equal.

equilateral
Said of a polygon all of whose sides are equal.

diagonal
A straight line between two nonadjacent angles of a polygon or polyhedron.

square
A rectangle all four sides and four angles of which are equal.

quadrilateral
Said of a polygon with four sides and four angles.

parallelogram
A rectangle having both pairs of opposite sides parallel to each other.

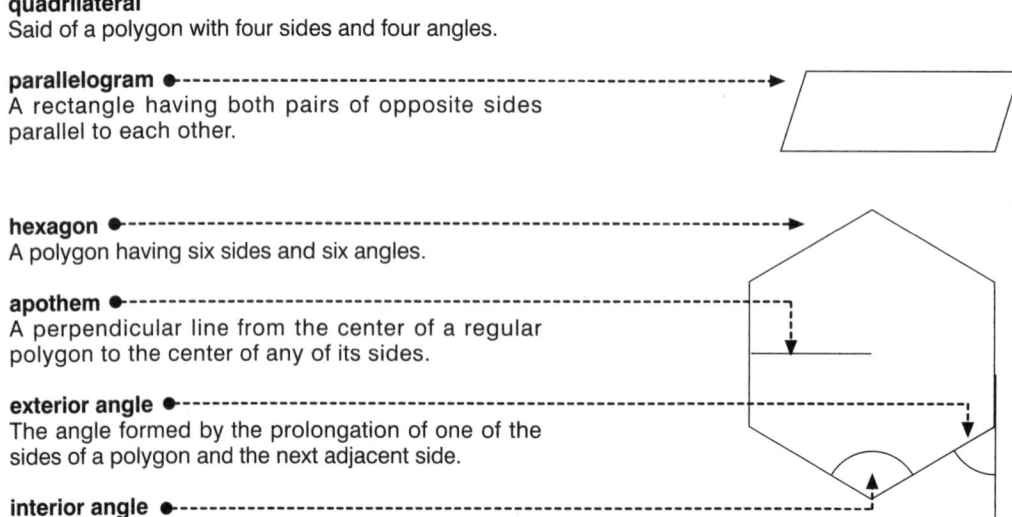

hexagon
A polygon having six sides and six angles.

apothem
A perpendicular line from the center of a regular polygon to the center of any of its sides.

exterior angle
The angle formed by the prolongation of one of the sides of a polygon and the next adjacent side.

interior angle
The angle formed inside the perimeter of the figure by two adjacent sides of a polygon.

Euclidean geometry

hexagram
A figure resembling a six-pointed star, obtained by prolonging each of the sides of a hexagon until they intersect, creating six equilateral triangles.

pentagon
A polygon having five sides and five angles.

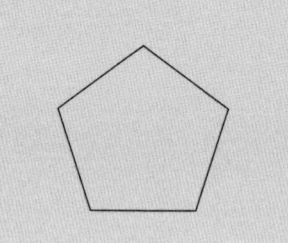

octagon
A polygon having eight sides and eight angles.

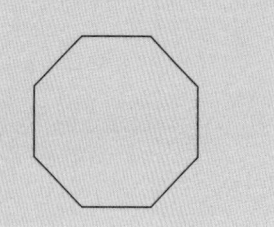

circle
A closed plane curve all points of which are equidistant from one point called the center; the portion of a plane limited by such a curve.

center (USA)
In a circle, the point from which all points of the circle are equidistant; also called centre (G.B.)

diameter
A straight line crossing the center of a circle, dividing it in two equal halves.

circumference
A closed plane curve all points of which are equidistant from one point called the center; the outer boundary of a circular area.

arc
Any unbroken segment of the circumference of a circle or other curved line.

ellipse
A plane curve such that the sums of the distances of each point in its periphery from two fixed points, the foci, are equal.

major axis
In an ellipse, the axis that crosses the two foci.

minor axis
In an ellipse, the axis that is perpendicular to the major axis and equidistant from the two foci.

hyperbola
The set of points in a plane whose distances to two fixed points in the plane have a constant difference; a curve consisting of two distinct and similar branches, formed by the intersection of a plane with a right circular cone, the plane making a wider angle with the base than the generator of the cone.

parabola
A plane curve formed by the intersection of a right circular cone with a plane parallel to a generator of the cone.

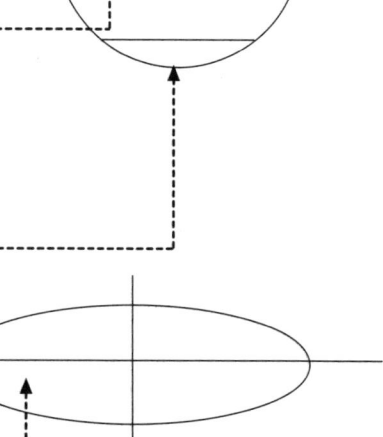

Euclidean geometry

solid geometry
The geometry of solid figures; the geometry of three dimensions; the branch of mathematics studying the properties of forms having width, length and depth, expressed in measures, to define the relations between points, angles, planes and solids in space.

solid
A geometrical figure consisting of three dimensions: length, height and depth. Also called body.

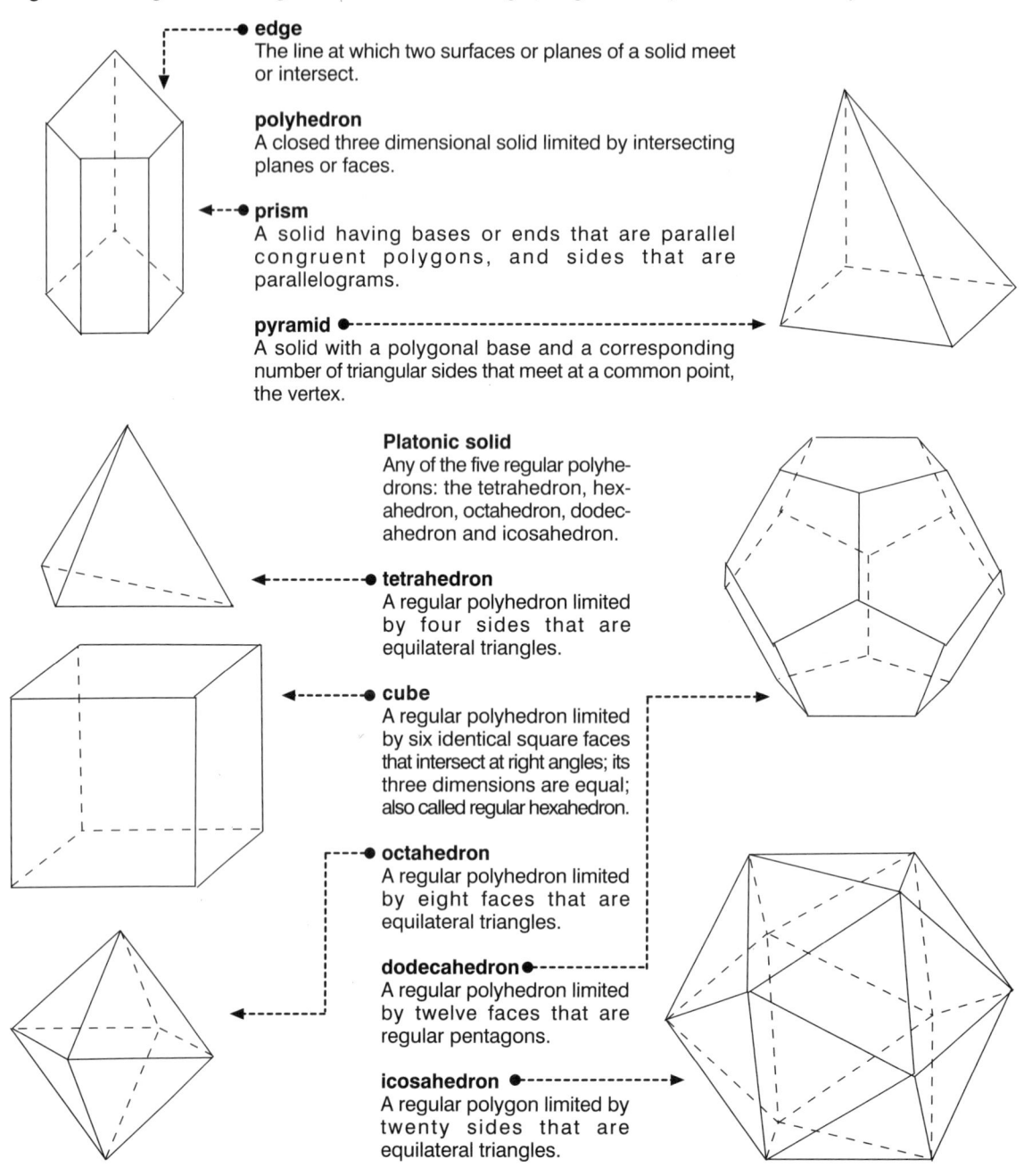

edge
The line at which two surfaces or planes of a solid meet or intersect.

polyhedron
A closed three dimensional solid limited by intersecting planes or faces.

prism
A solid having bases or ends that are parallel congruent polygons, and sides that are parallelograms.

pyramid
A solid with a polygonal base and a corresponding number of triangular sides that meet at a common point, the vertex.

Platonic solid
Any of the five regular polyhedrons: the tetrahedron, hexahedron, octahedron, dodecahedron and icosahedron.

tetrahedron
A regular polyhedron limited by four sides that are equilateral triangles.

cube
A regular polyhedron limited by six identical square faces that intersect at right angles; its three dimensions are equal; also called regular hexahedron.

octahedron
A regular polyhedron limited by eight faces that are equilateral triangles.

dodecahedron
A regular polyhedron limited by twelve faces that are regular pentagons.

icosahedron
A regular polygon limited by twenty sides that are equilateral triangles.

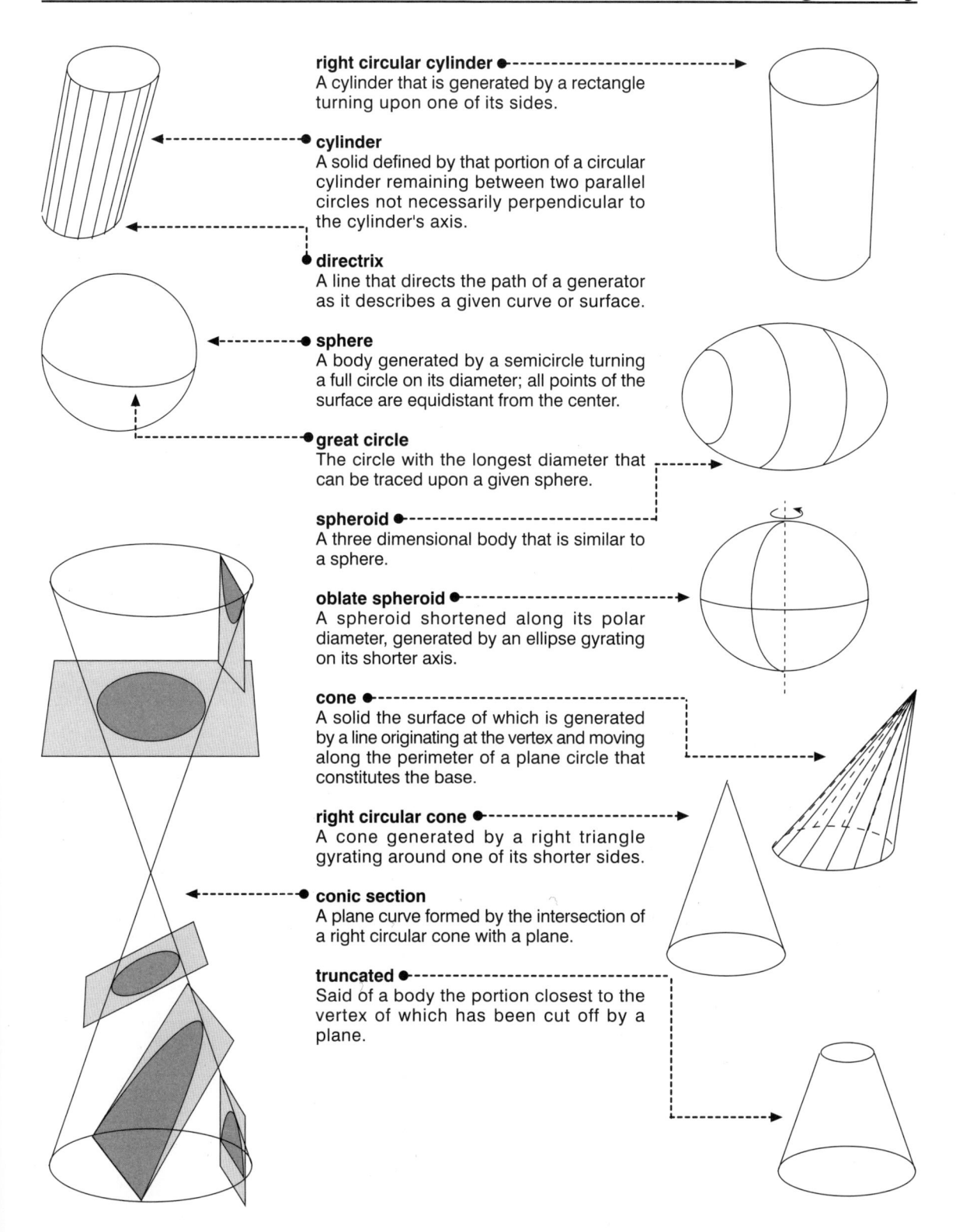

Euclidean geometry

right circular cylinder
A cylinder that is generated by a rectangle turning upon one of its sides.

cylinder
A solid defined by that portion of a circular cylinder remaining between two parallel circles not necessarily perpendicular to the cylinder's axis.

directrix
A line that directs the path of a generator as it describes a given curve or surface.

sphere
A body generated by a semicircle turning a full circle on its diameter; all points of the surface are equidistant from the center.

great circle
The circle with the longest diameter that can be traced upon a given sphere.

spheroid
A three dimensional body that is similar to a sphere.

oblate spheroid
A spheroid shortened along its polar diameter, generated by an ellipse gyrating on its shorter axis.

cone
A solid the surface of which is generated by a line originating at the vertex and moving along the perimeter of a plane circle that constitutes the base.

right circular cone
A cone generated by a right triangle gyrating around one of its shorter sides.

conic section
A plane curve formed by the intersection of a right circular cone with a plane.

truncated
Said of a body the portion closest to the vertex of which has been cut off by a plane.

Euclidean geometry

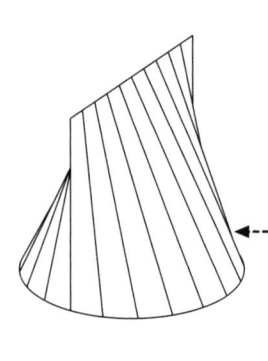

ruled surface
A surface that can be generated by a straight line, as a cylinder or a cone.

cylindrical surface
The surface generated by a sliding a perpendicular straight line along the perimeter of a plane circle.

conoid
A surface generated by sliding one end of a straight line along the perimeter of a closed plane curve, and the other along a straight line; the curve determines the conoid as circular, elliptic or parabolic.

translational surface
The surface that is generated by sliding a plane curve along a straight line or another plane curve.

elliptic paraboloid
A surface generated by sliding a vertical parabola opening upward, along another similar parabola on a plane perpendicular to the first, creating a figure with elliptical horizontal sections and parabolic vertical sections.

hypar
A surface generated by sliding a vertical parabola opening upward, along another parabola opening downward on a plane perpendicular to the first.

rotational surface
The surface generated when a plane curve is revolved around its axis.

paraboloid
A surface the plane sections of which are either parabolas and ellipses or parabolas and hyperbolas.

parabolic surface
A surface generated by the rotation of a parabolic arc around a vertical axis.

hyperboloid
Mathematically defined as a surface with a finite center, having an asymptotic cone, and the characteristic that some of its plane sections are hyperbolas while others are circles or ellipses.

torus
A solid generated by the revolution of a circle around an axis that lies outside its perimeter but on the same plane.

elliptical surface
A surface generated by the revolution of an elliptic arc around a vertical axis.

spherical surface
A surface generated by the revolution of a circular arc around a vertical axis.

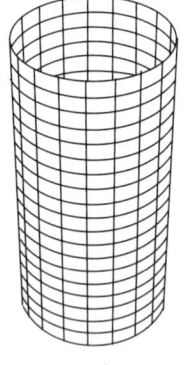

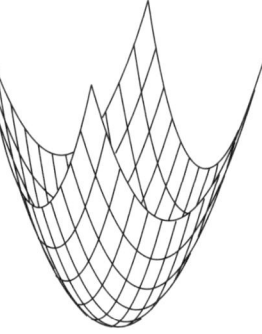

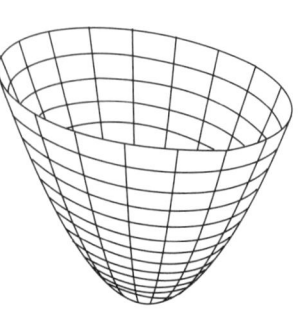

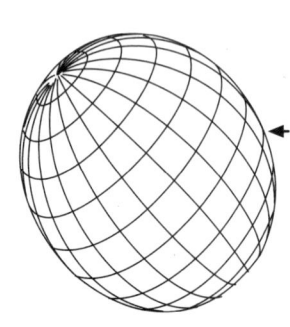

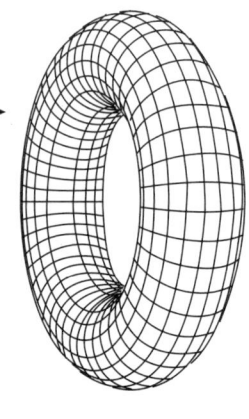

Euclidean geometry

symmetry
The identical correspondence of position and form between two bodies or figures situated on opposite sides of a plane, or a common axis or center.

bilateral symmetry
An identical distribution of the elements of a set on opposite sides of a common axis.

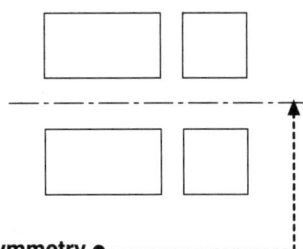

axis of symmetry
The imaginary line on opposite sides of which two sets of elements present a balanced correspondent distribution.

centerline (USA)
Any line bisecting a plane figure; a straight line taken as the center of a symmetrical composition; also called axis or centreline (GB).

radial symmetry
A balanced distribution of elements on opposite sides of one or more axes; also called central symmetry

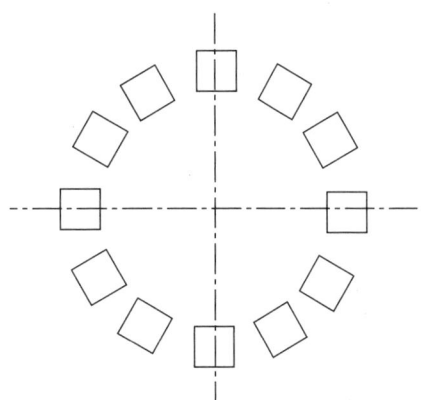

local symmetry
A symmetrical distribution that only applies in part of a design.

golden section
A ratio between two parts of a line or two dimensions of a plane figure, in which the lesser is to the greater as the greater is to the sum of both; a ratio approximating 0.618 to 1.000. Also called golden mean.

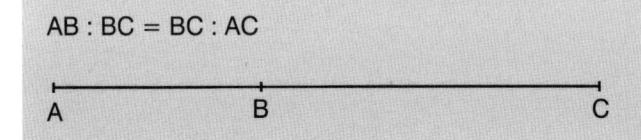

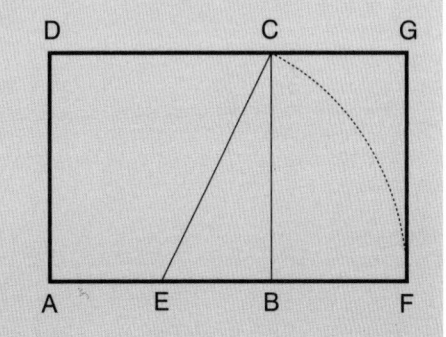

AB : BC = BC : AC

figure
1. Any given distribution of the elements of a geometrical figure. 2. The exterior form of a body as defined by its visible contour.

contour
The outline of a figure or body; the line that defines or bounds anything.

salient angle
An angle projecting out of a figure; any interior angle narrower than 180º; opposite of reentrant angle.

reentrant angle
An angle receding into of a figure or body; Any interior angle narrower than 180º; the opposite of salient angle; also called reentering angle.

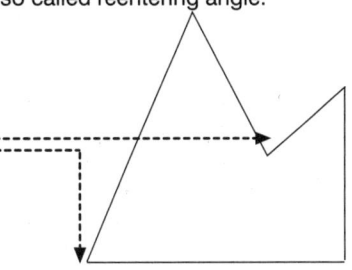

Euclidean geometry

descriptive geometry
A branch of geometry that studies the spatial relations of figures, based on their orthogonal projections on a plane; the representation of accurately defined figures by their projection on a plane so that the original figure's metrical properties can be deduced.

rectangular coordinate system
System of locating a point on a plane by its distance from two lines intersecting at a 90º angle, or in space by its distance from three planes likewise intersecting orthogonally at a point; also called Cartesian coordinates.

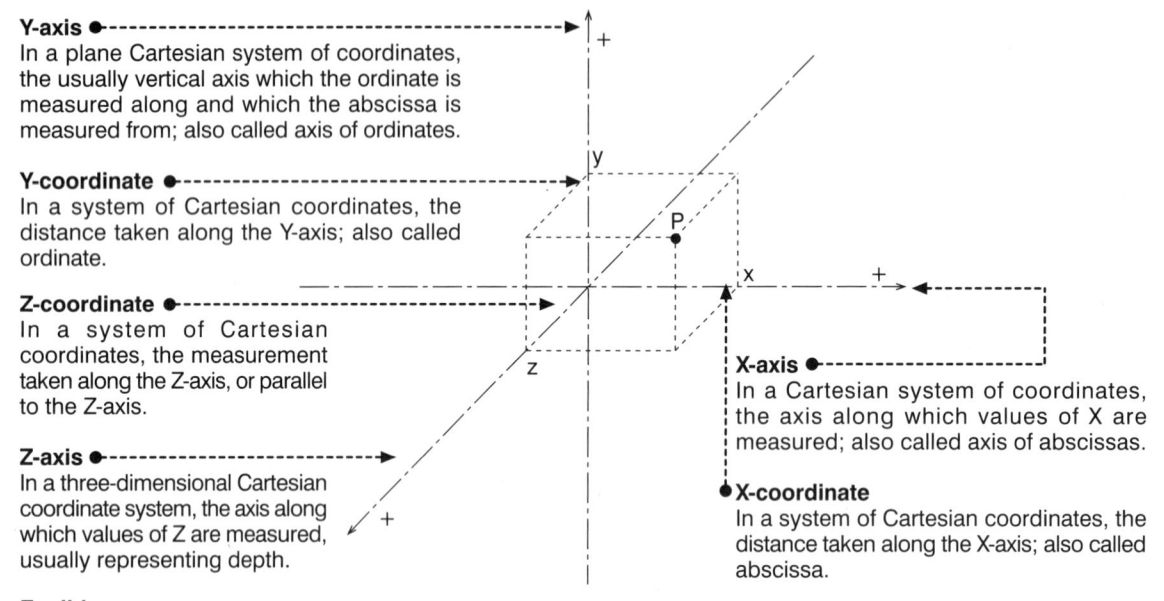

Y-axis
In a plane Cartesian system of coordinates, the usually vertical axis which the ordinate is measured along and which the abscissa is measured from; also called axis of ordinates.

Y-coordinate
In a system of Cartesian coordinates, the distance taken along the Y-axis; also called ordinate.

Z-coordinate
In a system of Cartesian coordinates, the measurement taken along the Z-axis, or parallel to the Z-axis.

Z-axis
In a three-dimensional Cartesian coordinate system, the axis along which values of Z are measured, usually representing depth.

X-axis
In a Cartesian system of coordinates, the axis along which values of X are measured; also called axis of abscissas.

X-coordinate
In a system of Cartesian coordinates, the distance taken along the X-axis; also called abscissa.

Euclidean space
Two dimensional (on one plane) or three dimensional space which conforms to the postulates of Euclid; also called Cartesian or three-dimensional space.

coordinate
One or all the lines traced in a system of coordinates, to define a point's location on a plane, a surface, or in space.

Cartesian coordinate
Each of the lines traced between a point on a plane and two intersecting lines, called axes, to define it's location on the given plane; the lines are parallel to one axis and intersect the other. A point's location in space is likewise determined by three intersecting planes.

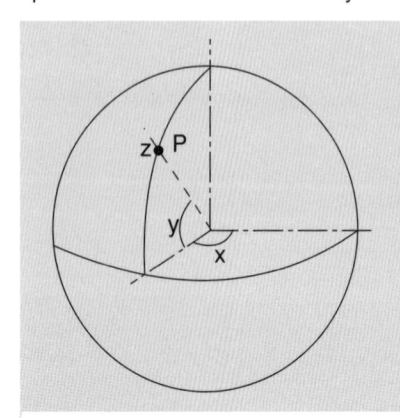

polar coordinate system
A system of coordinates for locating a point in a plane by the length of its radius vector and the angle this vector makes with a fixed line.

polar angle
The angle formed by the polar axis and a radius vector, in a system of polar coordinates.

polar axis
The fixed line in a polar coordinates system, from which the angle made by the radius vector is measured.

drawing

The art and the craft of using lines to represent a three dimensional real model upon a plane support.

pictorial space

The optical illusion of depth and space achieved by various graphic means such as linear perspective, outline, texture, etc.; the different means are often used in conjunction, reinforcing each other.

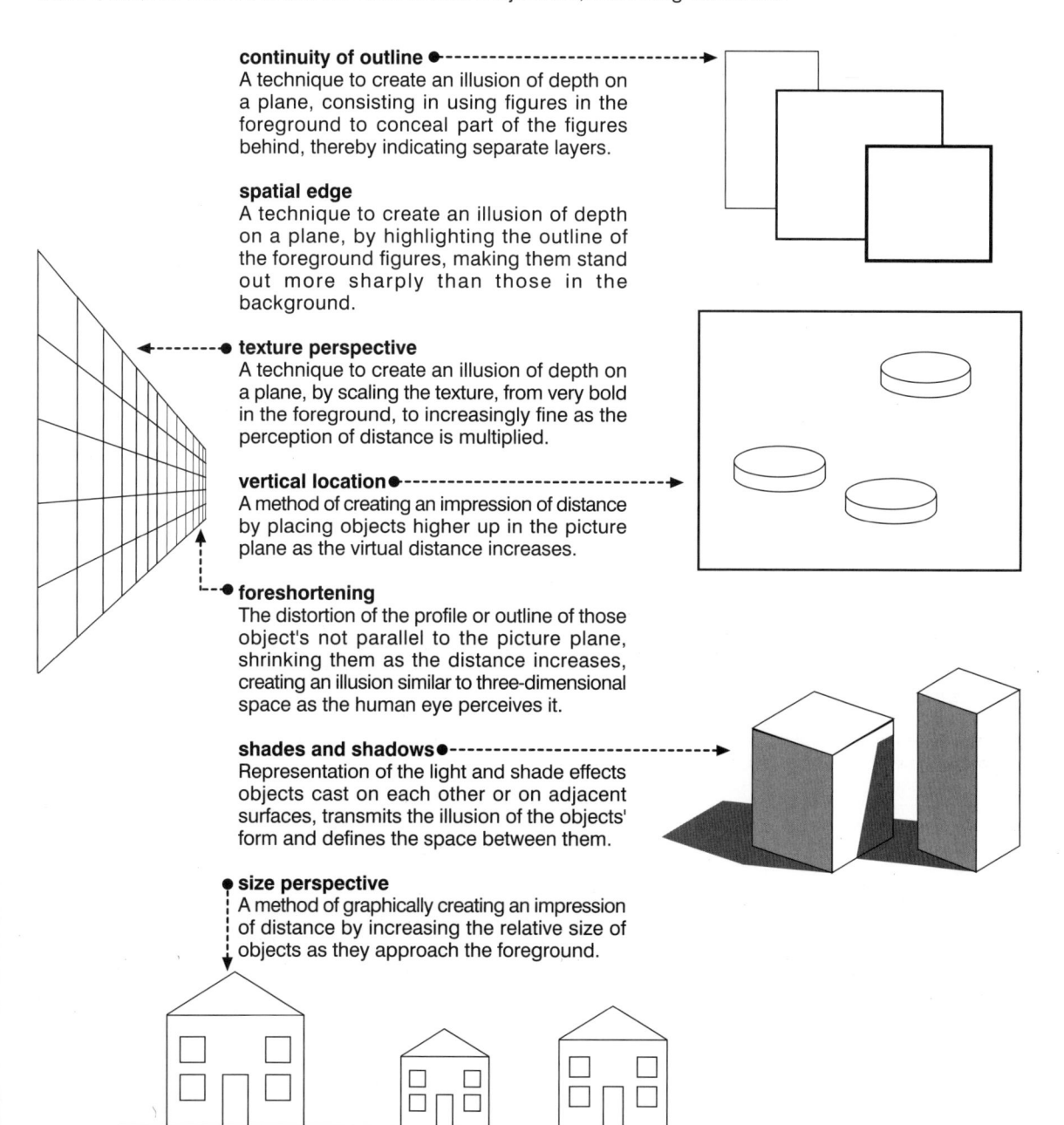

continuity of outline
A technique to create an illusion of depth on a plane, consisting in using figures in the foreground to conceal part of the figures behind, thereby indicating separate layers.

spatial edge
A technique to create an illusion of depth on a plane, by highlighting the outline of the foreground figures, making them stand out more sharply than those in the background.

texture perspective
A technique to create an illusion of depth on a plane, by scaling the texture, from very bold in the foreground, to increasingly fine as the perception of distance is multiplied.

vertical location
A method of creating an impression of distance by placing objects higher up in the picture plane as the virtual distance increases.

foreshortening
The distortion of the profile or outline of those object's not parallel to the picture plane, shrinking them as the distance increases, creating an illusion similar to three-dimensional space as the human eye perceives it.

shades and shadows
Representation of the light and shade effects objects cast on each other or on adjacent surfaces, transmits the illusion of the objects' form and defines the space between them.

size perspective
A method of graphically creating an impression of distance by increasing the relative size of objects as they approach the foreground.

drawing

perspective
A technique used to represent solid objects in space upon a flat surface, by making outlines converge into the distance and foreshortening objects that have a steep angle to the picture plane.

linear perspective
A mathematical method of representing three-dimensional objects on a flat surface, by capturing the model's outline on an orthogonal linear grid; the vertical lines are then depicted as converging on one, two or more points situated on an imaginary horizon line, as perceived by a given viewer.

center of vision (USA)
In linear perspective, the virtual point of intersection of the central axis of vision with the surface of the picture plane; also called centre of vision (G.B.).

picture plane
The flat surface upon which a system of lines representing an object are projected forming an image or picture.

sightline
In linear perspective, each one of the imaginary lines connecting the eye of the viewer to the defining points of the object.

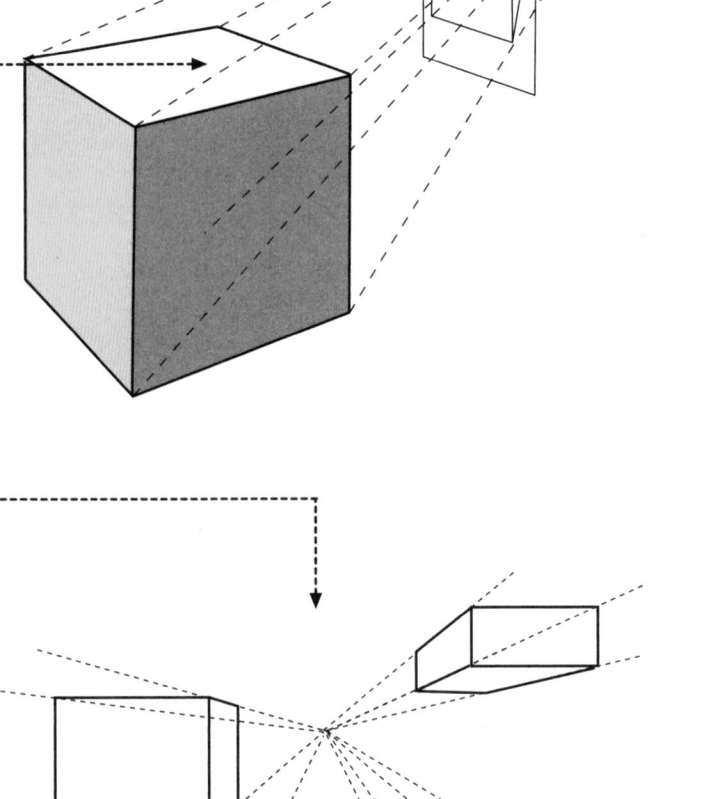

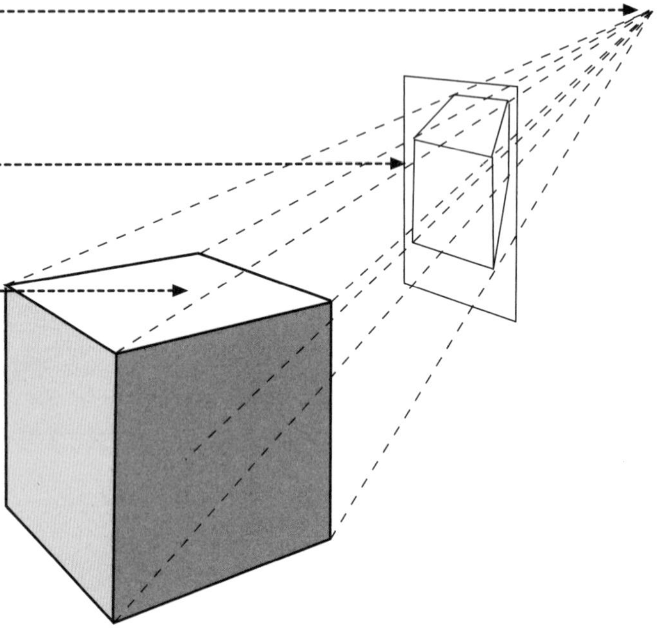

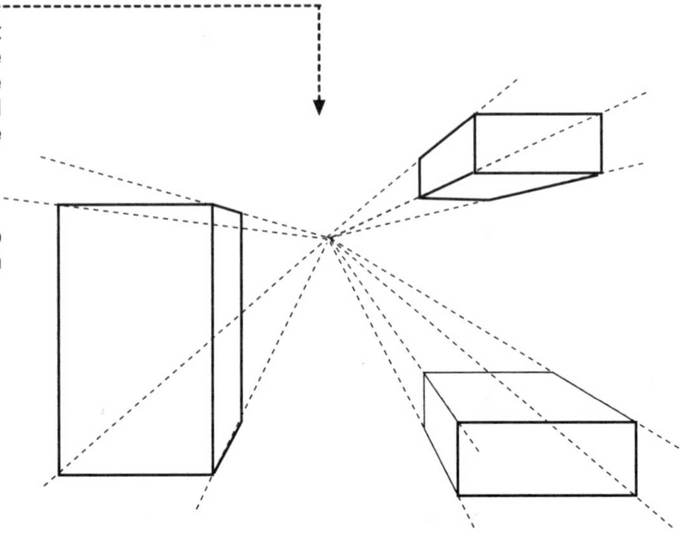

projection
The method of representing a three-dimensional object by projecting its defining points onto an orthogonal grid traced on the picture plane.

cone of vision
A visual field having its vertex in the eye of the viewer, the outer beams of which should form an angle of between 15º and 30º, which permits a definition of the object being drawn, without producing excessive distortion.

one-point perspective
The linear perspective of a rectangular object having two sides aligned obliquely to the picture plane, in which the lines perpendicular to the picture plane converge in a central point, and the vertical and horizontal lines parallel to the picture plane remain in that direction.

central axis of vision
In linear perspective, a beam perpendicular to the picture plane that defines the direction in which the viewer is looking.

drawing

two-point perspective
The linear perspective of a rectangular body with two sides oriented obliquely to the picture plane, so that vertical lines parallel to the picture plane remain so, while the oblique lines converge on two vanishing points to the left and right of the horizon line.

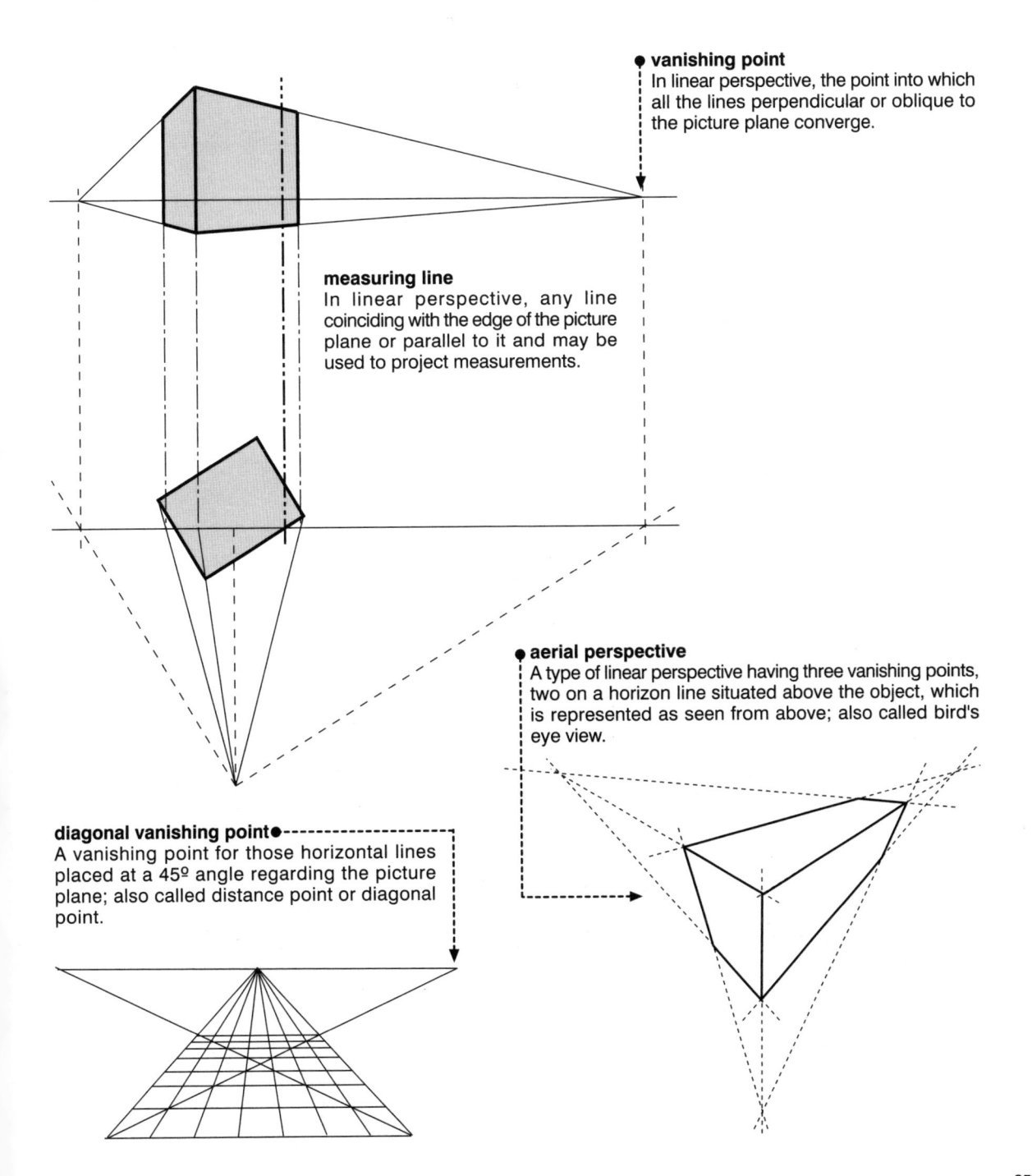

vanishing point
In linear perspective, the point into which all the lines perpendicular or oblique to the picture plane converge.

measuring line
In linear perspective, any line coinciding with the edge of the picture plane or parallel to it and may be used to project measurements.

aerial perspective
A type of linear perspective having three vanishing points, two on a horizon line situated above the object, which is represented as seen from above; also called bird's eye view.

diagonal vanishing point
A vanishing point for those horizontal lines placed at a 45º angle regarding the picture plane; also called distance point or diagonal point.

drawing

paraline drawing
A three-dimensional representation having the particularity that the parallel lines oblique to the picture plane don't converge as in linear perspective, remaining parallel.

cavalier drawing
A paraline drawing in which all equal lines of the object parallel to the picture plane remain of equal magnitude; perpendicular lines also remain parallel and maintain their dimensions; scale is maintained throughout, but visually the object appears distorted.

cabinet drawing
A paraline drawing in which all equal lines of the object parallel to the picture plane remain of equal magnitude; perpendicular lines also remain parallel but their dimensions are reduced by a ratio of ½; the scale is uncomplicated, and visually the object appears less distorted.

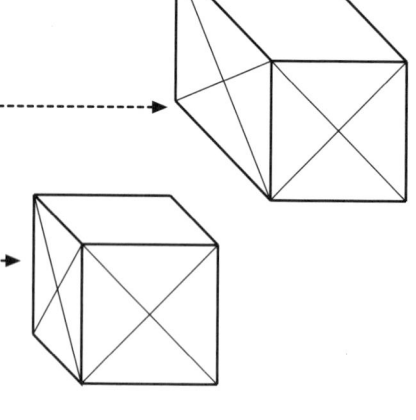

axonometric projection
The orthogonal projection on a plane of a three-dimensional object unequally inclined regarding the three main axes.

isometric projection
An axonometric projection in which the three main sides of the body have been drawn parallel to the three axes, so measurements can be taken directly from them without having to reverse reduction factors; horizontals are drawn at a 30º angle to the horizontal, verticals remain parallel to the vertical axis.

dimetric projection
An axonometric projection of a three-dimensional object inclined in relation to the picture plane so that two of its axes apply the same reduction factor, while the third, which is unaltered, seems shorter or longer than the other two.

trimetric projection
An axonometric projection of a three-dimensional object inclined in relation to the picture plane so that each of its three axes applies a different reduction factor.

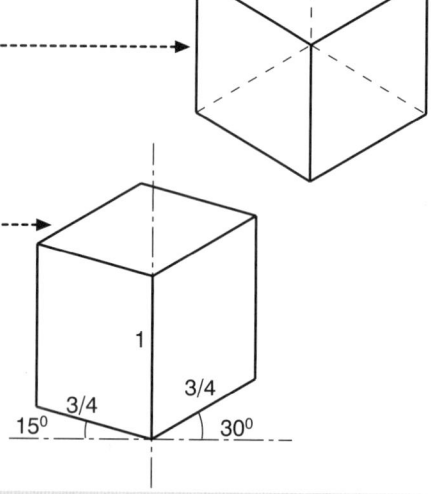

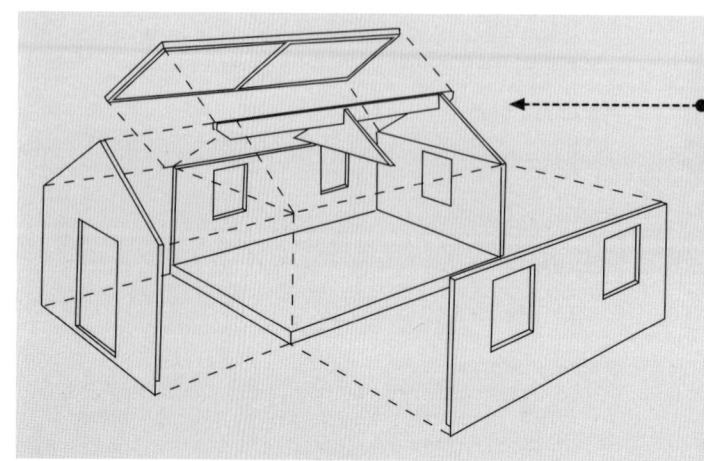

exploded view
A type of drawing that permits a view of the different components of a structure as well as the manner in which they are assembled and how they fit together.

drawing

architectural drawing
Any of the numerous drawings an architect produces for a building project, such as site plans, floor plans, sections and elevations, details, etc.).

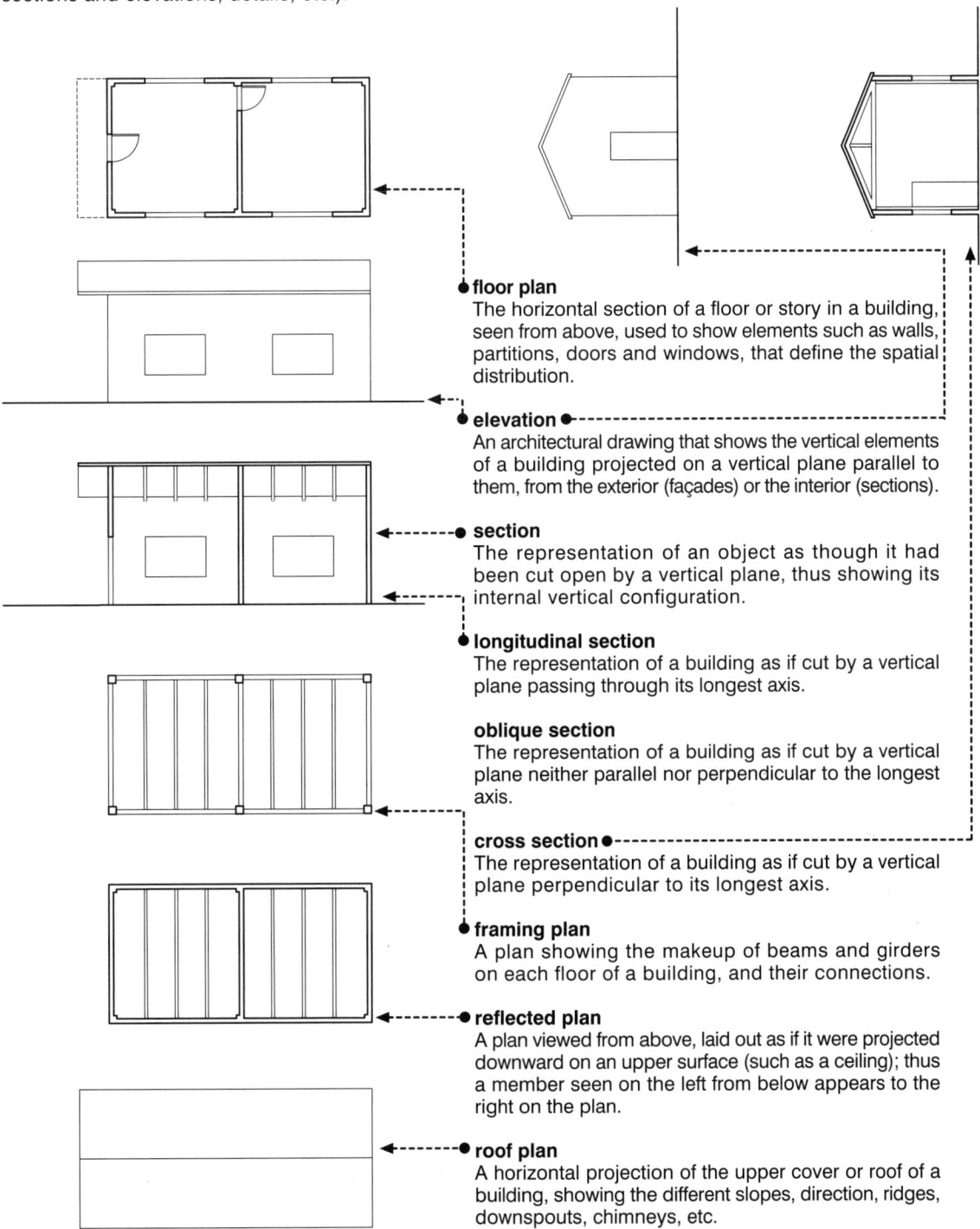

floor plan
The horizontal section of a floor or story in a building, seen from above, used to show elements such as walls, partitions, doors and windows, that define the spatial distribution.

elevation
An architectural drawing that shows the vertical elements of a building projected on a vertical plane parallel to them, from the exterior (façades) or the interior (sections).

section
The representation of an object as though it had been cut open by a vertical plane, thus showing its internal vertical configuration.

longitudinal section
The representation of a building as if cut by a vertical plane passing through its longest axis.

oblique section
The representation of a building as if cut by a vertical plane neither parallel nor perpendicular to the longest axis.

cross section
The representation of a building as if cut by a vertical plane perpendicular to its longest axis.

framing plan
A plan showing the makeup of beams and girders on each floor of a building, and their connections.

reflected plan
A plan viewed from above, laid out as if it were projected downward on an upper surface (such as a ceiling); thus a member seen on the left from below appears to the right on the plan.

roof plan
A horizontal projection of the upper cover or roof of a building, showing the different slopes, direction, ridges, downspouts, chimneys, etc.

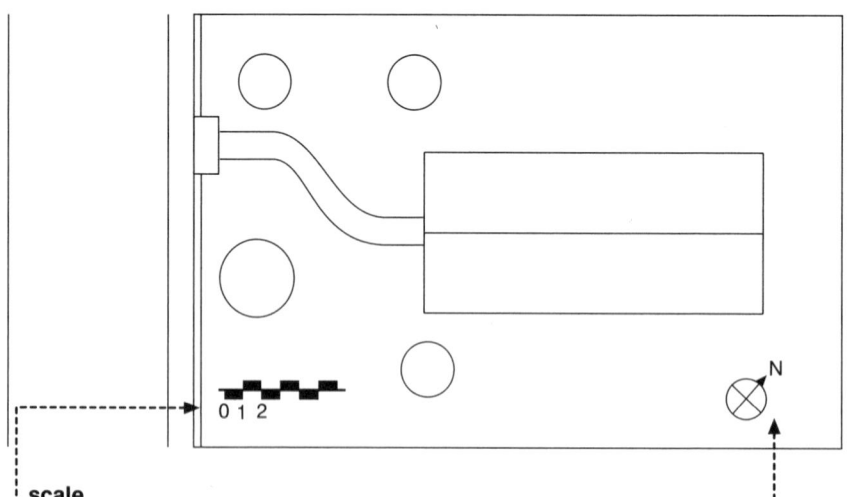

drawing

site plan
A plan showing the placement of the building regarding the boundaries of the property or the lot, the paths of access, the dimensions of the building and any significant features of the piece of land where the work will take place.

grading plan
A plan showing the projected finished profile of the ground surface of a given site, usually by means of contour lines and grade elevations

area plan
A plan or map, of a 1:10000 scale or similar, showing the building, the plot and the urban or rural context surrounding it.

scale
A proportional system or ratio that is defined on every architectural drawing, to be consistently applied in translating the dimensions of the plan into real size.

graphic scale
A graded line drawn into an architectural plan, representing the unit measures used, to avoid errors due to slight variations introduced when copies are made..

north arrow
A symbol drawn into architectural plans and maps indicating where the north lies.

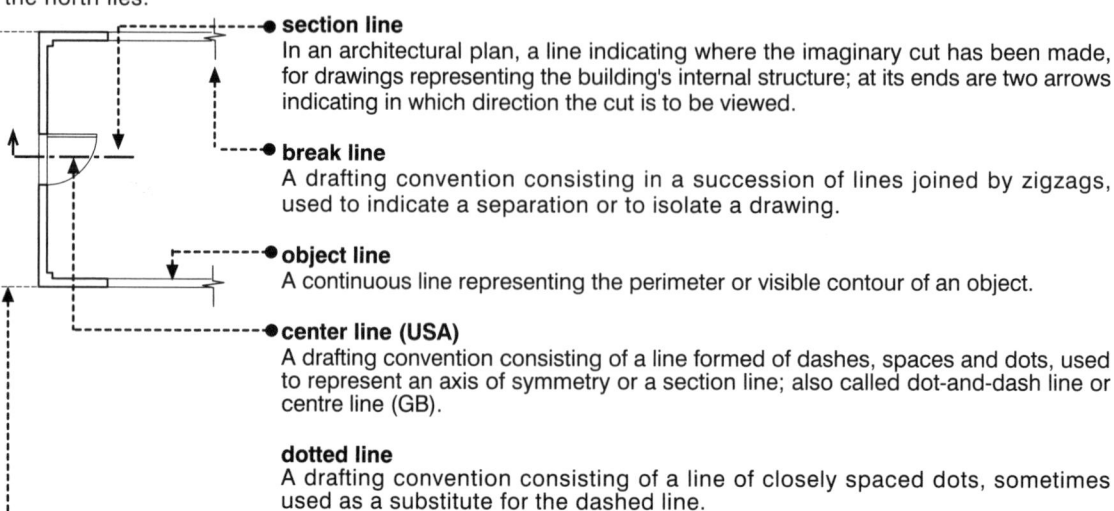

section line
In an architectural plan, a line indicating where the imaginary cut has been made, for drawings representing the building's internal structure; at its ends are two arrows indicating in which direction the cut is to be viewed.

break line
A drafting convention consisting in a succession of lines joined by zigzags, used to indicate a separation or to isolate a drawing.

object line
A continuous line representing the perimeter or visible contour of an object.

center line (USA)
A drafting convention consisting of a line formed of dashes, spaces and dots, used to represent an axis of symmetry or a section line; also called dot-and-dash line or centre line (GB).

dotted line
A drafting convention consisting of a line of closely spaced dots, sometimes used as a substitute for the dashed line.

dashed line
A drafting convention consisting in the use of a broken line to represent outlines that are behind something.

dimension line
A drafting convention consisting in a line limited by a dot, arrow or cross dash at each end, used to indicate the dimension of a wall or a door.

topographic survey

A record of the natural and man-made features of a piece of land, by means of contour lines indicating height above or below a fixed datum, and measuring techniques such as triangulation.

leveling (USA)
A procedure to establish the difference in elevation between two points, using a device consisting of a tripod, a spirit level, a telescope, a graded circle, a compass and a leveling rod; also called levelling or differential levelling (GB).

turning point
In leveling or plane tabling, a point temporarily located and marked in order to establish the elevation or position of a surveying instrument at a new station; abbr.: T.P.

station
In surveying, reference point where an observation is taken; also called set-up.

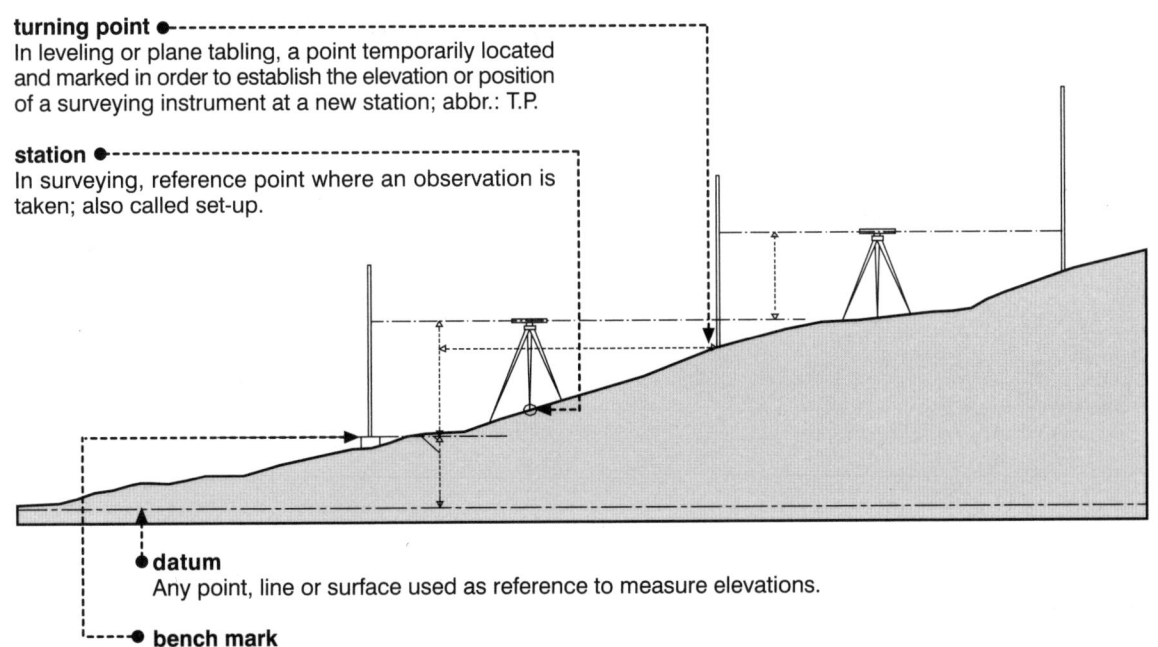

datum
Any point, line or surface used as reference to measure elevations.

bench mark
In surveying, a reference point on a permanently fixed object, such as a metal disk set in concrete, of known elevation and from which the elevation of other points may be determined.

triangulation
A surveying method in which the stations are points on the ground at the vertices of a network of triangles; the angles are measured instrumentally and the sides are derived by computation from selected sides called base lines, whose lengths are measured directly on the ground.

trilateration
A surveying method in which the lengths of all sides of a chain of triangles, or other polygons, are measured with an electronic instrument; the angles are then determined by computation of these field measurements.

base line
A very precisely established survey line, that is to serve as reference for the correlation of other surveys; also called baseline.

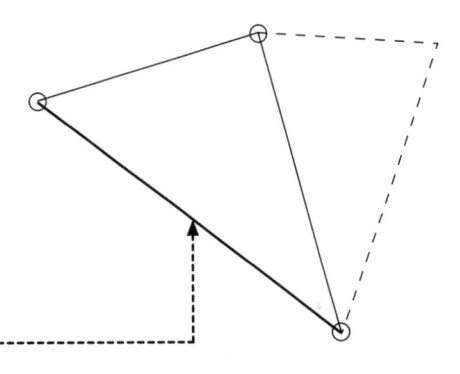

topographic survey

cadastral survey
The survey of landed property, defining units suitable for transfer, limitations of title, as events may require, establishing or reestablishing boundary lines usually defined by ownership.

land survey
The science of land measurement, often to establish or reestablish boundary lines as defined by ownership; also an official agency charged with such measurement.

stadia
A land surveying method in which distance is read by noting the interval of two parallel cross hairs, mounted in the eye of the survey telescope, as they seem to intersect a graduated rod held at the opposite end of the distance being measured.

government system
A land survey system applied where land has not been arbitrarily subdivided by developers; in 1785 Thomas Jefferson divided the North American continent into "quadrangles", with a linear grid, defined by north/south "principal meridians" and east/west "base lines"; also called rectangular system.

metes-and-bounds survey
A survey system used for irregular parcels of land, it records distances (metes) in feet from an established starting point (boundary, bounds) in a given direction (bearings), tracing an irregular polygon around the plot and back to the start.

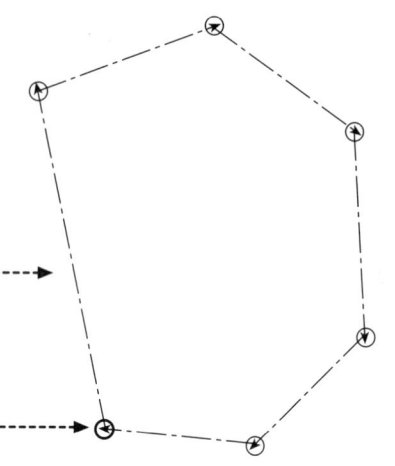

plat
A map or plan of a city, an area or a subdivision showing the boundaries of each individual property.

contour map
A topographic map that portrays relief by using contour lines, to record irregularities of the land surface; more closely spaced lines indicate steep slopes.

contour line
A curved line joining points of equal elevation in the land represented by a contour map or topographic survey.

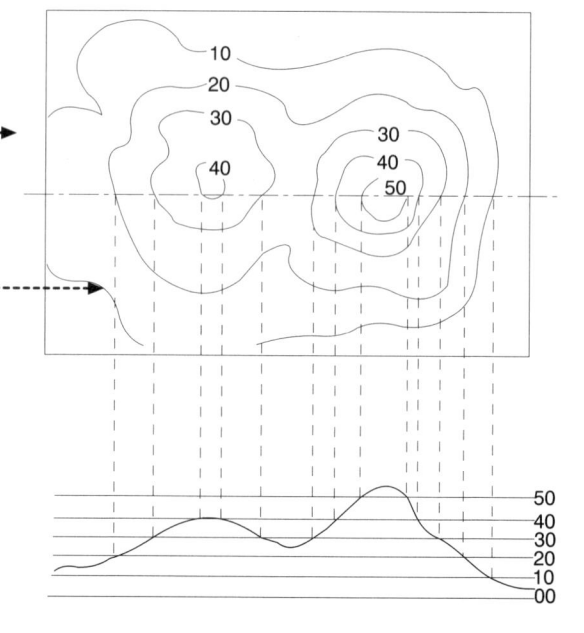

topographic survey

theodolite
A precision surveying instrument consisting of a tripod, telescopic sight, horizontal and vertical levels, and a device to measure horizontal (sometimes also vertical) angles.

alidade
The part of a surveying instrument consisting of a sighting device with index and reading and recording accessories.

horizontal circle
The graduated circle fixed to the base of the alidade of a surveying instrument, to measure horizontal angles.

optical plummet
A device some theodolites provide, to center the instrument over topographic reference points in a strong wind.

transit
A surveying instrument used to measure horizontal and vertical angles, distances, directions and differences in elevation; a type of theodolite having an alidade with a telescope that can be reversed.

spirit level
A glass tube containing alcohol or ether with an air bubble, to indicate if a plane is horizontal or not; used on its own or as part of a more complex device such as a theodolite; also called level.

Gunter's chain
A measuring device in land surveying, consisting of a chain of 100 equal sized links measuring a total of 66 feet (20 meters); also called surveyor's chain.

engineer's chain
A chain used to measure distance in land surveying; in the U.S.A., each link is 1 ft long; the length of the chain is 100 ft; also called a measuring chain.

chain
A distance measuring instrument in land surveying, consisting of a chain of identical links of a specified length.

artificial horizon
A device to indicate the horizon, such as a bubble, a pendulum or the flat surface of a liquid.

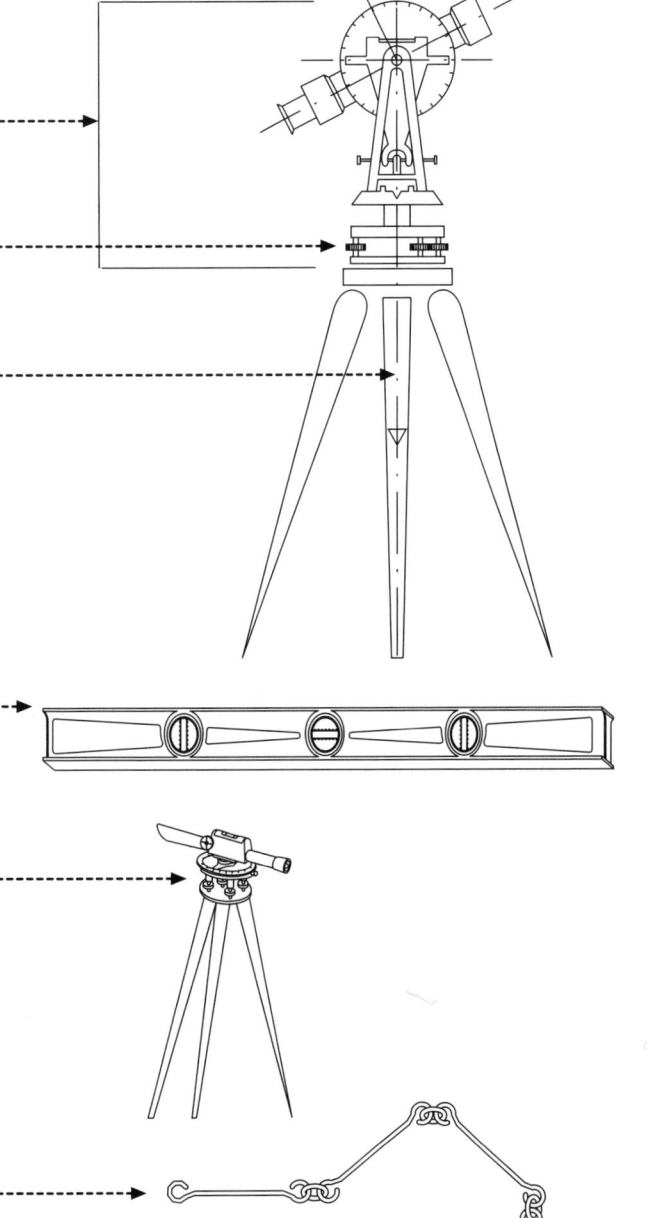